KING RICHARD II

Edited by

ANDREW GURR

Professor of English,
University of Reading

CAMBRIDGE
UNIVERSITY PRESS

CAMBRIDGE UNIVERSITY PRESS
Cambridge, New York, Melbourne, Madrid, Cape Town, Singapore, São Paulo

Cambridge University Press
The Edinburgh Building, Cambridge CB2 8RU, UK

Published in the United States of America by Cambridge University Press, New York

www.cambridge.org
Information on this title: www.cambridge.org/9780521532488

First published 1984
Reprinted 1988, 1990,1992, 1995, 1996, 2000 (twice)
Updated edition 2003
Fifth printing 2007

Printed in the United Kingdom at the University Press, Cambridge

Library of Congress catalogue card number: 83-23974.

British Library Cataloguing in Publication data
Shakespeare, William.
[Richard II]. King Richard II. – (The New Cambridge Shakespeare).
I. Title. II. Gurr, Andrew. III. King Richard II.
822.3′3 – PR2820

ISBN-13 978-0-521-82541-2 hardback
ISBN-13 978-0-521-53248-8 paperback

THE NEW CAMBRIDGE SHAKESPEARE

GENERAL EDITOR
Brian Gibbons, *University of Münster*

ASSOCIATE GENERAL EDITOR
A. R. Braunmuller, *University of California, Los Angeles*

From the publication of the first volumes in 1984 the General Editor of the New Cambridge Shakespeare was Philip Brockbank and the Associate General Editors were Brian Gibbons and Robin Hood. From 1990 to 1994 the General Editor was Brian Gibbons and the Associate General Editors were A. R. Braunmuller and Robin Hood.

KING RICHARD II

To Shakespeare's contemporaries, *Richard II* was a balanced dramatisation of the central political and constitutional issue of the time: how to cope with an unjust ruler. But over the last century or so, the play has come to be regarded as the poetic fall of a tragic hero. The introduction to this edition provides a full context for both the Shakespearean and the modern views of King Richard's fall.

For this updated edition Andrew Gurr has added a new section to the Introduction in which he describes the growing interest in re-historicising and re-politicising the play, surveys a number of important professional theatre productions and guides the reader through the scholarly criticism of recent years. The Reading List has also been revised and augmented.

THE NEW CAMBRIDGE SHAKESPEARE

All's Well That Ends Well, edited by Russell Fraser
Antony and Cleopatra, edited by David Bevington
As You Like It, edited by Michael Hattaway
The Comedy of Errors, edited by T. S. Dorsch
Coriolanus, edited by Lee Bliss
Hamlet, edited by Philip Edwards
Julius Caesar, edited by Marvin Spevack
King Edward III, edited by Giorgio Melchiori
The First Part of King Henry IV, edited by Herbert Weil and Judith Weil
The Second Part of King Henry IV, edited by Giorgio Melchiori
King Henry V, edited by Andrew Gurr
The First Part of King Henry VI, edited by Michael Hattaway
The Second Part of King Henry VI, edited by Michael Hattaway
The Third Part of King Henry VI, edited by Michael Hattaway
King Henry VIII, edited by John Margeson
King John, edited by L. A. Beaurline
The Tragedy of King Lear, edited by Jay L. Halio
King Richard II, edited by Andrew Gurr
King Richard III, edited by Janis Lull
Macbeth, edited by A. R. Braunmuller
Measure for Measure, edited by Brian Gibbons
The Merchant of Venice, edited by M. M. Mahood
The Merry Wives of Windsor, edited by David Crane
A Midsummer Night's Dream, edited by R. A. Foakes
Much Ado About Nothing, edited by F. H. Mares
Othello, edited by Norman Sanders
Pericles, edited by Doreen DelVecchio and Antony Hammond
The Poems, edited by John Roe
Romeo and Juliet, edited by G. Blakemore Evans
The Sonnets, edited by G. Blakemore Evans
The Taming of the Shrew, edited by Ann Thompson
The Tempest, edited by David Lindley
Timon of Athens, edited by Karl Klein
Titus Andronicus, edited by Alan Hughes
Twelfth Night, edited by Elizabeth Story Donno
The Two Gentlemen of Verona, edited by Kurt Schlueter

THE EARLY QUARTOS

The First Quarto of Hamlet, edited by Kathleen O. Irace
The First Quarto of King Henry V, edited by Andrew Gurr
The First Quarto of King Lear, edited by Jay L. Halio
The First Quarto of Othello, edited by Scott McMillin
The First Quarto of King Richard III, edited by Peter Davison
The Taming of a Shrew, edited by Stephen Roy Miller

THE NEW CAMBRIDGE SHAKESPEARE

The *New Cambridge Shakespeare* succeeds *The New Shakespeare* which began publication in 1921 under the general editorship of Sir Arthur Quiller-Couch and John Dover Wilson, and was completed in the 1960s, with the assistance of G. I. Duthie, Alice Walker, Peter Ure and J. C. Maxwell. *The New Shakespeare* itself followed upon *The Cambridge Shakespeare*, 1863–6, edited by W. G. Clark, J. Glover and W. A. Wright.

The New Shakespeare won high esteem both for its scholarship and for its design, but shifts of critical taste and insight, recent Shakespearean research, and a changing sense of what is important in our understanding of the plays, have made it necessary to re-edit and redesign, not merely to revise, the series.

The *New Cambridge Shakespeare* aims to be of value to a new generation of playgoers and readers who wish to enjoy fuller access to Shakespeare's poetic and dramatic art. While offering ample academic guidance, it reflects current critical interests and is more attentive than some earlier editions have been to the realisation of the plays on the stage, and to their social and cultural settings. The text of each play has been freshly edited, with textual data made available to those users who wish to know why and how one published text differs from another. Although modernised, the edition conserves forms that appear to be expressive and characteristically Shakespearean, and it does not attempt to disguise the fact that the plays were written in a language other than that of our own time.

Illustrations are usually integrated into the critical and historical discussion of the play and include some reconstructions of early performances by C. Walter Hodges. Some editors have also made use of the advice and experience of Maurice Daniels, for many years a member of the Royal Shakespeare Company.

Each volume is addressed to the needs and problems of a particular text, and each therefore differs in style and emphasis from others in the series.

PHILIP BROCKBANK
Founding General Editor

CONTENTS

ILLUSTRATIONS

PREFACE

King Richard II is one of the most extraordinary of all the Shakespearean crown jewels. It is the first link in the chain sometimes called 'The Henriad' which was the single most ambitious project Shakespeare ever undertook. *Richard II* launched his second and final attempt to identify the human element in the politics of English monarchy.

La Fontaine's best known fable is the story of the mice who solved the problem of the local cat by deciding to tie a bell round its neck, and who found that this left them with the fresh problem of who might do the tying. La Fontaine was wryly commenting on the most agonising political problem of his time. In a monarchy, if the king as lawgiver should break his own laws and tyrannise over his subjects, who could govern the governor? Sixteenth-century Catholics appealed to the Pope, but although he excommunicated Elizabeth in 1570, she lost little by it. Calvin said the lesser magistrates should prevail over the chief magistrate, but in England Parliament could not rule the ruler until thirty years after Shakespeare's death. The ultimate test of political power in monarchies was the usurpation of a ruler. There were three such tests in English history after William the Conqueror: King John, Richard II and Henry VI. Shakespeare dramatised all three. And the sharpest and most human of the three forms of that infinitely complex human interaction which is what we try to signify by the inadequate word 'dramatisation' is the story of Richard II.

Seen in its political context the 'Henriad' begins with a constitutional problem – an unjust ruler – and answers it in human terms with the all-conquering descendant of Richard's usurper, Henry V. The first play in the sequence is the most political, touching more painfully than any other the most sensitive issue in contemporary politics. Evidence for the pain is there in the fact that it is alone amongst Shakespeare's plays in bearing the marks of political censorship. That pain has now gone. With the political problems of monarchy far in the past it is the play's human element which directs our responses. We find it easier now to view it as a tragic fall rather than as the belling of an unjust cat. One of the functions of an edition such as this is to provide some of the context which made Shakespeare's contemporaries see it as they did.

Responses in the eye and ear to the play's powerful spectacle and poetry have changed less than the mind's responses. Its verse was gathered into anthologies within five years of its being written. Its scenic and poetic power, however, need not make us overlook the fine detailing of the play's language and structure, both in the delicately articulated balance of Richard's fall and Bullingbrook's rise and in the minutely patterned imagery. By their nature, editions are designed for the reader with more time to pause over such detailing than a theatre audience usually has. This edition therefore directs attention to the structural and political details, though always inside the framework of the dramatic performance. A section of the Introduction deals with the Shakespearean staging, emphasising the ritualistic and emblematic features which would have made the political issues more obvious then than they can be now.

Study of *Richard II* has consumed quite a few well-spent scholarly lifetimes. To my debt to those dying generations, I should like to add my endless thanks to all the friends and colleagues at home and abroad, especially Brian Gibbons, who have helped to deliver any of the useful things which might be found in this edition.

A.J.G.

ACKNOWLEDGEMENTS

Twenty-five editors across nearly four centuries have added their mites both to the text and the context of *King Richard II* in this edition. The biggest contributions were the earliest and the most recent. I acknowledge my greatest debts first to the editor who prepared the copy for the 1623 Folio text, and secondly to the two editors of the most substantial modern editions, Matthew Black (1955) and Peter Ure (1956). From the editor of the First Folio we have the best text of the deposition scene, a record of the playhouse adjustments to the stage directions, and alterations in the quarto text made with a care which confirms how respectful a memorial to Shakespeare the 1623 Folio was. Matthew Black's edition of *Richard II* provides, in its collation of variants and its detailed annotation, a solid basis on which all subsequent editors can gratefully build. Peter Ure's elegant and searching annotations to the text and the language, and to Shakespeare's use of his sources both historical and literary, are a model in their kind.

Even before Alexander Pope immortalised the extremes of editorial enterprise from slashing Bentley to piddling Theobald, editors of Shakespeare have tended to settle closer to the scholarly and cautious Theobald than to the corrector of Milton's metre. Pope himself flowed more like Bentley, and this edition owes something to the attention he gave to the play's metre and rhyme. Deciding that *Richard II* should appear in a version smoothed out on Popish lines involves the *a priori* assumption that the text was by intention more metrically regular than its first printers made it in effect. Most editors have been reluctant to make the Popish assumption because of the degree of editorial interference entailed. This edition has rather tentatively fingered that nettle.

The list of works which give help to editors is long and lengthening. The chief helps, together with the abbreviations used in referring to them, are recorded in the list of abbreviations and conventions. The basic help is of course the Oxford English Dictionary (*OED*), which has to be consulted with an eye on the corrections offered by Jürgen Schäfer, *Documentation in the OED: Shakespeare and Nashe as Test Cases*, 1980. M. P. Tilley's *A Dictionary of the Proverbs in England in the Sixteenth and Seventeenth Centuries*, 1950, with its Shakespeare appendix, is also a basic source of information, along with the additions and corrections provided by R. W. Dent, *Shakespeare's Proverbial Language: An Index*, 1981. On pronunciation, Fausto Cercignani's *Shakespeare's Works and Elizabethan Pronunciation*, 1981, is outstanding.

Stanley Wells has examined the question of modernising the spelling of Shakespearean texts in *Modernising Shakespeare's Spelling*, 1979, the prolegomena to the Oxford Shakespeare, and I should like to acknowledge my debt to his good sense, although I have not always adopted his preferences.

Citation of lines from other plays of Shakespeare are taken from G. Blakemore Evans (ed.), *The Riverside Shakespeare*, 1974. References to the Bible are by book, chapter and verse. All quotations are taken from the Bishops' Bible, which seems more likely to have been familiar at least to the early Shakespeare than the Geneva Bible.

ABBREVIATIONS AND CONVENTIONS

1. Shakespeare's plays

The abbreviated titles of Shakespeare's plays have been modified from those used in the *Harvard Concordance to Shakespeare*. All quotations and line references to plays other than *Richard II* are to G. Blakemore Evans (ed.), *The Riverside Shakespeare*, 1974, on which the *Concordance* is based.

Ado	*Much Ado about Nothing*
Ant.	*Antony and Cleopatra*
AWW	*All's Well that Ends Well*
AYLI	*As You Like It*
Cor.	*Coriolanus*
Cym.	*Cymbeline*
Err.	*The Comedy of Errors*
Ham.	*Hamlet*
1H4	*The First Part of King Henry the Fourth*
2H4	*The Second Part of King Henry the Fourth*
H5	*King Henry the Fifth*
1H6	*The First Part of King Henry the Sixth*
2H6	*The Second Part of King Henry the Sixth*
3H6	*The Third Part of King Henry the Sixth*
H8	*King Henry the Eighth*
JC	*Julius Caesar*
John	*King John*
LLL	*Love's Labour's Lost*
Lear	*King Lear*
Mac.	*Macbeth*
MM	*Measure for Measure*
MND	*A Midsummer Night's Dream*
MV	*The Merchant of Venice*
Oth.	*Othello*
Per.	*Pericles*
R2	*King Richard the Second*
R3	*King Richard the Third*
Rom.	*Romeo and Juliet*
Shr.	*The Taming of the Shrew*
STM	*Sir Thomas More*
Temp.	*The Tempest*
TGV	*The Two Gentlemen of Verona*
Tim.	*Timon of Athens*
Tit.	*Titus Andronicus*
TN	*Twelfth Night*
TNK	*The Two Noble Kinsmen*
Tro.	*Troilus and Cressida*
Wiv.	*The Merry Wives of Windsor*
WT	*The Winter's Tale*

2. Editions

Black	*A New Variorum Edition of Shakespeare, Richard II*, ed. Matthew H. Black, 1955
Cam.	*Works*, ed. William Aldis Wright, 9 vols., 1891–3 (Cambridge Shakespeare), IV
Capell	*Mr William Shakespeare his Comedies, Histories, and Tragedies*, ed. Edward Capell, 10 vols., 1767–8, V
Dyce	*The Works of William Shakespeare*, ed. Alexander Dyce, 6 vols., 1857, III
F	*Mr William Shakespeares Comedies, Histories, and Tragedies*, 1623 (First Folio)
F3	*Mr William Shakespeares Comedies, Histories, and Tragedies*, 1664 (Third Folio)
F4	*Mr William Shakespeares Comedies, Histories, and Tragedies*, 1685 (Fourth Folio)
Halliwell	*The Complete Works of Shakespeare*, ed. James O. Halliwell, 16 vols., 1853–65, IX
Hanmer	*The Works of Shakespear*, ed. Thomas Hanmer, 6 vols., 1743–4, III
Hudson	*The Complete Works of William Shakespeare*, ed. Henry N. Hudson, 11 vols., 1851–6, V
Irving	*The Works of William Shakespeare*, ed. Henry Irving and Frank A. Marshall, 8 vols., 1888–90, XI
Johnson	*The Plays of William Shakespeare*, ed. Samuel Johnson, 8 vols., 1765, IV
Johnson Var.	*The Plays of William Shakespeare*, ed. Samuel Johnson and George Steevens, 10 vols., 1773, V
Keightley	*The Plays of Shakespeare*, ed. Thomas Keightley, 6 vols., 1864, III
Kittredge	*The Complete Works of Shakespeare*, ed. George Lyman Kittredge, 1936
Malone	*The Plays and Poems of William Shakespeare*, ed. Edmond Malone, 10 vols., 1790, V
Neilson	*The Complete Dramatic and Poetic Works of William Shakespeare*, ed. William Allan Neilson, 1906
Pope	*The Works of Shakespear*, ed. Alexander Pope, 6 vols., 1723–5, III
Q1	*The Tragedie of King Richard the Second*, 1597 (first quarto)
Q2	*The Tragedie of King Richard the Second*, 1598 (second quarto)
Q3	*The Tragedie of King Richard the Second*, 1598 (third quarto)
Q4	*The Tragedy of King Richard the Second*, 1608 (fourth quarto)
Q5	*The Tragedy of King Richard the Second*, 1615 (fifth quarto)
Q6	*The Tragedy of King Richard the Second*, 1634 (sixth quarto)
Rowe	*The Works of Mr William Shakespear*, ed. Nicholas Rowe, 6 vols., 1709, III
Rowe[2]	*The Works of Mr William Shakespear*, ed. Nicholas Rowe, 3rd edn, 6 vols., 1714, III
Singer	*The Dramatic Works of William Shakespeare*, ed. Samuel Weller Singer, 10 vols., 1855–6, IV
Staunton	*The Plays of William Shakespeare*, ed. Howard Staunton, 3 vols., 1858–60, I
Steevens	*The Plays of William Shakespeare*, ed. George Steevens and Isaac Reed, 4th edn, 15 vols., 1793, VIII

Theobald	*The Works of Shakespeare*, ed. Lewis Theobald, 7 vols., 1733, III
Ure	*Richard II*, ed. Peter Ure, 1956 (Arden)
Wells	*Richard II*, ed. Stanley Wells, 1969 (New Penguin)
Wilson	*Richard II*, ed. John Dover Wilson, 1939 (New Shakespeare)

3. Other works, periodicals, general references

Capell	Trinity College, Cambridge, copy of Q1
Cercignani	Fausto Cercignani, *Shakespeare's Works and Elizabethan Pronunciation*, 1981
conj.	conjecture
Dent	R. W. Dent, *Shakespeare's Proverbial Language: An Index*, 1981 (references are to numbered proverbs)
ELH	*ELH: A Journal of English Literary History*
F (corr.)	First Folio, corrected state
Froissart	*The Chronicle of Froissart translated out of French by Sir John Bourchier Lord Berners* (1523–5)
F (uncorr.)	First Folio, uncorrected state
Holinshed	Raphael Holinshed, *The first and second volumes of Chronicles of England, Scotlande, and Irelande* (1587), II
Hunt.	Huntington Library copy of Q1
Huth	British Library copy of Q1 (Huth 46)
JEGP	*Journal of English and Germanic Philology*
Mahood	M. M. Mahood, *Shakespeare's Wordplay*, 1957
MLQ	*Modern Language Quarterly*
OED	*Oxford English Dictionary*
PBSA	*Papers of the Bibliographical Society of America*
Petworth	Petworth House copy of Q1
PMLA	*Publications of the Modern Language Association of America*
PQ	*Philological Quarterly*
Qq	Q1–5
Ren. Drama	*Renaissance Drama*
SB	*Studies in Bibliography*
SD	stage direction
SEL	*Studies in English Literature*
SH	speech heading
SP	*Studies in Philology*
SQ	*Shakespeare Quarterly*
S.St.	*Shakespeare Studies*
S.Sur.	*Shakespeare Survey*
subst.	substantively
2 Tamb.	Christopher Marlowe, *Tamburlaine* Part 2 (1590)
Tilley	M. P. Tilley, *A Dictionary of the Proverbs in England in the Sixteenth and Seventeenth Centuries*, 1950 (references are to numbered proverbs)
Woodstock	*Woodstock: A Moral History*, ed. A. P. Rossiter, 1946

Full references to other works cited in the Commentary in abbreviated form may be found in the Reading List at p. 225 below.

INTRODUCTION

Date

King Richard II was written in 1595 as the initial play in a sequence planned as three or four plays about the Lancastrian phase of English history. Shakespeare probably had a contract with the playing company formed in 1594, the Chamberlain's Men, in which he was one of the ten shareholders, to provide his players with about two plays a year, one tragedy and one comedy. The history plays – *Richard II, Henry IV* Parts 1 and 2 and *Henry V*, together with *Julius Caesar*, all written between 1595 and 1599 – fulfilled Shakespeare's commitment to provide tragedies for the last five years of the sixteenth century.

Besides the circumstantial evidence for the writing of the *Henry IV* plays in 1596–7, which would make 1595 the most likely date for Shakespeare to initiate his sequence of history plays, the debt he almost certainly owed to Daniel's *The Civil Wars* confirms that he started the sequence in 1595. Daniel used Lucan as a model for the opening of his poem (1, 1–2) and Shakespeare echoes Daniel rather than the original Lucan in Carlisle's speech, 4.1.140–1.[1] Examination of the links between the passages confirms the view that Shakespeare borrowed from Daniel rather than the other way about. Daniel's first four books of *The Civil Wars* were registered for publication on 11 October 1594, and were probably on sale some time in the following year. A letter of 3 November 1595 mentions them as one of the currently interesting new works available in London,[2] which suggests a date of publication towards the middle of that year. The fact that Shakespeare on average wrote two plays a year does not mean it took him six months for each play, and in practice it would have been quite possible for him to add Daniel to the list of authorities consulted for *Richard II* at a point well advanced in the play's composition.

That *Richard II* was on stage in 1595 is suggested most clearly in a letter written by Sir Edward Hoby on 7 December of that year. It was addressed to Sir Robert Cecil, son and successor to Elizabeth's chief minister Burghley,[3] and invites him to eat and be entertained:

Sir, findinge that you wer not convenientlie to be in London tomorrow night I am bold to send to knowe whether Teusdaie maybe anie more in your grace to visit poore Channon rowe where as late as it shal please you a gate for your supper shal be open: & K. Richard present

---

[1] See George M. Logan, 'Lucan–Daniel–Shakespeare: new light on the relation between *The Civil Wars* and *Richard II*', *S.St.* 9 (1976), 121–40.

[2] Rowland Whyte to Sir Robert Sidney, 3 November 1595, quoted in Arthur Collins, *Letters and Memorials of State*, 2 vols., 1746, 1, 357. I am indebted for this observation to John Pitcher.

[3] Cecil had been knighted and made a Privy Councillor in 1591. He became Secretary of State in 1596 and succeeded his father as Elizabeth's chief minister when his father died in 1598. If the connections made by some of his contemporaries between Elizabeth and Richard II had any cogency Cecil would have had good reason to be entertained by a performance of Shakespeare's play.

I

1 An engraving of Richard II. From Thomas Tymme, *A book…containing the true portraiture of the kings of England* (1597)

him selfe to your vewe. Pardon my boldnes that ever love to be honored with your presence nether do I importune more then your occasions may willingly assent unto, in the meanetime & ever restinge At your command Edw. Hoby.[1]

[1] Quoted in E. K. Chambers, *William Shakespeare*, 2 vols., 1930, II, 320–1.

The letter is endorsed '7 Dec. 1595...readile'. It is possible that Hoby, who collected historical portraits, had a painting to show his guest, and there is no indication which King Richard was intended. But the very lack of precision in specifying which King Richard he meant, together with the known popularity of Shakespeare's play and the circumstantial evidence for its composition late in 1595, make it most likely that Hoby was offering his guest a specially commissioned evening performance by Shakespeare's company of one of their newest plays.[1]

A measure of the play's popularity is the readiness with which its owners, the playing company, released it to the printers in 1597, presumably after its early success on stage had waned. The first edition (Q1) was promptly followed by two further issues in 1598 (Q2 and Q3). It was the first play-text to prove so popular as to warrant three printings in the space of two years, and the second quarto appeared with Shakespeare's name on its title page, the first time he was acknowledged as the author of one of his plays in print.

Also in 1598 Francis Meres issued his little survey of the arts in England, *Palladis Tamia*, and recorded the view that *Richard II* was foremost amongst the tragedies of the day. In 1600 six passages from the play, three by Gaunt, were anthologised in *England's Parnassus*. All this evidence for its popularity – Hoby's command performance, Meres's praise, the three editions in quick succession and the quotations – makes it likely that Elizabeth was thinking of Shakespeare's play in particular when she told William Lambarde, the antiquary and Keeper of the Tower of London, in the course of a conversation in 1601 that she was a second Richard II, and that 'this tragedy was played 40tie times in open streets and houses'.[2] A similar notion that Elizabeth was another Richard led the followers of the Earl of Essex to commission a performance of the play on the eve of the Essex rebellion, 7 February 1601. The relationship of Shakespeare's play to the current interest in the story of Richard II will be examined below.

1595 was a likely time in Shakespeare's career as a play-maker for him to launch such a substantial enterprise as the sequence about Lancastrian history. The years from 1590 to 1594 had been an unsettled time for writers, with the playing companies' fortunes frequently changing as the plague and other discomforts kept them on the move. Shakespeare's own uncertainty showed in his two attempts to advertise his status as a poet with the carefully supervised printings of *Venus and Adonis* in 1593 and *The Rape of Lucrece* in 1594. Curiously – he was alone in his time in doing so – he seems to have retained the ownership of all his early plays. Every other play-maker sold his texts to the exclusive ownership of the playing companies. Shakespeare's seem to have travelled with him. The unsettled times meant that Shakespeare's first sequence of history plays, *1*, *2* and *3 Henry VI* and *Richard III*, was performed piecemeal by different companies. The plays were probably never performed as a

---

[1] The question of what sort of 'K. Richard' Hoby had in mind has been the subject of some argument. See David M. Bergeron, 'The Hoby letter and *Richard II*: a parable of criticism', *SQ* 26 (1975), 477–80. A. N. Kincaid, *NQ* n.s. 28 (1981), 124–6, suggests that Hoby meant a lost tract by Bishop Morton about Richard III. It is unlikely that anything but a new and newsworthy 'K. Richard' would be offered to such a distinguished guest.   [2] Chambers, *Shakespeare*, II, 326–7.

sequence until he was settled with the Chamberlain's Men, the company he joined when it was formed in mid 1594. He stayed with them for the rest of his working life, and they prospered as no other company ever did. His early plays might well have been the capital with which he bought his share in the new company. The fact that he kept possession of them reflects both his own business acumen and also perhaps his own esteem for his early work. He probably saw the launching of a second sequence of history plays for the new company as both good art and good business.

History

By 1595 the Chamberlain's Men were firmly established in a London playhouse, with the protection of the most useful peer at Court, the Lord Chamberlain, to whom the Master of the Revels reported and who organised the Court's entertainments. It was a promising time which openly invited the launching of a second ambitious sequence of plays from English history. That *Richard II* was designed from the start to launch a sequence of plays can hardly be doubted. Young Harry Percy, the Hotspur of *1 Henry IV*, and young Prince Hal are foreshadowed in 2.3 and 5.3 as the antagonists they are to become in the following play. Their opposition involved Shakespeare in more juggling with the facts than he generally allowed himself in *Richard II*, since historically the prince was a whole generation younger than Harry Percy, who was two years older than Bullingbrook, and there was no evidence that the two ever even met, as they are described as doing in 5.3.13–14. It has been suggested that the Hotspur–Hal links in *Richard II* were late insertions made because the idea of a sequence came to Shakespeare only after the play was nearly finished,[1] but that seems unlikely in view of the careful preparation of such other links as the idea of pilgrimages and crusades to the Holy Land. This idea begins in 1.3 of *Richard II* and runs right through to the end of *Henry V*. Jerusalem forms a leitmotif through the whole sequence.

Essentially Shakespeare took the story of the old prophecy that Henry IV would die in Jerusalem and enlarged its frame of reference. It is mentioned by Holinshed, Shakespeare's main source for the whole sequence, only in the account of Henry's death, where it is offered with some scepticism. Daniel also refers to the story, though again only over Henry's death, and otherwise merely laments what might have been done by a united Christendom if Henry V's claim to France had been more substantial. Shakespeare makes it a recurrent question for Henry IV and his son. At the beginning of *1 Henry IV* Bullingbrook, now firmly Henry IV, refers to Cain's fratricide in the book of Genesis, with its evil precedent for the murder of his cousin Richard, and proposes not the expiatory pilgrimage to the Holy Land which he promises at the end of *Richard II* but a crusade (1.1.19–27). By the end of *2 Henry IV*, when he is about to die in the Jerusalem Chamber at Westminster, he bequeaths the task to his son, still as a crusade but now with the expedient purpose of keeping the nobles occupied, 'to busy giddy minds / With foreign quarrels' (4.5.213–14). In *Henry V*

---

[1] Guy Lambrechts, 'Sur deux prétendues sources de *Richard II*', *Etudes Anglaises* 20 (1967), 118–39.

the new king demotes the crusade still further into a campaign against his Christian neighbour France. After Agincourt he in his turn bequeaths the crusade, in characteristically flamboyant fashion, to his son. With more than a hint of his father's expediency he tells his French bride

if ever thou beest mine, Kate, as I have a saving faith within me tells me thou shalt, I get thee with scambling, and thou must therefore needs prove a good soldier breeder. Shall not thou and I, between Saint Denis and Saint George, compound a boy, half French, half English, that shall go to Constantinople to take the Turk by the beard?   (H5 5.2.203–10)

Henry's implication is that the scambling and disordered circumstances by which he secured his title to France are likely to demand yet more, though conveniently Christian, foreign quarrels in the future.

All these allusions are prepared for in *Richard II*. As the initiating play in the sequence it carefully presents both kinds of journey to Jerusalem, pilgrimage and crusade. Gaunt speaks of Richard's ancestors as royal crusaders (2.1.51–6), contrasting the wasteful king of peace with his militant namesake Richard I, the Lion-heart. Richard, who calls himself a lion at 1.1.174 and is exhorted by his queen to behave like one at 5.1.29–30, sets himself at 3.3.151 in the opposite role, offering to exchange his sceptre for 'a palmer's walking staff'. Palmers were pilgrims who had made the journey to Jerusalem. By contrast Mowbray, whom Bullingbrook describes along with himself as a pilgrim, ends his life of exile as a crusader according to Carlisle's account at 4.1.92–5. Mowbray and Bullingbrook are described as making a pilgrimage to death at 1.3.49. They both go on what Bullingbrook calls the 'enforcèd pilgrimage' of exile (1.3.263), a living equivalent of the journey to death which Gaunt (1.3.228–9) and Richard (2.1.154) describe as a pilgrimage. Mowbray's enforced pilgrimage turns into a crusade, while Bullingbrook wishes to convert his crusade at the end of the play (5.6.49–50) into a pilgrimage to Jerusalem to expiate his guilt over Richard's murder. That wish changes at the beginning of *1 Henry IV* into a crusade.

There are several verbal hints which link the alternatives of the militant journey to Jerusalem and the peaceable pilgrimage with the opposition between Christian patience and militancy in resisting an unlawful king. This is the underlying point of the leitmotif in the first play. Bullingbrook gives as the motive for his appeal against Mowbray in 1.1 the urge to revenge the murder of his kinsman Gloucester. Citing Cain's murder of Abel, Bullingbrook proposes to take vengeance with his own hand, not leaving it, as required in Genesis, to God. The scene which follows between Gloucester's widow and his brother Gaunt reinforces the point, since Gaunt's choice, Christian patience, is the opposite of his son's (it is also the opposite of the motivation given to the Gaunt of the anonymous play *Woodstock*, another of Shakespeare's sources). Gloucester's widow urges vengeance but Gaunt insists on the Christian posture. Precisely the same choice is put to Richard by his Queen in 5.1.26–34, and Bullingbrook's allusion to Abel is also balanced by his order in 5.6 that Richard's murderer should be exiled like Cain. Bullingbrook by the end of the play is, through his intermediary Exton, a murderer of his kinsman as was Richard at the beginning through his intermediary Mowbray. It is Cain's crime which first turns Bullingbrook to thoughts of Jerusalem. Similarly, Aumerle's request in 4.1 for a gage from 'some honest Christian' to allow more duelling challenges (83), and Carlisle's hope that England is 'a Christian climate' (30), together with Richard's claim in 5.1.20–5 that he is 'sworn brother' to necessity – a brotherhood simultaneously of chivalry and a monastic order – are other hints of the radical choice between prayer and the sword in the service of truth. Carlisle's prophecy in 4.1 about what will happen to the Christian climate if the sacred power of majesty is overturned with the sword is that 'peace shall go sleep with Turks and infidels' (139). The Christian patience invoked by Gaunt at 1.2.29 and 33–4 and by his brother York at 2.1.207 was the only choice offered, by the Homilies and the apologists for the crown, to the problem of an unjust king.[1] This issue, counterpoising pilgrimage against crusade, runs through all the sequence of history plays. The growth of expediency in the idea of a crusade is one of the many changes which the sequence traces.

Shakespeare launched a sequence which covered seventeen years of English history, from the contest between Bullingbrook and Mowbray in 1398 to the aftermath of Agincourt in 1415. The subject of the first play, however, the deposition of Richard II, had a special political interest in the 1590s which the later plays were free of, and *Richard II* had some trouble with the censors as a result. The interest developed out of a comparison between the position of Richard, surrounded by bad counsellors and lacking a direct heir, and Elizabeth. In the 1580s and 1590s the comparison was used to score political points chiefly about advice from favourites, but in the 1590s deposition also came into the question.[2] Towards the turn of the century it began to focus on the Earl of Essex.

Essex's distant ancestor was the Duke of Gloucester, youngest son of Edward III and Richard's victim. An anonymous play, *Woodstock*, which seems to have been chiefly composed in 1592–3, elevates Gloucester (also known as Thomas of Woodstock) into a plain truth-telling hero, the leading opponent and victim of Richard's flatterers.[3] In 1595 Daniel was more open and wrote a direct address to Essex at the end of Book II of *The Civil Wars*, calling him a leader capable of supplying better material for a poem than Bullingbrook.[4] Finally in the years following the staging of Shakespeare's play the historian Sir John Hayward wrote *The First Part of the Life and Raigne of King Henrie IIII* dealing substantially with Richard's deposition. Published in February 1599, it was dedicated to Essex as 'futuri temporis expectatione', a term suitable for an heir apparent to the throne. This was too much for Elizabeth, who not only accepted the identification of herself with Richard II but was acutely hostile to any open speculation about her successor. The Parliamentarian Peter Wentworth was already in the Tower for publishing a pamphlet arguing that James VI of Scotland was the heir with the best claim. Hayward's book was censored and its dedication removed. When the abortive Essex coup did take place, on 8 February 1601, both

[1] See Appendix 3, p. 225 below.
[2] See Lily B. Campbell, *Shakespeare's 'Histories': Mirrors of Elizabethan Policy*, 1947, pp. 168–94. The connections between the play and the Essex conspiracy were debated by Evelyn M. Albright and Ray Heffner in *PMLA* 42 (1927), 45 (1930), 46 (1931) and 47 (1932).
[3] See A. P. Rossiter (ed.), *Woodstock: A Moral History*, 1946.
[4] See Appendix 2, p. 202 below.

Hayward and Shakespeare's company were drawn into the trial which followed because of the publicity they had given to Richard's deposition.

Hayward's book was used in evidence against Essex, both in his trial over the failure of his 1599 campaign in Ireland and subsequently at his trial for treason. Hayward was put in the Tower in 1600 and remained there until after Elizabeth's death. The other publicists, Shakespeare's company, got off more lightly. Essex was said at Hayward's trial to have frequently attended performances of the play and to have applauded it warmly.[1] On the day before the coup his followers persuaded the company to stage the play once more, presumably as propaganda for their plans. According to Augustine Phillips, the player who testified on their behalf at the trial, the company objected that the play was now 'so old and so long out of use that they should have small or no company at it'.[2] The Essex conspirators agreed to pay an additional £2 to the players, and the play was performed. There is no certain evidence that the performance was of Shakespeare's play, but since it was a play 'of King Henry the Fourth, and of the killing of Richard the second',[3] it seems the most likely of the possible candidates and was certainly in the company's repertoire. In the event the players were cleared of any suspicion of complicity and went unpunished.

One other small piece of evidence about finding parallels in Shakespeare's play to contemporary political events is worth noting, because it emphasises the extent to which the parallels were in the eye of the beholder. Everard Guilpin, a young Inns-of-Court gallant, a satirist and frequenter of Shakespeare's company in the days when they performed at the Curtain, 1597–8, evidently knew *Richard II* quite well. In an epigram in *Skialetheia* (Sat. 1, sig. c3ᵛ) he adapted the account at 1.4.25–34 of Bullingbrook's journey into exile and his humble manner in order to make it fit Essex, very much to his disadvantage.

> For when great *Foelix* passing through the street,
> Vayleth his cap to each one he doth meet,
> And when no broom-man that will pray for him
> Shall have less truage than his bonnets brim,
> Who would not think him perfect curtesy?
> Or the honey suckle of humility?
> The devil he is as soone...

He is ambitious, and 'Signor Machiavell / Taught him this mumming trick.' If Elizabeth was Richard, then the earl was Bullingbrook. What Guilpin did was to adapt Shakespeare's Bullingbrook to fit contemporary Essex.[4] It confirms Elizabeth's own identification of herself with the deposed king, and makes Shakespeare's explicit reference to Essex in the prologue to Act 5 of *Henry V*, written in the summer of 1599 when Essex was campaigning in Ireland, seem almost like an apology for his identification with Bullingbrook.

Guilpin's association of Bullingbrook with Essex is no guarantee that most

---

[1] *Calendar of State Papers (Dom.) 1598–1601*, pp. 435–6   [2] *Ibid.*   [3] *Ibid.*, p. 575.
[4] An attack on Walter Raleigh in 1603 described Essex as Bullingbrook even more precisely: 'Renouned Essex, as he past the streets,'/Would vaile his bonnet to an oyster wife.' J. O. Halliwell (ed.), *Poetical Miscellanies*, 1845, p. 17.

THE
Tragedie of King
Richard the Second:

With new additions of the Parliament Sceane, and the deposing
of King Richard.

As it hath been lately acted by the Kinges
Maiesties seruantes, at the Globe.

By *William Shake-speare.*

AT LONDON,
Printed by W. W. for *Mathew Law*, and are to
be sold at his shop in Paules Church-yard,
at the signe of the Foxe.
1608

2   The title page of the fourth quarto, the Malone copy, advertising the addition of the deposition scene

audiences made the same identification, and in any case it is emphatically a hostile parallel. It was rather the underlying parallelism than anything in the content of the play itself which attracted attention. Nevertheless it confirms that the subject of the play was politically sensitive. It undoubtedly did attract the attention of the queen's censors. The editions published in Elizabeth's lifetime all lack the central deposition scene from 4.1.

The deposition scene poses several problems. It was evidently deleted from the early printed quartos as an act of censorship, but whether the same censorship affected the performed text is not known. Matthew Law, who first published the deposition scene in the fourth quarto (Q4) in 1608, was evidently not given access to any original manuscript, and relied on a transcription at least some of which was probably dictated and infected by memories of the staged version. That of course implies that the scene was appearing on stage in 1608. Possibly Law asked the players to supply him with a transcript once the censorship was lifted. The company certainly had a reasonable copy of their own, since a better version than the Q4 text was fitted into the edited copy of the third quarto (Q3, 1598) which the Folio printers used for the great collected edition of the plays in 1623. Perhaps the stage version of the play never lost the deposition scene, so that the playhouse always had a full version of the text. The supporters of Essex who commissioned the performance of the play which we assume to be Shakespeare's would have had much more reason to want it if they knew it contained the scene in which Richard hands over his crown to the new king. But there is unfortunately no clear indication whether the deposition scene stayed in the performed text when it was deleted from the printed versions, or alternatively whether it was deleted from the performed text in 1595 and restored after Elizabeth died in 1603.[1]

On the whole the latter of these alternatives is the less likely, if only because it would have required very positive action by the players. First they would need to have retained the censored scene in the expectation that at some future time they might be allowed to restore it, and then once they were free to do so they would have had first to secure fresh permission from the censor, then write it back not only into the promptbook and the 'plot' which hung in the playhouse recording entries, exits and properties used, but also into the players' 'parts' which were usually transcribed as soon as the text had been 'allowed' by the censor. The pattern of censorship in play-texts moreover was quite different from that of the censors of printed books. The bishops who descended on the verse satirists in 1599,[2] the Archbishop of Canterbury in particular, had a sharp and sophisticated eye for anything dangerous in theology or

[1] David Bergeron has conjectured that the deposition scene was not written until after 1601. The only evidence is negative, however. It would be more plausible if there were a real reason for the scene to have been created so late and so specially. See David Bergeron, 'The deposition scene in *Richard II*', *Renaissance Papers* (1974), 31–7. It is not inconceivable that the 'woeful pageant' as Westminster calls it (4.1.322) is alluded to by Duke Senior in *AYLI* before Jacques's 'All the world's a stage' speech. The Duke says 'This wide and universal theatre / Presents more woeful pageants than the scene / Wherein we play in.'

[2] See Richard A. McCabe, 'Elizabethan satire and the Bishops' ban of 1599', *Yearbook of English Studies* 11 (1981), 188–94.

politics. Their record in the last years of Elizabeth is a tribute to their sensitivity. Not so the censor of stage-plays. Edmund Tilney's record as censor is undistinguished, and that of his understudy from 1597 and eventual successor, George Buc, not much stronger. In the month when *Richard II* was entered in the Stationers' Register for printing, August 1597, *The Isle of Dogs* got several players and poets (not of Shakespeare's company) imprisoned and the play suppressed because it contained 'seditious' material. But sedition to the various Masters of the Revels was rarely anything much more dangerous than insults to foreign countries which had powerful ambassadors at Court. In the case of *The Isle of Dogs* it seems to have been the Polish ambassador.[1] An astonishing amount of political comment or display seems to have been acceptable. The censorship of plays hardened a little under James, but this was partly because James himself took a closer interest in plays and sponsored the 1606 act against stage profanity. The different records of the two kinds of censor make it entirely possible that a scene not acceptable to the bishops might be allowed by the Master of the Revels. If so, of course, the force of the contemporary parallels must have been less widely felt than Elizabeth and the Court politicians assumed.[2]

The restoration of a cut made through censorship in a performed text would have been unique, so far as we know, in the history of the drama at this time. For that admittedly circumstantial reason it seems likely that the deposition scene never was cut from the stage version. Its survival on stage would have given Matthew Law an impetus to secure leave to print it in 1608 which he might not have had if audiences were accustomed to the cut version. It was politically sensitive and therefore a good advertisement for Law's quarto. But it was not as explosive as Essex's followers thought.

Sources

Writing history even for such a populist medium as the stage, or turning it into epic poetry as Daniel set out to do, was a major undertaking in Tudor times, and Shakespeare took pains with his material. His primary source was the second edition (1587) of Raphael Holinshed's *Chronicles of England, Scotland and Ireland*, which covers the period of the play in about 24 double-column folio pages. He also made use of the anonymous play *Woodstock* for the first two acts dealing with Richard's injustices, and almost certainly consulted Berners's translation of Froissart's *Chronicle*, besides Daniel's *The Civil Wars*. It is possible that he also looked at Edward Halle's

[1] So E. K. Chambers, *The Elizabethan Stage*, 4 vols., 1923, III, 455. William Ingram, *A London Life in the Brazen Age*, 1978, pp. 179–84, gives the circumstantial evidence about the *Isle of Dogs* issue.

[2] In the 1609 edition of *The Civil Wars* Daniel wrote in the Epistle Dedicatorie: 'this Argument was long since undertaken (in a time which was not so well secur'd of the future, as God be blessed now it is) with a purpose, to showe the deformities of Civile Dissension, and the miserable events of Rebellions, Conspiracies, and bloudy Revengements, which followed (as in a circle) upon that breach of the due course of Succession, by the Usurpation of *Hen. 4*'. Bacon also raised the political issues relating to the deposition in 1615 (*Letters and Life of Francis Bacon*, ed. James Spedding, 7 vols., 1864, V, 145). Shakespeare had already dramatised the question as an irresolvable dynastic and legal tangle in *3H6*. The two sides of the question are given concisely in 1.1.132–50 by Henry, Bullingbrook's grandson, and York, Richard's descendant.

The union of the two noble and illustre famelies of Lancastre & Yorke, which begins its account of the Wars of the Roses with the quarrel between Mowbray and Bullingbrook as does Shakespeare, and he may have consulted any or all of three French chronicles in manuscript, to which Holinshed refers in his marginal notes.[1] He must also have known, but chose not to use, the stories of Richard, Mowbray and Henry IV in *A Mirror for Magistrates*.

Opinions differ over how much use Shakespeare made of other sources to supplement Holinshed. Some of Halle is reproduced almost verbatim in Holinshed, and the three French accounts all have a bias in favour of Richard which may marginally have influenced Shakespeare's analysis but which otherwise supplied him with little matter either of fact or language. Daniel and *Woodstock*, on the evidence of verbal echoes, seem to have made much more impact. Daniel, for instance, invented the idea of a grieving queen which Shakespeare developed. Queen Isabella, Richard's second wife, was barely ten at the time of the deposition. Daniel apologised in the preface to the 1609 enlargement of his poem (which repaid Shakespeare's debt by borrowing from him) for creating a queen with passions not suited to her years.[2] Shakespeare was also following Daniel when he used the name John of Gaunt instead of Holinshed's Duke of Lancaster. He similarly took Daniel's spelling 'Bullingbrooke' and his pun on the name as a river (*Civil Wars*, II, 8, and *R2* 3.2.109–10). Other verbal echoes of Daniel appear in Carlisle's prophecy (*Civil Wars*, III, 23, and *R2* 4.1.130–44) and in Richard's lament at 5.1.40–50. It is possible that Bullingbrook's ambiguous references to his fortune at 2.3.38 and elsewhere owe something to Daniel's conclusion (*Civil Wars*, I, 94–5) that his progress was the consequence of fortune, not ambition, although Shakespeare's Bullingbrook is consistently more materialistic than Daniel's. Shakespeare's omission of Northumberland's trickery in snaring Richard before the Flint Castle episode is, however, evidence for his independent shaping of his material, since the incident is given some emphasis in both Holinshed and Daniel. The omission makes Richard's fall more obviously self-inflicted.

Woodstock poses a few problems. It deals with Richard's abuses and ends with the downfall of his flatterers but it does not include Bullingbrook or Richard's deposition and death. Shakespeare evidently knew it, judging from the echoes at 1.4.45–51 and 2.1.60 and 113–14. In what circumstances he knew it, though, and whether it was ever staged in his time, is uncertain. The manuscript of the play, which is usually dated 1592 or 1593, is marked by several different hands, including that of George Buc, who acted as a censor only from 1597 onwards, and it has a stage direction calling for a 'tucket' which is thought not to be possible before about 1619. It was clearly

[1] For a detailed examination of the play's likely sources, see Matthew H. Black, 'The sources of Shakespeare's *Richard II*', in *Joseph Quincy Adams Memorial Studies*, ed. James G. McManaway, Giles E. Dawson and Edwin E. Willoughby, 1948, pp. 199–216. Geoffrey Bullough takes a similar view in *Narrative and Dramatic Sources of Shakespeare*, III, 1960. An adroit assessment of the evidence is Kenneth Muir's *The Sources of Shakespeare's Plays*, 1977, pp. 46–66.

[2] *The Civil Wars* (1609), Epistle Dedicatorie: 'And if I have erred somewhat in the draught of the young Q. *Isabel* (wife to *Ric. 2.*) in not suting her passion to her yeares: I must crave favour of my credulous Readers: and hope, the young ladies of *England* (who peradventure will thinke themselves of age sufficientt, at 14 yeares, to have a feeling of their owne estates) will excuse me in that point.'

prepared for the stage, but not necessarily for Shakespeare's company, and one of Shakespeare's borrowings seems to suggest that he read it rather than saw it on stage. Gaunt's condemnation of Richard at 2.1.60 is an echo of a passage in *Woodstock* 4.1.138–9[1] which is marked in the hand of a stage adapter as cancelled in the manuscript. So Shakespeare would most likely have seen it in the manuscript, not heard it on stage. What might have happened is that he served as his company's reader of play-texts submitted for possible purchase, and read the play under these circumstances but did not recommend it for performance. His own version simply uses *Woodstock* for details of the injustices which Holinshed refers to only in vague terms, and for little else. Half of the verbal resemblances occur in 2.1,[2] which suggests either a transient memory of the manuscript at the time Shakespeare was writing 2.1, or a fairly utilitarian borrowing of such small details as he found useful at a point where Richard's abuses were most in view. The personification of Gaunt as an antithesis to Richard's flatterers might owe something to *Woodstock*'s portrait of Gloucester, but it is a fairly notional debt.

It is probably sensible to see Shakespeare taking his story from Holinshed and grafting on to it a number of other features, some from other sources and some his own. The scenes with Richard's queen – 2.2, 3.4 and 5.1 – owe a debt to Daniel, but the other two scenes containing women – Gaunt's with the Duchess of Gloucester at 1.2 and York's with his duchess at 5.3 – are Shakespeare's creations. The two emblem scenes – the garden in 3.4 and Richard's mirror at 4.1.262–301 – are also Shakespeare's. Other recognisable innovations are the scene at Gaunt's deathbed and the participation of Northumberland and his son in the replacement of Richard with Bullingbrook. Other features of Shakespeare's version, notably the personalities of Richard and Bullingbrook, probably owe something to the various sources but not enough for them to be obvious influences.

Two of Shakespeare's innovations indicate the complexity involved in seeing the new shape he gave to his materials, and perhaps more usefully might show how the dramatic medium contributed to the reshaping. Gaunt's speeches in 2.1 give a human shape to an event reported only summarily in Holinshed. Richard's seizure of the dead Gaunt's property was an action which even contemporary historians regarded as his fatal mistake. It was a technical act of tyranny, putting the king's will above the law and denying the common rights of inheritance, as York protests (2.1.189–99). Moreover it gave Bullingbrook a pretext to return from exile to claim the rights of his new name. Holinshed puts it in a single paragraph:

In this meane time, the duke of Lancaster departed out of this life at the bishop of Elie's palace in Holborne, and lieth buried in the cathedrall church of saint Paule in London, on the northside of the high altar, by the ladie Blanch his first wife. The death of this duke gave occasion of increasing more hatred in the people of this realme toward the king, for he seized into his hands all the goods that belonged to him, and also received all the rents and revenues of his lands

---

[1] See *Woodstock*, p. 45.

[2] *Ibid.*, p. 50. A few verbal resemblances to the university play *Caesar's Revenge* have led to conjectures that *R2* is indebted to it. See Jacqueline Pearson, 'Shakespeare and *Caesar's Revenge*', *SQ* 32 (1981), 101–4. The resemblances are very slight and do not suggest any influence on *R2*.

which ought to have descended unto the duke of Hereford by lawfull inheritance, in revoking his letters patents, which he had granted to him before, by vertue whereof he might make his attorneis generall to sue liverie for him, of any maner inheritances or possessions that might from thenceefoorth fall unto him, and that his homage might be respited, with making reasonable fine: whereby it was evident, that the king meant his utter undooing.[1]

Shakespeare makes Richard say, before the confrontation with Gaunt, how useful a contribution from Gaunt's estate would be to add to the money from blank charters for the Irish wars (1.4.60-1), but he carefully sets up Richard's confiscation of Gaunt's entire estate as a consequence of Gaunt's dying speech aimed at correcting Richard. Gaunt (2.1.93-115) tries to deliver to Richard the truths which the flatterers Bushy, Bagot and Green have helped him to ignore. The effect, particularly painful to Richard in the presence of the flatterers, is to sting him to fury and the spiteful reprisal of total confiscation of Gaunt's estate. Shakespeare supplies a whole sequence of circumstances for the crucial act of tyranny.

By contrast with the exhibition of an uncontrolled Richard in this expansion of Holinshed, the mirror episode of 4.1 shows Richard behaving as adroitly and deviously as he does when he is handling the duellists in 1.3. Several details in Holinshed are set together in 4.1, the chief purpose being the confrontation of Bullingbrook and Richard in Parliament, which is not in the sources. In Shakespeare's most potent addition Northumberland tries to make Richard read out loud the thirty-three 'Articles' which Holinshed itemises and which were later turned into a 'bill of renouncement' which the historical Richard signed in private. Shakespeare makes Richard evade Northumberland by calling for a mirror and putting on a display of self-pity which eventually forces Bullingbrook to let him depart without reading the Articles. The iconography of the mirror develops some of the play's themes, notably in Richard's shadowy existence once unkinged, while as an evasive tactic it both matches the historical facts and adds a nuance to Richard's character. It is a *coup de théâtre* which makes a characteristically Shakespearean use of source material.

The study of sources has tangible value in allowing some measurement of the changes and choices made by the author. What can usefully be deduced, however, is limited when a wide range of possible sources is available, because the negative fact of the author choosing not to use a particular detail or colouring is a consideration of doubtful weight. Shakespeare seems to have been unusually thorough by his own standards in the amount of material he consulted for *Richard II*. How much we can learn from his selection or omission of significant detail depends to a large extent on our presuppositions about his underlying attitudes. Neither Holinshed nor Froissart makes any allusion to the divine right which Shakespeare's Richard invokes in 3.2. Daniel only refers to it in two lines (*Civil Wars*, II, 5): 'O *Majestie* left naked all alone / But with th'unarmed title of thy right'. Presumably Shakespeare emphasised it only as an element in Richard's personality, since the emblematic garden scene (3.4), while making the point that Richard's deposition is a consequence of his mismanagement of the national garden, has no reference at all to divine right. The

[1] Holinshed, *Chronicles*, 1587, II, 496. See Appendix 1, p. 197 below.

3 Richard II, from the tomb in Westminster Abbey, modelled from Richard's corpse. The tomb could have been seen by Shakespeare

4   Bullingbrook as Henry IV, from the effigy in Canterbury Cathedral. The effigy could have been seen by Shakespeare

emphasis given to it by an earlier generation of royalist critics such as Tillyard and Bullough[1] reflects their own presuppositions and their interpretation of the evidence of the source material. My own supposition, in contrast to previous Cambridge editors, is that Shakespeare chose his materials with a very precise idea of the structure

[1]   See for instance E. M. W. Tillyard, *Shakespeare's History Plays*, 1944, pp. 60–1, and Geoffrey Bullough, *Narrative and Dramatic Sources*, III, 355. A balanced view of the debate over royalism and orthodoxy is offered by Robert P. Merrix, 'Shakespeare's histories and the new bardolators', *SEL* 19 (1979), 179–96. For all Merrix's balance, the current political estimate is probably better represented by the essays in John Alvis and Thomas G. West (eds.), *Shakespeare as a Political Thinker*, 1981. Two essays, by Allan Bloom and Louise Cowan, see a problematic play which resolves the problems in an indeterminate way.

he wanted to create, and that this choice depended more on dramatic form and the principle of balance than on any political predisposition. The complete form of the play is all we can really rely on.

Structure

Dramatic form is a challenge to audiences (including readers and critics) who wish to identify an extrinsic political point in it, because of all the forms of fiction it is the one in which the author's presence is least apparent. Shakespeare has been recognised as a 'politic' historian like John Hayward and Francis Bacon,[1] but if he is one it is because his medium does what Bacon praised Machiavelli for, and portrays 'what men do, and not what they ought to do'.[2] Bacon was echoing Machiavelli's own claim in chapter 15 of *Il Principe*, and acknowledging the advantages of starting with earthly realism rather than godly moralising. Shakespeare's history plays follow the same principle of dealing only with earthly causes and effects. In the process they leave the authorial design apparent only in the total construct of what men say and do. It is from such evidence that deductions about political or human bias have to be drawn. Richard's faith in his divine right to rule is no evidence for Shakespeare's faith.

If a single word could be found to describe the structure of *Richard II* it would have to be 'balance'. There is the emblematic image of Fortune's scales, which the Gardener offers at 3.4.84–9; there is Richard's own emblem of the two buckets at 4.1.183–8, which he expounds as he and Bullingbrook hold the crown between them; there are the many verbal and situational images set up in Acts 1 and 2 and renewed or reversed in Acts 4 and 5. And more basic than all these is the image-pattern of the four elements, which presents Richard starting as fire and air and ending in water and earth, and Bullingbrook ascending through the contrary elements. Richard's fire (the sun) and air (words) descend to become water (tears) and earth (a grave). This reversal of positions is the most clear-cut evidence for the pattern of balance which Shakespeare imposed on his material.[3]

The elemental imagery and the images linked to it are described in detail below. The two emblems of Fortune's changing balance are patterns in the play's structure, which is not the usual two-strand plot that Shakespeare used for the next plays in the sequence, the Henry IV plays, where the Court, Hotspur and the rebellion are the main or serious plot and Eastcheap and Falstaff the comic sub-plot. Instead it comprises two equal and crossing plots of Richard and Bullingbrook. This fact helps to explain some of the play's peculiarities. It progresses through talk rather than action; it omits from Act 3 Northumberland's trick in capturing Richard; it lacks comedy apart from York's bumbling and the subtle burlesque of the Aumerle

---

[1] F. J. Levy, *Tudor Historical Thought*, 1967, p. 233.

[2] *De Augmentis* VII, ch. 2, in *Works*, ed. Spedding, 14 vols, 1857–74, V, 17.

[3] In a substantial article on the Christian imagery in the play, Stanley R. Maveety, 'A second fall of cursed man: the bold metaphor in *Richard II*', *JEGP* 72 (1973), 175–93, examines the integrative religious pattern and concludes (p. 187) that the play condemns both Richard and Bullingbrook, and (p. 193) is concerned with history more than with personalities.

conspiracy in 5.2 and 5.3;[1] and it omits any explicit reference to Bullingbrook's dubious claim by blood to be Richard's heir.[2] Extraneous historical details and intrusive comedy are kept out in order to emphasise the competition between the two occupants of Fortune's scales. Even the difference in the contenders' attitudes to Fortune is stressed. Where Richard sees it as fate which has him on its wheel and therefore determines his fall, Bullingbrook by contrast sees it in materialistic terms as the object of his return from exile and the means to reward his allies (2.3.48, 66). Richard's descent from Act 2 onwards is passive, 'patient' and fatalistic while Bullingbrook's ascent is active, bloody and materialistic.

Their paths cross in 3.3. On either side of that point there are visual and emblematic parallels which emphasise the change. Richard sits as judge in 1.1 while the contenders for truth throw down their gages in front of him. Bullingbrook does the same in 4.1. Richard tells them to 'freely speak' at 1.1.17 and Bullingbrook uses the identical phrase at 4.1.2, with no better result. After Richard's act of injustice in seizing Gaunt's estates in 2.1 three nobles agree to conspire against him. After Bullingbrook's act of injustice in seizing the crown in 4.1 three conspirators agree to plot against him. The contrasting roles of loyal father and treacherous son in Act 1, where Gaunt advocates Christian patience against the royal murderer of his brother Gloucester while Gaunt's son Bullingbrook attempts bloody revenge, are counter-balanced in 5.3.59 when Bullingbrook himself praises York in contrast to Aumerle as a 'loyal father of a treacherous son'. More narrowly verbal repetitions include the queen welcoming grief as a guest at 2.2.7 and complaining of it at 5.1.14. The most striking verbal feature of the balance pattern is the frequency, unique to this play, of invented negative verbs. Gaunt hopes to 'undeaf' Richard's ear (2.1.16). Bullingbrook's wealth on his first landing back in England is 'unfelt thanks' (2.3.61). In 3.1.9–10 Bullingbrook calls himself a 'happy [i.e. fortunate] gentleman' who has been 'unhappied' by the flatterers. Richard is urged to 'uncurse' his flatterers (3.2.137), and also asks the queen to 'unkiss' their marriage oath (5.1.74). Most conspicuously he calls himself 'unkinged' twice, both times exploiting the change of names, when he declares 'God save King Henry, unkinged Richard says' at 4.1.219 and 'I am unkinged by Bullingbrook' at 5.5.37.

A rather less distinct feature of the shifting balance in the play is the generation gap. The sons diverge from their fathers in subtle variations of the loyal father and treacherous son pattern. Besides the treachery of Bullingbrook to his king Richard and of his cousin Aumerle to his king Bullingbrook, Richard himself is called 'degenerate' (2.1.262) to his descent from Edward III and the Black Prince his father.

[1] See Sheldon P. Zitner, 'Aumerle's conspiracy', *SEL* 14 (1974), 239–57.

[2] Roger Mortimer, Earl of March, had the nearest claim to be Richard's heir as a descendant of the next eldest son of Edward III after the Black Prince, Richard's father. He was killed in Ireland in 1398, his death prompting Richard's expedition there. His son Edmund Mortimer was only three years old at the time. Holinshed, just before his account of the Percy rebellion which features in *1H4*, explains: 'this Edmund was sonne to Roger earle of March, sonne to the ladie Philip, daughter of Lionel duke of Clarence, the third sonne of King Edward the third; which Edmund at king Richards going into Ireland, was proclaimed heire apparant to the crowne and realme' (II, 521). Bullingbrook as the son of Gaunt, Edward III's fourth son, could not claim precedence over a descendant of the third son.

Aumerle's treachery to Bullingbrook is simultaneously loyalty to Richard, until the discovery of his share in the conspiracy against the new king leads him to beg for pardon and swear an expedient loyalty to him.[1] His father York by contrast is an honest turncoat. From being a reluctant and 'patient' (2.1.163) supporter of Richard he shifts when Regent into the stance of 'neuter' (2.3.158), voicing the dilemma of alternative loyalty to his two nephews at 2.2.111–15.[2] By 4.1 he becomes a tacit supporter of Bullingbrook. The path of York with his comic old man's dithering and his old man's fury against his son in 5.2 and 5.3 traces the shifting balance of loyalties through the length of the play.[3]

This structure throws some points of light on the personalities of Richard and Bullingbrook and provides a means of avoiding the turgid theorising about Richard as an actor or poet which entered twentieth-century readings of the play under the promptings of Pater and Yeats.[4] It also gives a perspective on the consequent division which some readers have seen between the real self and real language – the private individual Richard – and the public self and false language – the kingly persona. At the very least it puts into a larger and more luminous perspective the vexed question of the relationship between Richard and the play as a whole. Richard has been seen as a tragic martyr,[5] and as a clever politician.[6] The play is variously the tragedy of Richard, separate from the plays which followed it in the sequence, or a history of England the reading of which is distorted if it is presented as a tragedy. It has been shown to be inseparably of both genres,[7] and it has been seen as a distinct genre of its own.[8] The excuse that Richard's 'personage is so sore intangled'[9] was recorded as early as the 1559 edition of the *Mirror for Magistrates*.

The question of Richard as an actor, whose words are divorced from the political realities which in his role as king he should command, involves the question how far

---

[1] See Warren J. McIsaac, 'The three cousins in *Richard II*', *SQ* 22 (1971), 137–46.

[2] Shakespeare makes York submit to Bullingbrook because his forces are weak, as would be expected of a comic bumbler. In *A Mirror for Magistrates* York actually invites Bullingbrook to come back from exile.

[3] Norman Rabkin, *Shakespeare and the Common Understanding*, 1967, pp. 87–8, and Michael F. Kelly, 'The function of York in *Richard II*', *Southern Humanities Review* 6 (1972), 257–67, see York as representative of England. A. R. Humphreys, *Shakespeare: Richard II*, 1967, pp. 44 ff., and Roy Battenhouse, 'Tudor doctrine and the tragedy of *Richard II*', *Rice University Studies* 60 (1974), 31–53, see him as comic. Zitner's analysis of the function of 5.2 and 5.3 strengthens the comic view. At the other extreme James A. Riddell, 'The admirable character of York', *Texas Studies in Literature and Language* 21 (1979), 492–502, sees York as a model of Christian stoicism in contrast to Richard.

[4] Pater, vividly remembering Charles Kean's spectacular 1857 production, published his essay in 1889 in *Scribner's Magazine* and the same year in his collection of essays *Appreciations*. Yeats wrote about *Richard II* in 'At Stratford-on-Avon' (1901), *Essays and Introductions*, 1961, pp. 96–110.

[5] See Moody E. Prior, *The Drama of Power*, 1973, ch. 9; Sidney Homan, '*Richard II*: the aesthetics of judgement', *Studies in the Literary Imagination* 5 (1972), 65–71; Donald H. Reiman, 'Appearance, reality and moral order in *Richard II*', *MLQ* 25 (1964), 34–45; and Karl F. Thompson, 'Richard II, martyr', *SQ* 8 (1957), 159–66.

[6] See Harold F. Folland, 'King Richard's pallid victory', *SQ* 24 (1973), 390–9; S. Schoenbaum, '*Richard II* and the realities of power', *S.Sur.* 28 (1975), 1–13; Lois Potter, 'The antic disposition of Richard II', *S.Sur.* 27 (1974), 33–41; and Nicholas Brooke, *Shakespeare's Early Tragedies*, 1968, pp. 110–33.

[7] Michael Quinn, '"The king is not himself": the personal tragedy of Richard II', *SP* 55 (1959), 169–86.

[8] John R. Elliott, Jr, 'History and tragedy in *Richard II*', *SEL* 7 (1968), 253–71.

[9] *A Mirror for Magistrates*, ed. Lily B. Campbell, 1938, p. 110.

the whole sequence of plays is concerned with 'metadrama', the dramatisation of the problem of writing and language.[1] Some account of this view is given below in the section on the play's language. Its relevance here is to the political concept of the king's two bodies. This concept has been gruellingly examined by E. H. Kantorowicz[2] who sees *Richard II* as centrally concerned to explore and indeed explain it. In essence it was a legal fiction developed in the Middle Ages, an artificial separation of the king's physical body from his spiritual or legal existence as ruler. It was endorsed by the assumption of the king's divine right to rule because his divinity prevented any separation of the two bodies and gave a mystical sanction to inheritance of the title. Once England shifted, as it did in 1272, from an elective monarchy to a hereditary throne, the assumption of divine authority to rule became a needful accessory. Primogeniture as a natural law was also a divine law. The two bodies gave divine sanction to the idea of the crown as inherited property.[3]

Philip Edwards in a judicious essay on 'Person and office in Shakespeare's plays'[4] makes the point that the identity between the man and his office was a matter of *ought* rather than *is*. By Elizabethan criteria Richard's royal nature should have made the two indistinguishable. He himself is led in the course of the play to shift his own view from the assumption that his person is sacred, regardless of what he might do, into an acceptance that like 'glistering Phaëton' he might not be able to fulfil his office, and finally to a recognition of the need for the 'concord of my state and time' (5.5.47), a concurrence between his role (the throne of state) and conduct. The play is stretched by the tension between the *ought*, the continuum of person and office, and the *is* of the 'autonomous and plastic self'[5] which can choose to mould itself to its office, as Henry V does, or not, like Richard with his catalogue of injustices against his subjects. Politics and language both suffer when person and office are separate.

This tension stretches between the distinct views of kingship held by the Richardian and Lancastrian parties. Richard calls his blood 'sacred' and proclaims divine protection in 3.2 and 3.3. Carlisle makes the same claim in 4.1, that the man cannot be separated from his office, though Carlisle's speech is made at a time when Richard himself is prepared to admit precisely the opposite by abdicating. The view which separates the man from the office is first voiced by York at 2.1.198 when he protests against Richard's misconduct, and more ominously by Northumberland 43 lines later. Both say bluntly that the king is not himself. Northumberland follows this at 295 with the announcement that he will, by joining Bullingbrook, 'make high majesty look like itself'. The office needs a new man. At the end of the play he speaks of Bullingbrook's

---

[1] J. L. Calderwood, *Metadrama in Shakespeare's Henriad: 'Richard II' to 'Henry V'*, 1979.

[2] E. H. Kantorowicz, *The King's Two Bodies: A Study in Medieval Political Theology*, 1957.

[3] An apt summary of the main conflicts in Elizabethan political thought is Arthur Humphreys, 'Shakespeare's political justice in *Richard II* and *Henry IV*', *Stratford Papers on Shakespeare*, 1964, 30–50, especially pp. 33–8. An interpretation of the opposing views about the deposition as contrary ideals rather than one ideal violated is in Helmut and Jean Bonheim, 'The two kings in Shakespeare's *Richard II*', *Shakespeare Jahrbuch* (Heidelberg), 1971, pp. 169–79. Edna Zwick Boris, *Shakespeare's English Kings, The People and the Law*, 1978, includes a judicious survey of the legal background to the English history plays.

[4] Philip Edwards, 'Person and office in Shakespeare's plays', *Proceedings of the British Academy* 56 (1972), 93–109.   [5] *Ibid.*, p. 105.

'sacred state', the throne, not his sacred person.[1] Bullingbrook, like his father Gaunt, sees England as a piece of property which its owner has neglected and abused. His materialism, which makes him kill the flatterers who misused his estate, also lets him see the crown as the title to a property which can be bequeathed by will like the property of an ordinary title-holder. Elizabethan constitutional law was uneasy over this question. It never came to terms with the implications of Henry VIII's will. Henry bequeathed his crown to his children in a named succession – Edward, Mary, Elizabeth – as an alternative to the law of primogeniture. In the event no real conflict ensued, but the question whether a monarch had the right to bestow his title where he pleased was never settled. It was a question which ignored the metaphysics of the two bodies doctrine just as the Lancastrians in the play choose to ignore it.[2]

Between these two views, along the tightrope between the man and his office, stands the view of the Gardener in 3.4. There is no assumption of divinity there, only the responsibility of the royal gardener to keep his garden orderly and to prune the too-fast-growing sprays. If it has any political point, this scene, poised between the political realism of the confrontation at Flint Castle and the attempted legalisms of the Parliament scene, expresses the realistic political need for the man to fit the office. There is no divine right in the Gardener's concept of kingship, only good husbandry.[3] The vanities which made Richard light, and the narrow circle of flatterers who kept the weight of England's nobility at a distance from him, show the discordance of his state and his neglect of his good earth.

Richard's 'state' was essentially judicial. His office was to act as his country's lawgiver and judge. Bullingbrook's concept of the office is narrowly legalistic, like Gaunt's, York's and Northumberland's. He challenges law against the lawgiver, first covertly through his accusation of Richard's agent Mowbray in Act 1, then for his own property in Acts 2 and 3, and finally through 'the high court of Parliament', summoned to investigate Gloucester's murder, in Act 4. Gaunt's charge against Richard in 2.1 is that he has renounced his office as lawgiver by leasing his property to his flatterers and therefore ceding to them his legal authority. 'Thy state of law [the judicial throne] is bondslave to the law', he tells Richard in a sharply two-edged assertion of Richard's enslavement into bondage under the law he should command. Gaunt has already implicitly questioned Richard's justice in Act 1, over the duel, itself a practice uniformly condemned in the sixteenth century as unjust.[4] His argument with Gloucester's widow in 1.2 makes it clear that he saw the basis for the duel in

---

[1] The word 'sacred' appears more often in *R2* than in any other of Shakespeare's plays. The 'sacred' blood of kinship is invoked several times. Richard uses it of himself at 1.1.119. The murdered Gloucester's widow uses it at 1.2.12 of Edward III, father of the seven sons one of whom has shed his sacred blood through the agency of his blood kin, Edward's grandson Richard. Thus sacred blood has already been shed at the outset of the play.

[2] Shelley's case, a lawsuit of 1579–81 which was regularly quoted for three centuries, laid it down that property rights could be bequeathed to others than the heirs presumptive. Marie Axton, *The Queen's Two Bodies*, 1977, describes the problem of Henry VIII's will (p. 35), and gives an acute reassessment of the 'two bodies' question as it emerged in the 1590s succession debate (pp. 88–115).

[3] See Graham Holderness, 'Shakespeare's history: *Richard II*', *Literature and History* 7 (1981), 2–24, p. 19.

[4] See Diane Bornstein, 'Trial by combat and official irresponsibility in *Richard II*', *S.St.* 8 (1975), 131–41.

the murder, and that he cannot enforce justice on the royal judge, leaving it instead
to the supreme authority, 'the will of heaven' (1.2.6). Gaunt's thoughts follow the
line implied by Bullingbrook's reference (1.1.104) to Abel's blood, the punishment
for which Genesis declares is in God's hands. Gaunt in this way puts together the
concept of sacred majesty and judicial rule. His adoption of Christian 'patience'
(1.2.29) upholds the view of kingship proclaimed by Carlisle in 4.1. It had Biblical
sanction, for instance in Hosea 13.11, where evil rulers are said to be God's affliction
on erring mankind and therefore not to be actively opposed. That view was put
forcefully by the Homilies and James I.[1] The two arguments appear in open conflict
in 3.3, where Richard's assertion of kingly rights (72–100) is met by Northumberland's
assertion of subject's rights, at the pivotal point of the play.[2]

The alternatives of justice and divinity in kingship both focus attention on the
personality which will not be moulded by the office. Shakespeare sets out Richard's
injustices in the first two acts, making his murder of his uncle Gloucester the
underlying cause of the quarrel between Bullingbrook and Mowbray, and displaying
his rash wilfulness against Gaunt in 2.1. The flatterers do little in the way of flattering
and nothing to guide Richard in his unjust ways. They mirror his ego and support
his waywardness but their passivity leaves the full responsibility in Richard's hands.[3]
In this respect Shakespeare's play differs markedly from *Woodstock*, which supplied
him with some details of Richard's abuses but which laid all the blame on the flatterers.
Richard is fully responsible for his own fall. He words himself into abdication in the
face of the 'silent king'.

Richard's words carry his own denial of his divinity. He gives his crown to
Bullingbrook with a willingness that presents another version of Christian patience
under God's will. In 3.2 he counters the urging of Carlisle, translated by Aumerle
(27–35), to take positive action in endorsement of heaven's will, with the claim that
heaven will do all the work itself. It is this implicit fatalism which leads directly to
the despair with which he receives the news of Bullingbrook's advance. These shifts,
from the arrogant and self-willed exercise of injustice against the duellists in 1.3 and
against Gaunt in 2.1 to the acquiescence with which he accepts Bullingbrook's return,
have evoked among the play's critics a flurry of analysis of his failure to 'act' like
a king, his role-playing in and out of office and his acting more like a poet than a
king.[4] His complaint even after handing the crown to Bullingbrook that if not a king

---

[1] See Appendix 3. In *The Trew Law of Free Monarchies* (1598) James I made the same broad claims.
[2] Humphreys, *Richard II*, makes this point (p. 48). E. W. Talbert, *The Problem of Order*, 1962, suggests
    there is an alternation in 4.1 between Yorkist (Richardian and divine right) views and Lancastrian; first
    Lancastrian (162–7), then Yorkist (167–76), Lancastrian (177–80), Yorkist (181–90), and Lancastrian
    (190–222). This is perhaps too exact, but it does affirm the balanced presentation of the arguments. By
    comparison the debate between Peter Ure and A. L. French in *Essays in Criticism* 17 (1967) and 18 (1968)
    reads like straightforward Yorkist (Ure) versus Lancastrian (French). A useful summary of the Yorkist
    and Lancastrian interpretations of English history is in Henry Ansgar Kelly, *Divine Providence in the
    England of Shakespeare's Histories*, 1970, p. 205.
[3] Paul Gaudet, 'The "parasitical" counselors in Shakespeare's *Richard II*: a problem of dramatic
    interpretation', *SQ* 33 (1982), 142–54.
[4] Examinations of Richard as actor–king are numerous. See for instance Leonard F. Dean, 'Richard II:
    the state and the image of the theater', in *Shakespeare: Modern Essays in Criticism*, 1957, pp. 159–68,

he is 'nothing' has attracted to him all, or almost all, the sympathy due to a tragic hero, victim of his own illusion.[1]

To a great extent this view depends on the notion of the king's two bodies, the moral equation between what a man is and what he does. It is perhaps most aptly summarised by Alvin Kernan,[2] who sees the sequence of plays from *Richard II* to *Henry V* as epic in scale, a 'Henriad' tracing the dynastic, cultural and psychological transitions from medieval to modern England, from ritualistic feudalism to uncertain individualism and from the certainties of the past to the role-playing identity-crisis of the fallen world. In the first play of this sequence Richard thinks his world immutable while undermining it by his abuses. He ends in isolated darkness trying to 'hammer't out' into a new coherence, and finds only endless mutability, as his successors with their complex role-playing must also do. Richard's tragic discovery is every man's. He 'traces the way that the other major characters must each follow in their turn'.[3]

There is substantial evidence in the play to support Kernan's overview. It can paint with too broad a brush, though, and in particular it needs testing along with the Paterian concept of Richard as an actor, a man misled by his fascination with words. Theodore Weiss, when he says that *Richard II* 'is Shakespeare's most thoroughgoing study of the absorption in words and of the perils such absorption invites',[4] summarises the idea of Richard which is based on his behaviour at the end of the play and ignores what goes before. Such a view projects sympathy for a dead king backwards and puts a gloss on his conduct which is not warranted by the body of the play. It evokes a simple pity for the Richard of the mirror scene in 4.1, for instance, and so allows us to overlook the fact that Richard calls for the mirror in order to evade Northumberland's insistence that he read the Articles listing his misdeeds. It also invites a reading of 1.3 making Richard stop the duel merely out of histrionic self-regard, a desire to exercise arbitrary power and to keep the centre-stage for himself. It thus ignores the essential point of the duel. Richard has used Mowbray to murder Gloucester. If Mowbray won the duel Richard would be open to Mowbray's blackmail, as his enigmatic lines at 1.1.132–4 and 175–6 and 1.3.155–8 indicate. Equally if Bullingbrook won, Richard's guilt would be made evident. Richard cannot afford to have either man win, and therefore chooses to send both into the silence of exile for his own political safety.[5] The balance in *Richard II* is not between a

and Thomas F. Van Laan, *Role-Playing in Shakespeare*, 1978. Richard speaks of Death allowing him only 'a little scene/To monarchise' at 3.2.164–5. York broaches the image – in the form of a simile – at 5.2.23–8.

[1] The specific aspect of Richard's tragedy of namelessness is well set out by James Winny, *The Player King*, 1968, pp. 48–9, following a telling essay by Donald J. Gordon, 'Name and fame: Shakespeare's *Coriolanus*', in *Papers Mainly Shakespearean*, ed. G. I. Duthie, 1964, pp. 40–57. Names shift in the play amongst all three cousins descended from Edward III.

[2] Alvin Kernan, 'The Henriad: Shakespeare's major history plays', *Yale Review* 59 (1969), 3–32, reprinted in *Modern Shakespearean Criticism*, ed. Alvin B. Kernan, 1970.

[3] Kernan, 'Henriad', p. 10.

[4] Theodore Weiss, *The Breath of Clowns and Kings*, 1971, p. 260.

[5] See Larry S. Champion, 'The function of Mowbray: Shakespeare's maturing artistry in *Richard II*', *SQ* 26 (1975), 3–7.

medieval and out-of-date Richard and a modern, practical Bullingbrook.[1] The man Richard has no more moral right to his office than Bullingbrook has legal right.

Looking too closely at Richard as the play's tragic hero has the effect of distorting the balance between the two figures, an equivalence which is also concealed by their contrasting conduct. Richard talks while Bullingbrook acts. Richard dies and Bullingbrook lives.[2] These features, however, confirm the play's symmetry quite as much as they appear to conceal it. Richard's words, for instance, his wonderful verbalising of his emotions, are countered by Bullingbrook's actions. Bullingbrook's taciturnity in words is balanced by Richard's passivity in actions. Richard's two main actions, stopping the duel and seizing Gaunt's estate, both are reactions to an outside stimulus, not actions which he initiates. Otherwise he is passive when in danger and 'patient' in adversity up to the point of his death.[3] Bullingbrook by contrast takes initiatives, challenging Mowbray, returning from banishment, executing the flatterers, confronting Richard at Flint and summoning Parliament for a judicial airing of the question of Gloucester's murder. The language the two men use is not radically different except for the different forms of cover it provides for their respective passivity and activity, and in Richard's greater quantity of words.[4]

Imagery

Most of the images of the play are organised in relation to the four elements: earth, air, fire and water.[5] Richard, the sun-king of fire, contends with Bullingbrook, the flood. Their stormy conflict drowns Richard's fire in the water of tears and changes Bullingbrook into the sun, though a sun which can make rebels burn villages as quickly as did Phaëton, the 'son' who stole his father Apollo's sun-chariot, burned the earth when he lost control of it and was killed by a bolt from Zeus. Fire and water struggle for the earth of England and conduct their fight with the airy breath of words.

Each of the four elements possesses properties contrary to the others. Fire, the dominant element, is hot and its natural movement is upward. Air while cold also aspires (a pun used at 1.3.130) upward. Earth is dry and its natural tendency is downward, and water is wet and also tends downward. The theory of physical humours, which held that human character is fixed by the combination of these elements, also appears in the play as an aspect of the elemental pattern. Blood, the product of the hot and moist humours and therefore naturally related to fire and water,

---

[1] See Peter G. Phialas, 'The medieval in *Richard II*', *SQ* 12 (1961), 305–10. Phialas's point is developed by Robert D. Hapgood, 'Three eras in *Richard II*', *SQ* 14 (1963), 281–3.

[2] Sidney Homan's essay is a lucid analysis of the 'impossible equipoise between achievement in the public world and self-realisation in a private world' for both men (Homan, 'Aesthetics of judgement', p. 71).

[3] Shakespeare makes his Richard markedly weaker than Holinshed's or Daniel's, by omitting the trickery of Northumberland in capturing Richard before the Flint episode and by inventing his volatility in 3.2.

[4] The language of Richard and Bullingbrook has been analysed in a variety of ways. See below, p. 34.

[5] R. D. Altick, 'Symphonic imagery in *Richard II*', *PMLA* 62 (1947), 339–65, was the first commentator to identify a systematic pattern in the imagery. Arthur Suzman added to Altick's pattern in 'Imagery and symbolism in *Richard II*', *SQ* 7 (1956), 355–70, as did Kathryn M. Harris, 'Sun and water imagery in *Richard II*', *SQ* 21 (1970), 157–65. The best close study of the imagery and of the language generally remains Mahood.

inevitably predominates in the conflict between Richard and Bullingbrook. Blood and choler, the hot and dry humour, rule their early exchanges. Once Bullingbrook's flood overcomes Richard's fire Richard's temperament changes to the cold and pensive humour of melancholy. The warmth of England's earth under the benign sun of a proper king is lost first by Mowbray and Bullingbrook as they are forced into the cold silence and namelessness of exile, and finally by Richard in the cold silence of a hollow grave in the cold earth.

The basic images of the elements appear in different forms, some perhaps less recognisable than others. Fire is most obviously represented in Richard as the sun, and later in 'Bullingbrook's fair day' (3.2.218). The contest with Bullingbrook's flood produces storms (2.1.263–9, 2.4.19–22 and 3.3.43–6), in accordance with the idea that thunder and lightning are the product of the elements fire and water (sea or rain) in conflict with each other in the air. The sun warms the earth's garden, but when the king is only a Phaëton, fires break out on the earth (3.3.178–9 and 5.6.2–3). The choler of the duellists in 1.1 and their 'high blood' are features of the upward tendency of the hot element. The second of the upward-moving elements, air, appears as breath, tongues and words. Mowbray in 1.1.47 urges that his 'cold words' should not conceal the heat of his choler. Tongues, using air, and hearts, using blood, are too often distinct from each other (1.3.255–6, 5.5.97). Gaunt's mood in 2.1 is inspired whilst his breath and soul expire (31–2), and Richard calls to his soul to 'mount' to heaven while his body remains for the earth when he is killed by Exton (5.5.111–12). Bullingbrook's aspiration to the height of a crown is implied in references to one of the Lancaster emblems, a white falcon.[1] Richard's derisive comment at 1.1.109, 'How high a pitch his resolution soars!', has a hidden allusion not only to the falcon emblem which Bullingbrook alludes to at 1.3.61 but to the 'stoop' which was the falcon's dive on its prey, and also the visual gesture Bullingbrook had demanded of Mowbray, that he must stoop to take up Bullingbrook's gage (line 74). Stooping and kneeling on the earth as gestures of loyalty and respect are emblematic gestures which the play exploits through their links with the elements nearly as much as it does through their function in defining social status and attitude. The element of air indirectly recurs through words relating to voice, breath and tongue, just as earth recurs in references to land and England. As the land is wounded by the actions which take place on it, so the tongues of men misuse the air when language labours to express or to suppress reality and the 'breath of kings' in Richard gives away everything to the 'silent king' Bullingbrook. The same tongues find things sweet or sour as Fortune changes the earth for them. Earth, the heavy element, sustains all that walk on it, whether it appears as England itself, as the cultivated garden of 3.4 or as the little hollow grave which receives Richard. It has its sour venom in snakes, toads and spiders as well as its sweet Edenic fertility as a 'teeming womb of royal kings' (2.1.51), a 'blessed plot' which has become a 'tenement or pelting farm' under Richard's management. The other downward-tending element, water, appears as a flood when Bullingbrook invades the

---

[1] Holinshed reports an entertainment for Richard at Windsor before he went to Ireland of a joust of forty knights dressed in green with a white falcon as their emblem (II, 496).

land (3.2.106–10), and as rain in Bullingbrook's own account of his return (3.3.58–60).
Amongst those who suffer the flood, Richard's queen is the first to speak (2.2.27) of
the tears which come to dominate Richard's own humour. When Bullingbrook comes
to the confrontation with Richard he announces how harmless his arrival will be in
terms based on all four elements.

> Methinks King Richard and myself should meet
> With no less terror than the elements
> Of fire and water when their thundering shock
> At meeting tears the cloudy cheeks of heaven.
> Be he the fire, I'll be the yielding water.
> The rage be his, whilst on the earth I rain
> My waters; on the earth and not on him.   (3.3.54–60)

But once Richard's fire is quenched he is left with the cold melancholy of water and
earth, tears and the grave. Water and earth also interact through the play in blots
and spots, whether the blots on England's legal parchments (2.1.64), and the spots
on Mowbray's leopard coat and the 'spotless reputation' (1.1.178) that he hopes for,
or the spotted souls of the vipers (3.2.134) who occupy the earth like poisonous
caterpillars.

The elemental imagery is deployed most fully in two scenes, 1.1 and 3.2, which
mark the beginning and end of Richard's dominance. It is worth noting now
systematically they are emphasised and how exactly they interact. At 1.1.14 Richard
describes the contestants Bullingbrook and Mowbray as 'In rage deaf as the sea, hasty
as fire', the condition of the elements appropriate to a storm. In 37–8 Bullingbrook
speaks of his body on earth and his soul in heaven both asserting his truth, and at
41–2 calls Mowbray an ugly raincloud in the honest clarity of the sky. Mowbray picks
up the imagery with the 'cold words' of air and tongues, and at 58 introduces the
humours image in Bullingbrook's 'high blood's royalty'. At 74 Bullingbrook tells
Mowbray to 'stoop' (to the earth, as if in homage and humility or shame) to pick
up his enemy's gage, and at 82 Mowbray speaks of mounting his horse against
Bullingbrook as if he is ascending in honour. Bullingbrook accuses Mowbray of
Gloucester's murder, suggesting that the corpse calls for revenge from its grave in
'the tongueless caverns of the earth' (105). Richard returns to the humours imagery
at 153 with his ghoulish and implausible hope that the choler can be purged without
using the drastic expedient of bloodletting, and the scene ends with a marked
difference over kneeling. Mowbray kneels to Richard, his king and employer in the
murder of Gloucester at 165, but Bullingbrook, accuser of Mowbray over the murder
and thus obliquely the accuser of Richard himself, will not kneel. His speech at 187–95
contains assertions of his height in his refusal to be 'crestfallen', and of blood and
air in his readiness to bite out his tongue and spit it bleeding in Mowbray's face before
he will talk to him. Such defiance is an ominous assertion of 'high' Herford's
arrogance and his own idea of his height compared with his king's.

In 3.2 Richard's height and heat are measured against Bullingbrook's rising waters.
The scene opens with Aumerle asking how the king enjoys the air of England's earth
'After your late tossing on the breaking seas'. Storms have already been heralded at

5   A sun emblem on Richard's cloak, from the tomb in Westminster Abbey. It might have been seen as the sun emerging from behind a cloud, though its location on the upper side of the tomb makes it inaccessible to the casual visitor

1.1.14, 2.1.263–9 and 2.4.19–22, and Bullingbrook includes thunder and lightning in his elements speech at 3.3.54–60. At first Richard weeps for joy and stoops to touch the earth with his hand. He contrasts the land's sweets with its poisons (12–22). When Aumerle sourly warns ('Discomfortable cousin') of Bullingbrook's power Richard broaches the sun-king image of himself as 'the searching eye of heaven' (37–53), with Bullingbrook working in the darkness of Richard's absence like a thief. Bullingbrook will turn red with guilt, the blood rising to his face, when Richard confronts him at sunrise. This elaborately dressed image is immediately followed by a blunt refusal to acknowledge Bullingbrook's flood:

> Not all the water in the rough rude sea
> Can wash the balm off from an anointed king.   (3.2.54–5)

It is another fifty lines before Scroope arrives with his image of Bullingbrook in flood, but Richard evidently already feels his fire to be threatened. In the next line he also condemns the thought that 'The breath of worldly men' can depose God's heavenly deputy. At once Salisbury enters with the news of the Welsh soldiers dispersing, news which, using the terms of Richard's own sun-king image, Salisbury says has 'clouded all thy happy days on earth'. The blood leaves Richard's sun-face (76–9). Then Scroope enters with his image of Bullingbrook 'like an unseasonable stormy day', a summer tempest which makes the brook overflow its bank and flood the land with steel. Scroope's further news about the flatterers evokes from Richard images of the bitter earth, 'Snakes in my heart blood warmed', which leads Scroope to comment on how quickly sweet love turns to sour hate. When he learns that the flatterers are dead Richard weeps and thinks of graves and worms. He rejects the idea of inheritance (a tacit linkage with the imagery of blood) because all the land is Bullingbrook's and so all the king's party can bequeath is their bodies to the ground (148–50). At 168–70 he compares his body to a walled enclosure which death bores through with a mere pin. When raised again by his comforters he is finally thrown down by Scroope's last piece of news, which is to be seen in the messenger's eye in the way that 'the complexion of the sky' (194) predicts the day's weather. With this news Richard half concedes the transfer of the sun image from himself to Bullingbrook, 'From Richard's night to Bullingbrook's fair day'. The sun image of 37–53 which set up Richard as the sun and Bullingbrook as a thief in the night is now reversed. The elemental images are in balance and upward Bullingbrook is ready to pass downward Richard.

Later developments of the elemental images confirm the shifting balance. In 3.3.62 Richard is made to 'appear' like the red sun rising, but his ascent is like 'glistering Phaëton' and he soon descends to the 'base court'. The Gardener's image of the scales in the garden scene which follows (3.4.84–9) reinforces the concept of the altered balance, and gives odd resonances to the image of Fortune's buckets which Richard deploys later, in 4.1.183–8, where Richard's bucket is down 'drinking my griefs' while Bullingbrook is up and full of air. The Gardener's image had used the opposite elements, making Richard light with airy vanities and Bullingbrook heavy with his supporting nobles. Richard's bucket image is more apt to his own conceit of the sun-king, which he reiterates at 4.1.259–61:

> Oh that I were a mockery king of snow
> Standing before the sun of Bullingbrook,
> To melt myself away in water drops.

In the final act of the play Richard melts in tears. He ends consigning his body to the earth and hoping his soul will mount to heaven.

Most of the other groups of images have some linkage with the elemental pattern. The various associations of blood and inheritance, the food images of sweet and sour, with their implications in Richard's surfeiting, the visual impact of the recurrent kneeling, the contrast of kings sitting on their thrones and on the ground, and the frequent swearing of oaths all relate to the elements.

Blood is the humour combining fire and water, the elements which Richard and Bullingbrook exchange in the course of the play. It has a double significance, as the guarantor of lineage and inheritance on the one hand and as the mark of political disruption on the other. At 3.3.94 Richard warns Bullingbrook that his landing will open 'The purple testament of bleeding war'. The lineage aspect is emphasised by the Duchess of Gloucester's insistence on the descendants of Edward as 'seven vials of his sacred blood' (1.2.12). The coincidence of Edward having seven sons with the seven children of Jesse and the ancestry of Christ figured in medieval iconography was registered in the title page of Stow's *Annales of England* in 1592 (see illustration 6). Family trees, starting (at the bottom) with Jesse and ascending to Christ, were familiar in Shakespeare's time in church windows. One in Dorchester Abbey, for instance, south of Oxford on the Thames, has the figure of Jesse in stone on the sill of a north window, with the tree extending upwards in the stone tracery. The duchess's allusion to the tree of Jesse probably reflects equally the old iconography and Stow's adaptation.[1]

The descendants of Edward III in the play share the blood ties and the enmity of Cain and Abel. The issue is fair inheritance. Edward's living sons, Gaunt and York, preserve that inheritance against the grandsons, Richard and Aumerle, who wielded 'murder's bloody axe' (historically a pillow, but Shakespeare needed blood) in killing their uncle Gloucester. Richard himself denies Bullingbrook the acknowledgement of his blood right of inheritance until Bullingbrook forces him to it. Historically Bullingbrook was a marginally plausible heir to Richard after Roger Mortimer died in Ireland. Shakespeare makes no mention of Mortimer, and gives Richard instead that emphatic distancing which underlies both scenes of the quarrel between Bullingbrook and Mowbray:

> Were he my brother, nay, my kingdom's heir,
> As he is but my father's brother's son,
> Now by my sceptre's awe I make a vow
> Such neighbour nearness to our sacred blood
> Should nothing privilege him nor partialise
> The unstooping firmness of my upright soul. (1.1.116–21)

In 1.3 Richard addresses Bullingbrook cheerfully as 'Cousin of Herford', and makes

---

[1] See F. H. Crossley, *English Church Craftsmanship*, 1941, pp. 67, 70.

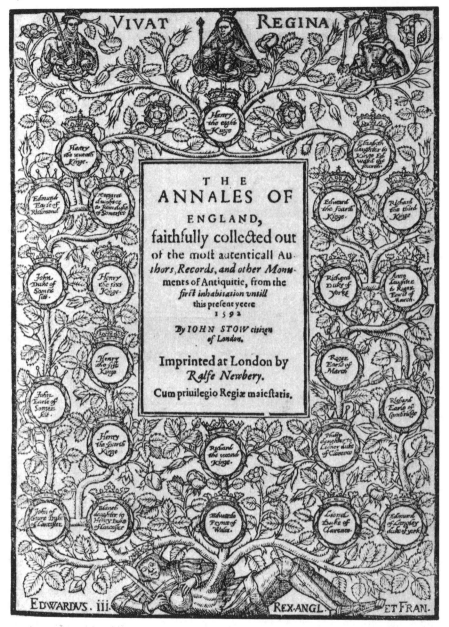

6   Edward III in an imitation of a Jesse tree. From the title page of John Stow, *Annales of England* (1592)

some play with the kinship signalled by the word cousin. At 3.3.189 he says that his cousin debases his 'princely knee' by touching the earth with it, an allusion to Bullingbrook's share in the royal blood of Edward. At the end of the play the blood on Bullingbrook's hands is that of Cain, shedder of family blood.[1]

Blood is also behind the references to self and to hearts. The disjunctions heart from tongue, heart from hand, and heart from knee all involve deception and change from the honesty of the Gaunt and York generation. And the high choler of Bullingbrook and Mowbray in 1.1 – 'In rage deaf as the sea, hasty as fire' – links the hot and moist humour of blood to the elemental imagery which is the play's most basic metaphorical pattern. All the images of blood, kinship, kingship and time run together in York's protest to Richard over his seizure of Gaunt's property and Bullingbrook's inheritance in 2.1.189–99.

The play is also crowded with the antithesis of sweet and sour. Although tied to the element of earth, which gives man its sweet or bitter harvest, it is primarily an image of feasting, which turns Richard's surfeit of sweetness into sour misfortune. At 2.2.84 York says 'Now comes the sick hour that his surfeit made.' In 3.2, the scene most packed with elemental images, Richard returns to look for more sweets from his land but finds only earth's poisons. He urges the earth not to comfort Bullingbrook with its sweets and calls Aumerle 'discomfortable' when the duke points out the need for military preparations. Salisbury and Scroope bring more 'discomfort' with their news until Richard orders 'Of comfort no man speak.' The emphasis on sweet and sour in this scene (12–15, 135–6, 193, 205) makes it likely that 'comfort' here is a homonym for 'comfit', the sweetmeat eaten at the end of an English feast, in contrast with the Dutch who ended their feasts with salt meat (2.1.13). In the dynamics of the play the sweets go to Bullingbrook and the sour diet is Richard's. In 3.4.105 the queen's rue is a 'sour herb of grace'. The change of diet is a fasting after the feasting, and links with the image of Richard's extravagance over time and care for his royal garden. 'I wasted time and now doth time waste me', he acknowledges (5.5.49).

The emblematic garden scene, 3.4, much discussed by the play's critics, serves the primary function in this context of emphasising the neglect of his land which accompanied Richard's surfeiting.[2] As 'landlord of England...not king' (2.1.113) the gardeners suggest that he has enjoyed the fruits of the garden while neglecting to prune its 'too-fast-growing sprays' (34). The servant's speech (40–7) makes the analogy exact, and echoes both Gaunt's sceptred isle speech (2.1.47–8) in its reference to 'our sea-wallèd garden' and Bullingbrook's complaint about the caterpillars of the commonwealth (2.3.165).

The elements of earth and air are behind the ceremonies attached to kingship and appear visually on stage in the kneeling, the hat-doffing in the various royal presences and in the enthroned kings. All the duties appropriate to subjects around their king, kneeling on the ground, swearing oaths to the air, remaining bareheaded in the presence, are displayed in 1.1 and 1.3 towards Richard, and in 4.1 and after towards

---

[1] See Robert B. Pierce, *Shakespeare's History Plays: The Family and the State*, 1971, p. 150.
[2] See Ure, pp. li–lvii. R. J. Dorius 'A little more than a little', *SQ* 11 (1960), 16–20, has a useful note on the relations of the garden symbol to the rest of the play.

Bullingbrook. Richard sits on the throne, raised several steps or 'degrees' above the ground in Act 1. In Act 3 he sits on the bare earth. In Act 4 Bullingbrook stands beside the throne and Richard stands bareheaded before him as Bullingbrook had done to him in 1.1. Kneeling is the subject's 'duty' of loyalty to the king. In 3.3.73 Richard demands that Northumberland kneel to him, but does not get this 'duty' until he has submitted to Bullingbrook's demands, by which point (175) it is an empty formality. Bullingbrook then kneels to Richard (for once the quarto text supplies the appropriate direction) at 187 when the king has descended to the base court, the place of servants. In 4.1 when Bullingbrook takes the throne from Richard (113) nobody kneels and Carlisle instead speaks sarcastically of 'this royal presence', changing the term to 'this noble presence' two lines later (115, 117). Richard himself says later (165) that he has not yet learned the subject's duty of kneeling. The scene is all words. Like 1.1 and 1.3, 4.1 is full of oaths about speaking the truth, and Richard's abdication takes the form of releasing everyone from their oaths of allegiance to him. But between 3.3.187 where Bullingbrook kneels to Richard and 5.3 where Aumerle kneels for mercy to Bullingbrook, nobody kneels either in duty or reverence to anyone. In the latter scene when Aumerle's mother kneels to secure his pardon the dutiful gesture becomes farcical. It has changed from a token of service to a histrionic plea for a promise or oath of mercy. There is no more kneeling in the play after that debasement.

A complex little linkage of concepts also derives from the posture of kneeling itself. Richard in 2.1 finds Gaunt bowed with age and not with respect. 'Crooked age' (133) does not bow Gaunt's 'unreverent shoulders' (123), a posture of disrespect which produces Richard's threat to cut his head off (an act performed with the victim kneeling and his head bowed over the block), as Richard had already done to Gaunt's brother. A more complex play on the same concept appears in the references to stooping. There is a hint of the falcon's flight, linked with the airy and upward ambition of falsely stooping Bullingbrook, in his 'stooping duty' at 3.3.48. Bullingbrook's stoop is an act of prey, not of homage.

The recurrent oath-taking gives to the air the true and false gestures which kneeling gives to the earth. The tongue and the heart and the hand and the heart are pairings which do not always speak the same language. The truth of actions contrasts in the play with the truth of words, to the detriment of language.

Language

Richard II is written entirely in verse, makes extensive use of rhyme, and has numerous set speeches. The formal language of the ceremony of duelling in 1.3, Richard's formal declaration absolving his followers from their oaths of loyalty to him at 4.1.203–14, Carlisle's oration in the style of the *sermo humilis* (4.1.115–49), the stichomythic exchanges between Gaunt and Richard in 2.1 and between Richard and his queen in 5.1, are all instances of formal rhetorical speeches which, although overtly stylised, do not stand out as markedly more artificial than their contexts. Even the rhymes, which have driven some critics (notably Dover Wilson) to dismiss the thought that Shakespeare could have written them, have a proper function in a play which is in many respects centred on the use of language and which puts it on display as the most important single instrument of Richard's fall.

Rhyme is the most conspicuous example in the play of formal verse, formal in the sense of verse which is overtly not a rhythmical version of ordinary speech. Its basic function is apparent in the opening scene of the play. There Bullingbrook and Mowbray make their accusations and counter-accusations against each other, in controlled anger and in terms which make it clear that at least one of them is speaking dishonestly, since clearly both cannot be offering the simple truth. The first appearance of rhyme is the couplets which close off speeches by each contender and their judge, Richard, at 1.1.18–19, 67–8, 82–3, 122–3 and 150–1. Bullingbrook has three successive couplets at 41–6 which conclude his initial charge against Mowbray with repetitions – 'Once more, the more to aggravate the note, / With a foul traitor's name stuff I thy throat.'[1] Pleonasmus or pointless duplication of words, and the application of names, a central feature of the use of language in the play, are both emphasised in this burst of rhyming. The formality of the ceremony of accusation rises to its peak in 154–95, which consists of twenty-one couplets. First Richard launches the judge's attempt to reconcile the opposing parties, drawing Gaunt into the exercise so that Richard exhorts his follower Mowbray while Gaunt does the same to his son Bullingbrook. Both make formal demands which hang momentarily in suspense at 164 while the contestants consider. Then Mowbray kneels to his interlocutor with two rhyming speeches. The act of refusing to do his king's bidding is not an easy one and the rhymes give his responses the weight of consideration which the situation demands. When Richard turns to Bullingbrook for his response he again hears it given in measured and stilted language. Richard's reaction then comes in four lines of hard, angry blank verse. The ceremonious formality returns with an effort in the three couplets with which he closes the scene.

Rhyming couplets, imposing a ceremonious formality on a tense confrontation which cannot be resolved but which has to be kept within bounds, reappear in the following scene between Gaunt and the widowed Duchess of Gloucester. Once the quarrel between them weakens into resignation the duchess says farewell in a couplet which has the standard winding-up function, the poetic full stop current in most plays of the 1590s. But the duchess cannot break off so smoothly, and returns for a final speech of grief delivered by means of an unusual variation. Her seventeen-line speech begins in blank verse, and gains more frequent couplets as the speaker gains control of herself. Two unrhymed lines are followed by a couplet, then an unrhymed line and another couplet, and one last unrhymed line before the three couplets which supply climax and emphasis for the scene's close. The lines which separate the couplets indicate the duchess's broken and distracted mind while the couplets indicate her more connected thoughts.

Gaunt, who speaks more couplet rhymes than any other character, and who also delivers up the most proverbial sayings and commonplaces, uses them for emphasis and also to display his settled confidence in his own rightness. In his main scene,

---

[1] See John Baxter, *Shakespeare's Poetic Styles: Verse into Drama*, 1980, pp. 155 ff.

the first part of 2.1, he starts with a structured recitation, even using a cross-rhyming quatrain in the first of his generalisations at 7–16. He caps Richard's replies with rhymes in the stichomythia of 84–93, but the two great passages, his 'sceptred isle' speech (40–68)[1] and the accusation against Richard (93–114), are in blank verse. This is not because they are more passionate and intense – though they have these qualities – but because they are less conventional. Gaunt is an honest man who uses couplets to express conventional wisdom. Blank verse is for him an intense and personal form of expression. The scene of his dying is a ceremony which needs no conventional couplets to assert the ceremonious nature of the occasion as Richard uses them in 1.1 and 1.3. Gaunt's two great speeches show his honest passion breaking through the veneer of ceremony. Only when Gaunt weakens and withdraws from the scene do couplets become the right form again.

The honesty of Gaunt's blank verse and its contrast with the trivialising character of his rhymes is one aspect of what is probably the play's most fundamental concern, the distance between words and what they represent. That distance is measured in a range of details, from the process of naming, through the unsuccessful attempts at maintaining ceremonial order,[2] to the kind of questioning of the role in art of language itself which has led some commentators to call the Henriad a 'metadrama', a form 'in which the playwright subjects the nature and materials of his art to radical scrutiny'.[3] All the points along this range warrant some scrutiny. Shakespeare made Richard's fall a matter of words by eliminating historical incidents such as Northumberland's ambush on the way to Flint Castle and inventing others such as Gaunt's deathbed and the deposition scene. Language is a central concern whatever the focus one looks for in the play.

Names work in their context as an index of value and a register of order. In the early part of the play they proclaim identity, as Mowbray asserts at 1.1.167, Gaunt at 2.1.86–7 and Bullingbrook at 3.1.24–7.[4] The progression of Bullingbrook from Herford to Lancaster and to king reflects changes in his identity, as does Richard's loss of name and Aumerle's change to Rutland. The changes indicate instability in the order of the state, the loss of the reality which gave strength to the ritual and ceremony. When Bullingbrook in 4.1 adopts Richard's rituals from 1.1 he not only stresses the separation of the man from the office but unsettles the security of names. When Richard is 'unkinged' the name of king becomes a name only, not a person. It is the corollary to the loss of identity as a man which Richard suffers when he loses his office, and Mowbray when he goes into tongueless exile.[5] York's protest 'be not

---

[1] There are many studies of Gaunt's deathbed speech, the best of which is by Donald M. Friedman, 'John of Gaunt and the rhetoric of frustration', *ELH* 43 (1976), 274–99.

[2] Leonard Barkan, 'The theatrical consistency of *Richard II*', *SQ* 29 (1978), 5–19, calls it 'a play of attempted ritual' (p. 6 n.).

[3] Calderwood, *Metadrama*, p. 1. The view that Shakespeare is tackling problems of language by means of politics rather than the reverse is broadly shared by Terence Hawkes, *Shakespeare's Talking Animals: Language and Drama in Society*, 1973, ch. 7.

[4] See T. P. McAlindon, *Shakespeare and Decorum*, 1973, pp. 23–5.

[5] Mowbray registers the price of exile from the homeland and the consequent loss of the power of speech at 1.3.160–70.

thyself' when Richard seizes Lancaster's inheritance, and Northumberland's echo of York (2.1.198 and 241), form the political equivalent of Richard's metaphysical formulation in prison, setting the word against the word (5.5.13–14).[1]

When names lose stability, language is equally unstable. The ceremonial denunciations of 1.1, which necessarily conceal lies, start a process of questioning and interpretation of meaning which runs throughout the play. It reaches its height at the point of balance in 3.3, where first Northumberland interprets Bullingbrook's message to Richard (101–20), and then Richard interprets Northumberland's meaning (143–75). This process of interpreting and hearing more than is spoken extends to Exton and the murder of Richard. Bullingbrook as 'the silent king' invites the hearing of more than is actually said, by Northumberland, by Richard and inevitably by Exton. There are many mentions of tongues in this play, and many assertions of the distance of tongue from heart.

Hardin Craig, and after him Tillyard, John Baxter and others,[2] saw the difference between Richard and Bullingbrook reflected not only in the contrast of the one's poetic eloquence and the other's silence but in their styles. Richard relies on words and they deceive him when the name loses touch with its referent. His style is eloquent, metaphorical, and in Craig's implication at a remove from reality, while by contrast Bullingbrook speaks plainly and uses a plain style quite unlike Richard's rhetoric. This view does not fit the evidence. Bullingbrook's speeches in 1.1 are like Mowbray's, bombastic, over-assertive, with formal rhyming. His subsequent speeches are structured with the rhetorical tropes of pleonasmus, macrologia, bomphilogia and periergia, all figures of inflation and elaboration.[3] He no more uses a plain style than Richard.[4]

The failure of language to match reality, the distance of tongues from plain truth and honesty, seen against the story of a king who talks himself into his grave, is what justifies Calderwood, Hawkes and others in regarding *Richard II* as the first study in a sequence which sets out the exploration of truth through fiction. The divorce of names from their referents and of language from plain meaning invites consideration of metaphor as a falsification of truth. In Calderwood's terms, 'The breakdown of an ontological language in *Richard II* brings into divided focus both the lie and the metaphor as verbal symbionts.'[5] Richard studies metaphors which seem to fit his case in prison at Pomfret 'because metaphor is the language of the unnamed'.[6] Fiction itself is open to all kinds of challenge when seen in the context of Richard's linguistic disintegration.

[1] Richard's comment on the Biblical 'word' echoes York's duchess at 5.3.121, where she is more mundane.

[2] Hardin Craig (ed.), *R2*, 1912, pp. xiv–xv; E. M. W. Tillyard, *Shakespeare's History Plays*, pp. 252–9; John Baxter, *Shakespeare's Poetic Styles*, esp. chs. 2 and 3. The best characterisation of Richard's 'poetic' mode is Stanley Wells, 'The lamentable tale of Richard II', *S.St.* 17 (1982), 1–23.

[3] McAlindon, *Shakespeare and Decorum*, p. 41. George Puttenham, *The Arte of English Poesie*, 1589, ch. 22, lists these tropes as examples of misused rhetoric.

[4] See Dorothy C. Hockey, 'A world of rhetoric in *Richard II*', *SQ* 15 (1964), 179–91, p. 189.

[5] Calderwood, *Metadrama*, p. 169.

[6] *Ibid.*, p. 14. All Richard's metaphors of course have their bearing on issues in the play as a whole. On Richard's thoughts about time, for instance (5.5.42–60), see Robert L. Montgomery, 'The dimensions of time in *Richard II*', *S.St.* 4 (1969), 73–85, and Michel Grivelet, 'Shakespeare's "war with time": the Sonnets and *Richard II*', *S.Sur.* 23 (1970), 69–78.

Staging

Shakespeare wrote *Richard II* while his company was performing at the Theatre.
James Burbage, father of Richard Burbage, the company's leading player and
shareholder, had built the Theatre in Shoreditch, a northern suburb of London,
nineteen years before, in 1576. It was the first of the open-air amphitheatres built
especially for playing. In 1596–7, when the lease on the land on which it was built
expired, the company played at the Swan, built in 1595 on the Bankside, or the
Curtain, built near the Theatre in 1577, until the Theatre could be dismantled and
rebuilt on the Bankside as the Globe. All four playhouses, Theatre, Curtain, Swan
and Globe, were substantial buildings about 100 feet in external diameter capable of
holding as many as three thousand spectators. Their internal configurations were
probably all similar to those of the Swan, which was built in 1595 and sketched by
a Dutch visitor, Johannes de Witt, soon after. It is likely that *Richard II* was written
to be performed on a stage very like the Swan's, and may well actually have been
performed there in the autumn of 1596.[1]

There is nothing in the play which could not have been accommodated at the Swan.
It needs no more than an open platform with two substantial entry doors, and a
balcony. The entry doors had to be wide enough to admit processions, and to allow
the chair of state or canopied throne used for all Court and 'presence' scenes to be
carried or trundled on stage. Possibly small pavilions, which in Holinshed are called
'chairs', might have been provided for the contestants in the duel scene, 1.3, though
they were not necessary features in this scene and there are no indications that anything was actually done to house the combatants. No other properties were needed
apart from Richard's 'warder' or short staff, the royal crown and regalia, two lances,
swords, gages (probably gauntlets), a hand-mirror, bills or bladed staves, some papers,
a dish of food and a coffin. More often than was usual in Shakespeare a locality is indicated in the dialogue – Coventry for the lists of 1.3 (1.1.199, 1.2.56), the Cotswolds near
Berkeley (2.3.1, 3), Barkloughly (Harlech) Castle (3.2.1), Flint Castle for 3.3 (indicated
at 3.2.209), a garden, mentioned in the opening line of 3.4, London for 4.1 (3.3.207
and 3.4.97), London near the Tower for 5.1 (5.1.2), and Pomfret (Pontefract) Castle
for 5.5 (5.1.52 and 5.4.10). Mostly these indications simply support Holinshed's
account. Only the garden scene, 3.4, and Pomfret ('This prison', 5.5.2) require a
scene-setting phrase that indicates the actual environment rather than the geographical
locality. Flint Castle, which is gestured at in 3.3.20 ('this castle'), 26 ('yon lime and
stone') and 32, would have been the tiring-house façade on the balcony of which
Richard appears at 61. There has been some controversy about whether trees might
have been brought on stage to represent forest or garden scenes. To have done so
for 3.4 would have been cumbersome and time-consuming, and would have made it
unnecessary for the queen to mention as she does that she is 'here in this garden'
in her opening line. The indication of 'these trees' where they can hide to overhear

---

[1] Ingram, *A London Life*, pp. 143–50, claims that Shakespeare's company most likely performed at the
Swan between October 1596 and January 1597. For a comment on the de Witt drawing of the Swan,
see *ibid.*, p. 111.

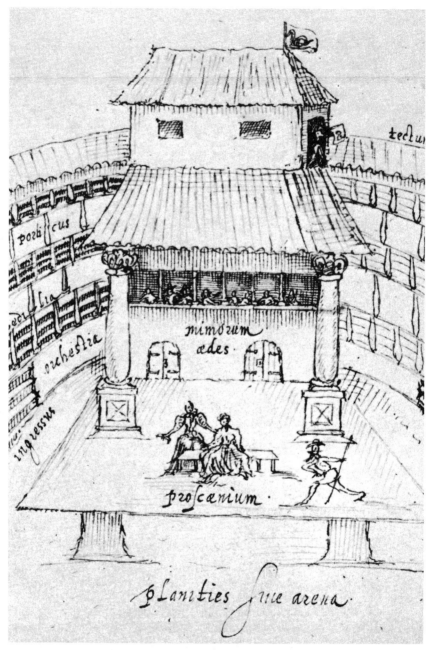

7 The stage and balcony of the Swan playhouse, according to Johannes de Witt. The Swan was built at the time *Richard II* was being written, in 1595. It is likely that the play was designed for performance on a stage similar to the Swan's, and it may have been performed at the Swan between October 1596 and January 1597.

the gardeners (25) could simply have been a gesture towards the stage posts which upheld the 'heavens' or 'shadow' covering the stage. There is no other call for garden properties in the scene, if we accept the first quarto reading 'yong apricocks' (29) for the Q2–5 'yon apricocks', and even the implied gesture of Q2–5 (which the Folio text renders as 'yond apricocks') hardly requires an actual object for the literal-minded to look at.

In the history of the play's staging the scene which receives the most variable handling is 1.3, the combat scene. The contestants have even been mounted on real horses. In the 1590s there would have been lances, as the ceremonials in the scene require, but no horses, and the only special feature which might have been utilised would be the two contestants' pavilions. These 'chairs' as Holinshed calls them were canopied seats decorated in the colours of each knight, and they sat inside them waiting to be summoned to the lists. Tents or small pavilions do seem to have been used in some playhouses at the time, and it is possible that such a ceremonial scene might have prompted the players to set up such structures. But there is nothing in either Q1's or F's stage directions or dialogue to suggest that any structures were used.

Besides the one piece of scene-setting for the garden, the play has little concern for locality. Most of the dialogue which describes something not easily exhibited on stage refers to the behaviour of the characters rather than the appearance of the stage. We are told that the Duchess of Gloucester is weeping at 1.2.58 and 74, as is the queen at 2.2.25, Richard at 3.2.4, Richard at 4.1.243, and the queen at 5.1.10. Travellers arrive hot and breathless according to the dialogue at 2.3.58 (Ross and Willoughby) and in 5.3 (Aumerle 'amazed' at 23 and then successively York and his duchess). Scroope is a gloomy messenger at 3.2.196. Most notably we are told that Richard changes colour, looking pale at 3.2.75 and hotly angry at 3.3.63.

The play is remarkable in the Shakespearean canon for its lack of movement on stage. Most of the action consists of speeches made under varying degrees of formality. There is strikingly little stage business other than the gestures which belong to the various situations in which characters stand and address one another. Most entries are formal, and some are processional (1.1, 1.3, 4.1, and the two military scenes 3.2 and 3.3). Very few scenes open at mid speech. Only 1.4, a conversational scene between Richard and his flatterers which makes an emphatic contrast to the scenes on either side of it, has a distinctly mid-speech entry where Richard comes on acknowledging something said to him by one of the flatterers ('We did observe'). Twenty-three lines later he explains what they observed to the man they meet, Aumerle, who has entered by one door as Richard and his flatterers enter by the other. Each scene is clearly separated from the next by the stage emptying for new characters to come on. The Folio text, for instance, supplies a rather awkward *Exit* for Gaunt at 1.1.195 so that he can re-enter with the Duchess of Gloucester ten lines later in 1.2. It is likely too that Aumerle should exit at 1.3.249 when he says farewell to Bullingbrook in order to re-enter at the beginning of the next scene. Despite this pattern of emptying the stage for a new scene the action was continuous, and the pace must have been fast. At 2,750 lines *Richard II* was an average length for a play of the time and would have run for about two hours, which was the common length

8 A possible Elizabethan staging of Act 1, Scene 3, the combat scene, by C. Walter Hodges, showing the Lists at Coventry, as upon a stage derived from the contemporary sketch of the Swan playhouse (*c.* 1595).

of a performance, between two and four o'clock in the afternoon, the hours of optimum daylight.

The only major piece of property needed to stage the play at Burbage's Theatre was a throne. Set on a small platform and canopied, the royal throne or chair of state would have been the centrepiece in 1.1 and 1.3, 4.1 and 5.6. Commonly called the 'state' it is the 'state of law' in Gaunt's charge against Richard at 2.1.114, part of the 'state and crown' which York says Richard must resign to Bullingbrook at 4.1.179,

9   A possible Elizabethan staging of Act 3, Scene 3, the Flint Castle scene, by C. Walter Hodges

Richard [To Northumberland]
We are amazed, and thus long have we stood
To watch the fearful bending of thy knee
Because we thought ourself thy lawful king...

and the 'sacred state' on which Bullingbrook is sitting when Northumberland
addresses him at 5.6.6. Emblematically the play opens with Richard entering to sit
on his throne, and closes with Bullingbrook descending from his throne to follow
Richard's coffin in the funeral procession with which tragedies commonly ended.

  The existence of the throne on stage dictated a number of ceremonial gestures which

10 The 'chair of state' used by Elizabeth for the opening of Parliament in 1586

emphasise the process of changing the throne's occupant. It was traditional in the royal 'presence', a technical term for the enthroned king and his court (1.1.15, 34 and elsewhere), for all the attendants to keep their hats in their hands. Richard at 3.2.171 when he feels himself unkinged tells his followers 'Cover your heads.' Carlisle at 4.1.115, when he hears Bullingbrook declare 'In God's name I'll ascend the regal throne', cries out in protest, invoking 'this royal presence' sarcastically because it is only 'My lord of Herford here, whom you call king' (134). Such a reference to the 'presence' would have most point if all the courtiers bared their heads as Bullingbrook went up the steps to the throne. For emblematic purposes throughout 4.1 the throne remained empty. Bullingbrook never actually sits in it, since he stands alongside Richard to hold the crown at 181, and departs with the announcement of his coronation, which would have been the correct moment for him to ascend the throne. We do not see Bullingbrook enthroned until the final scene when Richard is dead.

Ceremony required other gestures besides uncovering in the royal presence, the most frequent of which was kneeling. It too has its emblematic point, in relation to the elemental imagery, resting the knee on England's earth, and lowering one's height below that of the king. In 1.1 while Mowbray and Bullingbrook are declaring their charges against each other Mowbray kneels to Richard at 165, but when his turn comes Bullingbrook refuses to kneel (188–92), using images of his height and his wish not to look 'crestfallen'. This visually indicates on the one hand Mowbray's link with Richard as his supporter and executioner of the king's order to kill Gloucester, and on the other Bullingbrook's reluctance to affirm his loyalty to Richard for the same reason. In 1.3.47 before the duel Bullingbrook does kneel to Richard who 'descends' from his throne to embrace his kinsman, with evident insincerity on both sides. Mowbray presumably also kneels, to affirm the equivalence of the two combatants, when he declares his loyalty at 86–7. At 2.3.82 Bullingbrook kneels to York as the king's Regent, a gesture which York tetchily rejects as 'deceivable and false'. At 3.3.72–3 Richard reproves Northumberland for not kneeling in his presence, and in 187 when Bullingbrook himself confronts Richard he kneels before him as he did to York. The ceremony of kneeling is thoroughly burlesqued by York and his duchess to Bullingbrook in 5.3. A similar ceremoniousness, and on occasions a similar disingenuousness, attended the frequent swearing of oaths. These were taken either by raising the right hand or, as in the oath Richard exacts from the two exiles at 1.3.179, on the cross made by the guard and hilt of the king's sword.

All the properties held in the tiring-house of an Elizabethan playhouse were portable. The stage itself was bare except for a layer of rushes on the boards and hangings at the rear. They had to be portable if the players were to perform in noblemen's houses as the Chamberlain's Men probably did with *Richard II* for Sir Edward Hoby in December 1595. The largest property the play needed apart from the canopied throne was probably a chair for Gaunt, when he enters '*sick*' in 2.1. At 137 he asks to be helped away to his bed, so the canopied bed which was the other main item of Elizabethan staging was evidently not used. All the other properties could be carried by individuals. The central items were the royal regalia, notably the crown and sceptre. Richard's sceptre is mentioned at 1.1.118, and in 4.1 both sceptre and

11   A possible Elizabethan staging of Act 4, Scene 1, the Parliament scene, by C. Walter Hodges

Richard
As brittle as the glory is the face
For there it is, cracked in an hundred shivers.

crown are central emblems. The initial entry for 4.1 *as to the Parliament* would have meant a procession headed by an attendant carrying the crown. It remains in view but untouched until Richard asks for it at 181 to make the emblematic transfer to Bullingbrook. The sceptre, on the other hand, is brought in by York at 109–10 as the token of Richard's abdication. Apart from the gages of 1.1 and 4.1 and the contestants' lances in 1.3 the chief emblematic property was the mirror in 4.1.264–87.

It is likely that trumpet-calls also had an emblematic function, but how consistently they were used is not clear from the texts of the play. A flourish normally heralded the king's arrival and departure, and Richard is so heralded in 1.1 and 1.3. But no royal flourish is marked for his arrival to visit the sick Gaunt at 2.1.68, though his departure is accompanied by a flourish according to the Folio at 223. Other trumpet-calls, such as charges and parleys, are used for instance in 1.3.6, 25, 117 and 122. There must also have been trumpets in 3.2 and 3.3 since trumpet and drum were the routine instruments for the music of war and battlefield signals.

Less visually significant than these were the swords which all nobles, including Bullingbrook in 5.3, always wore, together with bills for the murderers of Richard. There is no indication in the text that bills were used, but they are described by Holinshed and were standard equipment for ordinary soldiers. A contemporary drawing of a scene from *Titus Andronicus*, a Roman play, includes Elizabethan soldiers carrying bills. There was full armour for the combatants in 1.3 and a presumably more portable variety for 3.2 and 3.3. York's 'signs of war about his agèd neck' (2.2.74) might have been a gorget, an iron neck-piece. The other items used are papers, in the form of Northumberland's 'Articles' of 4.1.222, Aumerle's sealed scroll at 5.2.56 and Northumberland's report to Bullingbrook at 5.6.10. Richard has a dish of food at 5.5.94, and a coffin for the funeral procession which concludes the play.

Costumes were the most substantial of the portable properties. *Richard II* has a higher than usual number of parts for the kings and nobles, who wore the most colourful apparel. In some instances costume was used to signal points of staging. As the threat of war develops in Act 2 courtly costume changes into military gear. York enters at 2.2.74 'With signs of war about his agèd neck', and for the rest of Acts 2 and 3 most of the nobles would have been dressed for travel, booted and spurred. In 5.2 York's boots are used for a tragicomic burlesque of all the travelling which took the crown from Richard to Bullingbrook. Other standard signals would have appeared in the garb of the gardeners in 3.4 – a rake seems to have been the routine tool to signal gardeners. Similarly the Keeper of Richard's prison in 5.5 would have carried a bunch of keys.

Two other features of the staging are worthy of note. Noises 'off' are heard in 5.3 when first York and then the duchess knock for admission to the presence chamber where Aumerle has locked himself in with Bullingbrook. In 5.5 music plays off stage during Richard's soliloquy, a device which probably involved strings behind one of the entry doors. And the most visually spectacular scene of all, 3.3, the central scene of the play when Richard's downward fall takes him past the climbing Bullingbrook, is notable for the way it patterns the presentation of Richard and his supporters on high, on the balcony above the entry doors. Northumberland stands in centre stage below to address Richard and draw him down to the 'base court' on a level with Bullingbrook, who all the time marches around the stage with colours held high and drums muffled, the embodiment of the earthly forces which are bringing Richard down.

Stage history

There are testimonials to the early popularity of *Richard II* from the quarto printers, from Edward Hoby and from Elizabeth herself. The representative of Shakespeare's company who spoke at Essex's trial and claimed to have objected in 1601 that the play was old and out of use was probably exaggerating in his company's defence. It certainly stayed in the repertory, and may indeed have returned to prominence when Elizabeth died, judging by the speed with which Matthew Law bought the printing rights. The Captain of the East India Company's ship the *Dragon* staged it on board in 1607, along with *Hamlet*. If Hoby's entertainment for Cecil was Shakespeare's play, he set a precedent in using it for special occasions which others soon followed. There is no record of it at Court, but few of the plays so honoured are named at this time. Essex was said at his trial to have seen it often. Presumably it stayed in the repertory throughout the life of Shakespeare's company, and stayed popular. There is a record of it being performed at the Globe on 12 June 1631 before a good audience.[1]

It evidently lost nothing of its political force even after the Restoration. Permission for it to be acted was granted in 1669 but when Nahum Tate tried to put it on stage he immediately ran into censorship trouble. It was staged in an adapted version on about 11–13 December 1680, and banned on 14 December.[2] Tate had already modified the play to eliminate almost all of Richard's misdeeds and to dwell on the pathos of the scene between Richard and his queen, but evidently not enough at a politically sensitive time. A month later he tried again. This time it was staged under a different name, *The Tyrant of Sicily* or *The Sicilian Usurper*, but it had no better luck and suffered a more severe penalty than before, the theatre being closed for ten days. In the course of that year Tate published his version with a preface defending his loyalty and probity, and disclaiming any attempt to identify the present reign with Richard's:

I am not ignorant of the posture of Affairs in King *Richard* the Second's Reign, how dissolute then the Age, and how corrupt the Court; a Season that beheld *Ignorance* and Infamy preferr'd to *Office* and *Pow'r*, exercis'd in Oppressing Learning and Merit; but why a History of those Times shou'd be supprest as a Libel upon Ours, is past my Understanding.[3]

Tate could bite back. Nonetheless his Richard is certainly not Shakespeare's. Almost all of the first two acts and their picture of Richard's misdeeds vanished. Gaunt's deathbed scene ends with Richard first forgiving Gaunt and then, after York has supported his brother, promising to reform. The seizure of Gaunt's estate becomes a forced loan. Tate replaced the cuts with an expansion of the queen's part, including several songs inserted at pathetic moments such as the parting of the royal couple and Richard in prison. Tate's York was emphatically a comic figure, a tradition which

[1] Chambers, *Shakespeare*, II, 334, 348.
[2] See William Van Lennep, *The London Stage 1660–1800*, 1965, pp. lxiii, cxxx, 293–4.
[3] Quoted in Brian Vickers, *Shakespeare: The Critical Heritage*, 6 vols., 1974–81, I: *1623–1692*, p. 322.

stayed with the play well into the eighteenth century, if a comment by Steevens is anything to go by.[1]

Despite the sentimentalising and the comedy, Tate's version did not evade the political implications of the story. His preface, admittedly defensive, puts the emphasis squarely on the Tyrant rather than the Usurper.

Nor cou'd it suffice me to make him speak like a King (who as Mr. *Rymer* says in his *Tragedies of the last Age considered*, are always in Poetry presum'd Heroes) but to *Act so too*, viz. with *Resolution* and *Justice*. Resolute enough our *Shakespeare* (copying the History) has made him, for concerning his seizing old *Gaunt's* Revennues, he tells the wise Diswaders,
> Say what ye will, we seize into our Hands
> His Plate, his Goods, his Money and his Lands.

But where was the Justice of this Action? This Passage I confess was so material a Part of the Chronicle (being the very Basis of *Bullingbrook's* Usurpation) that I cou'd not in this new Model so far transgress Truth as to make no mention of it; yet for the honour of my Heroe I suppose the foresaid Revennues to be *Borrow'd* onely for the present Exigence, not *Extorted*.[2]

At the same time Tate protests that his object was to rouse pity for the falling hero.

Politics, whether open or subterranean, have always influenced attitudes to *Richard II*. It might be loosely claimed that in the eighteenth century it lost favour because it portrayed a bad king, and that it returned in the nineteenth century because Charles Kean and Walter Pater made a tragic poet–king out of the old story of the tyrant–king. The records of its life in the eighteenth century support this view, with one notable exception. First Lewis Theobald produced an adaptation even more ameliorative than Tate's, eliminating the first two acts entirely, in 1719. It was revived in London once, and probably toured the provinces for some time afterwards. Apart from occasional provincial revivals there was only one major London production in the whole century, and most theatre managers as well as readers seem to have concurred with Johnson's view of it as a dull piece not worth staging. The exception was the strikingly scrupulous 1738 production at Covent Garden by John Rich, the impresario who had staged Gay's *The Beggar's Opera* a decade before. Again the production seems to have been a political issue. The stage licensing laws which Walpole had introduced in the wake of *The Beggar's Opera* were under attack, because only two theatres had been licensed in 1737. In particular a letter from *The Craftsman* for 2 July 1737 ridiculed the Theatre Licensing Bill by quoting passages from plays which it claimed would have to be censored under the new regulations. The plays quoted included *Richard II*. The printer and others concerned with *The Craftsman* were imprisoned and the matter went to the courts. It had plenty of publicity, and Rich seems to have chosen to stage *Richard II* to take advantage of the furore.[3] Thomas Davies, in his *Dramatic Miscellanies* (1783) confirmed the play's topicality.

---

[1] Steevens, *Private Correspondence*, II, 122, refers to 'old *puss in boots*, who arrives so hastily in the fifth act'. Quoted by A. C. Sprague, *Shakespeare's Histories*, 1964, p. 29.
[2] Vickers, *Critical Heritage*, I, 323.
[3] A full account of Rich's venture and the surviving records is in James G. McManaway, '*Richard II* at Covent Garden', *SQ* 15 (1964), 161–75. See also A. H. Scouten, *The London Stage 1660–1800, Part 3: 1729–1747*, 1961, pp. 701, 702, 704, 706, 717, 746, 750, 761, 796.

When he pronounced the following words,
> The king is not himself, but basely led
> By flatterers, –

the noise from the clapping of hands and clattering of sticks was loud and boisterous. And when Ross said,
> The Earl of Wiltshire hath the state in farm, –

it was immediately applied to Walpole, with the loudest shouts and huzzahs I ever heard.[1]

However fitting for Walpole's time, its staging, judging from sketches of the combat scene and the Parliament scene which have survived, seems to have been not unShakespearean. The throne was positioned in centre stage for both scenes, and for the second it remained empty, with the supporters of Bullingbrook and Richard ranged on either side.

In the nineteenth century Richard's part was recognised as a good tragedian's role, and Edmund Kean reintroduced it to London in 1815. His version, in a text by Richard Wroughton which omitted the Aumerle conspiracy from Act 5 and gave the queen more emoting after Richard's death, ran with revivals up to 1828 and was taken to New York in 1820 and 1826. Macready also played Richard in the provinces at this time, in a version which concluded with Richard's death. His production finally reached London in 1850. Perhaps the most influential revival the play has ever had began in 1857, when Charles Kean staged a spectacular gothic–historical production. Kean provided dummy horses for the combat scene, 1.3, and a spectacular entry to London to open Act 5 which used nearly six hundred walk-ons, including the young Ellen Terry who swarmed up a lamp-post, and pealing church bells. To a necessarily curtailed text it supplied the romanticised colour of the Victorian idea of medieval history. As Pater recorded,

in the painstaking 'revival' of *King Richard the Second*, by the late Charles Kean, those who were very young thirty years ago were afforded much more than Shakespeare's play could ever have been before – the very person of the king based on the stately old portrait in Westminster Abbey, 'the earliest extant contemporary likeness of any English sovereign', the grace, the winning pathos, the sympathetic voice of the player, the tasteful archaeology confronting vulgar modern London with a scenic reproduction, for once really agreeable, of the London of Chaucer. In the hands of Kean the play became like an exquisite performance on the violin.[2]

Pater's recollection was influential. Sympathy for Richard as tragic hero, which had been lost under the weight of Victorian disapproval of histrionics and moral laxity voiced by Dowden and others,[3] gained strength from Pater's praise of the play's music. 'It belongs to a small group of plays', he wrote, 'where, by happy birth and consistent evolution, dramatic form approaches to something like the unity of a lyrical ballad, a lyric, a song, a single strain of music'.[4] At the centre of this 'symphony' is Richard, the 'graceful, wild creature', the beautiful child-like poet.

Pater's view prevailed into twentieth-century interpretations of the play both in

[1] Thomas Davies, *Dramatic Miscellanies*, 3 vols., 1783–4, I, 152–3.
[2] Walter Pater, 'Shakespeare's English Kings', in *Appreciations*, 1889, p. 195.
[3] Sprague, *Shakespeare's Histories*, p. 32. Sprague's account of the play's stage history is sensitive and thorough.   [4] Pater, 'Shakespeare's English Kings', p. 203.

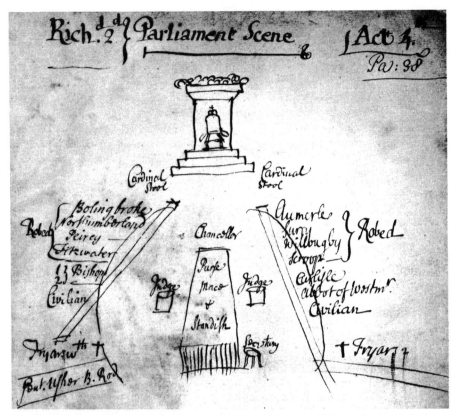

12   The stage layout for the Parliament scene (Act 4, Scene 1) in the 1738 Covent Garden production.
Bullingbrook and his supporters line up on stage right, Richard's supporters on stage left, while the
throne stands empty, dominating the scene

criticism and in performance. Hardin Craig's edition in 1912 embodied the view of
Richard the tragic poet which Pater had from Charles Kean, and Craig's view was
transferred back to the stage in the 1951 Stratford production of the whole sequence.[1]
It was inevitable that, once the monarchy lost its central place in the British political
system as it did in the eighteenth century, interest in *Richard II* would shift from
the politics of deposition to the psychology of the deposed. Censorship ceased to be
a problem after 1738. When the play resurfaced in the nineteenth century, it was not
as a history, and its staging has generally been as a tragedy, a star vehicle for the actor
of Richard, ever since.

In the twentieth century it has also been the vehicle for spectacle. Beerbohm Tree
used real horses for the combat scene in 1903, and, falling for the same temptation
as Charles Kean, invented a pageant scene for Bullingbrook's coronation to make a
contrast with the pathos of solitary Richard in the fifth act. Solitary Richard, however,

[1]   Hockey, 'A world of rhetoric', p. 179.

was the central focus in the 1930s, to such a degree that Harold Hobson in 1948 claimed that the play was almost the public's favourite in the Shakespearean repertory because it matched the new age's capacity for self-pity.[1] More recent productions have never entirely removed this feature of the play's appeal, and the political issues which dominated the first two centuries of its life have not been successfully resurrected. In details modern productions vary widely. Few directors allow comedy to break up the solemnity, though a comic York and even comic gardeners turn up occasionally. The Aumerle conspiracy, which for some critics brilliantly burlesques the solemnity of Act 5 and calls the nature of loyalty in question, is still usually cut.

Probably the most ambitious and certainly the most influential version of recent years was John Barton's production for the Royal Shakespeare Company, staged at Stratford in 1973 and transferred to London in the following year. Very markedly a piece of director's theatre, it put the balance of Richard and Bullingbrook to the test by interchanging the actors of the two roles. Richard Pasco and Ian Richardson exchanged parts, playing Richard and Bullingbrook on alternate nights through both seasons of the play's run. It was a device which worked for the company better than for the audiences, perhaps, but it served as more than just a reminder of how the director saw the play's balanced structure. Through the interaction of two emphatically different personalities playing out their opposing stories, the drama of word against deed, tongue against heart and the private passions under the public rituals developed an unprecedented subtlety and delicacy of nuance.

Barton surrounded the two protagonists with an array of staging devices designed as a double framework of poetic symbolism and social ritual. The visual symbols were blatant. They included two ladders reaching up behind the contestants in the combat scene with between them a platform on which Richard literally rose and fell. A bowl of earth stood downstage throughout, beside which Gaunt spoke his sceptred isle speech. Death appeared with the Duchess of Gloucester who entered as a ghost from the grave, in the Gardener's servants who were dressed as monks in a monastery garden, and most blatantly in the crowning of an antic Death at the finale, standing between the two uncrowned protagonists. This literal representation of Richard's antic from 3.2.162 was matched by a snowman (4.1.259's 'mockery king of snow') in 5.2 Listing such blatant devices, however, does an injustice to a production which never used its symbolism randomly. When Richard broke his mirror Bullingbrook took the empty frame and lowered it over Richard's head, first making it a halo, then a crown and finally a noose.

The ritual features were as suggestive as the visual symbolism. Ceremonial became the outward show of an orderly state in which the balance of power shifts step by unseen step behind the dazzle of a divinely ordained rule. The effect was operatic in the sense that it showed real emotions constrained by ceremonial forms of presentation. Richard entered at Coventry, at Barkloughly and at Flint with the panoply of a sun-god. In the Parliament scene the splendour faded as Bullingbrook's uncrowned dominance made it incongruous, and Pomfret showed a ragged Richard

---

[1] Sprague, *Shakespeare's Histories*, p. 37.

13 The combat scene (Act 1, Scene 3) in John Barton's 1973 Stratford production. Mowbray (Denis Holmes) is at stage left, Bullingbrook (Ian Richardson) at stage right; the king (Richard Pascoe) sits holding his warder, while the Marshal (Richard Mayes) gestures with the baton which was his badge of office

getting false reassurance from the groom who turned out to be Bullingbrook in disguise. Both judgement scenes, 1.1 and 4.1, displayed the pageantry of a rich and ordered state and resounded with speeches which seemed as regulated by style as an operatic aria. Under the glittering pageantry the balance could be felt shifting all the time. In the combat scene, for instance, the contestants were mounted on ingeniously mobile brightly coloured hobby-horses, in an appealingly stylised representation of the reality behind the ceremonial. The nobles in the travelling scenes of Act 2, however, were on tall black horses with a menace which raised the image above the level of a blandly clever trick which was all it seemed to be in the ceremonial combat scene. Barton did not always avoid the danger of a too-literal demonstration of what he took the text to signify. Making the disguised Bullingbrook at Pomfret give Richard a toy horse in answer to his complaint about roan Barbary and providing a child-size coffin for Richard's corpse at the end was only one example of this. But the obtrusively symbolic staging did its work of framing the social and political order in which the protagonists were balanced, and giving a context to the journey of discovery which each undergoes.

Pasco's Richard was closer to the traditional tragic hero than Richardson's. He began light-hearted, developed tearfully and ended close to contemptible, a superb evocation of the actor–king. Richardson's Bullingbrook was unwavering in his taciturn ambition. Together they offered, in Richard David's words, 'the traditional contrast, the likeable Richard who did everything wrong and the unsympathetic Bolingbroke who did everything right'.[1] When the roles were reversed the play became much more a half-hidden game of political manoeuvring and sly calculation. Richard threw his warder down to stop the combat because he had planned it. In the Parliament scene it was his cunning which made him call for the mirror as an escape from Northumberland's demand to read the incriminating Articles. This Richard fought against his fate right to his death, while seeking in his soliloquies to comprehend it. Pasco matched this calculating Richard with a hesitant Bullingbrook. He read out the charges against the flatterers in 3.1 distastefully, as if it was not by his own choice. He inserted the speech from *2 Henry IV* 3.1 about the sleepless cares of kingship to adjust the imbalance created by Richard's long Pomfret speech in Act 5.

Curiously, as the production went on, its two Richards changed and began to resemble each other more closely. Pasco's weak king became younger and stronger. Richardson's cunning fighter lost some of his cleverness. Transferred to London some of the play's visual symbolism was removed, notably the ladders and Fortune's platform, and as the ritualism receded the human conflict strengthened. The symbolic trappings of two tragic falls remained, but the strong Richard easily made up for the loss of stylised social symbolism and it became more powerfully the story of a political struggle, the human elements shifting fatally under the rigid social framework.

Recent critical and stage interpretations

Critical History

Over the last twenty years *Richard II*'s context has received far more attention than its text. Almost nothing has been added to ideas about the text beside some reconsideration of the origins of the two versions of the 'deposition scene', first inserted into the quartos of 1608 and after, and then in a more polished version into the Folio. The context, by contrast, has been given intense study as a crucial revelation of Elizabethan and Shakespeare's own politics, and more generally the role and subversive power of theatre in the political and cultural movements of the 'Early Modern' period. This term, an innovation since 1984, reflects the general concern to rehistoricise Shakespeare's plays. In that process *Richard II* has become a major concern in particular for New Historicists and Cultural Materialists (not to mention their many successors, including Neohistoricists).

---

[1] Richard David, *Shakespeare in the Theatre*, 1978, p. 168. David gives 10 rewarding pages to John Barton's production (pp. 164–73). A less immediately informative but much more wide ranging resource for studying the history of productions is the record of cuts and other changes made in many of the surviving promptbooks, in William P. Halstead's *Shakespeare as Spoken: A Collation of 5000 Acting Editions and Promptbooks of Shakespeare*, 12 vols. (University Microfilms), 1977–80. The records for *R2* are in vol. V, 1979.

The aim for many scholars is to re-politicise Shakespeare by finding evidence of a subversive intent in the immediate historical circumstances of play production. In Phyllis Rackin's words, 'In such a history, Shakespearean texts are reconstituted as playscripts designed for performance in a volatile theatrical setting where the erasures in the official historical record could be restored and the voices silenced by the repressions of the dominant discourse could speak and be heard.'[1] *Richard II*'s historical and political context has been studied from two angles, close to each other but distinct, and both of them with much to say about our concept of the play. The first is the question of the play's 'application' to Elizabeth I in the last years of her reign, along with the constraints that imposed in the light of Tudor censorship and authorial self-censorship. The second has entailed an intensive revaluation of how the Tudor historiographers, especially the authors who assembled the Holinshed chronicles, thought about their work, and what that suggests about Shakespeare's use of their work.

In 1982, at the outset of the New Historicist movement, Stephen Greenblatt instigated this approach through his focus on the decision by Essex's followers to have the Chamberlain's Men stage *Richard II* on the eve of Essex's attempted coup in February 1601.[2] His Introduction to the collection of essays that initiated New Historicism began with Elizabeth's identification of herself with Richard, and the 'Aesopian indirection' of contemporary comment. It found a new approach to counter the still-current assumption[3] that '*Richard II* is not at all subversive but rather a hymn to Tudor order.' Greenblatt's challenge launched the questioning about the subversive role of plays that has become a characteristic of the New Historicist approach.

Much of the material for such revisionism is supplied in the Introduction that precedes this section from the 1984 edition, but the New Historicist case warrants a fresh look at the story. The parallels that Elizabethans found between Richard's misrule and Elizabeth's were even more numerous than the 1984 edition noted. They ranged from complaints about her misuse of the law in order to finance government to the parallel, so evident in the play, between Richard's murder of his uncle Woodstock and Elizabeth's execution of her cousin Mary Queen of Scots in 1587.[4] Through the later 1590s the parallels seemed to grow even closer, as the heirless Elizabeth was compared with the childless Richard, and Essex began to loom as a new Bullingbrook. It was Bullingbrook's dubious but profitable act of deposition that lay behind the conspirators' commissioning of a performance on the day before Essex's attempted coup, and behind Elizabeth's own complaint to William Lambard after Essex's execution, cited by Greenblatt in his essay, that Richard's story was applied to her on stage.

[1] Phyllis Rackin, *Stages of History: Shakespeare's English Chronicles*, 1990, p. xi.
[2] Stephen Greenblatt (ed), *The Power of Forms in the English Renaissance*, 1982, p. xi.
[3] i.e., Tillyard's and Dover Wilson's view of the plays as upholding the 'Elizabethan World Order'.
[4] Lily Campbell (*Shakespeare's 'Histories'*, p. 201) noted long ago that the reference in 2.1 to extortion by benevolences was registered at the Essex trial as a specific instance of Elizabethan practices being used to pose as Richardian, so 'the times of Elizabeth rather than those of Richard II were in question'. The even more potent parallel between the killing of Woodstock and that of Mary, for all its impact on Catholics in England, has received much less attention.

A further but no less easily recognisable parallel in the play was the interpretation that Piers of Exton chose to lay on Bullingbrook's meaningful look about Richard living in prison at Pomfret. The story of Henry II's complaint about Thomas à Beckett was on record at Canterbury Cathedral, and not a few Elizabethans saw the Queen's use of her Secretary Davison in 1587 as a comparably indirect expression of her readiness to execute Mary. In 1604, soon after Elizabeth's death, William Camden gave the then standard defensive version of what happened:

she delivered a Writing to *Davison*, one of her Secretaries, signed with her own Hand, commanding a Warrant under the Great Seal of *England* to be drawn up for the Execution, which should lie in readiness if any Danger chanced to break forth in that time of Jealousie and Fear; and commanded him to acquaint no man therewith. But the next day, while Fear seemed to be afraid of her own Counsels and Designs, her Mind changed, and she commanded *Davison* by *William Killegrew* that the Warrant should not be drawn. *Davison* came presently to the Queen, and told her that it was drawn and under Seal already. She was somewhat moved at it, and blamed him for making such Hast. He notwithstanding acquainted the Council both with the Warrant and the whole matter, and easily perswaded them, who were apt to believe what they desired, that the Queen had commanded it should be executed. Hereupon without any Delay *Beale* (who in respect of Religion was of all others the Queen of *Scots* most bitter Adversary) was sent down, with one or two Executioners, and a Warrant, wherein Authority was given to the Earls of *Shrewsbury*, *Kent*, *Derby*, *Cumberland*, and others, to see her executed according to the Law; and this without any Knowledge of the Queen at all.[1]

The Davison intervention was seen as comparable to Piers of Exton's in the play (a version ignored by Holinshed), and to the knights who rode to Canterbury to kill Beckett. Henry II, Henry IV in Shakespeare's play, and Elizabeth were seen as of a sort in wanting themselves rid of a threat to their crown, but reluctant to give a direct order. The resemblances between Richard and Elizabeth make it no wonder that material about Richard's deposition was censored out of the 1587 republication of Holinshed's *Chronicles*.

The comparison made any account of Richard's reign potentially dangerous, especially in the 1590s when the succession had become a major issue, and official silence about it a matter of reproach to Elizabeth. Moreover, part of the Queen's fear and her refusal to allow the succession to be discussed in public was the chronic hostility of many courtiers to her encirclement by protective flatterers. Her own cousin Henry Carey, Lord Chamberlain and founder of the Shakespeare company, renewed his pose of bluff simplicity at court in the 1580s by declaring 'I was never one of Richard II's men.' He meant that he was no flatterer, not a Bushy, Bagot or Greene.[2] It was a comment that needed no elaboration. Evelyn May Albright called Richard

---

[1] William Camden, *The HISTORY of the most Renowned and Victorious PRINCESS ELIZABETH, Late Queen of England* . . . The Third Edition, 1675, p. 382. Usually known as the *Annales*, it was written in Latin in 1604. This quotation is from the first version published in English.
[2] Cited by Evelyn M. Albright, 'Shakespeare's *Richard II* and the Essex conspiracy', *PMLA* 42 (1927), 686–720, p. 691.

Elizabeth's 'political nickname.' Many courtiers were doing precisely what Carey disavowed.

The danger of applying Richard's downfall to Elizabeth was most evident in the fate of John Hayward, who suffered much more than Shakespeare's company did for their performance in 1601. We might wonder whether the alternative play about Richard's reign that Simon Forman saw at the Globe in 1611 was staged to distract attention from the Essex–Bullingbrook parallel. According to Forman's summary,[1] it started with the Jack Straw rebellion and continued with Richard's deception of the rebellious Earl of Arundel, ending with John of Gaunt setting the nobility against the king in order to put his own son on the throne, and Gaunt's killing of the wise man who told him he should not be king but that his son would be. It appears to have stopped short of the deposition, and was certainly not designed as a prequel to Shakespeare's play. One wonders whether the absence of *Richard II* from the records of Tudor and Stuart performances at court is a mark of its sensitivity for monarchs. Its banning under Charles II affirms that view.

Besides the well-known parallels of insulating and isolating flatterers, and complaints about landlordism in the sale of benevolences and unjust taxes, two other features of Elizabeth's reign made her identification with Richard particularly explosive. Shakespeare took care to depict both of them in the sequence of plays that he began to write in 1595. One was the question of royal hands red with the blood of their kindred. Richard's killing of his uncle Woodstock, the Duke of Gloucester, was paralleled by Elizabeth's execution of her cousin Mary Queen of Scots. The other was the question of succession after a ruler who had no clear heir. Richard had no son at his death in 1399, a lack that led to the Wars of the Roses between the usurping Lancastrian Henries and the dubiously patrilinear Yorkist Richards and Edwards, descendants of the Mortimers who feature as claimants in *1 Henry IV* and more tacitly in *Henry V* in the form of the treacherous Cambridge. It was boldly adroit of Shakespeare, when Elizabeth had forbidden any discussion of her likely successor, to write a play showing how the door had first been opened to disgorge the horrors of long and bloody civil war when no legitimate heir could be found. The historical parallel was a warning. Later he used a similar tactic with *King Lear*, when he set out the questions inherent in James's wish to unify his two kingdoms by showing its opposite: what could happen to a divided state.

That these were all questions bearing heavily on the play was reaffirmed by Greenblatt's essay and the flood of argument that followed. It became the central issue in the subsequent debate over the political potency of Early Modern plays. Much of that debate has focussed on what happened to the play in the years following its composition, especially its use in the Essex rebellion. According to Barbara Hodgdon, by 1598, when the play reached its third printing, the Earl of Essex appeared to resemble Bullingbrook in more ways than Shakespeare can have expected in 1595. As she puts it, Bullingbrook's 'situation closely corresponds to what Essex saw as his grievances against the Crown: exile from court, if not from England;

---

[1] Quoted in full by E. K. Chambers, *William Shakespeare*, 2 vols, 1930, II.339–40.

loss of revenue, royal favor, and title; disgraced honor. And indeed, the questions Essex posed in his 18 October letter to the Lord Keeper, Sir Thomas Egerton – a letter brought against him later as evidence of seditious interest – sound remarkably like Bolingbroke: "When the vilest of all indignities are done unto me, doth religion enforce me to sue? Doth God require it? Is it impiety not to do it? What, cannot princes err? Cannot subjects receive wrong? Is an earthly power or authority infinite? Pardon me, pardon me, my good Lord, I can never subscribe to these principles.""[1] This letter, quoted by Camden in his *Annales*, made it predictable that the Essex followers should want to see Shakespeare's play before the coup began, and similarly that the staging should be queried at Essex's trial. How important that commission from the conspirators might have been has become a test of how potent was drama as a social instrument capable of challenging and subverting the political establishment.

Recent readers of the play have concentrated on how seriously the judges at Essex's trial took the play's enactment on the eve of the coup, and how readily they accepted Augustine Phillips's plea that the performance was done simply for money. The assumption by Greenblatt, Barbara Hodgdon and many others that it was a demonstration of the drama's power was first challenged by J. Leeds Barroll in 1988,[2] when he asserted that it was not the play but John Hayward's book, *The First Part of the Life and Raigne of King Henrie IIII*,[3] that the judges saw as a sign of danger from Essex. Hayward's book got into trouble after its first publication in 1599, when it sold a remarkable 1,500 copies in a very short time. All copies of the immediately launched second and revised edition were seized and burned that June at the time of the 'Bishops' Ban' on erotic poetry and dangerous history. Barroll, backed by Paul Yachnin, Phyllis Rackin and others, sees that story as evidence for where the chief political contest took place, not over the play but over the history. As Margaret Healy put it, *Richard II* has become 'a key text over which the battle between right- and left-wing critics for the political body of the Bard has been, and still is being fought'.[4]

Where the truth lies is probably unknowable. Camden's own summary, written three years after the event, gives the standard Elizabethan reading. His account says nothing about the play and its performance, except when he notes the accusations laid against Essex's steward, Gilly Meyricke, 'That he had at his own Charge procured an old out-worn Play, of the Tragicall Deposing of King *Richard* the Second, to be acted upon the publick Stage before the Conspiratours: which the Lawyers interpreted to be done by him, as intending to signifie to them, they should now behold that acted upon the

[1] Barbara Hodgdon, *The End Crowns All. Closure and Contradiction in Shakespeare's History*, 1991, p. 124.
[2] 'A new history for Shakespeare and his time', *Shakespeare Quarterly* 39 (1988), 441–64.
[3] Hayward's book and its manuscript continuation (*The Second Part*) have been finely edited by John J. Manning, as *John Hayward's The Life and Raigne of King Henrie IIII*, Royal Historical Society (Camden Fourth Series, vol. 42), London, 1992. On pp. 17–34 he gives a full account of the book's publication, censoring and burning. Richard Dutton (*Licensing, Censorship and Authorship in Early Modern England*, London, 2000) also devotes a chapter to the story and the censorship of Hayward's *Life*, though he makes no note of Manning's edition.
[4] Margaret Healy, *William Shakespeare: Richard II*, Writers and their Work, 1998, p. x.

Stage, which was the next day to be acted by themselves in Deposing the Queen. And the like Censure was given upon a Book of the same Argument set forth a little before by one *Hayward*, a learned man, and dedicated to the Earl of *Essex*; as if it had been written purposely to shew them the Way and incite them to the Deposing of the Queen: a dear Book to the Authour, who was punished by a tedious Imprisonment for his unseasonable publishing of it, and for those Words in his Preface to the Earl, *Great thou art in Hope, greater in Expectation of future time.*' (p. 627). That was Camden's English translation of Hayward's Latin '*futuri temporis expectatione*', quoted on page 6 above. Camden seems to be citing an equal level of concern over the two illustrations of a precedent for Essex deposing Elizabeth.

On the other side, a notable addition to this flurry of concern for the play's political use in Shakespeare's time is Annabel Patterson's study of the compilers of Holinshed's *Chronicles*, and especially the new text published and then revised after censorship in 1587. This second edition was what Shakespeare made chief use of for his play. Patterson identifies the 1587 Holinshed's political alignment with remarkable clarity. It was a politically alert work with a sophisticated political philosophy, which might easily be seen as a form of dramatisation.[1] In her analysis, the compilers were concerned to preserve in print as 'documentary history' the limited records from the national archive. Secondly, in the light of radically divergent interpretations of the same events in post-Reformation England, their design was to represent fairly that diversity of opinion. 'Wherever possible . . . diversity should be expressed as multivocality, with the *Chronicles* reporting verbatim what they found in earlier historians or contemporary witnesses.' Thirdly, Patterson sees them as giving voice to the opinions of the common people, and fourthly she says they asserted the 'right to know' by providing the evidence on which modern judgements of past actions could be made.[2] It is this last principle, if her reading of the *Chronicles* is correct, that Shakespeare most clearly renewed in his composition of *Richard II*, with its scrupulous (if imaginative) detailing of the events that led to Richard's deposition, and the precise balancing in the play's chiasmic structure of the tyrant *in exercitio* against the tyrant *absque titulo*.

Most of the other matters set out in the 1984 Introduction need little revision. There is no reason to reconsider the dating of the play, for instance, although we might exercise more caution about the assumption that it was Shakespeare's play that was staged at Hoby's house in the Strand in December 1595. Sir Edward Hoby certainly invited Robert Cecil, who was one of his close friends, to dinner on 7 December 1595, just a few months before Elizabeth made him her chief Secretary. Hoby's offer was 'as late as it shall please you, a gate for your supper shall be open, and K. Richard present himself to your view'.[3] What remains unclear is whether Hoby's offer was the play or a portrait.[4] The timeliness of *Richard II* as one of the company's latest offerings in 1595 makes the link enticing, but the alternative is

[1] Annabel Patterson, *Reading Holinshed's Chronicles*, 1994, especially p. 115.
[2] *Ibid.*, p. 7. The extent of Patterson's disagreement with Rackin is registered in footnote 10 on page 279.
[3] *Salisbury MSS*, v.487.
[4] For a comment on some over-ready interpretations of Hoby's letter, see David M. Bergeron, 'The Hoby letter and *Richard II*: a parable of criticism', cited on p. 3.

equally so, and there is fresh information about that. In 1593 Hoby was made Constable of Quinborough Castle in Kent and commissioned a series of pictures of former Constables to hang there, starting with Edward III and John of Gaunt and ending with himself. By 1595 his series of commissioned pictures might have included either Richard II or Richard III, and he may have planned to show one of them to Cecil. On the other hand, the fact that 1595 was also the time when Shakespeare's *Richard II* first came to the stage at the Theatre could mean that a special performance might have been a feature of the entertainment for Cecil. Hoby's friends included the two Privy Councillors who set up the Lord Admiral's and Lord Chamberlain's companies the year before. Hoby himself was the Lord Chamberlain's son-in-law. Showing off one of his company's latest offerings to Cecil would be a neat gesture of loyalty to all three of Hoby's friends. The question must remain open whether it was the play or a portrait that Hoby had ready for Cecil.

Assessments of the text have received less attention than the context. Donna B. Hamilton has clarified the concept of the law that Gaunt expounds in his death scene.[1] Less has been done with the patterning of the elemental images, earth, air, fire and water, that are so carefully set out in the play. As part of the new scrutiny of the play's politics it has become almost a cliché that the opening scene depicts the ceremony of a medieval England soon to be lost to a more 'politic' world of Machiavellian realism, and some critics have noted how carefully Richard's ritualist court conceals a brutal murder. As part of that, Clayton MacKenzie draws attention to the loss of the well-ordered "demi-Paradise" that Gaunt sees in the older England.[2] More critics now see the York scenes in Act 5 as burlesque, David M. Bergeron finding Bahktinian 'carnival' in the inverted rule of Bullingbrook through Act 5. Other critics find the York scene with Bullingbrook (5.2) a wild burlesque of order, and note the mock-ballad rhyming of the Duchess's plea to the new king.

Sources

In recent years *Edward III* has been given close attention. Thought an early Shakespeare play, or one on which he may have collaborated, new editions confidently ascribing it to the Shakespeare canon have appeared in series including the New Cambridge (1998, ed. Giorgio Melchiori). Entered in the Stationers' Register for Cuthbert Burby on 1 December 1595 and first published as a quarto in 1596, it may have been written around 1593 during a long closure for plague. Like *2 Henry VI* and *3 Henry VI*, published in 1594 and 1595, it has links with the Pembroke's company who broke up while on tour in August 1593. Shakespeare very likely belonged to that company along with Richard Burbage and several lesser players named in the 1595 text of *3 Henry VI* who later worked with Burbage and Shakespeare in the Chamberlain's. If so, Shakespeare must have known and per-

---

[1] Donna B. Hamilton, 'The state of law in *Richard II*', *Shakespeare Quarterly* 34 (1983), 5–17.
[2] See Clayton G. MacKenzie, 'Paradise and paradise lost in *Richard II*', *Shakespeare Quarterly* 37 (1986), 318–39.

formed in *Edward III*. Knowledge of *Edward III*, as well as Marlowe's *Edward II*, published in 1594 as performed by the 1593 Pembroke's, would certainly have been there when he composed *Richard II*.

A similar concern, and similar doubts, apply to *King John*. Views are still divided over whether Shakespeare wrote this play in 1590 or in 1595, the same year as *Richard II*. If it was composed in 1590, the Queen's Men's *Troublesome Raigne of King John*, published as a two-part play in 1591, must have been an imitation of Shakespeare's play. If it was written in 1595, along with *Richard II*, it must be a belated rewrite of the Queen's Men's play (a company he may also have worked in, along with John Heminges, also a member of the Chamberlain's). Since Shakespeare did rewrite the Queen's *King Leir*, *Hamlet*, and *Famous Victories of Henry V*, a plausible case can be made for his *King John* being a rewrite of the earlier Queen's one. *King John*'s two main political subjects, national sovereignty against the authority of the Pope and the nationalism that overrides evidence of royal culpability, are reflected in complex ways in *Richard II* and the sequence of plays that developed from it. But whether any of these earlier plays, *Edward II*, *Edward III*, and *The Troublesome Raigne of King John*, may have influenced the thinking behind the composition of *Richard II* is a matter for speculation, however fertile.

Textual History

Views about the 'deposition scene' (4.1.154–317) have on the whole upheld the conclusion that it was written down from dictation, in one version for the printer of Q4, and in a better one for the Folio printer. It is agreed that the F version is superior to Q4's, but there is no consensus about the precise origin of either. Laurie Maguire counts what she calls the 'Abdication Scene' as a 'suspect text', said to be written down from an actor's memory of the play in performance, but concludes that it was not copied down from memory.[1] Her table of variants from the F text (p. 298) lists none of any significance. The differences that exist between the Q and F versions might as readily come from the use of dictation to make the copy as from memory. Dictation for speed of transcription is a feature of several so-called 'bad' quartos, confirmed in the quarto of *Henry V* (1600).[2]

Attention to the issue of censorship has renewed the question whether it was the stage text or the printed text or both which lost the deposition scene. It is both highlighted and befogged by the dispute over the political role of the plays. Work on the role of the Master of the Revels, notably by Richard Dutton,[3] identifies him as a fairly lenient censor of plays for the stage. This has also clarified the distinction, relevant for 1595 and the printing of the first three quartos in 1597 and 1598, between the censoring of plays for performance and for printing. The Master was only concerned with staging, the Company of Stationers and the Church, usually the

---

[1] Laurie E. Maguire, *Shakespearean Suspect Texts: The 'Bad' Quartos and their Contexts*, 1996, p. 325.
[2] See Gurr, ed. *The First Quarto of King Henry V*, 2000, pp. 15–18.
[3] *Mastering the Revels*, 1991, especially pp. 124–7.

Bishop of London, with any contentious texts for the press. In my view, the fact that the deposition scene could be reinserted twice, first in the fourth quarto (1608) and then in the First Folio, strongly hints that the Master did originally allow it for the stage, and that it was the press censors who ordered it deleted from the early quartos while Elizabeth was still living. The Q4 text would have been roughly copied by dictation from the 'allowed' manuscript playbook which had the Master's signature on it, while the Folio copyists made a more leisurely version.

Stage History

Richard II on stage presents a peculiar difficulty in that its political significance for its own time has been lost for modern audiences. As a result the actorly focus on Richard alone as a tragic hero unbalances the play's delicate presentation of the gradual shift in political control from one kind of tyrant to another. In recent years its chief stagings have been incorporated as a prelude to the second sequence of English history plays and the central confrontation between Prince Hal and Falstaff. The Royal Shakespeare Company has maintained its tradition of staging all the histories in sequence, most recently in 1999–2000. To some extent this appears to be a long-term consequence of the idea that for educational purposes knowledge of English history comes best from Shakespeare, creating some confusion for modern playgoers. The New Education Code for England of 1882–3 laid it down that the study of English history was an essential part of a British education and, specified the reading of a history play by Shakespeare as the best way of ensuring it. In the nineteenth century that usually meant studying *Richard II* or *Henry V*, since neither has the difficulty that the Eastcheap scenes in the *Henry IV* plays were thought to have for innocent schoolchildren. Modern playgoers, lacking the knowledge of Shakespeare's historical sources and the politics of monarchy that go with them, are left finding their pleasure in the characterization of Richard, and sometimes his interplay with his antagonist, the shadowy Bullingbrook. The RSC's production of the series in 1999–2000 used *Richard II* as a preface to the *Henry IV* plays, giving David Troughton, as Bullingbrook, a strongly manipulative role, counterbalancing their Richard. But it was a slow, drab production, making no attempt to show the shifting balance of power as central to the story.

Through the last twenty years *Richard II* has been staged in widely varying ways, though the focus on Richard as tragic hero still predominates. Critical views of the play in performance have shifted too. Admirable studies have appeared, chiefly of plays staged at Stratford and London through the 1970s and 1980s. In *In One Person Many People* Liisa Hakola writes about John Barton's Stratford production of 1973–4, Terry Hands' of 1980–81, and Barry Kyle's of 1986–7. Margaret Shewring's neat book in the 'Shakespeare in Performance' series writes about productions up to Michael Bogdanov's, praising Michael Pennington's performance for the touring English Shakespeare Company in 1987–8.[1] It also looks at the generally unhappy television versions by the NBC in 1954 and the BBC in 1979.

[1] Margaret Shewring, *Richard II: Shakespeare in Performance*, 1996.

14   Fiona Shaw as Richard II, in the 1998 National Theatre production in London.

In spite of the remoteness of direct political applications of the play, its psychological politics and its transfer of power have had plenty of attention. The chief effect has been to emphasise the play's careful balance between tyrant king and usurper king, at some cost to the performance tradition, which always favours Richard as the tragic hero. Insistence on the play as Richard's tragedy was maintained when Fiona Shaw took the title role at the National Theatre in London in 1998, when the cross-dressed Richard's verbalised anguish ruled at the cost of the shift of power. A finely spoken production, elegantly directed by Deborah Warner, it made much of the ceremonial colour of the opening and Richard's gradual descent to the dungeon at Pomfret.

One of the most politically minded productions in England was staged in 2000 by the Almeida, using the old Gainsborough Film Studios in Islington, London. Ralph Fiennes played Richard as a self-regarding and posturing neurotic, aware that his role is only to act the part of a king, and always finely sensitive to the power game he plays with his opposite. Fiennes was much better cast for this role than for the other he took in that season, Coriolanus. The production was heavily over-designed, as is (regrettably) common in subsidized theatre. It used the interval to lay green turf across the entire stage, presumably in order to make a literal truth of Bullingbrook's reference in 3.3 to 'the fresh green lap of fair King Richard's land', and 'the grassy carpet of this plain'. Audiences should have been grateful that Bullingbrook's threat to rain on the earth was not taken literally as well.

NOTE ON THE TEXT

Richard II's popularity is indicated by the five quarto editions which appeared before it joined thirty-five other plays of Shakespeare in the 1623 Folio. Unlike some of the thirteen plays printed in quarto in Shakespeare's lifetime it was published in a clean, accurate text with the blessing of its owners, the Chamberlain's Men. The manuscript supplied to the printer was close to the author's own manuscript, and shows no sign of being adapted for use in the playhouse. Each of the four quartos which appeared subsequently was printed from its predecessor. Apart from the deposition scene added to the fourth quarto (Q4) none of the later texts has any independent authority, and each adds its own crop of misprints to its predecessor.

The Folio text (F) by contrast was independently collated with a copy profoundly influenced by playhouse use. It is basically a copy of the third quarto (Q3), corrected in most of its stage directions, its metre and in occasional words or lines, and with some passages cut. It has a better version of the deposition scene than Q4. Whoever did the collation was generally bold and competent, though not really thoroughgoing. The Folio text is thus an important check against the occasional stumbles of the first quarto (Q1), and gives substantial evidence of what was done with the play in the playhouse.

On the principle that the author's text is in the main preferable to the playhouse text, Q1 forms the basis for this edition. It is true of course that the copy used to print Q1 was to some extent a less than fully finished artefact. Its stage directions were patchy, there are two or three minor inconsistencies and in places the Q1 printing has left the original almost indecipherable. On the whole Q1 is a clean text, and shows ample evidence that the manuscript which lies behind it was a careful and precisely constructed version of the original design. *Richard II* Q1 is a more meticulously finished product than most of the early Shakespeare quartos. By contrast the Folio text shows some evidence of the finished product as it was worn on the stage through twenty or so years of playing. It is based on a derivative quarto containing errors introduced by three sets of quarto compositors and less than perfectly adjusted to conform to a playhouse manuscript of the performed text. By and large it gives an accurate record of what its first handlers did with it after Shakespeare handed it over, both the performers who arranged the staging and adjusted words and rhythms and the Folio editor who sought to record the stage version in print and who made his own sense of muddling passages. For the modern reader the optimum text must be Q1 corrected by a judicious mixture of F's alternative readings and conjectures, with substantial augmentation by F's stage directions. The choices are considered in detail in the Textual Analysis, pp. 185–93 below.

The text for this edition modernises the spellings and regularises abbreviations and punctuation. The spelling of characters' names in speech headings and stage directions has been made uniform. Where a modernised spelling conceals word-play it has been registered in the Commentary. Punctuation has been kept as light as possible, except where it is necessary to use commas to clarify the syntax. Any significant departure from the QI or F punctuation is recorded in the collation. In the format of the collations, the authority for this edition's reading follows immediately after the square bracket enclosing the quotation from the text. Other readings, if any, follow in chronological order. Exclamation marks, which Elizabethan compositors did not always distinguish from question marks, have been kept to a minimum. Elisions in QI have generally been retained, especially where they affect the metre. Conventionally all -ed endings are assumed to be elided. On the few occasions where the metre requires otherwise, the syllable is printed with an accent.

King Richard II

LIST OF CHARACTERS
in order of appearance

RICHARD
GAUNT
BULLINGBROOK
MOWBRAY
DUCHESS OF GLOUCESTER
MARSHAL
AUMERLE
2 *Heralds*
GREEN
BAGOT
BUSHY
YORK
QUEEN
ROSS
WILLOUGHBY
NORTHUMBERLAND
PERCY
BERKELEY
SALISBURY
Welsh CAPTAIN
CARLISLE
SCROOPE
Queen's LADIES
GARDENER
Gardener's SERVANTS
FITZWATER
SURREY
WESTMINSTER
DUCHESS OF YORK
EXTON
GROOM
KEEPER
Attendant nobles, soldiers, servants, murderers

Notes
Neither Q nor F supplies a list of characters. Almost every character is identified in the dialogue at the first entry, and very few are not in Holinshed. The notes which follow list them in the order of their appearance, and are chiefly historical.

RICHARD 1367–99, king 1377–99. Known as Richard of Bordeaux, where he was born; a grandson of Edward III and a younger son of the Black Prince, Edward's eldest son. The events of the play cover the last two years of his reign.

GAUNT John of Gaunt (Ghent), Duke of Lancaster, younger brother of the Black Prince and fourth son of Edward III. The sons of Edward are listed in *2H6* 2.2.10–17.

BULLINGBROOK Henry, eldest son of Gaunt, named after his birthplace. Holinshed spelt it 'Bullingbrooke', and Shakespeare followed him, using its watery associations. The spelling 'Bolingbroke' became standard in the eighteenth century. He was created Duke of Hereford in 1397.

MOWBRAY Thomas Duke of Norfolk. The Mowbray of *2H4* was his eldest son. He died in Venice in 1399. He was Captain of Calais when Gloucester was imprisoned there, and was responsible for his death, if not himself the murderer. Holinshed and most Elizabethan commentators make him the murderer, though *Woodstock* has Gloucester killed by 'Lapoole'.

DUCHESS OF GLOUCESTER Widow of the murdered duke, who was the Black Prince's youngest brother.

MARSHAL Historically the Duke of Surrey replaced Mowbray as Marshal in 1398. In the play he has a purely ceremonial function.

AUMERLE Spelt 'Aumarle' at first in Q1 after Holinshed, probably reflecting the pronunciation. Son of the Duke of York, named from Albemarle in Normandy, he was made a duke by Richard, and was one of Richard's closest supporters. He was made Constable after Gloucester's arrest. The historical Aumerle was probably not involved in the conspiracy which followed Richard's deposition, and lived to become the Duke of York who died at Agincourt.

GREEN Sir Henry, Northamptonshire M.P. and royal councillor, a member of the Council of Regency during Richard's absence in Ireland.

BAGOT Sir William, Sheriff of Leicester and M.P., king's minister and councillor, and a member of the Regency Council.

BUSHY Sir John, Sheriff of Lincoln and M.P., Speaker of the House of Commons and Richard's chief agent there, and a member of the Regency Council.

YORK Edmund Langley, Duke of York, fifth son of Edward III (see 2.1.171–2). The historical York was more interested in hunting than in politics.

QUEEN Shakespeare's queen is a conflation of Richard's first wife, Anne of Bohemia, and his second, Isabella of France, who was barely ten when the events of the play took place. Daniel gave a precedent for Shakespeare's queen.

ROSS or Roos, seventh Lord, of Helmsley in Yorkshire, M.P. and Lord Treasurer under Henry IV.

WILLOUGHBY fifth Lord, of Eresby, an M.P. and northern lord like Ross. All Bullingbrook's chief supporters were from the north.

NORTHUMBERLAND Henry, first Earl. Shakespeare omits mention of the ambush by which he captured Richard near Flint but otherwise his character is presented as in Holinshed. He became the leading rebel in the reign of Henry IV.

PERCY Son of Northumberland, the Hotspur of *1H4*. The historical Hotspur was two years older than Bullingbrook.

BERKELEY fifth Lord and M.P. Shakespeare's use of him is straight from Holinshed.

SALISBURY John Montagu, third Earl.

Welsh CAPTAIN Leader of the Welsh contingent. Editors speculate, partly because of the reference at 3.1.43, that he should have been the Glendower of *1H4*. A Welsh accent also appears in *Wiv.* and *H5*. The portents described by the Captain, which are taken from Holinshed and Daniel, would be appropriate for the Glendower of *1H4*.

CARLISLE Thomas Merkes, made Bishop of Carlisle in 1397. He was pardoned by Henry IV in 1400 and given a country vicarage.

SCROOPE or Lescrope, Sir Stephen, a famous fighter, brother to the Earl of Wiltshire.

GARDENER Visually distinct as the first figure on stage not either a noble, soldier or priest. Sometimes staged as a comic, though there is no support for this in the text.

FITZWATER Walter, fifth Lord and M.P. Holinshed uses the old form for the standard Fitzwalter, probably reflecting Elizabethan pronunciation (Walter Raleigh punned on the pronunciation of his first name as 'Water'). Judging from Q1 Shakespeare may have spelled him 'Fitzwaters'.

SURREY Thomas, third Earl of Kent, made Duke of Surrey in 1397. He was the son of Richard's half-brother, and was made Lord Marshal in 1398 before the Mowbray–Bullingbrook quarrel.

WESTMINSTER The Abbot of, according to Holinshed.

DUCHESS OF YORK The historical Duchess of York was Aumerle's step-mother, sister of the Duke of Surrey. She later married Willoughby.

EXTON Sir Piers. Holinshed tells the story of the murder of Richard by Exton (II, 517). Nothing else is known of the historical Exton, though he may have been related to Sir Nicholas, Sheriff of London, an opponent of Richard.

KING RICHARD THE SECOND

1.1 *Enter* KING RICHARD, JOHN OF GAUNT, *with other Nobles and Attendants.*

RICHARD Old John of Gaunt, time-honoured Lancaster,
    Hast thou according to thy oath and band
    Brought hither Henry Herford, thy bold son,
    Here to make good the boisterous late appeal,
    Which then our leisure would not let us hear,   5
    Against the Duke of Norfolk, Thomas Mowbray?
GAUNT I have, my liege.
RICHARD Tell me moreover hast thou sounded him
    If he appeal the Duke on ancient malice,
    Or worthily as a good subject should   10
    On some known ground of treachery in him?
GAUNT As near as I could sift him on that argument,
    On some apparent danger seen in him
    Aimed at your highness, no inveterate malice.
RICHARD Then call them to our presence. Face to face   15

Act 1, Scene 1   **15** presence. Face to face] *Neilson;* presence face to face, Qq, F; presence; *Pope*

Act 1, Scene 1

1.1 Q marks neither act nor scene divisions. F marks them as in this edition except that it leaves 5.4 as part of the preceding scene.

o SD Located by Holinshed at Windsor, this would have been a throne-room scene on stage. The 'chair of state' would be placed at centre-stage and the king would enter at the head of a procession of nobles to take his seat for the formal hearing of the 'appeal' (4). The content of the scene is close to Holinshed, II, 493–4.

1 Old...Gaunt The historical Gaunt was 58. His age and his brother York's are set in contrast to Richard's 'youth', 2.1.69.

2 band bond. An archaic form. As at 4.1.76 and 5.2.65.

3 Herford A disyllable, judging from the metre. Q and F both use the modern spelling 'Hereford' here and at 28, but F has 'Herford' at 1.2.46 and 53. The shorter form reflects the pronunciation. But see Stanley Wells, *Modernising Shakespeare's Spelling*, p. 29.

4 late recent.

4 appeal accusation, a criminal charge made under penalty of supplying proof. See 4.1.79, and 'repeal', 4.1.85–7.

5 leisure lack of leisure.

7 liege The feudal term is apt both for Gaunt's outlook and for the occasion, in that his son's loyalty is being called in question.

8 sounded enquired of.

9 on ancient malice on the basis of long-established personal enmity.

11 known ground facts, not animosity.

12 An alexandrine. Editors have conjectured either that 'him on' is intrusive by infection from 'on' in the line following, or that 'argument' is a dissyllable, giving a decasyllabic line with feminine ending.

12 sift find by examining. See *Ham.* 2.2.58.

12 argument subject-matter.

13 apparent self-evident.

15 our presence The vicinity of the king had the attributes of a courtroom. Its protocols included the

And frowning brow to brow ourselves will hear
The accuser and the accusèd freely speak.
High stomached are they both and full of ire,
In rage deaf as the sea, hasty as fire.

Enter BULLINGBROOK *and* MOWBRAY.

BULLINGBROOK Many years of happy days befall   20
    My gracious sovereign, my most loving liege.
MOWBRAY Each day still better other's happiness,
    Until the heavens, envying earth's good hap,
    Add an immortal title to your crown.
RICHARD We thank you both. Yet one but flatters us,   25
    As well appeareth by the cause you come,
    Namely to appeal each other of high treason.
    Cousin of Herford, what dost thou object
    Against the Duke of Norfolk, Thomas Mowbray?
BULLINGBROOK First, heaven be the record to my speech.   30
    In the devotion of a subject's love,
    Tendering the precious safety of my prince,
    And free from other misbegotten hate,
    Come I appellant to this princely presence.
    Now Thomas Mowbray do I turn to thee,   35
    And mark my greeting well; for what I speak
    My body shall make good upon this earth,
    Or my divine soul answer it in heaven.

requirements that subjects stood, were hatless, and never turned their backs on the king. Bullingbrook alludes to its judicial function speaking of 'this princely presence' at 34. See *OED* sv *sb*. 2b, c and d.

18 High stomached haughty, full of self-regard and valour.

19 rage...sea See *John* 2.1.451: 'The sea enragèd is not half so deaf.' Both phrases are proverbial (Dent s169.2, F246.1).

19 SD BULLINGBROOK Q and F spell the name 'Bullingbrooke' throughout. The modern spelling 'Bolingbroke' was popularised in the eighteenth century by the family of Henry St John, first Viscount Bolingbroke, Pope's friend. This edn follows the spelling first adopted by Riverside.

19 SD MOWBRAY According to *2H4* 3.2.26 Mowbray's page was Falstaff.

21 loving liege Kings were assumed to love their subjects. The adjective and noun together summarise the feudal relationship.

22 Each day still May each day always.

23 hap fortune.

24 an immortal...crown immortality to your name of king. With a suggestion of enthronement in heaven.

25 flatters Shakespeare always uses 'flattery' to mean deceit.

26 the cause you come the judicial claim which brings you.

28 object bring as an accusation.

30 First Both Bullingbrook and Mowbray start counting but do not get past the first item. Conceivably Mowbray at 54 is parodying his rival.

32 Tendering Cherishing and offering. See Polonius's word-play, *Ham.* 1.3.106–9.

33 other...hate any hatred other than concern for the prince's safety.

34 appellant making a formal appeal. See 4 n. above.

36 greeting form of address. As given at 39.

Thou art a traitor and a miscreant,
Too good to be so, and too bad to live.   40
Since the more fair and crystal is the sky,
The uglier seem the clouds that in it fly.
Once more, the more to aggravate the note,
With a foul traitor's name stuff I thy throat,
And wish (so please my sovereign) ere I move,   45
What my tongue speaks my right drawn sword may prove.
MOWBRAY Let not my cold words here accuse my zeal.
'Tis not the trial of a woman's war,
The bitter clamour of two eager tongues,
Can arbitrate this cause betwixt us twain.   50
The blood is hot that must be cooled for this.
Yet can I not of such tame patience boast
As to be hushed, and naught at all to say.
First, the fair reverence of your highness curbs me
From giving reins and spurs to my free speech,   55
Which else would post until it had returned
These terms of treason doubled down his throat.
Setting aside his high blood's royalty,
And let him be no kinsman to my liege,
I do defy him, and I spit at him,   60
Call him a slanderous coward and a villain,
Which to maintain I would allow him odds

---

53 hushed] Q2–5, F; huisht Q1   57 doubled] Qq; doubly F   60 and I] Q1, F; and Q2–5

40 **good** high-ranking.
41–2 Couplet rhyming begins here, along with the elemental imagery. See pp. 31–3 above.
41 **crystal** The Ptolemaic idea of the cosmos assumed that the heavenly bodies were fixed on transparent crystal spheres revolving one inside the other with the earth at their centre.
43 **aggravate** emphasise (by repetition of the word 'traitor').
43 **note** stigma. From Latin *nota*, the term for the Roman Censor's public reproof of individuals.
44 **stuff…throat** choke and prevent from speaking. With a hint at the forcible swallowing of an insult.
46 **right drawn** justly drawn.
47 **accuse** undermine the strength of.
47 **zeal** (1) ardour, (2) loyalty. The second meaning was already archaic in Shakespeare's day.
48 **trial** (1) test by combat, (2) judgement, as in legal dispute (with tongues).

49 **eager** sharp, cutting (like a sword).
50 **Can arbitrate** That can reach a judicial decision.
51 **cooled** i.e. by spilling. Medicinal bloodletting, purgation by bleeding, was thought to cool the body as well as releasing the excessive 'humour'.
53 **hushed** The Q1 spelling 'huished' probably reflects the pronunciation.
54 **fair reverence** Compare 'loving liege' at 21.
56 **post** Develops the imagery of 'curbs', 'reins' and 'spurs'. Posting meant travelling fast by using relays of horses.
57 **terms of treason** 'traitor' and 'miscreant' (39 and 44).
57 **doubled** redoubled (Bullingbrook has already called Mowbray a traitor twice), and folded thickly.
58 **his…royalty** his high rank and high anger. See 71 below.

And meet him were I tied to run afoot
Even to the frozen ridges of the Alps,
Or any other ground inhabitable   65
Where ever Englishman durst set his foot.
Meantime, let this defend my loyalty:
By all my hopes most falsely doth he lie.

BULLINGBROOK Pale trembling coward, there I throw my gage,
Disclaiming here the kindred of the king,   70
And lay aside my high blood's royalty,
Which fear, not reverence, makes thee to except.
If guilty dread have left thee so much strength
As to take up mine honour's pawn, then stoop.
By that and all the rites of knighthood else   75
Will I make good against thee, arm to arm,
What I have spoke, or thou canst worse devise.

MOWBRAY I take it up, and by that sword I swear
Which gently laid my knighthood on my shoulder
I'll answer thee in any fair degree   80
Or chivalrous design of knightly trial;
And when I mount, alive may I not light
If I be traitor or unjustly fight.

RICHARD What doth our cousin lay to Mowbray's charge?

---

63 tied] Q1; tide Q2–5, F   70 the king] Q1; a King Q2–5, F   73 have] Qq; hath F   75 rites] Qq; rights F
77 spoke...devise] Q1; spoke, or thou canst deuise Q2; spoke, or what thou canst deuise Q3–5; Spoken, or thou canst
deuise F

---

63 **tied** obliged. See *OED* sv *v* 5.

65 **inhabitable** not habitable.

67 **this** Possibly Mowbray here throws down a gage, in the form of a glove or hood, though since Bullingbrook gives no sign of taking anything up it is more likely that Mowbray touches his sword, or else is heralding the declaration of the next line.

69 **gage** Holinshed says that the gages used in the Parliament scene were hoods, but the reference at 4.1.25 to a 'manual seal' makes it likely that gloves were used on stage.

71 **lay...royalty** See 58 above.

72 **makes...except** holds you back (by making the exception at 58). Bullingbrook is freeing Mowbray from the danger of shedding royal blood.

74 **pawn** the gage which holds his honour in pawn. The same term is used at 4.1.55 and 70 when the situation is reversed and Bullingbrook has to preside over the challenges between unruly nobles.

74 **stoop** bend (to pick up the gage). At 3.3.48 'stooping' means 'kneeling in homage'. A stoop was

also a hawk's predatory dive, a term relevant to Bullingbrook, one of whose badges was a white falcon.

75 **rites** The homonym was commonly spelt in either way. F's 'rights' normalises the meaning but is a not unreasonable alternative.

77 **or...devise** The text and the meaning are both unclear. A misreading in Q2 was compounded in subsequent quartos. F, using a copy of Q3, made an independent correction which might derive from an unknown source superior to Q1, but more likely was the F editor's invention. See Richard E. Hasker, 'The copy for the First Folio *Richard II*', *SB* 5 (1952), 57. Bullingbrook presumably means 'any lies worse than those you have already devised'.

78 **that sword** The sword used in dubbing a knight was normally the king's. See William Segar, *The Booke of Honor and Armes* (1590), V, 54, 74.

82 **light** alight.

83 **unjustly** in an unjust cause.

It must be great that can inherit us   85
So much as of a thought of ill in him.
BULLINGBROOK Look what I speak, my life shall prove it true:
That Mowbray hath received eight thousand nobles
In name of lendings for your highness' soldiers,
The which he hath detained for lewd employments   90
Like a false traitor and injurious villain.
Besides I say, and will in battle prove
Or here or elsewhere to the furthest verge
That ever was surveyed by English eye,
That all the treasons for these eighteen years   95
Complotted and contrivèd in this land
Fetch from false Mowbray their first head and spring.
Further I say, and further will maintain
Upon his bad life to make all this good,
That he did plot the Duke of Gloucester's death,   100
Suggest his soon-believing adversaries,
And consequently like a traitor coward
Sluiced out his innocent soul through streams of blood,
Which blood, like sacrificing Abel's, cries
Even from the tongueless caverns of the earth   105
To me for justice and rough chastisement;
And, by the glorious worth of my descent,
This arm shall do it, or this life be spent.

---

87 speak] Q1 ; said Q2–5, F   97 Fetch] Q1 ; Fetcht Q2–5 ; Fetch'd F   99 good,] Qq ; good. F   104 Abel's,] Q4–5 ; Abels Q1–3, F

---

85 inherit bequeath, with a hint of the blood kinship in 'cousin'.

87 Look what Whatever.

88 nobles Gold coins, worth one-third of a pound sterling.

89 lendings advances on pay. Holinshed says he should have paid the Calais garrison.

90 lewd improper.

95 eighteen years Since 1381 and the rising of Wat Tyler and Jack Straw when Richard was a boy. Shakespeare may simply have taken the figure from Holinshed.

97 Fetch Draw, as water.

100 Gloucester's death Bullingbrook is ignoring the part Richard played in ordering Mowbray to kill Gloucester. See p. 22 above. In Holinshed there is no mention of the murder amongst the charges Bullingbrook lays against Mowbray.

101 Suggest Tempt, incite. See 3.4.75.

103 through...blood This reference together with 1.2.21 and 2.2.102 all assume Gloucester was beheaded. Of the possible sources Shakespeare might have consulted Holinshed, Froissart and *Woodstock* all say Gloucester was smothered. Le Beau, one of the French sources to whom Holinshed refers, has him beheaded. Presumably Shakespeare wanted the blood.

104 sacrificing Abel's Abel the shepherd sacrificed his beasts to God. Cain's murder of his brother stemmed from jealousy, since as a tiller of the earth he had no beasts to sacrifice. See Gen. 4.10. It is Richard rather than Mowbray who has shed his kinsman's blood.

106 To me Bullingbrook asks for revenge as Gloucester's nephew, which Richard also is. In Genesis it is God who punishes Cain and sends him into exile. See Stanley R. Maveety, 'A second fall of cursed man: the bold metaphor in *Richard II*', *JEGP* 72 (1973), 175–93.

RICHARD How high a pitch his resolution soars!
     Thomas of Norfolk, what say'st thou to this?   110
MOWBRAY Oh let my sovereign turn away his face
     And bid his ears a little while be deaf,
     Till I have told this slander of his blood
     How God and good men hate so foul a liar.
RICHARD Mowbray, impartial are our eyes and ears.   115
     Were he my brother, nay, my kingdom's heir,
     As he is but my father's brother's son,
     Now by my sceptre's awe I make a vow
     Such neighbour nearness to our sacred blood
     Should nothing privilege him nor partialise   120
     The unstooping firmness of my upright soul.
     He is our subject, Mowbray; so art thou.
     Free speech and fearless I to thee allow.
MOWBRAY Then, Bullingbrook, as low as to thy heart
     Through the false passage of thy throat thou liest.   125
     Three parts of that receipt I had for Calais
     Disbursed I duly to his highness' soldiers.
     The other part reserved I by consent,
     For that my sovereign liege was in my debt
     Upon remainder of a dear account   130
     Since last I went to France to fetch his queen.
     Now swallow down that lie. For Gloucester's death,

116 my kingdom's] QQ; our kingdomes F   118 my] F; *not in* QQ   127 duly] Q1; *not in* Q2–5, F

109 **pitch** The highest point in the flight of a hawk. The image combines height and air with Bullingbrook's falcon badge (see 74 n. above). Richard is slightly derisive.

113 **this slander…blood** disgrace to the royal blood.

114 **God and good men** Proverbial.

115 **eyes and ears** In response to Mowbray's 'face' (111) and 'ears' (112).

117 **my father's…son** Richard states the relationship in the most distant terms. In fact Bullingbrook was a possible heir after Roger Mortimer, the Earl of March, who was killed by the Irish in 1398 and whose death prompted Richard to go to Ireland. See 1.4.35–6 n.

119 **sacred blood** Divinity in the kingship has already been implied by Bullingbrook's renunciation of his blood's royalty at 71.

121 **unstooping…upright** The king kneels to nobody but God. The play has many gestures of kneeling in duty or submission. See 1.4.33.

124–5 The lie is in Bullingbrook's heart, not just his mouth. See *2H4* 4.1.134 ff. 'To lie in one's throat' was proverbial.

126 **Three parts** three-quarters.

126 **receipt** sum received.

126 **Calais** The spelling 'Callice' in QQ and F reflects the pronunciation.

128 **by consent** Mowbray suggests that Richard accepted the deal, a point not to be found in Holinshed's account.

130 **remainder** the balance.

130 **dear** expensive and precious.

132–4 Mowbray is deliberately ambiguous. According to Holinshed he actually delayed carrying out Richard's order to kill Gloucester for three weeks. His 'sworn duty' must be his loyalty to the king. It is an oblique way of reminding Richard of his involvement in Gloucester's death and implies that it is for Richard to restore his honour. In 4.1 Bagot accuses Aumerle of complicity in the murder too. For a consideration of the

I slew him not, but to my own disgrace
Neglected my sworn duty in that case.
For you, my noble lord of Lancaster,   135
The honourable father to my foe,
Once did I lay an ambush for your life,
A trespass that doth vex my grievèd soul.
But ere I last received the sacrament
I did confess it, and exactly begged   140
Your grace's pardon, and I hope I had it.
This is my fault. As for the rest appealed,
It issues from the rancour of a villain,
A recreant and most degenerate traitor,
Which in myself I boldly will defend,   145
And interchangeably hurl down my gage
Upon this overweening traitor's foot,
To prove myself a loyal gentleman
Even in the best blood chambered in his bosom.
In haste whereof most heartily I pray   150
Your highness to assign our trial day.
RICHARD Wrath-kindled gentlemen, be ruled by me.
Let's purge this choler without letting blood.
This we prescribe though no physician.
Deep malice makes too deep incision.   155
Forget, forgive, conclude and be agreed.
Our doctors say this is no month to bleed.

133 my] Q1; mine Q2–5, F   137 did I] Qq; I did F   139 But] Q1 *(Huth)*, F; Ah but Q1 *(Capell, Hunt., Petworth)*
146 my] Q1, F; the Q2–5   152 gentlemen] F; gentleman Qq   157 month] Qq; time F

likelihood that Mowbray is hinting at Richard's
obligations to him, see Larry S. Champion, 'The
function of Mowbray: Shakespeare's maturing
artistry in *Richard II*', *SQ* 26 (1975), 3–7.
  137 Referred to by Holinshed.
  139 But A press-correction from Q1 Compositor
S's *seriatim* stint. The Huth reading is metrically
correct.
  140 exactly begged asked pardon specifically
for the ambush of Gaunt.
  142 the rest appealed the other charges.
  144 recreant coward, one who yields in a fight.
  144 degenerate traitor betraying his own royal
blood.
  146 interchangeably reciprocally.
  146–7 Neither Q nor F notes the contestants'
actions with the gages in their stage directions.
Bullingbrook evidently picks up Mowbray's gage,
as Mowbray must have picked up Bullingbrook's at

78. Gaunt tells his son to throw down Mowbray's
at 161.
  153 purge purify medicinally and clear of guilt.
  153 choler The hot and dry humour, yellow
bile.
  154 though no physician Kings were traditionally healers of their people. James I referred to the
king as the physician of the politic body in his
Counterblast (1604).
  155 too deep incision Medicinal bleeding was
by shallow cuts in veins.
  156 Forget, forgive Proverbial. See Tilley
F597.
  156 conclude come to terms.
  157 doctors Learned men, including astro-
logers.
  157 month F's reading normalises, but reduces
what is probably Richard's joke about astrological
influence in medicine.

Good uncle, let this end where it begun,
We'll calm the Duke of Norfolk, you your son.
GAUNT To be a make-peace shall become my age.   160
    Throw down, my son, the Duke of Norfolk's gage.
RICHARD And, Norfolk, throw down his.
GAUNT   When, Harry, when?
    Obedience bids I should not bid again.
RICHARD Norfolk, throw down we bid; there is no boot.
MOWBRAY Myself I throw, dread sovereign, at thy foot.   165
    My life thou shalt command, but not my shame.
    The one my duty owes, but my fair name,
    Despite of death, that lives upon my grave,
    To dark dishonour's use thou shalt not have.
    I am disgraced, impeached and baffled here,   170
    Pierced to the soul with slander's venomèd spear,
    The which no balm can cure but his heart blood
    Which breathed this poison.
RICHARD   Rage must be withstood.
    Give me his gage. Lions make leopards tame.
MOWBRAY Yea, but not change his spots. Take but my shame   175
    And I resign my gage. My dear, dear lord,
    The purest treasure mortal times afford
    Is spotless reputation; that away,
    Men are but gilded loam, or painted clay.
    A jewel in a ten times barred up chest   180

162–3 When…bids] *Pope;* When Harry? when obedience bids / Obedience bids Q1; When *Harrie* when? Obedience bids, / Obedience bids Q2–5, F

159 Richard is not entirely detached and impartial. Mowbray is his man on the evidence of the Gloucester murder, and Bullingbrook is implicitly attacking Richard through his agent.

162–3 Pope's emendation simplifies what seems to have been an accumulation of compositor errors in Q1 and Q2, beginning with a mistake over lineation which led the Q1 compositor (S) to set 'Obedience bids' twice and then forget to delete the first block.

163 Obedience The duty of son to father.

164 boot advantage, point.

165 Myself Not his gage. Mowbray kneels as a visual signal of his particular loyalty to Richard.

170 impeached accused in law.

170 baffled dishonoured in public for cowardice; a chivalric term. Turpine in *The Faerie Queene*, VI, vii, 27, is baffled. The procedure involved hanging either the knight or his image upside down by the heels, a reversal of the imagery of height.

172 balm antidote. Poisons and their antidotes were thought to exist in close proximity. Thomas Browne's *Vulgar Errors* (*Works*, 1964, II, 536) states 'if we look upon the words of the most High, there are two and two, one against another; that one contrary hath another, and poyson is not without a poyson unto it self'.

174 Lions…tame In heraldry Norfolk's crest was a *lion leopardé*. Holinshed (II, 495) describes Mowbray's horse's coat as embroidered with silver lions.

175 change his spots Proverbial (Tilley L206), and in Jer. 13.23. Mowbray is punning on spots as stains on his reputation (see 178), and possibly the 'spot' of killing Gloucester.

175 Take…shame Mowbray appeals to Richard to take responsibility for his 'spots'.

Is a bold spirit in a loyal breast.
Mine honour is my life, both grow in one.
Take honour from me and my life is done.
Then, dear my liege, mine honour let me try.
In that I live, and for that will I die.   185
RICHARD Cousin, throw up your gage. Do you begin.
BULLINGBROOK O God defend my soul from such deep sin!
Shall I seem crestfallen in my father's sight?
Or with pale beggar fear impeach my height
Before this out-dared dastard? Ere my tongue   190
Shall wound my honour with such feeble wrong,
Or sound so base a parle, my teeth shall tear
The slavish motive of recanting fear
And spit it bleeding in his high disgrace,
Where shame doth harbour, even in Mowbray's face.   195

                                         Exit Gaunt

RICHARD We were not born to sue, but to command,
Which, since we cannot do to make you friends,
Be ready, as your lives shall answer it,
At Coventry upon Saint Lambert's Day.
There shall your swords and lances arbitrate   200
The swelling difference of your settled hate.

---

186 up] Qq; downe F   187 God] Qq; heauen F   187 deep] Qq; foule F   188 sight?] Qq; sight, F   189 beggar fear]
Q1, F; begger-face Q2–5   191 my] Qq; mine F   192 parle] F; parlee Qq   195 SD] *not in* Qq   198 lives] Q1, F; life
Q2–5

---

186 **Cousin** Richard reaffirms the blood relation
in turning to Bullingbrook.

186 **throw up** F normalises as 'throw down', but
makes it a gesture of challenge not withdrawal. The
assumption made by some editors that Richard
was on the stage balcony and that he asks for the gage
to be tossed up to him is too literal-minded. 'Up'
has the sense of putting away, as in *Oth.* 1.2.59.

187 **God** F's alteration to 'heaven' here and
elsewhere reflects the theatrical censorship introduced in the 1606 Act against blasphemy on stage.
See Textual Analysis, p. 176 below.

188 **crestfallen** Bullingbrook does not kneel as
Mowbray did at 165. His speech is based on the
contrast of his height (189: high rank) and the depth
of the disgrace of speaking rather than fighting.

190 **dastard** coward.

192 **parle** truce. F's monosyllable fits the metre
better than Q's French pronunciation, and was the
standard anglicised form.

193 **motive** moving limb, his tongue. See *Tro.*
4.5.57.

194–5 Stories about a philosopher who bit off his
tongue and spat it in a tyrant's face can be found
in Thomas Elyot, *The Governor*, Lyly's *Euphues* and
Kyd's *Spanish Tragedy*.

194 **his** its.

195 **SD** F adds an exit for Gaunt here so that he
can enter to start the next scene.

199 **Saint Lambert's Day** 17 September, one
of three dates offered by Holinshed. Lambert was
unjustly deprived of his bishopric. See David
E. Lampe, 'Ironic saint's lore in *Richard II* 1.i', in
Studies in English and American Literature, ed. John
L. Cutler and Lawrence S. Thompson, 1978, pp.
79–80.

200 **lances** Both the tilting weapon and the
surgeon's instrument for lancing a swelling (201).

200 **arbitrate** On the controversy over duelling
as a means to justice see Diane Bornstein, 'Trial
by combat and official irresponsibility in *Richard
II*', *S.St.* 8 (1975), 131–41. In *2H4* 4.1.131–3
Westmorland suggests that 'fortune', not justice,
would have decided the issue.

Since we cannot atone you, we shall see
Justice design the victor's chivalry.
Lord Marshal, command our officers at arms
Be ready to direct these home alarms.   205

Exeunt

1.2 *Enter* JOHN OF GAUNT *with the* DUCHESS OF GLOUCESTER.

GAUNT Alas, the part I had in Woodstock's blood
Doth more solicit me than your exclaims
To stir against the butchers of his life.
But since correction lieth in those hands
Which made the fault that we cannot correct,   5
Put we our quarrel to the will of heaven,
Who when they see the hours ripe on earth
Will rain hot vengeance on offenders' heads.
DUCHESS Finds brotherhood in thee no sharper spur?
Hath love in thy old blood no living fire?   10
Edward's seven sons, whereof thyself art one,
Were as seven vials of his sacred blood,
Or seven fair branches springing from one root.
Some of those seven are dried by nature's course,

---

202 we shall] Q1; you shall Q2–5, F   205 SD] F; *Exit.* Qq   Act 1, Scene 2   0 SD] Qq; *Enter Gaunt, and Dutchesse of Gloucester* F   1 Woodstock's] Qq; *Glousters* F

202 **atone** set at one, reconcile.
203 **design** mark out, signify.
203 **chivalry** victory in chivalric combat.
204 **Lord** Ure (p. xviii) suggests that the extra-metrical 'Lord' may be a memorial error in Q anticipating 1.3.46 where Bullingbrook uses the term, which is in Holinshed. Richard elsewhere (1.3.7, 26 and 99) addresses him as plain 'Marshal'. Q's spelling 'Martiall' suggests it may have been pronounced as a trisyllable, which would certainly make the use of 'Lord' redundant metrically.
205 **home alarms** calls to arms at home, as distinct from the Irish alarms.

Act 1, Scene 2
1.2 This scene is not in any of the sources. It serves to emphasise both the murder of Gloucester which underlies the previous scene and the contrasting choices of Christian patience or revenge. See p. 5 above.
1 **part** share.
1 **Woodstock's** This is the only occurrence of

the name in Q. F normalises to the form used at 16 and 36 and 4.1.3. Possibly the abandonment of the name after this one use in Q represents an authorial change.
1 **blood** kinship (not murder).
3 **stir** take action. See *Ham.* 4.4.54.
4 **those hands** Richard's.
6 In contrast to the duellists of 1.1.
7 **hours** A disyllable, usually spelt 'howers'.
8 **rain hot vengeance** Biblical, principally with reference to Sodom and Gomorrah. See Gen. 19.24–5, Luke 17.28–9, Ps. 11.7, 140.10.
13 A genealogical tree of the *planta genista*, the House of Plantagenet. The extended simile, 12–21, equates the seven sons of Edward III with the Tree of Jesse. Jesse, the father of David, had seven sons and was the first name at the root of the genealogical tree ending in Christ which was a common medieval emblem in stained glass windows. A good example is in Dorchester Abbey near Oxford. See also illustration 6, p. 29 above.

Some of those branches by the Destinies cut,   15
But Thomas, my dear lord, my life, my Gloucester,
One vial full of Edward's sacred blood,
One flourishing branch of his most royal root,
Is cracked, and all the precious liquor spilt,
Is hacked down, and his summer leaves all faded,   20
By envy's hand, and murder's bloody axe.
Ah, Gaunt, his blood was thine; that bed, that womb,
That mettle, that self mould, that fashioned thee
Made him a man; and though thou liv'st and breath'st
Yet art thou slain in him. Thou dost consent   25
In some large measure to thy father's death
In that thou seest thy wretched brother die,
Who was the model of thy father's life.
Call it not patience, Gaunt. It is despair.
In suffering thus thy brother to be slaughtered   30
Thou showest the naked pathway to thy life,
Teaching stern murder how to butcher thee.
That which in mean men we entitle patience
Is pale cold cowardice in noble breasts.
What shall I say? To safeguard thine own life   35
The best way is to venge my Gloucester's death.

GAUNT   God's is the quarrel, for God's substitute,
His deputy anointed in His sight,
Hath caused his death, the which if wrongfully
Let heaven revenge, for I may never lift   40
An angry arm against His minister.

DUCHESS   Where then, alas, may I complain myself?

GAUNT   To God, the widow's champion and defence.

---

37 God's...God's] Qq; Heauens...heauens F   42 then...complain] Q1 *(Hunt. and Petworth)*, Q2–5; then may I
complaine Q1 *(Capell and Huth)*; then (alas may I) complaint F   43 God...and] Qq; heauen...to F

---

15 **Destinies** The Fates with their shears. The
word may be a disyllable.

23 **self** same.

25 **consent** accept, acquiesce.

28 **model** perfect copy.

29 **patience** A word with specifically Biblical
connotations. See 6–8 above and Appendix 3, p.
215.

31 **naked** clear, defenceless.

33–4 These lines give point to the emphasis on
cowardice by the quarrelling nobles in 1.1.

36 **venge** avenge. An archaic form.

37–41 Gaunt anticipates York at 2.3.95 and
Carlisle at 4.1.121–33 in affirming what Richard
relies on in 3.2 and 3.3.

38 **in His sight** At Westminster Abbey, God's
house.

39 **if wrongfully** if the cause of death is
wrongful.

42 **complain myself** lodge a legal complaint on
my own behalf.

43 A Biblical saying. See Eccles. 35.14, Ps. 68.5,
146.9.

DUCHESS Why then I will. Farewell, old Gaunt.

        Thou goest to Coventry, there to behold   45

        Our cousin Herford and fell Mowbray fight.

        Oh, set my husband's wrongs on Herford's spear,

        That it may enter butcher Mowbray's breast!

        Or if misfortune miss the first career

        Be Mowbray's sins so heavy in his bosom   50

        That they may break his foaming courser's back,

        And throw the rider headlong in the lists,

        A caitiff recreant to my cousin Herford.

        Farewell, old Gaunt. Thy sometime brother's wife

        With her companion grief must end her life.   55

GAUNT Sister, farewell. I must to Coventry.

        As much good stay with thee as go with me.

DUCHESS Yet one word more. Grief boundeth where it falls,

        Not with the empty hollowness, but weight.

        I take my leave before I have begun,   60

        For sorrow ends not when it seemeth done.

        Commend me to thy brother Edmund York.

        Lo, this is all. Nay, yet depart not so;

        Though this be all, do not so quickly go.

        I shall remember more. Bid him, ah, what?   65

        With all good speed at Plashy visit me.

        Alack, and what shall good old York there see

        But empty lodgings and unfurnished walls,

        Unpeopled offices, untrodden stones,

        And what hear there for welcome but my groans?   70

        Therefore commend me, let him not come there,

        To seek out sorrow that dwells everywhere.

---

47 set] Qq; sit F   54 sometime] *Pope;* sometimes Qq, F   58 it] Q2–5, F; is Q1   59 empty hollowness] Q1 *(Hunt. and Petworth),* Q2–5, F; emptines, hollownes Q1 *(Capell and Huth)*   62 thy] Q1; my Q2–5, F   65 ah] Qq; Oh, F   70 hear] Q1 *(Hunt. and Petworth),* Q2–5, F; cheere Q1 *(Capell and Huth)*   72 sorrow that] Q1–3; sorrow, that Q4–5, F

    46 fell deadly.

    47 set place (like a banner or favour). F 'sit' is a normalisation. See 5.5.27 n.

    49 career charge or encounter in a tilt. Technically a career is a gallop ending in a sudden stop.

    53 caitiff recreant captive coward.

    54 sometime Neither Q nor F consistently differentiates between 'sometime' meaning 'once' or 'formerly' and 'sometimes' meaning 'occasionally'.

    58 boundeth rebounds (like a ball).

    60–74 For the versification of this passage see p. 32 above.

    66 Plashy The Gloucester home in Essex. It is mentioned in *Woodstock* 1306–11 and Holinshed.

    68 unfurnished walls walls bare of tapestry or arms. The three adjectives begin the sequence of words prefixed by un- in the play. See p. 17 above.

    69 Unpeopled offices Duties without servants to perform them.

Desolate, desolate will I hence and die.
The last leave of thee takes my weeping eye.

Exeunt

1.3 *Enter Lord* MARSHAL *and the Duke* AUMERLE.

MARSHAL My Lord Aumerle, is Harry Herford armed?
AUMERLE Yea, at all points, and longs to enter in.
MARSHAL The Duke of Norfolk, sprightfully and bold,
　　　Stays but the summons of the appellant's trumpet.
AUMERLE Why then, the champions are prepared and stay   5
　　　For nothing but his majesty's approach.

The trumpets sound and the King [RICHARD] *enters with his nobles; when
they are set, enter* [MOWBRAY] *the Duke of Norfolk in arms defendant.*

RICHARD Marshal, demand of yonder champion
　　　The cause of his arrival here in arms.
　　　Ask him his name, and orderly proceed
　　　To swear him in the justice of his cause.   10
MARSHAL In God's name and the king's say who thou art,
　　　And why thou com'st thus knightly clad in arms,
　　　Against what man thou comest and what thy quarrel.
　　　Speak truly on thy knighthood and thy oath,

Act 1, Scene 3 0 SD] Qq; *Enter Marshall, and Aumerle.* F   6 SD] Qq; *Enter King, Gaunt, Bushy, Bagot, Greene,
& others: Then Mowbray in Armor, and Harrold* F   13 what thy] Q1; *what's thy* Q2–5, F   14 thy oath] Qq; *thine*
oath F

Act 1, Scene 3
　1.3 In Holinshed this scene occupies four days.
On two of them the contestants visited the king, on
the third came the abortive combat and the
sentences of exile, and on the fourth, some weeks
later, came the remission of Bullingbrook's sentence.
It might be noted here that in *2H4* 4.1.123–7
Mowbray's son attributes Richard's fall to his
intervention in the duel.
　0 SD AUMERLE Q1–4 spell it Aumarle, the
likely pronunciation.
　2 enter in enter the lists for the combat.
　3 sprightfully full of high spirits.
　4 Mowbray is impatient. He should wait for the
summons of the herald, not his opponent.
　6 SD.2 *set* seated. Richard would again have
occupied the chair of state. Conceivably here the
nobles might have been seated too, as audience for
the show. According to Holinshed, each of the
combatants had a 'chair' or canopied pavilion. Had

they been used on stage they would have obscured
much of the audience's view.
　6 SD.2 *defendant* Normally the appellant would
enter first, as he does in Holinshed and as the
Marshal describes them at 1 and 3–4.
　7 demand of The term used in formal enquiry.
See 26 n. below.
　9 Ask…name Part of the formalities of the
challenge.
　10 swear him make him swear.
　11–24 F alters none of the references to God in
this passage, probably by accident rather than
because of the ceremonious nature of the language.
Bullingbrook's 'God of heaven' at 40 in the
equivalent speech is retained but his other reference
to God becomes 'heaven'.
　13 quarrel cause of complaint.
　14 knighthood chivalry.
　14 thy oath swearing the justice of your cause.

And so defend thee heaven and thy valour.   15
MOWBRAY My name is Thomas Mowbray, Duke of Norfolk,
    Who hither come engagèd by my oath
    (Which God defend a knight should violate)
    Both to defend my loyalty and truth
    To God, my king, and my succeeding issue,   20
    Against the Duke of Herford that appeals me,
    And by the grace of God, and this mine arm,
    To prove him, in defending of myself,
    A traitor to my God, my king, and me.
    And as I truly fight, defend me heaven.   25

The trumpets sound. Enter [BULLINGBROOK] Duke of Herford
appellant in armour.

RICHARD Marshal, demand of yonder knight in arms
    Both who he is and why he cometh hither
    Thus plated in habiliments of war,
    And formally according to our law
    Depose him in the justice of his cause.   30
MARSHAL What is thy name? And wherefore com'st thou hither
    Before King Richard in his royal lists?
    Against whom comest thou, and what's thy quarrel?
    Speak like a true knight, so defend thee heaven.
BULLINGBROOK Harry of Herford, Lancaster and Derby   35
    Am I, who ready here do stand in arms
    To prove by God's grace and my body's valour
    In lists, on Thomas Mowbray, Duke of Norfolk,
    That he's a traitor foul and dangerous

---

15 thee] Q2–5, F; the Q1   17 come] Qq; comes F   18 God] Qq; heauen F   20 my succeeding] Qq; his succeeding
F   25 SD] Qq; *Tucket. Enter Hereford, and Harold.* F   26 demand of] *Irving;* aske Qq, F   28 plated] Qq; placed F
29 formally] Q1–4; formerly Q5, F   32 lists?] F; lists, Qq   33 comest] Q5; comes Q1–4; com'st F   37 God's] Qq;
heauens F   39 he's] F; he is Qq

15 so accordingly.
18 defend forbid.
20 my succeeding issue my children who will
succeed me (with my honourable name). F's reading
makes Mowbray pledge loyalty to the king's heirs,
which is plausible, though the many references in
the play to inheritance never include any succession
from Richard.
21 appeals See 1.1.9 n.
25 SD *The trumpets sound* F calls for a 'tucket',
a flourish of trumpets.
26 demand of Irving adopts a conjecture by

Joseph Ritson who suggested that the irregular
metre in Q and F results from a normalisation by the
Q compositor (A), and that the formulaic 'demand
of' used at 7, which would restore the metre, was
the original text. It is the final line of sig. B2ʳ in Q1.
Possibly Compositor A associated the 'demand of'
in 7 with the 'Ask' of 9, and the memory confused
him at 26.
28 plated...war wearing plate armour.
30 Depose him Take his deposition on oath.
34 so...heaven so that heaven may defend you.

To God of heaven, King Richard and to me;   40
And as I truly fight, defend me heaven.
MARSHAL On pain of death, no person be so bold
    Or daring-hardy as to touch the lists,
    Except the Marshal and such officers
    Appointed to direct these fair designs.   45
BULLINGBROOK Lord Marshal, let me kiss my sovereign's hand
    And bow my knee before his majesty,
    For Mowbray and myself are like two men
    That vow a long and weary pilgrimage.
    Then let us take a ceremonious leave   50
    And loving farewell of our several friends.
MARSHAL The appellant in all duty greets your highness,
    And craves to kiss your hand and take his leave.
RICHARD We will descend and fold him in our arms.
    Cousin of Herford, as thy cause is right   55
    So be thy fortune in this royal fight.
    Farewell, my blood, which if today thou shed
    Lament we may, but not revenge the dead.
BULLINGBROOK Oh, let no noble eye profane a tear
    For me, if I be gored with Mowbray's spear.   60
    As confident as is the falcon's flight
    Against a bird do I with Mowbray fight.
    My loving lord, I take my leave of you.
    Of you, my noble cousin, Lord Aumerle,

---

43 daring-hardy] *Theobald;* daring, hardy, Qq; daring hardie F   44 Marshal] F; Martiall Qq   46 Marshal] F; Martiall
Qq   55 right] Qq; iust F   58 the] Q1–2; thee Q3–5, F

---

42 **On...death** Under penalty of death.
43 **touch** interfere in.
49 **pilgrimage** See p. 4 above.
51 **several** separate, and various.
54 **descend** The chair of state was raised on a dais several 'degrees' or steps above floor level. But the height may have been more symbolic than real, since Richard is condescending in rank rather than in physical height.
56 **royal fight** It is not royal because of Bullingbrook's kinship with the king but because of the royal presence. If there is a hint of Mowbray fighting on behalf of his royal master, the line following balances that thought with Richard's claim to a blood link with Mowbray's opponent. The vocative 'my blood' in 57 assumes that all subjects are the king's and that subjects' blood in the body politic is shared with the king.

58 **revenge** Since the duel is a trial of truth the outcome must be acknowledged as just, so there can be no question of revenging the death of the loser. Richard may have in mind Bullingbrook's demand for revenge over Gloucester, who was also 'my blood'.
58 **the dead** F's 'thee' makes Richard's reference to 'my blood' apply to Bullingbrook but not his opponent, which would make Richard's unctuous sentiment too specific. On the other hand Q is certainly incorrect at 1.3.15, 4.1.109, 5.1.41 and 5.2.11 in printing 'the' for F's 'thee'.
59 **profane a tear** weep a tear which would be impure because shed for a traitor and liar.
61 **falcon's flight** See 1.1.74 n. A possibly proverbial phrase (Dent F34.1).
63 **My loving lord** Richard. Some editors assume he addresses the Marshal.

Not sick, although I have to do with death,   65
But lusty, young and cheerly drawing breath.
Lo, as at English feasts so I regreet
The daintiest last, to make the end most sweet.
Oh thou, the earthly author of my blood,
Whose youthful spirit in me regenerate   70
Doth with a twofold vigour lift me up
To reach at victory above my head,
Add proof unto mine armour with thy prayers,
And with thy blessings steel my lance's point
That it may enter Mowbray's waxen coat,   75
And furbish new the name of John a Gaunt
Even in the lusty haviour of his son.
GAUNT God in thy good cause make thee prosperous.
Be swift like lightning in the execution
And let thy blows, doubly redoubled,   80
Fall like amazing thunder on the casque
Of thy adverse pernicious enemy.
Rouse up thy youthful blood, be valiant and live.
BULLINGBROOK Mine innocency and Saint George to thrive.
MOWBRAY However God or Fortune cast my lot   85
There lives or dies, true to King Richard's throne,
A loyal, just and upright gentleman.
Never did captive with a freer heart
Cast off his chains of bondage and embrace

---

69 earthly] Qq; earthy F   71 vigour] Qq; rigor F   72 at] Q1–2, F; a Q3–5   76 furbish] Qq; furnish F
78 God] Qq; Heauen F   82 adverse] Qq; amaz'd F   84 innocency] *Capell*; innocence Qq, F   85 God] Qq;
heauen F

67–8 See Bacon, *Life and Letters*, ed. Spedding,
III, 215: 'Let not this Parliament end, like a Dutch
feast, in salt meats, but like an English feast, in sweet
meats.'
67 **regreet** salute, welcome.
68 **daintiest** sweetest-tasting. 'Dainties' were
appetisers or sweetmeats.
69 **thou** Gaunt.
70 **spirit** A monosyllable, pronounced 'sprite'.
70 **regenerate** reborn, renewed.
71 **twofold** i.e. father's and son's.
71 **lift me up** As a parent does a child.
73 **proof** impenetrability, as with 'proved'
armour. There is also a hint of the armour of truth.
74 **steel** Literally 'make into steel'; metaphorically 'strengthen'.
75 **waxen** as if made of wax; a soft and false
coating unlike truth.

76 **furbish** polish.
77 **lusty haviour** vigorous actions.
79 **lightning** In this context, the vengeance of
God.
81 **amazing** bemusing. See SD for Aumerle at
5.3.23 (Q1).
81 **casque** helmet.
82 **adverse** (1) opposing (as 'adversary'), (2)
unfortunate.
84 **innocency** Capell's emendation restores the
metre.
84 **Saint George** Meaning England, as Henry V
before Harfleur (*H5* 3.2.34). One of Holinshed's
French sources, the *Traïson*, states that Bullingbrook's coat-of-arms was 'like unto the arms of
St George'.

His golden uncontrolled enfranchisement   90
More than my dancing soul doth celebrate
This feast of battle with mine adversary.
Most mighty liege and my companion peers,
Take from my mouth the wish of happy years.
As gentle and as jocund as to jest   95
Go I to fight. Truth hath a quiet breast.
RICHARD Farewell, my lord. Securely I espy
    Virtue with valour couchèd in thine eye.
    Order the trial, Marshal, and begin.
MARSHAL Harry of Herford, Lancaster and Derby,   100
    Receive thy lance, and God defend the right.
BULLINGBROOK Strong as a tower in hope, I cry amen.
MARSHAL Go bear this lance to Thomas Duke of Norfolk.
1 HERALD Harry of Herford, Lancaster and Derby
    Stands here, for God, his sovereign and himself,   105
    On pain to be found false and recreant,
    To prove the Duke of Norfolk, Thomas Mowbray,
    A traitor to his God, his king, and him,
    And dares him to set forward to the fight.
2 HERALD Here standeth Thomas Mowbray, Duke of Norfolk,   110
    On pain to be found false and recreant,
    Both to defend himself, and to approve
    Henry of Herford, Lancaster and Derby
    To God, his sovereign, and to him disloyal,
    Courageously and with a free desire,   115
    Attending but the signal to begin.
MARSHAL Sound trumpets, and set forward combatants.
        A charge sounded.

---

94 mouth] Q1–4, F; youth Q5   **99 trial, Marshal**] *Rowe;* triall Marshall Q5, F; triall Martiall Q1–4   **101 God**] Qq; heauen F   **101 the**] Q1; thy Q2–5, F   **108 his God**] Q1 *(Hunt. and Petworth),* Q2–5, F; God Q1 *(Capell and Huth)*   **109 forward**] Q1; forwards Q2–5, F   **117 forward**] Q1, F; forth Q2–5   **117 SD**] F *(at 116);* not in Qq

90 enfranchisement release from imprisonment. See *John* 4.2.52.

95 to jest to play a game, to masquerade.

96 quiet calm.

97 Securely The adverb for the verb in the line following.

98 couchèd levelled in readiness (as a lance).

99 Order Organise, set in order.

99 trial, Marshal Q consistently spells 'Marshal' as 'Martiall', and the Q1 compositor (A) is here led by the spelling into a misreading of the whole phrase, which implies that the Q1 spelling is authorial. See Cercignani, p. 347.

102 Strong...hope From Ps. 61.3.

104 Lancaster That is, heir to the Duke of Lancaster, Gaunt.

108 An echo of Mowbray at 24; hence the third-person pronouns. 'Him' means 'himself'.

112 approve test.

Stay, the king hath thrown his warder down.
RICHARD Let them lay by their helmets and their spears,
And both return back to their chairs again.   120
Withdraw with us, and let the trumpets sound
While we return these dukes what we decree.
                    A long flourish.
Draw near,
And list what with our Council we have done.
For that our kingdom's earth should not be soiled   125
With that dear blood which it hath fosterèd,
And for our eyes do hate the dire aspect
Of civil wounds ploughed up with neighbour's sword,
And for we think the eagle-wingèd pride
Of sky-aspiring and ambitious thoughts   130
With rival-hating envy set on you
To wake our peace, which in our country's cradle
Draws the sweet infant breath of gentle sleep,
Which so roused up with boisterous untuned drums,
With harsh resounding trumpet's dreadful bray   135
And grating shock of wrathful iron arms,
Might from our quiet confines fright fair peace,

---

122 SD] F; *not in* Qq   123–4] *Theobald;* Draw neere and list / What...Qq, F   124 Council] F4; counsell Qq; Councell F   128 civil] Q1 *(Hunt. and Petworth),* Q2–5, F; cruell Q1 *(Capell and Huth)*   128 sword] Qq; swords F   129–33] *not in* F   133 Draws] Q1 *(Hunt. and Petworth),* Q2–5; Draw Q1 *(Capell and Huth)*   136 wrathful iron] Q1 *(Hunt. and Petworth),* Q2–5, F; harsh resounding Q1 *(Capell and Huth)*

118 warder A baton held either by the king, the Constable or the Marshal ready to throw between the combatants if it was felt necessary to stop them. See *2H4* 4.1.123–7.

120 chairs According to Holinshed the 'chairs' were canopied like pavilions, Bullingbrook's in green, Mowbray's with red and white damasked curtains.

121 Withdraw with us An order to the Council of Lords.

122 While we return Until we report.

123 Draw near An order to the two contestants. The brevity of the line possibly indicates the distance of stage area each would have to cover – from the downstage corners to upstage centre – to reach the king's throne. In Holinshed the contestants waited for two hours until the Council's decision was announced.

124 Council Q1's spelling does not differentiate between the body of nobles and its advice. See 2.2.60 n.

125 For that In order that.

129–33 Not in F. Dover Wilson and other editors have suggested that some imperfect revision is indicated, and that some part of 129–38 was meant to be deleted. The chief problem is the repetition of 'peace' at 132 and 137. The first 'peace' has two dependent clauses beginning 'which' attached to it, the second having the second 'peace' in it, so that the subject 'peace' of 132 frights the fair peace of 137. This is probably a misreading of the full sentence, which runs from 129 to 139. The subject is the 'eagle-wingèd pride' of 129 which Richard says has set the contestants on to 'wake our peace', and which (the 'Which' of 134) is roused with drums and trumpets to 'fright fair peace' and therefore has evoked the sentence of banishment. Since 129–39 are a single syntactical unit no deletion is called for.

131 set on you set you on.

132 wake keep awake.

136 shock The impact of horses in combat.

136 wrathful iron The uncorrected form of Q1's text repeats a phrase from the preceding line.

And make us wade even in our kindred's blood,
Therefore we banish you our territories.
You, cousin Herford, upon pain of life,   140
Till twice five summers have enriched our fields
Shall not regreet our fair dominions,
But tread the stranger paths of banishment.

BULLINGBROOK Your will be done. This must my comfort be:
That sun that warms you here shall shine on me,   145
And those his golden beams to you here lent
Shall point on me and gild my banishment.

RICHARD Norfolk, for thee remains a heavier doom,
Which I with some unwillingness pronounce.
The sly slow hours shall not determinate   150
The dateless limit of thy dear exile.
The hopeless word of never to return
Breathe I against thee, upon pain of life.

MOWBRAY A heavy sentence, my most sovereign liege,
And all unlooked for from your highness' mouth.   155
A dearer merit, not so deep a maim
As to be cast forth in the common air,
Have I deservèd at your highness' hands.
The language I have learnt these forty years,
My native English, now I must forgo,   160
And now my tongue's use is to me no more
Than an unstringèd viol or a harp,
Or like a cunning instrument cased up,

---

140 life] Qq; death F

139 you Richard addresses both contestants.
140 pain of life pain of losing life. F's reading normalises the phrase, though F retains it at 153.
142 regreet greet again. Compare 67 and 186.
143 stranger foreign, alien.
146–7 A proverbial saying (Tilley s985).
149 with some unwillingness Richard here seems to make his only concession to the debt which Mowbray has been hinting he owes. See 154–5 n.
150 sly slow not visibly moving.
150 determinate put a limit to. The phrase appears in *Woodstock* 2750.
151 dateless endless. See *Sonnets* 30.6: 'For precious friends hid in death's dateless night'.
151 dear deeply felt.
154 sentence Mowbray both evokes the legal sense and quibbles on Richard's 'word' at 152.
154–5 Mowbray's response is unrhymed, in contrast to Bullingbrook's two conventional couplets.

The spontaneous nature of his reaction, his open declaration that it was unexpected, brings the undercurrent of threat, which he hinted at 1.1.132–4 and which Richard admits at 149, close to the surface.
156 merit reward.
156 maim wound.
159 forty years Mowbray was about 32 in 1398. Other figures are similarly rounded upwards at 2.4.1 and in Richard's change at 3.2.76 from Salisbury's 12,000 to 20,000.
160–2 These lines introduce the imagery of curbed or broken language which recurs in the play. They also hint at Mowbray's silence over the murder of Gloucester.
162 viol A stringed instrument played with a bow.
163 cunning ingenious.

Or being open, put into his hands
That knows no touch to tune the harmony.   165
Within my mouth you have engaoled my tongue,
Doubly portcullised with my teeth and lips,
And dull unfeeling barren ignorance
Is made my gaoler to attend on me.
I am too old to fawn upon a nurse,   170
Too far in years to be a pupil now.
What is thy sentence then but speechless death,
Which robs my tongue from breathing native breath?

RICHARD It boots thee not to be compassionate.
After our sentence plaining comes too late.   175

MOWBRAY Then thus I turn me from my country's light
To dwell in solemn shades of endless night.

RICHARD Return again, and take an oath with thee.
Lay on our royal sword your banished hands.
Swear by the duty that you owe to God   180
(Our part therein we banish with yourselves)
To keep the oath that we administer.
You never shall, so help you truth and God,
Embrace each other's love in banishment,
Nor never look upon each other's face,   185
Nor never write, regreet nor reconcile
This louring tempest of your home-bred hate,
Nor never by advisèd purpose meet
To plot, contrive or complot any ill
'Gainst us, our state, our subjects or our land.   190

---

167 portcullised] Q1 *(Hunt. and Petworth)*, Q2–3; portculist Q1 *(Capell and Huth)*; percullist Q4–5, F   172 then] F;
not in Qq   180 you owe] F; y'owe Qq   180 God] Qq; heauen F   183 God] Qq; Heauen F   185 never] Qq; euer
F   186 never] Qq; euer F   186 nor] Qq; or F   188 never] Qq; euer F

164 his hands the hands of someone.

165 touch fingering, skill.

167 portcullised A portcullis was an iron grille dropped across a castle gateway to defend it.

170 a nurse The first person to teach a child to talk.

172 sentence Picking up the word-play of 154. It is Richard's spoken 'sentence' which makes Mowbray silent, his 'speechless death' being a form of execution through the enforcement of silence in life.

174 boots is pointless. Richard has already used the term to Mowbray at 1.1.164.

174 be compassionate demand sympathy.

175 plaining complaining.

178 with thee Richard recalls Mowbray ('thee') as he turns to go, bringing the two contestants together for the last time to swear the oath.

179 on...sword On the hilt, which together with the guard makes the shape of a cross.

181 The question whether exiles had any continuing obligation of loyalty to the ruler who exiled them was a matter for debate under Roman or international law.

187 louring frowning.

188 advisèd considered.

189 complot plot jointly, conspire.

190 our state Richard has come forward from his chair of state to administer the oath.

BULLINGBROOK I swear.

MOWBRAY   And I, to keep all this.

BULLINGBROOK Norfolk, so far as to mine enemy:
  By this time, had the king permitted us,
  One of our souls had wandered in the air,
  Banished this frail sepulchre of our flesh,   195
  As now our flesh is banished from this land.
  Confess thy treasons ere thou fly the realm.
  Since thou hast far to go, bear not along
  The clogging burthen of a guilty soul.

MOWBRAY No, Bullingbrook. If ever I were traitor,   200
  My name be blotted from the book of life
  And I from heaven banished as from hence.
  But what thou art, God, thou and I do know,
  And all too soon, I fear, the king shall rue.
  Farewell, my liege. Now no way can I stray.   205
  Save back to England all the world's my way.   *Exit*

RICHARD Uncle, even in the glasses of thine eyes
  I see thy grievèd heart. Thy sad aspect
  Hath from the number of his banished years
  Plucked four away. [*To Bullingbrook*] Six frozen winters
          spent,   210
  Return with welcome home from banishment.

BULLINGBROOK How long a time lies in one little word.
  Four lagging winters and four wanton springs
  End in a word, such is the breath of kings.

---

192 far] F2; fare Qq, F   192 enemy:] Q1–2, Q4–5; enemie, Q3, F   197 the] Qq; this F   203 God] Qq; heauen F
210 SD] *Johnson; not in* Qq, F

192 **so far** let me say this much. Q and F both reflect the Q1 compositor (S) normalising his copy.

195 **sepulchre** Presumably spoken with the accent on the second syllable, although at 2.1.55 the stress is required on the first and third. See Cercignani, p. 41.

195 **sepulchre...flesh** The flesh is the temple or mausoleum of the soul.

196 **this land** Bullingbrook is emphasising an aspect of the elemental imagery, whereby souls inhabit the air but flesh is on earth.

199 **clogging burthen** A clog was a wooden block tied to a prisoner's leg to impede his movements. See 5.6.20, 'clog of conscience'.

201 **blotted...life** See Rev. 3.5, in the English

of the Bishops' Bible: 'He that overcometh shall be thus clothed in white array, and I will not blot out his name out of the book of life.' See 'blot', 2.1.64 n., and 1.1.175.

204 **shall rue** regret what you are.

205 **no way...stray** (1) cannot take a wrong road, (2) cannot sin.

207 **glasses** windows. The conceit is proverbial (Tilley E231).

208–10 Holinshed gives no reason for the remission of Bullingbrook's sentence. Froissart states that it was made on the Council's recommendation because of Bullingbrook's popularity with the people.

214 **breath** Both words and air.

GAUNT I thank my liege that in regard of me   215
　　　　He shortens four years of my son's exile;
　　　　But little vantage shall I reap thereby,
　　　　For ere the six years that he hath to spend
　　　　Can change their moons and bring their times about
　　　　My oil-dried lamp and time-bewasted light   220
　　　　Shall be extinct with age and endless night,
　　　　My inch of taper will be burnt and done,
　　　　And blindfold Death not let me see my son.
RICHARD Why uncle, thou hast many years to live.
GAUNT But not a minute, king, that thou canst give.   225
　　　　Shorten my days thou canst with sullen sorrow,
　　　　And pluck nights from me, but not lend a morrow.
　　　　Thou canst help time to furrow me with age,
　　　　But stop no wrinkle in his pilgrimage.
　　　　Thy word is current with him for my death,   230
　　　　But dead thy kingdom cannot buy my breath.
RICHARD Thy son is banished upon good advice,
　　　　Whereto thy tongue a party verdict gave.
　　　　Why at our justice seemst thou then to lour?
GAUNT Things sweet to taste prove in digestion sour.   235
　　　　You urged me as a judge, but I had rather
　　　　You would have bid me argue like a father.
　　　　Oh, had it been a stranger, not my child,
　　　　To smoothe his fault I should have been more mild.
　　　　A partial slander sought I to avoid   240
　　　　And in the sentence my own life destroyed.
　　　　Alas, I looked when some of you should say

---

221 extinct] Q2–5, F; extint Q1   221 night] Q4–5, F; nightes Q1–3   226 sullen] Qq; sudden F   232 upon] Q1, F;
with Q2–5   236 urged] Q1, F; vrge Q2–5   238–41] *not in* F   240 partial slander sought] Q1 *(Hunt. and Huth)*; partiall
slander ought Q1 *(Capell and Petworth)*, Q2–5

---

219 bring…about introduce their regulated
and scheduled seasons.
220 oil-dried empty. The proverb is Tilley O29.
See *1H6* 2.5.8.
221 extinct (1) extinguished, (2) died out.
222 taper A cheap candle.
223 blindfold Death Both death as the agent
removing sight and the image of death as an eyeless
skull.
225 king An angrily abrupt form of address,
which emphasises both the royal power (of
sentencing) and its limits.

226 sullen This word occurs four times in the
play, once as a noun (2.1.139).
230 current As money, an image extended in
'buy' in the next line.
233 a party verdict a share in the Council's
verdict of banishment.
235 A proverbial phrase introducing the antithesis of sweet and sour, which recurs especially in
3.2. See Tilley M1265.
239 smoothe gloss over, appease.
240 partial slander false accusation of bias.
242 looked when waited for the time when.

I was too strict to make mine own away,
But you gave leave to my unwilling tongue
Against my will to do myself this wrong.   245
RICHARD Cousin, farewell, and uncle, bid him so.
        Six years we banish him and he shall go.   *Exit. Flourish*
AUMERLE Cousin, farewell. What presence must not know,
        From where you do remain let paper show.   [*Exit*]
MARSHAL My lord, no leave take I, for I will ride   250
        As far as land will let me by your side.
GAUNT Oh, to what purpose dost thou hoard thy words,
        That thou returnst no greeting to thy friends?
BULLINGBROOK I have too few to take my leave of you,
        When the tongue's office should be prodigal   255
        To breathe the abundant dolour of the heart.
GAUNT Thy grief is but thy absence for a time.
BULLINGBROOK Joy absent, grief is present for that time.
GAUNT What is six winters? They are quickly gone.
BULLINGBROOK To men in joy; but grief makes one hour ten.   260
GAUNT Call it a travail that thou tak'st for pleasure.
BULLINGBROOK My heart will sigh when I miscall it so,
        Which finds it an enforcèd pilgrimage.
GAUNT The sullen passage of thy weary steps
        Esteem as foil wherein thou art to set   265
        The precious jewel of thy home return.
BULLINGBROOK Nay, rather every tedious stride I make

---

247 SD] F; *Exit.* Q1 *(Hunt. and Huth); not in* Q1 *(Capell and Petworth),* Q2–5   249 SD] *This edn; not in* Qq, F
265 as foil] Q1; a foyle Q2; a soyle Q3–5, F   267–92] *not in* F

---

243 make…away do away with, sacrifice, exile.

248–9 Aumerle asks Bullingbrook to write privately the news of his location in exile which 'presence', the royal Court, has no official concern for. Richard's release of each exile from the dubious obligation of continuing loyalty (181) is countered by Aumerle's care to keep track of Bullingbrook, on the grounds of their blood kinship ('Cousin').

249 SD Aumerle has to leave the stage in order to re-enter in the next scene, like Gaunt at 1.1.195.

250–1 The lord who accompanies Bullingbrook the length of England on his departure matches the lords who join him as soon as he touches the land again. This sign of warmth from the Marshal suggests that Shakespeare was not thinking of him as the historical Marshal, Surrey, who was Richard's man as much as Aumerle.

252 hoard thy words Gaunt's metaphor begins

an extended word-play, based on the concealed image of 'spending' words. 'Prodigal' (255) and probably 'dolour' (256) extend the metaphor. See Mahood, p. 78.

255 office function.

257 grief grievance.

258 grief unhappiness.

261 travail labour and travel. The metaphor is developed in 'pilgrimage' (263), 'apprenticehood' (270), 'freedom' (272) and 'journeyman' (273). See Mahood, p. 78. An apprentice, once freed from his bond of service, became a journeyman, a craftsman on day-labour rates.

262 miscall it so describe it as a journey not as a labour.

265 as foil as a defeat (in wrestling); as a setting. Q2's text misreads or normalises Q1. Q3, followed by F, misreads Q2.

Will but remember me what a deal of world
I wander from the jewels that I love.
Must I not serve a long apprenticehood   270
To foreign passages, and in the end,
Having my freedom, boast of nothing else
But that I was a journeyman to grief?
GAUNT All places that the eye of heaven visits
Are to a wise man ports and happy havens.   275
Teach thy necessity to reason thus:
There is no virtue like necessity.
Think not the king did banish thee,
But thou the king. Woe doth the heavier sit
Where it perceives it is but faintly borne.   280
Go, say I sent thee forth to purchase honour,
And not the king exiled thee; or suppose
Devouring pestilence hangs in our air
And thou art flying to a fresher clime.
Look what thy soul holds dear, imagine it   285
To lie that way thou goest, not whence thou com'st.
Suppose the singing birds musicians,
The grass whereon thou treadst the presence strewed,
The flowers fair ladies, and thy steps no more
Than a delightful measure or a dance,   290
For gnarling sorrow hath less power to bite

268 a] Q1–3; *not in* Q4–5 276 thus:] *Pope;* thus, Qq; thus – *Wilson* 279 king. Woe] Q1–3; King, who Q4–5

268 **remember me** remind me. 'Remind' is a tempting editorial emendation since it restores the metre, but it is unlikely since the same usage occurs at 3.4.14, a passage set by Q1 Compositor A, whereas this passage was set by S. Memorial contamination is therefore ruled out, and it stands as authorial practice.

271 **passages** Stretches of time as well as space.

272 **freedom** i.e. from apprentice indentures and from exile.

274–5 A paraphrase of the stock *sententiae*, in this case from Ovid's *Fasti* ('Omne solum forti patria est'), noted in the quotation books under *patria*. See T. W. Baldwin, *Shakspere's 'Small Latine & Lesse Greeke'*, 1944, II, 427–8. Gaunt adds a play on 'son' and 'sun' to enliven the sentiment, as does Richard using the same 'eye of heaven' periphrasis at 3.2.37. For a detailed examination of the use of sources for this passage see Kenneth Muir, *The Sources of Shakespeare's Plays*, pp. 54–8.

277 A saying used by Chaucer, *Knight's Tale*,

3041–2, and *TGV* 4.1.62. Wells identifies borrowings from Lyly's *Euphues*, here and twice later, at 278–9 (the Diogenes story), and 293–8 (the frosty Caucasus image). The last two occur on the same page in *Euphues*.

278–9 Lyly tells the story of the philosopher Diogenes who, when told that the Synoponetes had banished him from Pontus, replied that he banished them from Diogenes.

280 **faintly** feebly, wearily.

281 **purchase** acquire by labour. Bullingbrook uses the same verb to describe his acquisition of the crown in *2H4* 4.5.199.

282 **suppose** pretend.

285 **Look what** Whatever.

288 **the presence strewed** The royal presence chamber, its floor covered in rushes, as was the Elizabethan stage.

290 **measure** slow dance step.

291 **gnarling** snarling (as a dog). See extract 1560 from *England's Parnassus* at p. 234 below.

The man that mocks at it and sets it light.
BULLINGBROOK Oh, who can hold a fire in his hand
  By thinking on the frosty Caucasus?
  Or cloy the hungry edge of appetite   295
  By bare imagination of a feast?
  Or wallow naked in December snow
  By thinking on fantastic summer's heat?
  Oh no, the apprehension of the good
  Gives but the greater feeling to the worse.   300
  Fell Sorrow's tooth doth never rankle more
  Than when he bites but lanceth not the sore.
GAUNT Come, come, my son, I'll bring thee on thy way.
  Had I thy youth and cause I would not stay.
BULLINGBROOK Then England's ground farewell, sweet soil adieu, 305
  My mother and my nurse that bears me yet.
  Where'er I wander, boast of this I can,
  Though banished, yet a true born Englishman.

                                                    Exeunt

1.4 *Enter the King* [RICHARD] *with* [GREEN *and* BAGOT] *at one door, and the Lord* AUMERLE *at another.*

RICHARD We did observe. Cousin Aumerle,
  How far brought you high Herford on his way?
AUMERLE I brought high Herford, if you call him so,
  But to the next highway, and there I left him.

301 never] Qq; euer F   302 he] Q1; it Q2–5, F   306 that] Qq; which F   308 SD] Qq; *not in* F   Act 1, Scene 4
0 SD] *Hanmer; Enter the King with Bushie &c at one dore, and the Lord Aumarle at another.* Qq; *Enter King, Aumerle,*
Greene, and Bagot. F

292 **sets it light** regards it lightly.
295 **cloy** surfeit, clog; with a visual image of a
knife used to cut food.
298 **fantastic** imaginary.
299 **apprehension** understanding and anticipation.
301–2 An image of snake bite, where the flesh is
pricked but there is no open wound to release the
swelling pus inside. See *R3* 1.3.290: 'His venom
tooth will rankle to the death.'
304 **stay** linger, delay.
306 **bears** carries as if pregnant or suckling a
child.

Act 1, Scene 4
0 SD F supplies the names of the characters

entering and Q the mode of entry. Q's entry for
Bushy is a problem related to the entry at 52 and
the textual crux at 23. Q may signal an unresolved
confusion in the writing of the scene.
  1 **We did observe** Richard enters in the middle
of a conversation about Bullingbrook's departure, as
we learn from his explanation to Aumerle at 23–4.
Richard is only interested in Bullingbrook, not at
all in Mowbray. The ostensible balance and
impartiality of the first scenes, already affected by
the difference in their sentences, is now openly set
aside.
  2 **high** elevated, as in the bucket image of
4.1.183–8, and proud. Pride and ambition as height
are implied in Richard's imagery at 1.3.129–39.
  4 **next** nearest.

RICHARD And say, what store of parting tears were shed?   5
AUMERLE Faith, none for me, except the northeast wind,
          Which then blew bitterly against our faces,
          Awaked the sleeping rheum and so by chance
          Did grace our hollow parting with a tear.
RICHARD What said our cousin when you parted with him?   10
AUMERLE 'Farewell',
          And, for my heart disdainèd that my tongue
          Should so profane the word, that taught me craft
          To counterfeit oppression of such grief
          That words seemed buried in my sorrow's grave.   15
          Marry, would the word 'farewell' have lengthened hours
          And added years to his short banishment,
          He should have had a volume of 'farewells'.
          But since it would not he had none of me.
RICHARD He is our cousin, cousin, but 'tis doubt,   20
          When time shall call him home from banishment,
          Whether our kinsman come to see his friends.
          Our self and Bushy, Bagot here and Green,
          Observed his courtship to the common people,

7 blew] Qq; grew F   7 faces] Q1–2; face Q3–5, F   8 sleeping] Q1–2; sleepie Q3–5, F   10 our] Q1, F; your Q2–5
11–12] *Pope; one line* Qq, F   15 words] Qq; word F   20 cousin, cousin] F; Coosens Coosin Qq   22 come] Q1, Q5,
F; comes Q2–4   23 Bushy, Bagot here and Green] Q6; Bushy, Qq; *Bushy:* heere *Bagot* and *Greene* F

6 **for me** on my part.
8 **rheum** A watery discharge.
9 **hollow** insincere. The adjective recurs with
varying connotations.
11 **'Farewell'** The baldest of parting words.
Its extra-metrical position emphasises the bald-
ness.
12 **for** because.
13 **that** my disdain.
14 **counterfeit** pretend, act a part.
15 **words** more words than 'farewell' (the
'word' of 13). F's reading makes 'farewell' itself the
buried word.
18 **volume** book.
20 **cousin, cousin** Richard has already called
Aumerle cousin at 1 and Bullingbrook at 10.
23 Q6 restores metrically what F supplies with
less evident success to the defective Q1 reading.
Editors conjecture that the Q compositor misread a
correction in his copy designed to allow for Bushy's
entry as messenger at 52. There was evidently a
change of plan between the initial entry in Q1, which
includes Bushy, and 52 when he enters with news.
If the change was not made until the writing came
close to 52 a correction of 23 would be necessary,
and could have been misread as a deletion of Bagot

and Green. F's reading looks like a different
misreading of the same correction.
24 It has been suggested that here Shakespeare
uses Froissart's explanation for the reduction of
Bullingbrook's sentence, that he was dangerously
popular with the people. If so, Shakespeare is
careful to avoid making any direct link.
24–36 More can be made of this speech as a
revelation of Richard than of Bullingbrook. Some
of Richard's words ('courtship', 'craft') suggest
that he sees Bullingbrook's behaviour as disingenu-
ous acting of a role which Richard himself would
never play. There is a direct sneer at the 'reverence'
(bowing) thrown away on 'slaves', and the
'tribute', the payment made by a subject to his lord,
of his kneeling. He describes this abasement as a
positive act of Bullingbrook's, 'wooing' the people
and diving into their hearts like a cormorant or
osprey. Gestures of false courtesy such as bowing
or kneeling to one's inferiors are not Richard's style.
His conclusion, however, that Bullingbrook in
behaving this way is acting like the heir apparent,
hardly matches this assumption that he is misusing
his height. Richard is reading more into Bullingbrook's behaviour than his observation would seem
to show.

How he did seem to dive into their hearts   25
With humble and familiar courtesy,
What reverence he did throw away on slaves,
Wooing poor craftsmen with the craft of smiles
And patient underbearing of his fortune,
As 'twere to banish their affects with him.   30
Off goes his bonnet to an oysterwench.
A brace of draymen bid God speed him well
And had the tribute of his supple knee,
With 'Thanks, my countrymen, my loving friends',
As were our England in reversion his,   35
And he our subjects' next degree in hope.
GREEN Well, he is gone, and with him go these thoughts.
Now, for the rebels which stand out in Ireland,
Expedient manage must be made, my liege,
Ere further leisure yield them further means   40
For their advantage and your highness' loss.
RICHARD We will ourself in person to this war,
And, for our coffers, with too great a court
And liberal largesse, are grown somewhat light,
We are enforced to farm our royal realm,   45
The revenue whereof shall furnish us
For our affairs in hand. If that come short
Our substitutes at home shall have blank charters

27 What] Q1 *(Hunt. and Huth)*, F; With Q1 *(Capell and Petworth)*, Q2–5   28 smiles] Qq; soules F   47 hand. If] F;
hand if Qq

29 **underbearing** carrying, enduring.

30 **affects** affection.

31 **bonnet** A contemptuous term. Bonnets were brimless and made of wool. Nobleman's hats were more elaborate in Elizabethan times.

33 **supple** easily bent.

35 **in reversion** as heir. The legal term for expectation of an inheritance.

36 **our...hope** the nearest to us and the next after us in our subjects' expectations. Roger Mortimer, son of the third son of Edward III, had a claim to the crown prior to Bullingbrook, son of Edward's fourth son. After Roger Mortimer's death in Ireland (see 1.1.116 n.) Richard named as his heir Roger Mortimer's son Edmund, then aged only three, who became the pretender against Bullingbrook and appears with the rebels in *1H4*. Holinshed explains this in his account of the Percy rebellion which features in *1H4*. See *1H4* 1.3, especially 145–57.

38 **stand out** hold out, make a stand.

39 **Expedient manage** Proper and speedy management, as of horses.

43 **too...court** At 4.1.283 Richard boasts of having 10,000 retainers.

44 **liberal largesse** Under a conspicuously parsimonious queen, Elizabethans were acutely sensitive to the moral and even institutional requirement that monarchs should make generous grants to their subjects.

45 **farm** allocate sections of the country to tax-farmers, who pay for the right to extort taxes on their own behalf. *Woodstock* goes into detail on this device.

48 **substitutes** See 1.2.37.

48 **blank charters** This term comes from Holinshed, where it is emphasised by a marginal note. They were actually papers issued by the counties, granting the right to unspecified levies. See Anthony Tuck, *Richard II and the English Nobility*, 1973, p. 197.

Whereto when they shall know what men are rich
They shall subscribe them for large sums of gold   50
And send them after to supply our wants,
For we will make for Ireland presently.

Enter BUSHY.

Bushy, what news?
BUSHY Old John of Gaunt is grievous sick, my lord,
Suddenly taken, and hath sent post haste   55
To entreat your majesty to visit him.
RICHARD Where lies he?
BUSHY   At Ely House.
RICHARD Now put it, God, in the physician's mind
To help him to his grave immediately.
The lining of his coffers shall make coats   60
To deck our soldiers for these Irish wars.
Come, gentlemen, let's all go visit him.
Pray God we may make haste and come too late.
[ALL] Amen.

Exeunt

---

52 SD–53] F; *Enter Bushie with news* Qq   53 Bushy, what news?] F; *not in* Qq   54 grievous] Qq; verie F   58 God]
Qq; heauen F   58 in the] Q1; into the Q2–5; in his F   63 God] Qq; heauen F   64 ALL Amen] *Staunton;*
Amen Qq; *not in* F

---

50 **subscribe them** fill in the blanks with names
and money.

52 **presently** immediately.

52 SD–53 Q1's stage direction is oddly verbose,
at a point where the manuscript might well have
been corrected in the wake of the entry stage
direction and 23. Wilson conjectured that the Q1
compositor misread 'wt' as *with* and assumed that
it was a continuation of the stage direction. It is also
possible that the decision to use Bushy as a
messenger was made late and so required the
insertion of a phrase identifying him, 53. More care
is taken in *R2* than in most of Shakespeare's plays

to identify characters and localities. The use of
Bushy as messenger also has the advantage of
showing that Richard is kept in touch only with his
own followers and flatterers.

57 **Ely House** The house in London where
Holinshed says Gaunt died.

60 **lining** contents. Richard puns on the
secondary meaning, a cloth lining, with 'coats' and
'deck'.

64 Staunton's ascription of the response to
Richard's prayer corrects Q1's omission. The
response was given by the clerk and congregation,
not the priest.

2.1 *Enter* JOHN OF GAUNT, *sick, with the* DUKE OF YORK, *etc.*

GAUNT Will the king come that I may breathe my last
    In wholesome counsel to his unstaid youth?
YORK Vex not yourself, nor strive not with your breath,
    For all in vain comes counsel to his ear.
GAUNT Oh, but they say the tongues of dying men   5
    Enforce attention like deep harmony.
    Where words are scarce they are seldom spent in vain,
    For they breathe truth that breathe their words in pain.
    He that no more must say is listened more
    Than they whom youth and ease have taught to glose.   10
    More are men's ends marked than their lives before.
    The setting sun, and music at the close,
    As the last taste of sweets, is sweetest last,
    Writ in remembrance more than things long past.
    Though Richard my life's counsel would not hear   15
    My death's sad tale may yet undeaf his ear.
YORK No, it is stopped with other flattering sounds,
    As praises, of whose taste the wise are fond,
    Lascivious metres, to whose venom sound
    The open ear of youth doth always listen,   20
    Report of fashions in proud Italy,
    Whose manners still our tardy-apish nation

Act 2, Scene 1   12 at] Qq; is F   18] Q1 (found); As praises of whose state the wise are found Q2; As praises of his
state: then there are found Q3–5; As praises of his state: then there are sound F

Act 2, Scene 1

2.1 The death scene of Gaunt is not in
Holinshed, though there are precedents in *Woodstock*
and Froissart if any were needed. The seizure of
Gaunt's property and York's reaction to it are in
Holinshed.

o SD *sick* Gaunt would either have remained
standing or, more likely, have rested in a sick
'chair'. He is not in a bed since he says at 137
'Convey me to my bed.' Tamburlaine sat in 'my
fatal chair' for his funeral (*2 Tamb.* 5.3.211). In 1.1
and 1.3 Richard sits while all the Court stand. In
4.1, 5.3 and 5.6 Bullingbrook sits while everyone
else stands. Here Gaunt sitting while Richard stands
is a reversal of decorum which emphasises Gaunt's
status as a sick elder of the state.

1 breathe A sick man's difficulty in breathing is
well represented by Gaunt's ponderous rhymes at
7–16. It augments the imagery of words, tongues
and breath.

2 unstaid uncontrolled.

4 counsel advice. Both Gaunt and York were
members of Richard's Council.

7–8 Gaunt's first couplet paraphrases proverbial
wisdom, as most of the subsequent couplets do.

10 glose talk superficially.

12 close The conclusion of a piece of music.
Each of the instances here has a link with a thematic
image.

14 Writ in remembrance Words written about
things in living memory.

16 death's sad tale serious last words.

18 taste Homonymic with 'test'. See *Tro.*
3.3.13.

18 the...fond The line was progressively
corrupted in Q2, Q3 and F.

19 metres verses.

19 venom poisonous.

22 tardy-apish belatedly copying.

Limps after in base imitation.
Where doth the world thrust forth a vanity –
So it be new there's no respect how vile –   25
That is not quickly buzzed into his ears?
Then all too late comes counsel to be heard
Where will doth mutiny with wit's regard.
Direct not him whose way himself will choose.
'Tis breath thou lackst and that breath wilt thou lose.   30
GAUNT Methinks I am a prophet new inspired,
And thus expiring do foretell of him.
His rash fierce blaze of riot cannot last,
For violent fires soon burn out themselves.
Small showers last long but sudden storms are short.   35
He tires betimes that spurs too fast betimes.
With eager feeding food doth choke the feeder.
Light vanity, insatiate cormorant,
Consuming means, soon preys upon itself.
This royal throne of kings, this sceptred isle,   40
This earth of majesty, this seat of Mars,
This other Eden, demi-paradise,
This fortress built by Nature for herself

27 Then] Qq ; That F

25 **there's no respect** nobody bothers to
consider.
28 **will...wit** 'Will', standing for the animal
passions, was commonly set against 'wit', man's
reason, as in Sidney's contrast of 'our erected wit'
and 'our infected will' in the *Apology for Poetry*.
31 **inspired** Literally and theologically 'inspira-
tion' was the breath of God's spirit in mankind.
Gaunt picks up York's point about saving his breath
and gives it a theological meaning, while acknowledging York's advice by the use of 'expiring',
breathing out and breathing his last, in the next line.
33 **riot** (1) misrule, (2) uproar.
33–9 As in 11–14, each of Gaunt's *sententiae*,
while expressing proverbial commonplaces, relates
to a thematic image.
36 **betimes...betimes** quickly...early in the
day.
38 **cormorant** A proverbially greedy feeder.
40–66 For comment on the word-play see
Mahood, p. 80, especially about a fertile Eden
unexpectedly occupied by the God of War. For
analysis of the use of sources for this set-piece
oration, see Muir, *The Sources of Shakespeare's
Plays*, pp. 58–64. For precedents of speeches in
praise of the *patria* or homeland, and the related

rhetorical forms, see William C. McAvoy, 'Form in
Richard II, II.i.40–46', *JEGP* 104 (1955), 355–61.
This speech became famous early enough to be the
longest passage from the play quoted in *England's
Parnassus* (see Appendix 4, p. 234 below), even if
the compiler did ascribe it to Drayton.
40–1 Gaunt emphasises the monarchy in the first
three of his descriptions, and the warlike nature of
the English in his fourth. The contrast with
Richard's conduct of the state underlies the whole
speech.
41 **earth of majesty** proper place for kings.
Besides its obvious link with the elemental imagery
of land, ground and England, 'earth' has a
paradoxical force from its use (*OED sb* 4) to denote
a fox's or badger's lair.
41 **seat of Mars** residence of the god of war.
42 **other Eden** second Paradise. This reference
is generally thought to broach the 'garden' image
which is developed in 3.4. In fact it begins with
Bullingbrook's reference to Genesis at 1.1.104. The
imagery of earth and garden begins even earlier, at
1.1.23, 37, etc.
43–4 The Armada in 1588 affirmed the common
notion of England's seas as a moat. The linkage of
'infection' with war suggests an echo of Daniel's

Against infection and the hand of war,
This happy breed of men, this little world,   45
This precious stone set in the silver sea
Which serves it in the office of a wall
Or as a moat defensive to a house
Against the envy of less happier lands,
This blessèd plot, this earth, this realm, this England,   50
This nurse, this teeming womb of royal kings
Feared by their breed and famous by their birth,
Renownèd for their deeds as far from home
For Christian service and true chivalry
As is the sepulchre in stubborn Jewry   55
Of the world's ransom, blessèd Mary's son,
This land of such dear souls, this dear, dear land,
Dear for her reputation through the world,
Is now leased out, I die pronouncing it,
Like to a tenement or pelting farm.   60
England, bound in with the triumphant sea
Whose rocky shore beats back the envious siege
Of watery Neptune, is now bound in with shame,
With inky blots and rotten parchment bonds,
That England that was wont to conquer others   65
Hath made a shameful conquest of itself.

48 a moat] Q4–5, F; moate Q1–3   52 famous by] Qq; famous for F   53 home] *This edn*; home, Qq, F

'contagion' (*Civil Wars*, IV, 43, 90) by civil wars. France in 1595 was concluding thirty years of internal religious wars. The infection is the specific plague of war. Gaunt thinks of the sea as a protection against invasion from outside, though his hearers might pick up the alternative of civil war through 'infection'.

45 breed race.

47 office function.

50 plot land for cultivation.

51 teeming fertile, abundant in progeny.

53–6 Gaunt sees England's greatness chiefly in terms of its royal crusaders, of whom the most notable were Richard I and Edward I. For the alternatives of pilgrimage or crusade as a theme running through all the histories from *R2* to *H5*, see pp. 4–6 above.

55 stubborn Jewry The residents of Jerusalem, who resisted both Christ and the crusaders.

56 world's ransom A phrase from the Bishops' Bible, Matt. 20.28.

57–8 dear (1) beloved, (2) expensive, and (by

extension) (3) invaluable. The repetition of the word prepares for the monstrous act of leasing, putting a commercial price on something beloved enough to be priceless.

59 leased out Both Daniel (*Civil Wars*, II, 19: 'And who as let in lease doe farm the crowne') and *Woodstock* use the same term for Richard's abuse of his fiscal authority.

60 tenement...farm Both terms are demeaning. A 'tenement' was a tenancy, a property used but not owned. A 'pelting' (paltry) farm is a smallholding. The adjective is in *Woodstock* 1888. Gaunt is fusing the concept of tax farming with debasement of landownership.

61–3 bound in...bound in bordered by... legally bonded.

64 Gaunt's image makes the blank charters visually as well as legally corrupted, and links up with the recurrent references to bonds (1.1.2; 5.2.65, etc.) and to blots (1.3.201; 3.2.81; 4.1.235, 325; 5.3.65).

Ah, would the scandal vanish with my life,
How happy then were my ensuing death!

Enter King [RICHARD], QUEEN, AUMERLE, BUSHY, GREEN, BAGOT,
ROSS *and* WILLOUGHBY.

YORK The king is come. Deal mildly with his youth,
    For young hot colts being reined do rage the more.   70
QUEEN How fares our noble uncle Lancaster?
RICHARD What comfort, man? How is't with agèd Gaunt?
GAUNT Oh, how that name befits my composition!
    Old Gaunt indeed, and gaunt in being old.
    Within me grief hath kept a tedious fast,   75
    And who abstains from meat that is not gaunt?
    For sleeping England long time have I watched.
    Watching breeds leanness; leanness is all gaunt.
    The pleasure that some fathers feed upon
    Is my strict fast, I mean my children's looks,   80
    And therein fasting hast thou made me gaunt.
    Gaunt am I for the grave, gaunt as a grave,
    Whose hollow womb inherits naught but bones.
RICHARD Can sick men play so nicely with their names?
GAUNT No, misery makes sport to mock itself.   85
    Since thou dost seek to kill my name in me
    I mock my name, great king, to flatter thee.
RICHARD Should dying men flatter with those that live?
GAUNT No, no, men living flatter those that die.

---

68 SD] F; *Enter king and Queene, &c.* Qq *(after 70)*   70 reined] *Singer;* ragde Qq, F   87 I] Q1, F; O Q2–5
88 with] Q1; *not in* Q2–5, F

68 SD Wells suggests that since Richard is given
an exit with a flourish of trumpets at 223, according
to F, he should enter with one here. The sound
would give York occasion for his next words.

70 **reined** Q1's version suggests a compositorial
transposition from 'rage' two words later. Probably
the manuscript read 'raigned'. In *The Mirror for
Magistrates*, ed. Campbell, p. 79, Richard is
described as 'not raygning but raging by youthfull
insolence'. Singer's emendation makes sense even
without this possible source for the phrase.

73 **composition** condition.

76 **meat** food.

77 **watched** kept awake, kept guard.

78 **Watching** Lack of sleep.

78 **all gaunt** lean and 'Gaunt'. The specific
charge, that the exile of Bullingbrook has caused

Gaunt's suffering, is part of the greater charge that
Gaunt has had to do Richard's work for him.
'Sleeping England' is the king as well as the land.
The word-play has a submerged link with Richard's
imagery of tasting sweet and bitter things. See
5.5.49.

83 **womb** We might expect 'tomb' here. They
are linked by the queen's image of giving birth to
grief at 2.2.10–66, and in the recurrence of 'hollow'
in the play.

83 **inherits** receives as its due.

84 **nicely** delicately, trivially.

86 **kill...in me** Bullingbrook's exile deprives
Gaunt of his heir. The loss of names runs through
the play, culminating in Richard's becoming
nothing in 5.5.

87 **flatter** deceive.

RICHARD Thou now a-dying sayest thou flatterest me.   90
GAUNT Oh no, thou diest, though I the sicker be.
RICHARD I am in health, I breathe, and see thee ill.
GAUNT Now He that made me knows I see thee ill,
   Ill in myself to see, and in thee, seeing ill.
   Thy deathbed is no lesser than thy land,   95
   Wherein thou liest in reputation sick,
   And thou, too careless patient as thou art,
   Commit'st thy anointed body to the cure
   Of those physicians that first wounded thee.
   A thousand flatterers sit within thy crown   100
   Whose compass is no bigger than thy head,
   And yet encagèd in so small a verge
   The waste is no whit lesser than thy land.
   Oh, had thy grandsire with a prophet's eye
   Seen how his son's son should destroy his sons,   105
   From forth thy reach he would have laid thy shame,
   Deposing thee before thou wert possessed,
   Which art possessed now to depose thyself.
   Why cousin, wert thou regent of the world
   It were a shame to let this land by lease,   110
   But for thy world enjoying but this land
   Is it not more than shame to shame it so?

92 and] Q1; *not in* Q2–5, F 95 thy] Q1; the Q2–5, F 102 encagèd] F; inragèd Qq 109 wert] Qq; were F
110 this] Qq; his F

93 **see thee ill** (1) see thee imperfectly, (2) see
thee sick. The next line makes the double meaning
clear. There is a firm suggestion of moral sickness
in Richard facing merely physical sickness in Gaunt.
97 **too...patient** See p. 6 above. Richard is
both a sick patient and an unsoldierly figure of
Christian patience.
98 **anointed body** The coronation ceremony
includes anointing the king with oil. Richard
half-remembers Gaunt's speech when in 3.2.55 he
declares that water cannot wash off the 'balm'
(medicinal ointment) from a king.
99 **physicians** Gaunt develops the secondary
meanings of both 'patient' and 'anointed' into this
scornful name, which emphasises Richard's mis-
placed trust in his lying flatterers.
101 **compass** scale, boundary.
102 **verge** A triple pun: a border or rim; the
twelve-mile radius around the king which was the
Lord Marshal's jurisdiction; and a measure of land
of between 15 and 30 acres.

103 **waste** (1) a desert, (2) a waist. The second
meaning picks up 'head' from 101. Waste was also
a legal term for prejudicial damage to property by
a tenant, a reference back to the charge in 60 above.
104 **thy grandsire** Edward III.
105 The open suggestion is that Richard is
destroying his own patrimony for his own children,
but grammatically 'his sons' could also be the sons
of Edward III, including Gloucester and Gaunt.
107 **Deposing** Technically 'disinheriting', but
the word has an ominous ring not intended by
Gaunt, judging from his arguments to the Duchess
of Gloucester in 1.2.
107–8 **possessed...possessed** A chiasmus, in
which the repeated words reverse their meaning.
The first 'possessed' (107) signifies 'in possession',
the standard meaning. The second (108) means (1)
obsessed (i.e. with deposing yourself), (2) possessed
by a devil.
109 **regent** governor.
111 **thy world** your earthly domain.

Landlord of England art thou now, not king,
Thy state of law is bondslave to the law,
And thou –

RICHARD   A lunatic lean-witted fool,   115
Presuming on an ague's privilege,
Dar'st with thy frozen admonition
Make pale our cheek, chasing the royal blood
With fury from his native residence.
Now, by my seat's right royal majesty,   120
Wert thou not brother to great Edward's son
This tongue that runs so roundly in thy head
Should run thy head from thy unreverent shoulders.

GAUNT Oh spare me not, my brother Edward's son,
For that I was his father Edward's son.   125
That blood already, like the pelican,
Hast thou tapped out and drunkenly caroused.
My brother Gloucester, plain well-meaning soul,
Whom fair befall in heaven 'mongst happy souls,

---

113 thou now, not king] *Theobald;* thou now not, not King Q1–4; thou now not, nor King Q5; thou, and not King F
115 And thou – / RICHARD A] *Capell;* And thou / *King.* A Q1; And – / *Rich.* And thou, a F   118 chasing] Qq;
chafing F   124 brother] Q2–5; brothers Q1, F   127 Hast thou tapped out] Q1; Hast thou tapt Q2–5; Thou hast
tapt out F

113 This line summarises the accusations of
tenancy (60), waste (103) and possession (107–8). It
echoes Daniel and *Woodstock* 2826 ('& thou no king
but landlord now become').

113 now, not king Theobald's conjecture is
better than Q5's adjustment and F's attempt to
correct the metre. None has any obvious authority.

114 state of law throne and seat of law.

114 bondslave The proper relationship of
lawgiver and subjects has been reversed by the act
of leasing the land, which has 'bound in' (63) the
king and made him subject to the law. Gaunt
believes, as did Elizabeth and James, that as
lawgiver the monarch is above the law.

115 Richard completes Gaunt's sentence by
reversing it and turning it on Gaunt by means of
his own word-play on his name. 'Lean-witted'
means 'thin in mind', i.e. gaunt of wits.

116 Presuming on Exploiting.

116 an ague's privilege the privilege of the sick
and feverish.

117 frozen sick (chilled) and hostile (cold).
Agues caused alternate fever and shivering. Both the
cold and the hostility make Richard lose colour. He
pales again at 3.2.75, and at 3.3.62–3 he goes red.

120 my seat my state of law (114). Richard's
threat is an implicit denial of Gaunt's accusation.

121 great...son The Black Prince, Richard's
father.

122 roundly bluntly, fluently.

123 unreverent not bowed in respect. There is
a complex visual pun here related to the iteration
of bowing and kneeling in the play. Gaunt is bowed
with age and sickness, the 'crooked age' of 133. He
should be bowed in awe of the throne, and he might
have to bow under the executioner's axe. The threat
to cut Gaunt's head off links to the execution of
Gloucester. See also York at 2.2.102.

124 brother This is the only obvious instance in
the text of an error shared by Q1 and F and no other
quarto. In the absence of any other evidence for F
consulting Q1 it must be accepted as a coincidence.

126 pelican The bird which was said to bite its
own breast in order to feed its children with its
blood was not only an emblem of parental care but
also, as here, of filial ingratitude. See *Lear* 3.4.75.

127 tapped out drawn like a drink from a barrel
(by the insertion of a spigot).

128 plain...soul Holinshed, Daniel and Froissart all describe Gloucester as a violent intriguer.
This account, while it fits his contribution as a
victim of murder, may be based on his characterisation in *Woodstock* as 'plain Thomas', the
antithesis of Richard in dress and conduct.

May be a precedent and witness good   130
That thou respect'st not spilling Edward's blood.
Join with the present sickness that I have
And thy unkindness be like crooked age
To crop at once a too long withered flower.
Live in thy shame, but die not shame with thee.   135
These words hereafter thy tormentors be.
Convey me to my bed, then to my grave.
Love they to live that love and honour have.   *Exit*

RICHARD And let them die that age and sullens have,
     For both hast thou, and both become the grave.   140
YORK I do beseech your majesty, impute his words
     To wayward sickliness and age in him.
     He loves you, on my life, and holds you dear
     As Harry Duke of Herford were he here.
RICHARD Right, you say true. As Herford's love, so his.   145
     As theirs, so mine, and all be as it is.

           Enter NORTHUMBERLAND.

NORTHUMBERLAND My liege, old Gaunt commends him to your
     majesty.
RICHARD What says he?
NORTHUMBERLAND   Nay nothing, all is said.
     His tongue is now a stringless instrument.
     Words, life and all old Lancaster hath spent.   150
YORK Be York the next that must be bankrupt so.
     Though death be poor it ends a mortal woe.
RICHARD The ripest fruit first falls, and so doth he.

146 all] Q1, F; *not in* Q2–5   146 SD] F; *not in* QQ

130 **May be** Must be. Gaunt is now openly
accusing Richard of the murder.
   133 **unkindness** unnatural feelings. Richard
will join with time ('crooked age') to destroy his kin.
   135 **die…thee** (1) shame will not leave you, (2)
shame will live after you.
   137 **Convey** Help, escort. If Gaunt is in a sick
chair, he would be carried off in it. The word is
repeated, and picked up by Richard, at 4.1.315–16.
   139–40 Richard reverses the rhymes of Gaunt's
final couplet.
   139 **sullens** Gaunt has used the word at 1.3.226.
   140 **become** suit, are fit for.
   143 **holds you dear** York means that Gaunt
holds Richard as warmly in his affection as his own
son. Richard chooses to hear an ambiguity, and

interprets him as saying that Bullingbrook loves
Richard no more than Gaunt evidently does.
   146 **As theirs, so mine** Richard will love Gaunt
and his son as little as they love him. 'Be it as it is'
is a proverbial dismissal (Dent B112.1).
   149 Tongues are called stringed instruments at
1.3.161–2 and 5.5.46.
   150 **spent** ended, expended.
   151 **bankrupt** York picks up the financial sense
of Northumberland's last word. Behind his
extension of the image in the next line to the poverty
of death is the Biblical commonplace about leaving
the world as naked as we enter it (e.g. Job 1.21).
   153 **ripest…falls** A proverbial saying (Tilley
R133).

His time is spent, our pilgrimage must be.
So much for that. Now, for our Irish wars,   155
We must supplant those rough rug-headed kern,
Which live like venom where no venom else
But only they have privilege to live.
And, for these great affairs do ask some charge,
Towards our assistance we do seize to us   160
The plate, coin, revenues and moveables
Whereof our uncle Gaunt did stand possessed.

YORK   How long shall I be patient? Ah, how long
Shall tender duty make me suffer wrong?
Not Gloucester's death nor Herford's banishment,   165
Nor Gaunt's rebukes, nor England's private wrongs,
Nor the prevention of poor Bullingbrook
About his marriage, nor my own disgrace
Have ever made me sour my patient cheek
Or bend one wrinkle on my sovereign's face.   170
I am the last of noble Edward's sons,
Of whom thy father, Prince of Wales, was first.
In war was never lion raged more fierce,

---

156 kern] Q1 *(Hunt., Huth, Capell),* Q2; kernes Q1 *(Petworth),* Q3–5, F   161 coin] Q1 *(Hunt., Huth, Capell),* F; coines
Q1 *(Petworth)*   168 my] Q1 *(Hunt., Huth, Capell),* F; his Q1 *(Petworth)*   171 of] Q1, F; of the Q2–5

---

154 pilgrimage Richard picks up the Biblical hint in York's speech, and perhaps recalls Bullingbrook's reference to a pilgrimage at 1.3.49.

155 Irish wars See 1.4.60–1. It is not clear whether Richard intended from the outset to take all of Gaunt's property. His anger at Gaunt's reproofs would make it plausible to see him as overreacting here. All the commentators regarded this act as the cause of his deposition.

156 rug-headed shaggy. Literally 'rug' was a coarse wool frieze.

156 kern footsoldiers. Most editors use F's plural, but Edmund Spenser, *A View of the Present State of Ireland,* uses it as a collective singular. In this gathering of Q1 the Petworth copy has the uncorrected state (see 161, 168, 186). Both the Q1 compositor (A) and the Q3 compositor who provided the copy for F normalised independently.

157–8 where no…only they Ireland has no snakes.

159 ask some charge demand some expenditure.

160 seize The legal term for taking possession of goods.

162 stand possessed Again Richard is using

legal terminology, possibly in reaction to Gaunt's accusation that he has changed from lawgiver to bondslave (114).

163 patient A word with Biblical resonance. See 1.2.29, and 5.1.34 n.

166 Gaunt's rebukes Richard's reproof of Gaunt in 115–23.

166 private wrongs the wrongs of individuals.

167–8 prevention…marriage Richard stopped the move to marry Bullingbrook to a cousin of the French king while he was in exile. It is noted in Holinshed, II, 495.

168 my own disgrace The only recognisable source for this detail is *Woodstock,* which has Gloucester saying to York and Lancaster that Richard has 'disgraced our names' (1301). A case might be made for the accuracy of the Petworth reading of Q1, which would refer the disgrace to Bullingbrook's exile, but 'own' would then be redundant.

170 bend aim. The metaphor is from archery.

170 wrinkle frown.

171 last The last surviving son. Gloucester was actually the youngest.

173 lion Possibly a concealed allusion to the contrasting figure of Richard I, Coeur-de-lion, is

In peace was never gentle lamb more mild
Than was that young and princely gentleman.   175
His face thou hast, for even so looked he,
Accomplished with the number of thy hours.
But when he frowned it was against the French
And not against his friends. His noble hand
Did win what he did spend, and spent not that   180
Which his triumphant father's hand had won.
His hands were guilty of no kindred blood
But bloody with the enemies of his kin.
Oh, Richard! York is too far gone with grief,
Or else he never would compare between.   185

RICHARD Why, uncle, what's the matter?

YORK   O my liege,
Pardon me if you please; if not, I, pleased
Not to be pardoned, am content with all.
Seek you to seize and gripe into your hands
The royalties and rights of banished Herford?   190
Is not Gaunt dead? And doth not Herford live?
Was not Gaunt just? And is not Harry true?
Did not the one deserve to have an heir?
Is not his heir a well-deserving son?
Take Herford's rights away and take from time   195
His charters and his customary rights.
Let not tomorrow then ensue today.

---

177 the] F; a, Qq   182 kindred] Qq; kindreds F   186] *not in* Q1 *(Petworth)*   186–8] *Theobald; King* Why...
matter? / *Yorke* Oh...please, / If...all, / Seeke Qq; *Rich.* Why Vncle, / What's... matter? / *Yor.* Oh...if not / I
pleas'd...all: Seeke F

---

intended here. He is certainly indicated by Gaunt
in his reference to crusader kings at 52–4. Kings as
lions are also mentioned at 1.1.174 and 5.1.29.

177 Accomplished Fully equipped. See *MV*
3.4.61.

178–83 A series of rhetorical tropes of antimeta-
bole, or reversals. Richard uses the same trope at
4.1.262 and 304–8 and at 5.5.49.

180 spend An echo of 150, 154.

182 York now also openly alludes to his brother
Gloucester's murder. His first reference at 165 is
equivocal.

186–8 Both Q1 and F got into difficulties in this
passage through a miscalculation of cast-off copy.
F had to stretch 186 'Why...matter' into two lines
to make up space while Q1 had to create an extra

line. The Petworth copy shows that this was done
as a press-correction. There is other evidence of
cramped spacing in the gathering (D). Six other
pages, one in each of the succeeding gatherings and
four in H, also have an extra line.

187 Pardon me Acknowledging his feudal lord
('my liege'), York asks to be forgiven for his
treasonable speech, though his grief still prompts
him to renew his protest.

189 gripe grasp.

190 royalties The rights granted by the
monarch, and the royal prerogative which goes with
royal blood.

195 rights Both of inheritance and succession.

196 His Time's.

197 ensue follow.

Be not thyself. For how art thou a king
But by fair sequence and succession?
Now, afore God – God forbid I say true –   200
If you do wrongfully seize Herford's rights,
Call in the letters patents that he hath
By his attorneys-general to sue
His livery, and deny his offered homage,
You pluck a thousand dangers on your head,   205
You lose a thousand well-disposèd hearts,
And prick my tender patience to those thoughts
Which honour and allegiance cannot think.

RICHARD Think what you will, we seize into our hands
His plate, his goods, his money and his lands.   210

YORK I'll not be by the while. My liege, farewell.
What will ensue hereof there's none can tell,
But by bad courses may be understood
That their events can never fall out good.   *Exit*

RICHARD Go, Bushy, to the Earl of Wiltshire straight.   215
Bid him repair to us to Ely House
To see this business. Tomorrow next
We will for Ireland, and 'tis time, I trow.
And we create in absence of ourself
Our uncle York lord governor of England,   220
For he is just, and always loved us well.
Come on, our queen; tomorrow must we part.
Be merry, for our time of stay is short.

> *Exeunt King [Richard] and Queen,*
> *[Aumerle, Bushy, Green and Bagot]*

---

200 say] Q1 *(Hunt., Capell, Petworth)*, F; lay Q1 *(Huth)*   201 rights] Q1; right Q2–5, F   202 the] Qq; his F
223 SD] Capell; *Exeunt King and Queene: Manet North.* Qq; *Flourish. / Manet North. Willoughby, & Ross.* F

198 **thyself** In Elizabethan texts the possessive
adjective plus 'self' was normally written as two
words, giving the idea of the self an emphasis now
lost. York is saying, as Gaunt has said, that Richard
is not the kingly self he should be, because he flouts
the law which makes kings.

201 **wrongfully...rights** The word-play about
wrongs and rights underlines York's point about
Richard's breach of law.

202–4 These items are close to Holinshed, II,
496, which has 'letters patents' and 'attorneis-
generall' to 'sue liverie'.

203–4 **sue...livery** act on his behalf with those

of his tenants who have knightly status until he can
claim his own right.

204 **deny** refuse.

211 **by** present.

214 **events** consequences.

215 **Earl of Wiltshire** The Lord Treasurer, the
first Lord Scroope or Lescrope, brother of the
Scroope of 3.2.90 and fourth of the flatterers.

217 **see** conduct. The 'business' is that of
seizing Gaunt's property.

217 **Tomorrow next** This next morning.

218 **trow** believe.

NORTHUMBERLAND Well, lords, the Duke of Lancaster is dead.

ROSS And living too, for now his son is duke.   225

WILLOUGHBY Barely in title, not in revenues.

NORTHUMBERLAND Richly in both if justice had her right.

ROSS My heart is great, but it must break with silence
      Ere't be disburdened with a liberal tongue.

NORTHUMBERLAND Nay, speak thy mind, and let him ne'er speak
         more   230
      That speaks thy words again to do thee harm.

WILLOUGHBY Tends that that thou wouldst speak to the Duke of
         Herford?
      If it be so, out with it boldly, man.
      Quick is mine ear to hear of good towards him.

ROSS No good at all that I can do for him,   235
      Unless you call it good to pity him,
      Bereft, and gelded of his patrimony.

NORTHUMBERLAND Now afore God 'tis shame such wrongs are borne
      In him, a royal prince, and many mo
      Of noble blood in this declining land.   240
      The king is not himself, but basely led
      By flatterers, and what they will inform
      Merely in hate 'gainst any of us all
      That will the king severely prosecute
      'Gainst us, our lives, our children and our heirs.   245

ROSS The commons hath he pilled with grievous taxes
      And quite lost their hearts. The nobles hath he fined

---

226 revenues] Qq; reuennew F   232 that that thou wouldst] *Keightley;* that thou wouldst Qq; that thou'dst F
232 the] Qq; th' F   238 God] Qq; heauen F   243 'gainst] Q1, F; against Q2–5   246 pilled] Qq (pild); pil'd F

228 great swollen with emotion.

228 break with silence burst through keeping silent. The distance of heart from mouth or tongue marks all the intriguing in the play.

229 liberal generous, free. The concealed metaphor is of handing out (disburdening) wealth, the opposite of Richard's act.

232 Keightley's emendation smoothes the metre of an awkward line. F's elisions attempt to do the same job by making 'Herford' trisyllabic.

237 gelded (1) deprived of gold, (2) castrated.

239 mo The plural and collective form of 'more'.

241–2 The king…flatterers This charge, developing York's point at 198, is the basis for the *Woodstock* story. It was a charge levelled against

Elizabeth and one of the chief reasons for comparing her with Richard. See Dent, Appendix B, 'To FORGET oneself'.

244 prosecute take redress on the basis of written depositions. Again the language is quasi-legal.

246 pilled despoiled. Cognate with modern 'pillage', the verb was linked by false etymology to 'caterpillars'. See 2.3.165 n. See also Gascoigne, *The Steele Glas* (1576): 'The stately lord which woonted was to keepe / A court at home, is now come up to courte, / And leaves the country for a common prey, / To pilling, polling, brybing, and deceit.' *Woodstock* (835) refers to 'these that pill the poor, to jet in gold'.

For ancient quarrels and quite lost their hearts.
WILLOUGHBY And daily new exactions are devised,
    As blanks, benevolences, and I wot not what.   250
    But what a God's name doth become of this?
NORTHUMBERLAND Wars hath not wasted it, for warred he hath
        not,
    But basely yielded upon compromise
    That which his ancestors achieved with blows.
    More hath he spent in peace than they in wars.   255
ROSS The Earl of Wiltshire hath the realm in farm.
WILLOUGHBY The king grown bankrupt like a broken man.
NORTHUMBERLAND Reproach and dissolution hangeth over him.
ROSS He hath not money for these Irish wars,
    His burthenous taxations notwithstanding,   260
    But by the robbing of the banished duke.
NORTHUMBERLAND His noble kinsman, most degenerate king!
    But lords, we hear this fearful tempest sing
    Yet seek no shelter to avoid the storm.
    We see the wind sit sore upon our sails   265
    And yet we strike not but securely perish.
ROSS We see the very wreck that we must suffer,
    And unavoided is the danger now
    For suffering so the causes of our wreck.
NORTHUMBERLAND Not so. Even through the hollow eyes of death   270

---

251 But] Q1–3, F; *North.* But Q4–5   251 a] QQ; o' F   252 SH NORTHUMBERLAND] Q1, F; *Willo.* Q2–5   254 his
ancestors] F; his noble auncestors QQ   257 king] Q1–2; King's Q3–5, F

249 new exactions A phrase from the Holinshed marginalia (II, 496).
  250 blanks blank charters. See 1.4.48 n.
  250 benevolences forced loans (*OED* sv *sb* 4).
  251 this the income from the new exactions.
  252–4 In Holinshed (II, 487) Gloucester com-
plains about the handing over of Brest to the Duke
of Brittany shortly before being murdered. Northumberland is adding to Gaunt's point about the
contrast of Richard with his crusading ancestors at
51–4 and the Tree of Jesse imagery for the sons of
Edward III.
  254 his ancestors Q1's 'noble' is extra-metrical
and may be an intrusion from the compositor's
memory of 246, or an anticipation of 262. The
compositor was A, whose error rate of 1 in 17 lines
included frequent recollections and anticipations of
adjacent lines.

257 king Q3 normalises with a verb,
unnecessarily.
  257 broken Cognate with 'bankrupt', according
to *OED* sv *ppl a* 7. The stress is partly on 'man'
in contrast with 'king'.
  258 dissolution bankruptcy, dissipation.
  262 degenerate i.e. inferior to his ancestors
Edward III and the Black Prince.
  266 strike take in. A nautical term (from taking
in sails), but used here with a hint of taking up arms
against the king.
  266 securely in the overconfident illusion of
security.
  267 wreck The Q and F spelling 'wrack' adds the
idea of an instrument of torture to the existing image
of shipwreck.
  268 unavoided impossible to avoid.
  270–1 through…peering The 'hollow eyes'

I spy life peering, but I dare not say
How near the tidings of our comfort is.
WILLOUGHBY Nay, let us share thy thoughts as thou dost ours.
ROSS Be confident to speak, Northumberland.
    We three are but thy self, and speaking so   275
    Thy words are but as thoughts. Therefore be bold.
NORTHUMBERLAND Then thus: I have from le Port Blanc,
    A bay in Brittaine, received intelligence
    That Harry Duke of Herford, Rainold Lord Cobham,
    [The son of Richard Earl of Arundel]   280
    That late broke from the Duke of Exeter,
    His brother, Archbishop late of Canterbury,
    Sir Thomas Erpingham, Sir John Ramston,
    Sir John Norbery, Sir Robert Waterton, and Francis Coint,
    All these well furnished by the Duke of Brittaine   285
    With eight tall ships, three thousand men of war,
    Are making hither with all due expedience
    And shortly mean to touch our northern shore.
    Perhaps they had ere this, but that they stay

---

271 spy] Q1, F; espie Q2–5   277 le Port Blanc] *Wright*; le Port Blan Qq; Port *le Blan* F   278 Brittaine] Q1; Brittanie Q2–4; *Britaine* F   280] *Malone*; *not in* Qq, F   283 Ramston] Qq; *Rainston* F   284 Coint] *Halliwell*; Coines Qq; *Quoint* F

of death are the sockets in a skull. Northumberland's image is the emblematic scheme of the soul trapped within the body. Francis Quarles, *Emblems Divine and Moral* (1634), v, no. 8, prints an emblem of a human body trapped inside a skeleton.

275 thy self See 198 n. A proverbial concept (Tilley F696).

276 Thy words...thoughts Since the three are one self and therefore one mind, their thoughts do not need putting into words. Heart and tongue in this instance speak the same things.

277 le Port Blanc Shakespeare started with the name as in Holinshed, Q1's compositor misread his manuscript and the F editor corrected with a conjecture.

278 Brittaine Brittany. The metre is no help over the pronunciation, since even as a disyllable it makes the line eleven syllables in all. The line can only be metrically normal if the second half of 'Brittaine' is elided, making the word effectively a monosyllable. The line reads most easily as an alexandrine, as does 285.

279 Rainold Holinshed spells 'Reginald'. All the details in 277–88 are from Holinshed (II, 498).

280 Shakespeare's copying of Holinshed here makes it clear that the Q1 compositor (A) missed

a line, and the F editor failed to restore it. It was not Cobham but Arundel who broke from Exeter. Malone's line is a conjecture based on Holinshed. Hudson suggested that a closer adoption of Holinshed would give 'Thomas, the son and heir to th'Earl of Arundel'.

281 Exeter Half-brother to Richard and brother-in-law to Bullingbrook. He was executed by Bullingbrook for his part in Westminster's plot. See 5.3.136.

282 His Arundel's.

283 Erpingham Sir Thomas reappears in *H5* before Agincourt.

284 Coint Holinshed's spelling. It has been conjectured that he could be the Poins of *1* and *2H4*.

285 Duke of Brittaine The Duke's widow became Bullingbrook's second wife once he was Henry IV.

286 tall large.

286 three...war Holinshed (II, 498) notes a dispute about the size of Bullingbrook's following. Some commentators claim he had 'not past fifteen lances'. Shakespeare gives Northumberland the maximum estimate.

289 stay wait for.

The first departing of the king for Ireland.   290
If then we shall shake off our slavish yoke,
Imp out our drooping country's broken wing,
Redeem from broking pawn the blemished crown,
Wipe off the dust that hides our sceptre's gilt,
And make high majesty look like itself,   295
Away with me in post to Ravenspurgh.
But if you faint, as fearing to do so,
Stay and be secret, and myself will go.

ROSS To horse, to horse! Urge doubts to them that fear.
WILLOUGHBY Hold out my horse, and I will first be there.   300

Exeunt

2.2 *Enter the* QUEEN, BUSHY, BAGOT.

BUSHY Madam, your majesty is too much sad.
You promised, when you parted with the king,
To lay aside life-harming heaviness
And entertain a cheerful disposition.

QUEEN To please the king I did. To please myself   5
I cannot do it; yet I know no cause
Why I should welcome such a guest as grief
Save bidding farewell to so sweet a guest

---

291 our] Q1, F; our Countries Q2–5   293 broking] Q1–2, F; broken Q3–5   294 gilt] F; guilt Qq   Act 2, Scene 2
3 life-harming] Q1–2; half-harming Q3–5; selfe-harming F

---

290 **The...king** The king to depart first.

292 **Imp out** Mend by inserting new feathers (in falconry).

293 **broking pawn** pawnbroking, lending money on the security of the crown. Northumberland's charge is similar to Gaunt's 'landlord', and he picks up Willoughby's 'broken man' from 257.

294 **gilt** gold leaf, with a hint of the homonymic 'guilt'. Q's spelling is the secondary meaning.

295 Northumberland's use of the adjective which Richard has applied to Bullingbrook (1.4.2) emphasises the ambiguity of his demand. To him, both here when Richard has the crown and at 5.6.6 when it is Bullingbrook's, kingship is an abstraction separate from the man who performs its duties.

296 **in post** in haste.

296 **Ravenspurgh** A port on the Humber near Spurn Head, now under the sea.

297 **faint** timid, faint-hearted.

299 **Urge** Persuade of.

300 **Hold...horse** If my horse will hold out.

Act 2, Scene 2

2.2 This scene is largely Shakespeare's invention, except for the details of people's movements reported at the end. Like Daniel, Shakespeare unhistorically makes the queen a grown woman.

0 SD As in 1.4 the flatterers are divided, with one entering late as a messenger. Using different messengers helps to differentiate the three. Bushy is the messenger in 1.4, Green in this scene, and Bagot has his separate role as the sole survivor in 4.1.

3 **life-harming heaviness** The popular belief was that every sigh consumes a drop of blood. See 5.5.49, and *Rom.* 3.5.58. The F text shows the editor adjusting his copy (Q3) without help from Q1 or any authoritative source, as at 2.1.18.

As my sweet Richard. Yet again methinks
Some unborn sorrow ripe in Fortune's womb   10
Is coming towards me, and my inward soul
With nothing trembles; at some thing it grieves,
More than with parting from my lord the king.
BUSHY Each substance of a grief hath twenty shadows
Which shows like grief itself but is not so,   15
For sorrow's eye, glazèd with blinding tears,
Divides one thing entire to many objects,
Like perspectives, which rightly gazed upon
Show nothing but confusion; eyed awry
Distinguish form. So your sweet majesty,   20
Looking awry upon your lord's departure,
Find shapes of grief more than himself to wail
Which, looked on as it is, is naught but shadows
Of what it is not. Then, thrice-gracious queen,
More than your lord's departure weep not. More's not
  seen,   25
Or if it be 'tis with false sorrow's eye
Which for things true weeps things imaginary.
QUEEN It may be so, but yet my inward soul
Persuades me it is otherwise. Howe'er it be
I cannot but be sad, so heavy sad   30
As, though on thinking on no thought I think,
Makes me with heavy nothing faint and shrink.

12 With] Q1 *(Hunt., Huth, Capell),* F; At Q1 *(Petworth)*   16 eye] F; eyes Qq   19 Show] Q1 *(Hunt., Huth, Capell),* F; Shews Q1 *(Petworth)*   24 Then...queen,] F; then thrice (gracious Queene), Qq   25 More's] F; more is Qq   26 eye] Q1, F; eyes Q2–5   27 weeps] Qq; weepe F   31 though] Q2–5, F; thought Q1

10 The emblem of sorrow about to be born like a monster from Fortune's womb continues until Green delivers his news (10–66).
12 **some thing** The stress is on 'thing': some unknown thing, not nothing.
14 **substance...shadows** See *Ham.* 2.2.258: 'The very substance of the ambitious is merely the shadow of a dream.'
17 **entire** complete in itself.
18 **perspectives** Bushy's simile refers specifically to paintings such as Holbein's *The Ambassadors*, which has a long greyish mark, twisted like a seashell, slantwise across the bottom of the picture. When viewed from the edge of the frame at an acute angle it appears compressed by perspective and proves to be a vivid illustration of a human skull. See Ernest B. Gilman, '*Richard II* and the

perspectives of history', *Ren. Drama* 7 (1976), 85–115.
18 **rightly** from the front, and correctly.
19 **awry** obliquely.
21 **Looking awry** Viewing obliquely, misjudging.
22 **himself** The original grief.
22 **wail** bewail, weep for.
25 **More than...not** Weep only for the one grief.
25 An alexandrine.
27 **for** because of.
31–2 A tortuous piece of word-play. 'Thought' was associated with sadness, as at 5.5.11 and *Ham.* 3.1.84. The conceit turns on the paradox of 'heavy nothing', the no-thought which is heavy, depressing.

BUSHY 'Tis nothing but conceit, my gracious lady.
QUEEN 'Tis nothing less. Conceit is still derived
    From some forefather grief. Mine is not so,   35
    For nothing hath begot my something grief,
    Or something hath the nothing that I grieve.
    'Tis in reversion that I do possess,
    But what it is that is not yet known what
    I cannot name; 'tis nameless woe I wot.   40

Enter GREEN.

GREEN God save your majesty, and well met, gentlemen.
    I hope the king is not yet shipped for Ireland.
QUEEN Why hopest thou so? 'Tis better hope he is,
    For his designs crave haste, his haste good hope;
    Then wherefore dost thou hope he is not shipped?   45
GREEN That he, our hope, might have retired his power
    And driven into despair an enemy's hope
    Who strongly hath set footing in this land.
    The banished Bullingbrook repeals himself
    And with uplifted arms is safe arrived   50
    At Ravenspurgh.
QUEEN   Now God in heaven forbid!
GREEN Ah madam, 'tis too true; and that is worse
    The Lord Northumberland, his son young Harry Percy,
    The lords of Ross, Beaumond and Willoughby,

33] Q1 (*Hunt., Huth, Capell*), F; *not in* Q1 (*Petworth*)   40 SD] F; *not in* QQ   41 God] Qq; Heauen F
50–1] F; *one line* Qq   53 son young] Q1; yong sonne Q2–5, F   54 lords] Q1 (*Hunt., Huth, Capell*), F; lord Q1
(*Petworth*)

33 conceit imagination.
34 Conceit Thinking.
36–7 An extension of the paradox in 31–2.
38 in reversion not yet gained as an inheritance.
It has been begotten (36) and is ready to be
inherited.
40 SD Q1's omission of an entry for the new
speaker, who clearly enters at this point, was
probably for lack of space because of a miscalculation
in casting-off copy. This page (D3ᵛ) has an extra
line.
46 retired withdrawn.
48 strongly with a strong force.
49 repeals himself repeals his sentence of
banishment. *OED* cites this passage as evidence for
the meaning 'recall from exile', but the legal term
more plausibly fits the sentence than the actual
punishment.

50 with…arms Either 'arms [weapons] raised'
as a military threat, or 'hands raised' in prayer.
Green might be expected to mean the first, but
'safe' implies the second.
52 that what.
53–5 See Holinshed, II, 498.
53 Another alexandrine. It has been conjectured
that either 'his son' or 'Harry' is a non-authorial
intrusion, but since most of the six-foot lines occur
when Holinshed is being echoed with lists of names
(2.1.278, 279, 284, 285, for instance) the insertions,
if that is what they are, were evidently made by
someone who consulted Holinshed. On balance it
is better to assume that they are authorial.
54 Beaumond The fifth Lord Beaumont.
Holinshed names these and others as joining
Bullingbrook in the north.

With all their powerful friends are fled to him.   55

BUSHY Why have you not proclaimed Northumberland
    And all the rest, revolted faction, traitors?

GREEN We have, whereupon the Earl of Worcester
    Hath broke his staff, resigned his stewardship,
    And all the Household servants fled with him   60
    To Bullingbrook.

QUEEN So, Green, thou art the midwife to my woe
    And Bullingbrook my sorrow's dismal heir.
    Now hath my soul brought forth her prodigy
    And I, a gasping new-delivered mother,   65
    Have woe to woe, sorrow to sorrow joined.

BUSHY Despair not, madam.

QUEEN   Who shall hinder me?
    I will despair, and be at enmity
    With cozening hope. He is a flatterer,
    A parasite, a keeper-back of death   70
    Who gently would dissolve the bands of life
    Which false hope lingers in extremity.

Enter YORK.

GREEN Here comes the Duke of York.
QUEEN With signs of war about his agèd neck.

57 all the...faction,] *This edn;* al the rest reuolted faction, Q1; the rest of the reuolted faction, Q2–3, F; the rest of the reuolting faction Q4–5   59 broke] Q2–5, F; broken Q1   60–1] *Pope; one line* Qq, F   60 Household] *This edn;* household Qq, F   62 to] Q1; of Q2–5, F   69 cozening] Q1–3, F; couetous Q4–5   72 hope lingers] Qq; hopes linger F   72 SD] F; *not in* Qq

57 Neither Q2, Q4 nor F seems to have any authority in emending Q1, and 'revolted faction' as a parenthetical phrase is acceptable grammatically.

58 **Worcester** The king's Steward, brother to Northumberland. In *1H4* he joins the Northumberland rebellion against Henry IV.

59–61 In Holinshed, II, 500. In this, as with the news in 2.1 of Bullingbrook's return, Shakespeare telescopes the events.

59 **broke** Q2's emendation is metrically better than Q1, though it has no intrinsic authority as a correction.

59 **staff** The white staff of office for the Steward of the royal Household.

60 **Household** The royal establishment, particularly one commanding the 10,000 retainers of which Richard boasts at 4.1.282, warrants a distinguishing capital letter. Those who defected to Bullingbrook with the Steward were many of them

more substantial nobles than the connotations of 'household servants' would admit.

61 The short line perhaps signifies a pause while the news sinks in.

63 **heir** child; i.e. the new-born object of the queen's grief. It picks up 'in reversion' at 38, and echoes Richard at 1.4.35–6.

64 **prodigy** monster, ominous birth.

66 As a mother adds to the pain of childbirth the grief of discovering that her child is a monster.

69 **cozening** deceitful. With a faint echo of the term 'cousin'.

71 **bands** The same word as 'bond' (see 1.1.2), cognate with bondage (2.1.114).

72 **lingers** makes to linger alive.

74 **signs of war** York enters with armour, presumably a gorget around his neck. A gorget was an iron collar which in Shakespeare's day soldiers were permitted to wear with civilian dress to denote their military status.

Oh, full of careful business are his looks!   75
Uncle, for God's sake speak comfortable words.
YORK Should I do so I should belie my thoughts.
Comfort's in heaven and we are on the earth
Where nothing lives but crosses, cares and grief.
Your husband, he is gone to save far off   80
Whilst others come to make him lose at home.
Here am I left to underprop his land
Who weak with age cannot support myself.
Now comes the sick hour that his surfeit made,
Now shall he try his friends that flattered him.   85

Enter a SERVINGMAN.

SERVINGMAN My lord, your son was gone before I came.
YORK He was? Why so, go all which way it will.
The nobles they are fled, the commons cold,
And will, I fear, revolt on Herford's side.
Sirrah, get thee to Plashy, to my sister Gloucester.   90
Bid her send me presently a thousand pound.
Hold, take my ring.
SERVINGMAN My lord, I had forgot to tell your lordship.
Today as I came by I callèd there –
But I shall grieve you to report the rest.   95
YORK What is't, knave?
SERVINGMAN .An hour before I came the duchess died.

76 God's] Qq; heauens F   77] Qq; *not in* F   78 on] Q1 *(Hunt., Huth, Capell),* F; in Q1 *(Petworth)*   79 cares] Q1;
care Q2–5, F   85 SD] F; *not in* Qq   88 commons cold] *Pope;* commons they are cold Qq, F
93–5] Q1; My...forgot / To...there, / But... F   94 as I...callèd] Q1; I came by and call'd Q2–5, F

75 **careful business** anxious bother.
76 **comfortable** capable of comforting. In 3.2
Richard asks his attendants to speak of comfort. See
p. 30 above.
79 **crosses** things that get in the way, burdens.
80 **to save...off** i.e. to keep Ireland under the
English crown.
81 York confirms the point made by Green
at 46–8.
82–3 The concealed metaphor is of the crutch
needed by crooked age.
84 **the sick...made** the consequences of his
overeating. See 2.1.37–9. York remembers Gaunt's
prophecy.
85 **try** test.
86 York has evidently sent for Aumerle to help
him rule in Richard's absence. Aumerle must have
gone to join Richard, whom he accompanies in 3.2.

York's need of him reflects his inability (often, and
I think rightly, played as comic) to control events,
and his ready defeatism.
88 **the commons cold** Pope's emendation
eliminates a phrase which looks like the kind of
memorial error common in Q1's Compositor A.
There is no obvious reason to make the line an
alexandrine, and Holinshed's marginal gloss, which
the text echoes, also lacks a verb: 'The harts of the
commons wholie bent to the duke of Lancaster'.
90 **Sirrah** A form of address to inferiors.
90 **sister** sister-in-law.
91 **presently** at once.
92 **take my ring** To guarantee the authority of
the request.
97 In Holinshed the duchess died later, through
grief at the death of her son. Transferred here, her
death adds to the tide of royal woes.

YORK God for His mercy! What a tide of woes
        Comes rushing on this woeful land at once!
        I know not what to do. I would to God,   100
        So my untruth had not provoked him to it,
        The king had cut off my head with my brother's.
        What, are there no posts despatched for Ireland?
        How shall we do for money for these wars?
        Come, sister – cousin I would say, pray pardon me.   105
        Go, fellow, get thee home. Provide some carts
        And bring away the armour that is there.
                                          [*Exit Servingman*]
        Gentlemen, will you go muster men?
        If I know how or which way to order these affairs
        Thus disorderly thrust into my hands   110
        Never believe me. Both are my kinsmen.
        T'one is my sovereign, whom both my oath
        And duty bids defend; t'other again
        Is my kinsman, whom the king hath wronged,
        Whom conscience and my kindred bids to right.   115
        Well, somewhat we must do. Come, cousin.
        I'll dispose of you. Gentlemen, go muster up your men
        And meet me presently at Berkeley Castle.

98 God] Qq; Heau'n F   99 Comes] Qq; Come F   100 God] Qq; heauen F   103 no] Q1; two Q2–5; *not in* F
107 SD] *Capell* (Servant); *not in* Qq, F   110 disorderly thrust] Qq, F; thrust disorderly *Steevens*   118 Castle] F; *not in* Qq

98 **God...mercy** An exclamation repeated by
York at 5.2.75, and used twice in *Woodstock*.
98 **tide** York anticipates the idea of Bullingbrook
as an overflowing river at 3.2.109–10.
101 **untruth** disloyalty.
102 In his despair York is presumably thinking
of his brother Gloucester, killed by beheading,
according to his widow at 1.2.21, but possibly he is
also thinking of Richard's threat to Gaunt at
2.1.123.
103 **What** A call to the attendants.
105 **sister** His distraction makes him think of the
queen as his dead sister-in-law. He refers to her
again at 119.
106 **home** The royal Household, which has just
been announced as abandoned.
106 **carts** Because the retainers have fled, all
York can command is their armour and weapons.
110 **disorderly thrust** Steevens conjectures
that the roughness of the metre results from a
transposition of these two words.

111–15 **Both...right** York's dilemma is a cause
of his dithering incompetence, just as his incompetence is a means of obscuring the need to make a
choice. His decision at 2.3.158 to stand 'as neuter'
is a tacit and subconscious act of choice in favour
of Bullingbrook. See p. 18 above.
112 **oath** Of allegiance to the king. See 4.1.209.
117 **dispose of** make arrangements for. York
registers the fact that the royal Household is
dispersed (60) and so the queen needs
accommodation.
118 **Berkeley Castle** The castle is by the town
of Berkeley, on the bank of the Severn. Edward II
was murdered there. F specifies the castle rather
than merely the town, probably because the castle
is mentioned at 2.3.53, although it also improves the
metre and may have been an accidental omission in
Q. Holinshed makes it clear that the castle is the
place referred to, not the town.

I should to Plashy too,
But time will not permit. All is uneven   120
And everything is left at six and seven.

Exeunt York and Queen

BUSHY The wind sits fair for news to go for Ireland
But none returns. For us to levy power
Proportionable to the enemy is all unpossible.

GREEN Besides, our nearness to the king in love   125
Is near the hate of those love not the king.

BAGOT And that's the wavering commons, for their love
Lies in their purses, and whoso empties them
By so much fills their hearts with deadly hate.

BUSHY Wherein the king stands generally condemned.   130

BAGOT If judgement lie in them then so do we,
Because we ever have been near the king.

GREEN Well, I will for refuge straight to Bristow Castle.
The Earl of Wiltshire is already there.

BUSHY Thither will I with you, for little office   135
Will the hateful commons perform for us,
Except like curs to tear us all to pieces.
Will you go along with us?

BAGOT No, I will to Ireland to his majesty.
Farewell. If heart's presages be not vain   140
We three here part that ne'er shall meet again.

BUSHY That's as York thrives to beat back Bullingbrook.

119–21] *Pope;* I should...permit: / All...seauen Qq, F   121 SD] *Rowe; Exeunt Duke, Qn man. Bush. Green,* Qq; *Exit* F   122 go for] Qq; go to F   124 unpossible] Qq; impossible F   127 that's] F; that is Qq   132 ever have been] Qq; haue beene euer F   133 Bristow] *Kittredge;* Brist. Qq; Bristoll F   137 to pieces] Q1; in pieces Q2–5, F

121 **at six and seven** Proverbial, from dicing. See Tilley A208.

122 **sits** is settled in one direction.

130 **Wherein** For emptying their purses.

131 **judgement...them** they are the judges. Parliament, in the form of king, lords and commons together, was regarded primarily as the High Court of the country. It was seen as a judiciary rather than as a legislative body.

133 **Bristow** F supplies the more modern spelling 'Bristoll', but Q1's 'Brist.' must be short for 'Bristow' as at 2.3.163.

134 In Holinshed Wiltshire goes with Green and Bushy. A supernumerary character, mentioned at 2.1.215 and 256 but never on stage, is thus written out of the scene.

135 **office** service.

136 **hateful** full of hate.

139 At 3.2.122 Richard indicates no knowledge of where Bagot may be. At 2.3.164 Bullingbrook says he is rumoured to be at Bristol, but if so he escapes the executions there to testify in the Parliament scene, 4.1. Holinshed records him as reaching Ireland (II, 497), being held in the Tower (II, 511) and testifying to Aumerle's activities as in 4.1. The historical Bagot was eventually pardoned by Parliament. Most editors conclude that Shakespeare was casual about his movements (Ure: 'sheer carelessness') but there is no error except in Bullingbrook's rumour about his presence in Bristol.

142 **beat back** As in battle – but with a suggestion of beating back the tide, like King Canute.

GREEN Alas, poor duke! The task he undertakes
          Is numbering sands and drinking oceans dry.
          Where one on his side fights thousands will fly.   145
          Farewell at once, for once, for all, and ever.
BUSHY Well, we may meet again.
BAGOT   I fear me never.

                                                        Exeunt

2.3 *Enter* BULLINGBROOK *and* NORTHUMBERLAND.

BULLINGBROOK How far is it, my lord, to Berkeley now?
NORTHUMBERLAND Believe me, noble lord,
          I am a stranger here in Gloucestershire.
          These high wild hills and rough uneven ways
          Draws out our miles and makes them wearisome.   5
          And yet your fair discourse hath been as sugar,
          Making the hard way sweet and delectable.
          But I bethink me what a weary way
          From Ravenspurgh to Cotshall will be found
          In Ross and Willoughby, wanting your company,   10
          Which I protest hath very much beguiled
          The tediousness and process of my travel.
          But theirs is sweetened with the hope to have
          The present benefit which I possess,
          And hope to joy is little less in joy   15
          Than hope enjoyed. By this the weary lords
          Shall make their way seem short as mine hath done
          By sight of what I have, your noble company.

146–7] Qq; *Bush. Farewell...euer. / Well,...againe.* F   147 SD] *Rowe; Exit* F; *not in* Qq   Act 2, Scene 3
0 SD BULLINGBROOK] *Hereford* Qq; *the Duke of Hereford* F   3 here] Q1, F; *not in* Q2–5   6 your] Qq; *our* F
9 Cotshall] Qq; *Cottshold* F; *Cotswold Hanmer*   14 which] Q1; *that* Q2–5, F

144 numbering...dry Both the earth and the water images are proverbial for impossible tasks (Tilley S91 and O9).

Act 2, Scene 3
2.3 The reintroduction of Bullingbrook is a scene largely invented from Holinshed's bare facts (II, 498).
4 These...hills The Cotswolds. As a northerner Northumberland would know his own much wilder Pennines better. Perhaps Shakespeare did not. He did know the Cotswolds.

6 fair discourse Bullingbrook's actual words are practical and almost monosyllabic. Northumberland is applying the flattery which he blamed Richard for at 2.1.241–2.
9 Cotshall The Cotswolds. Q1's spelling is repeated in *Wiv.* In *2H4* it is 'Cotsole'.
10 In By.
12 tediousness and process A doublet: the tedious process.
15 in joy enjoyable.
16 By this With this hope.

BULLINGBROOK Of much less value is my company
    Than your good words. But who comes here?   20

Enter HARRY PERCY.

NORTHUMBERLAND It is my son, young Harry Percy,
    Sent from my brother Worcester whencesoever.
    Harry, how fares your uncle?
PERCY I had thought, my lord, to have learned his health of you.
NORTHUMBERLAND Why, is he not with the queen?   25
PERCY No, my good lord, he hath forsook the court,
    Broken his staff of office and dispersed
    The Household of the king.
NORTHUMBERLAND   What was his reason?
    He was not so resolved when last we spake together.
PERCY Because your lordship was proclaimèd traitor.   30
    But he, my lord, is gone to Ravenspurgh
    To offer service to the Duke of Herford,
    And sent me over by Berkeley to discover
    What power the Duke of York had levied there,
    Then with directions to repair to Ravenspurgh.   35
NORTHUMBERLAND Have you forgot the Duke of Herford, boy?
PERCY No, my good lord, for that is not forgot
    Which ne'er I did remember. To my knowledge
    I never in my life did look on him.
NORTHUMBERLAND Then learn to know him now. This is the duke.   40
PERCY My gracious lord, I tender you my service,
    Such as it is, being tender, raw and young,
    Which elder days shall ripen and confirm
    To more approvèd service and desert.
BULLINGBROOK I thank thee, gentle Percy, and be sure   45

28–9] F; *North.* What...resolude, / When...togither? Qq   29 last we] Qq; we last F   35 directions] Qq; direction F   36 Herford, boy] Q3–5, F; Herefords boy Q1–2

---

22 **whencesoever** wherever Worcester may be.
26–30 Harry Hotspur reports the same news as Green at 2.2.58–61, with the same explanation for Worcester's defection.
36 boy The historical Hotspur was two years older than Bullingbrook. Shakespeare is preparing to set him in contrast with Bullingbrook's son Prince Hal, as at 5.3.1–12, where the king's complaint about his son's dissolute ways is delivered to Hotspur.

41 With such an offer Percy might be expected to kneel to Bullingbrook. At 50 however they shake hands. It is likely that at this point he does not make to the 'Duke' the gesture of loyalty he would make to the king.
41 tender See 1.1.32 n.
45–50 In *1H4* 1.3.251–4 Hotspur describes Bullingbrook's speech here as 'a candy deal of courtesy'. His 'candy' in that play echoes his father's 'sugar' at 6 in this scene.

I count myself in nothing else so happy
As in a soul remembering my good friends,
And as my fortune ripens with thy love
It shall be still thy true love's recompense.
My heart this covenant makes, my hand thus seals it.   50
NORTHUMBERLAND How far is it to Berkeley, and what stir
    Keeps good old York there with his men of war?
PERCY There stands the castle by yon tuft of trees,
    Manned with three hundred men as I have heard,
    And in it are the lords of York, Berkeley and Seymour,   55
    None else of name and noble estimate.

            Enter ROSS *and* WILLOUGHBY.

NORTHUMBERLAND Here come the lords of Ross and Willoughby,
    Bloody with spurring, fiery red with haste.
BULLINGBROOK Welcome, my lords. I wot your love pursues
    A banished traitor. All my treasury   60
    Is yet but unfelt thanks, which, more enriched,
    Shall be your love and labour's recompense.
ROSS Your presence makes us rich, most noble lord.
WILLOUGHBY And far surmounts our labour to attain it.
BULLINGBROOK Evermore thank's the exchequer of the poor,   65
    Which till my infant fortune comes to years
    Stands for my bounty. But who comes here?

            Enter BERKELEY.

NORTHUMBERLAND It is my lord of Berkeley, as I guess.
BERKELEY My lord of Herford, my message is to you.
BULLINGBROOK My lord, my answer is, to Lancaster,   70
    And I am come to seek that name in England,
    And I must find that title in your tongue

53 yon] Qq; yond F   56 SD] F; *not in* Qq   65 thank's] Q1–4; thankes Q5, F   67 SD] F; *not in* Qq

48 **my fortune** (1) spiritual luck, (2) material wealth. The latter sense is underlined in the next line with 'recompense'.

55 **Berkeley** The lord of the castle, named in Holinshed along with Seymour and the Bishop of Norwich (II, 498).

56 SD In Holinshed the northern lords join Bullingbrook at Ravenspurgh.

59 **wot** assume.

60–2 **All...recompense** An elaboration of the reference to 'fortune' in 48–9, emphasised by the repetition of 'recompense'.

63 **presence** Since the word is not only the antonym to 'absence' but has connotations of a royal Court, it contains a hint that the lords expect more than a financial return for their efforts.

65–7 **Evermore...bounty** Cited at *1H4* 1.3.253.

70 **Lancaster** Bullingbrook objects to Berkeley calling him by his old name, although he accepted Northumberland's use of 'Herford' at 36.

72 **title** Bullingbrook uses the term as a dignified form. Berkeley three lines later mocks his dignity by punning on 'tittle', a trifle.

Before I make reply to aught you say.
BERKELEY Mistake me not, my lord, 'tis not my meaning
 To raze one title of your honour out.   75
 To you, my lord, I come – what lord you will –
 From the most gracious regent of this land,
 The Duke of York, to know what pricks you on
 To take advantage of the absent time
 And fright our native peace with self-born arms?   80

      Enter YORK.

BULLINGBROOK I shall not need transport my words by you.
 Here comes his grace in person. My noble uncle. [*Kneels.*]
YORK Show me thy humble heart and not thy knee,
 Whose duty is deceivable and false.
BULLINGBROOK My gracious uncle –   85
YORK Tut, tut! Grace me no grace, nor uncle me no uncle.
 I am no traitor's uncle, and that word grace
 In an ungracious mouth is but profane.
 Why have those banished and forbidden legs
 Dared once to touch a dust of England's ground?   90
 But then, more why? Why have they dared to march
 So many miles upon her peaceful bosom,
 Frighting her pale-faced villages with war
 And ostentation of despisèd arms?
 Comest thou because the anointed king is hence?   95
 Why, foolish boy, the king is left behind
 And in my loyal bosom lies his power.

---

77 gracious regent of] Q1; ghorious of Q2; glorious of Q3–5, F 80 SD] F; *not in* Qq 82 SD] *Rowe; not in* Qq, F
86 no uncle] Qq; *not in* F 89 those] Qq; these F

75 **raze** erase, as with an inscription. See 3.1.25.

77 **gracious regent of** Q2 misprints Q1, Q3 guesses at a correction, and F copies Q3.

79 **the absent time** the king's absence. Bullingbrook's 'presence' has already been stressed at 63.

80 **our native peace** See 2.1.44 n. and 3.2.118 n.

80 **self-born** carried for self and not for country. With a pun on birth, presumably monstrous as at 2.2.64.

80 SD York's entry is another indication of his flustered state, since he has not waited for his messenger to return.

83 Bullingbrook's obeisance here is technically to show his 'duty' to the king's regent, and his elder kinsman. York doubts the honesty of either allegiance.

85 Bullingbrook begins a flowery speech which York in his fluster will not tolerate. From here on Bullingbrook speaks less and less until he has the crown.

88 **profane** 'Grace' had emphatically religious associations. To be in a state of grace was principally to be virtuous and truth-telling.

90 **a dust** a speck of dust.

94 **despisèd** contemptible (because self-born).

96 **the king...behind** An allusion to the concept of the king's two bodies. The king's role is filled by York. See p. 19 above.

Were I but now lord of such hot youth
As when brave Gaunt, thy father, and myself
Rescued the Black Prince, that young Mars of men,   100
From forth the ranks of many thousand French,
Oh then how quickly should this arm of mine,
Now prisoner to the palsy, chastise thee
And minister correction to thy fault!
BULLINGBROOK My gracious uncle, let me know my fault.   105
    On what condition stands it and wherein?
YORK Even in condition of the worst degree,
    In gross rebellion and detested treason.
    Thou art a banished man, and here art come
    Before the expiration of thy time   110
    In braving arms against thy sovereign.
BULLINGBROOK As I was banished, I was banished Herford;
    But as I come, I come for Lancaster.
    And, noble uncle, I beseech your grace
    Look on my wrongs with an indifferent eye.   115
    You are my father, for methinks in you
    I see old Gaunt alive. Oh then, my father,
    Will you permit that I shall stand condemned
    A wandering vagabond, my rights and royalties
    Plucked from my arms perforce and given away   120
    To upstart unthrifts? Wherefore was I born?
    If that my cousin king be king in England
    It must be granted I am Duke of Lancaster.
    You have a son, Aumerle, my noble cousin.
    Had you first died and he been thus trod down   125
    He should have found his uncle Gaunt a father
    To rouse his wrongs and chase them to the bay.

98 now] Qq; now the F   111 thy] Q1, F; my Q2–5   116 for] Q1–2, F; or Q3–5   117 my] Q1, F; *not in* Q2–5
122 in] Q1; of Q2–5, F   124 cousin] Qq; Kinsman F

99–101 There is no obvious source for this claim.
It contrasts the amity of the older generation of
brothers with the animosity of the younger
generation of cousins which is causing York's
difficulty.

103 prisoner...palsy The historical York had
hemiplegia. The palsy or shaking sickness has
imprisoned York as all the French army could
not.

106 On what...it What law have I broken.

107 in condition York adapts Bullingbrook's
legal use into its modern sense.

111 braving flaunting. 'Bravery' meant striking
costume or manner.

113 for (1) as, (2) to claim.

115 indifferent impartial.

119 my rights and royalties See 2.1.190.
Bullingbrook is echoing York's own words of
protest to Richard.

121 unthrifts spendthrifts.

122–3 Again Bullingbrook echoes York's own
argument to Richard about fair succession at
2.1.195–9.

127 rouse...bay A hunting metaphor: to start

I am denied to sue my livery here,
And yet my letters patents give me leave.
My father's goods are all distrained and sold, 130
And these and all are all amiss employed.
What would you have me do? I am a subject,
And I challenge law. Attorneys are denied me,
And therefore personally I lay my claim
To my inheritance of free descent. 135

NORTHUMBERLAND The noble duke hath been too much abused.

ROSS It stands your grace upon to do him right.

WILLOUGHBY Base men by his endowments are made great.

YORK My lords of England, let me tell you this:
I have had feeling of my cousin's wrongs 140
And laboured all I could to do him right.
But in this kind to come, in braving arms,
Be his own carver and cut out his way,
To find out right with wrong? It may not be.
And you that do abet him in this kind 145
Cherish rebellion and are rebels all.

NORTHUMBERLAND The noble duke hath sworn his coming is
But for his own, and for the right of that
We all have strongly sworn to give him aid.
And let him ne'er see joy that breaks that oath. 150

YORK Well, well. I see the issue of these arms.
I cannot mend it, I must needs confess,
Because my power is weak and all ill-left.

133 I] Qq; *not in* F   144 wrong] Qq; *wrongs* F   150 ne'er] Q3–5; *neuer* Q1–2; neu'r F

and drive a beast from its cover and pursue it until
it is cornered. 'Bay' comes from the barking of the
hounds who have cornered the prey.
128–9 Bullingbrook again echoes York at
2.1.202–4. The phrases are from Holinshed.
129 letters patents The phrase is as in
Holinshed. The letters were given to Bullingbrook
by Richard when he shortened the term of
banishment.
130 distrained seized by law.
132–3 I am...law In Daniel's *The Civil Wars*,
I, 91, Bullingbrook dreams of a weeping Genius of
England, and says 'I am thy Champion and I seeke
my right.' She replies that this is the pretence of an
ambitious man.
133 challenge law claim my legal rights.
135 of through.
137 stands...upon is incumbent on you.

138 endowments Gifts that are properly
Bullingbrook's.
142 braving arms See 111. York is repeating
himself.
143 Be...carver Kings did not carve their own
food. See *Ham.* 1.3.19–20: 'He may not, as
unvalued persons do, / Carve for himself.'
144 To find...wrong To get justice through
injustice. The end does not justify the means.
147–9 This is the first instance of Northumberland speaking for Bullingbrook. Holinshed (II, 498)
tells how Bullingbrook swore an oath to his
followers. Bullingbrook himself says the same to
Richard at 3.3.195. See *1H4* 4.3.60–5.
153 all ill-left everything left in poor condition.
Judging from 2.2.104 it was also poorly financed. In
Holinshed (II, 498) York had ample forces but could
not trust them to fight against Bullingbrook.

But if I could, by Him that gave me life
I would attach you all and make you stoop 155
Unto the sovereign mercy of the king.
But since I cannot, be it known unto you
I do remain as neuter. So fare you well,
Unless you please to enter in the castle
And there repose you for this night. 160
BULLINGBROOK An offer, uncle, that we will accept.
But we must win your grace to go with us
To Bristow Castle, which they say is held
By Bushy, Bagot and their complices,
The caterpillars of the commonwealth, 165
Which I have sworn to weed and pluck away.
YORK It may be I will go with you, but yet I'll pause,
For I am loath to break our country's laws.
Nor friends nor foes to me welcome you are.
Things past redress are now with me past care. 170

Exeunt

2.4 *Enter Earl of* SALISBURY *and a Welsh* CAPTAIN.

CAPTAIN My lord of Salisbury, we have stayed ten days
And hardly kept our countrymen together,

157 unto] Q1; to Q2–5, F   Act 2, Scene 4   0 SD] QQ; *Enter Salisbury, and a Captaine.* F

155 attach arrest.
155 stoop kneel for forgiveness. See 1.1.74 n.
158 as neuter (1) neutral, (2) unproductive, helpless.
159–60 York's afterthought changes him from Bullingbrook's enemy and sovereign to his host.
162 win persuade. Bullingbrook does not hesitate to push York further once he has begun to weaken.
164 Bagot See 2.2.139 n.
165 This term for the flatterers, besides its aptness to the image of England as a garden which appears in Gaunt at 2.1.42 and in 3.4, was a kind of catchphrase in the later sixteenth century. With precedents in the Bible (Isa. 33.14, Jer. 41.14, 27), caterpillars are spoken of in Harrison's *Description of England*, published as a part of Holinshed in 1587. The phrase is used in *An Alarum for Usurers* (1584) about usurers, in *The Jew of Malta* (1589) about money-minded friars, and in *A Knack to Know a Knave* (1592), a play featuring the clown Will Kemp which Shakespeare might have known, where its application is very similar to Bullingbrook's. Ironically the phrase also appeared on the title page of Stephen Gosson's *School of Abuse*,

Conteining a pleasaunt invective against Poets, Pipers, Plaiers, Jesters, and such like Caterpillars of a Commonwelth. Shakespeare also used the term with a fairly broad reference in *2H6* 3.1.90 and 4.4.37. With these precedents Shakespeare need not have been heavily indebted to *Woodstock*, where Bagot and Green are called 'Cankers! Caterpillars!' (516) and where the citizens are called caterpillars at 1638. By a false etymology 'caterpillar' was related to the French 'piller' and 'pillage'. See 2.1.246 n.
166 weed and pluck At 3.4.50 the Gardener refers to the flatterers as 'weeds' which Bullingbrook has 'plucked up root and all'.
169 Nor...nor Neither...nor.

Act 2, Scene 4
2.4 Largely from Holinshed, II, 499.
0 SD *a Welsh* CAPTAIN Bullingbrook's reference at 3.1.43 to Glendower has led editors to assume that this captain is Glendower. Holinshed twice refers to him as 'capteine' of the Welsh soldiers.
1 stayed waited.
1 ten days Fourteen, according to Holinshed. See 1.3.159 n.

And yet we hear no tidings from the king.
Therefore we will disperse ourselves. Farewell.
SALISBURY Stay yet another day, thou trusty Welshman.   5
The king reposeth all his confidence in thee.
CAPTAIN 'Tis thought the king is dead. We will not stay.
The bay trees in our country are all withered
And meteors fright the fixèd stars of heaven.
The pale faced moon looks bloody on the earth,   10
And lean looked prophets whisper fearful change.
Rich men look sad and ruffians dance and leap,
The one in fear to lose what they enjoy,
The other to enjoy by rage and war.
These signs forerun the death or fall of kings.   15
Farewell. Our countrymen are gone and fled
As well assured Richard their king is dead.   *Exit*
SALISBURY Ah, Richard! With the eyes of heavy mind
I see thy glory like a shooting star
Fall to the base earth from the firmament.   20
Thy sun sets weeping in the lowly west,
Witnessing storms to come, woe and unrest.
Thy friends are fled to wait upon thy foes
And crossly to thy good all fortune goes.   *Exit*

---

8 are all] Q1 ; all are Q2–5, F   15 or fall] Q1 ; *not in* Q2–5, F   17 SD] F; *not in* Qq   18 the] Q1 ; *not in* Q2–5, F
24 SD] F; *not in* Qq

3 yet still.

5–6 A paraphrase of Holinshed, II, 499.

8 Holinshed added a note on this curiosity to the 1587 edition of his history. Shakespeare's use of it confirms that it was the second edition of Holinshed he consulted. Holinshed in fact records that before Richard went to Ireland the bay trees in the west withered and then grew green again, an even more remarkable occurrence which, however, lacks the ominous point of the Welsh Captain's account. A crown of bay leaves was a Roman symbol of victory and immortal reputation.

9 Daniel has four stanzas on the omens at this time (the end of I, 114–17).

9 meteors unfixed stars.

11 prophets soothsayers (not Biblical prophets).

13 enjoy possess.

19 shooting star A simile developed from 'meteors' at 9, and hinting at the Phaëton image of 3.3.178.

21 Besides the thematic image of the king as a sun, now watery, this line has been taken to allude to the emblem engraved on Richard's cloak on the effigy in Westminster Abbey, a sunburst shining from clouds. See illustration 5, p. 26 above. It is not, however, easily visible on the tomb, and would certainly not have been visible without artificial light in Shakespeare's day.

22 Witnessing Forecasting, indicating.

23 wait upon serve, offer allegiance to.

24 crossly adversely. See 'crosses', 2.2.79.

3.1 *Enter* BULLINGBROOK, YORK, NORTHUMBERLAND, ROSS, PERCY, WILLOUGHBY, *with* BUSHY *and* GREEN *prisoners.*

BULLINGBROOK Bring forth these men.
    Bushy and Green, I will not vex your souls,
    Since presently your souls must part your bodies,
    With too much urging your pernicious lives,
    For 'twere no charity. Yet to wash your blood   5
    From off my hands, here in the view of men
    I will unfold some causes of your deaths.
    You have misled a prince, a royal king,
    A happy gentleman in blood and lineaments
    By you unhappied and disfigured clean.   10
    You have in manner with your sinful hours
    Made a divorce betwixt his queen and him,
    Broke the possession of a royal bed
    And stained the beauty of a fair queen's cheeks
    With tears drawn from her eyes by your foul wrongs. 15
    Myself, a prince by fortune of my birth,
    Near to the king in blood and near in love
    Till you did make him misinterpret me,
    Have stooped my neck under your injuries
    And sighed my English breath in foreign clouds,   20
    Eating the bitter bread of banishment

Act 3, Scene 1 0 SD] F; *Enter Duke of Hereford, Yorke, Northumberland, Bushie and Greene prisoners.* Qq 7 deaths]
Q1, F; death Q2–5 15 by] Q1; with Q2–5, F 18 you] Q1, F; they Q2–5

Act 3, Scene 1

3.1 The basic material for this scene is in Holinshed, II, 498 and 518. The absence of the Earl of Wiltshire (see 2.2.134) has led some editors to assume that Shakespeare confused him with Bagot, which is unlikely. See 2.2.139 n.

3 part leave, separate from.

4 urging emphasising, persuading (you of).

5–6 to wash…hands to make the executions a matter of justice, not revenge. See 5.6.50, and Richard's reference to Pilate at 4.1.238.

7 causes legal reasons.

9 happy fortunate, gifted.

10 unhappied See p. 17 above.

10 clean completely.

11 in manner in a way.

12 divorce breach, separation. Bullingbrook makes it clear by the words 'in manner' at 11 that he is using the term metaphorically.

13 A fairly specific extension of the breach implied in 'divorce'. Commentators have variously taken this allegation, not detailed in Holinshed, to mean adultery, homosexuality, or a relic from an old play. Every similar accusation levelled by one character against another in the play, for instance between Mowbray and Bullingbrook in 1.1, and by York to Richard at 2.1.167–8, includes a few extraneous charges. Holinshed says of Richard's time, 'there reigned abundantlie the filthie sinne of leacherie and fornication, with abhominable adulterie, speciallie in the king' (II, 508). This first stage in Bullingbrook's accusation relates to sin, and includes the destruction of marital concord. The injustices come second.

16 fortune See 2.3.48.

19 stooped Compare 2.3.155.

20 clouds (1) of breath, (2) in the sky. Both signify obscurity.

21 bitter…banishment A phrase from 1 Kings 22.27. For the imagery of sweet and sour see p. 30 above.

Whilst you have fed upon my signories,
Disparked my parks and felled my forest woods,
From my own windows torn my household coat,
Razed out my imprese, leaving me no sign   25
Save men's opinions and my living blood
To show the world I am a gentleman.
This and much more, much more than twice all this,
Condemns you to the death. See them delivered over
To execution and the hand of death.   30

BUSHY More welcome is the stroke of death to me
Than Bullingbrook to England. Lords, farewell.

GREEN My comfort is that heaven will take our souls
And plague injustice with the pains of hell.

BULLINGBROOK My Lord Northumberland, see them dispatched.   35
                    [*Exeunt Northumberland and prisoners*]
Uncle, you say the queen is at your house.
For God's sake fairly let her be intreated.
Tell her I send to her my kind commends.
Take special care my greetings be delivered.

YORK A gentleman of mine I have dispatched   40
With letters of your love to her at large.

BULLINGBROOK Thanks, gentle uncle. Come, lords, away,
To fight with Glendower and his complices.
A while to work, and after holiday.
                                             Exeunt

---

22 Whilst] Q1; While Q2–5, F   24 my own] Q1–2; mine owne Q3–5, F   25 Razed] F; Rac't Qq   25 imprese]
Q6; impreze Qq; Impresse F   32 Lords, farewell] Qq; *not in* F   35 SD] *Capell; not in* Qq, F   37 God's] Qq;
Heauens F

22 **signories** properties of which I am lord.
23 **Disparked my parks** Converted my hunting preserves to other uses.
24 Took out the glass showing the Bullingbrook crest.
25 **Razed** Berkeley's term at 2.3.75.
25 **imprese** Emblems painted on wood in versions of the household coat-of-arms. Probably a disyllable, judging by the metre, although the Italian plural requires three syllables. Both Q1 and F offer forms of the word which make it an anglicised singular when a plural is clearly indicated.
29 **the death** judicial execution.
33–4 Compare Gaunt's argument at 1.2.6.
36 **the queen...house** See 2.2.117 n.
37 **intreated** treated.
38 **commends** regards.

41 **at large** in full.
42–4 The existence of rhyming words for 42 and 44, and the lack of any other direct reference in the play to the subject of 43, have prompted the assumption that 43 may be a late insertion, evidence of belated preparation for *1H4* where Glendower appears. Holinshed says that Glendower supported Richard in Flint Castle and escaped to Wales when Richard surrendered. At the beginning of Bullingbrook's next scene, 3.3, before Flint Castle, he refers to the Welsh army's disbanding as if he had just heard of it. If the Welsh Captain of 2.4 is meant for Glendower, then 43 must be an intrusion. The idea of 'holiday' has a rather better point if the work is the weeding of the caterpillars. As the only reference to Glendower in the whole play, it may be a very late insertion indeed, and possibly not even authorial.

3.2 *Drums, flourish and colours. Enter* RICHARD, AUMERLE, CARLISLE *and soldiers.*

RICHARD Barkloughly Castle call they this at hand?
AUMERLE Yea, my lord. How brooks your grace the air
　　　　After your late tossing on the breaking seas?
RICHARD Needs must I like it well. I weep for joy
　　　　To stand upon my kingdom once again.　　　　　　　　　5
　　　　Dear earth, I do salute thee with my hand,
　　　　Though rebels wound thee with their horses' hooves.
　　　　As a long-parted mother with her child
　　　　Plays fondly with her tears and smiles in meeting,
　　　　So weeping, smiling, greet I thee, my earth,　　　　　10
　　　　And do thee favours with my royal hands.
　　　　Feed not thy sovereign's foe, my gentle earth,
　　　　Nor with thy sweets comfort his ravenous sense
　　　　But let thy spiders that suck up thy venom
　　　　And heavy-gaited toads lie in their way,　　　　　　15
　　　　Doing annoyance to the treacherous feet
　　　　Which with usurping steps do trample thee.
　　　　Yield stinging nettles to mine enemies,
　　　　And when they from thy bosom pluck a flower
　　　　Guard it, I pray thee, with a lurking adder　　　　　20

Act 3, Scene 2　0 SD] F; *Enter the King, Aumerle, Carleil, &c* Qq　1 they] Q1; you Q2–5, F　11 favours] Q1; fauour Q2–5, F

Act 3, Scene 2
3.2 The material for this scene is in Holinshed, II, 499.

1 Barkloughly Harlech, misprinted 'Barclow-lie' in Holinshed. There is a possible confusion with Berkeley, spelt 'Barkley'.

2 brooks enjoys. Usually with the sense of suffering or enduring.

2 grace An honorific usually applied to dukes as at 3.3.10, but not always specific. Kings might equally be addressed as majesty, highness or lord.

3 seas Aumerle is not only reminding us of Ireland but using the elemental imagery. He may be using the water image deliberately, since there is a hint of Bullingbrook in 'brooks', an unusual word for its context.

4 weep The first sign of Richard's conversion from fire to water. See p. 23 above.

9 fondly (1) affectionately, (2) foolishly.

13 sweets The antithesis to poisons, as suggested in 'venom' (14) and 'nettles' (18).

13 comfort A term linked with 'sweet' throughout the play. It may be associated with 'comfit', a sweet offered at the end of a feast.

13 ravenous sense strong appetite.

14 venom York is the first to use this word at 2.1.19 of Richard's listening to flattering sounds. It is then used by Richard of Ireland's human snakes (2.1.157), the other rebels.

15 heavy-gaited slow moving. With a hint in 'heavy' of closeness to the earth.

17 usurping Used specifically of the feet which occupy the piece of earth on which the toad squats; but the word also predicts the intentions of the rebels and their treachery towards the crown.

20 Guard it (1) Watch over it, (2) trim it with a braid.

20 adder Richard reverts to snakes and their venom as creatures who use the bitter or sour products of the earth, but he does so in differing ways. See 129, 131. The idea is proverbial (Tilley s585).

Whose double tongue may with a mortal touch
Throw death upon thy sovereign's enemies.
Mock not my senseless conjuration, lords.
This earth shall have a feeling and these stones
Prove armèd soldiers ere her native king   25
Shall falter under foul rebellion's arms.

CARLISLE Fear not, my lord. That power that made you king
Hath power to keep you king in spite of all.
The means that heavens yield must be embraced
And not neglected. Else heaven would   30
And we will not. Heavens offer, we refuse
The proffered means of succour and redress.

AUMERLE He means, my lord, that we are too remiss
Whilst Bullingbrook through our security
Grows strong and great in substance and in power.   35

RICHARD Discomfortable cousin, knowest thou not
That when the searching eye of heaven is hid
Behind the globe and lights the lower world
Then thieves and robbers range abroad unseen
In murders and in outrage boldly here.   40
But when from under this terrestrial ball
He fires the proud tops of the eastern pines
And darts his light through every guilty hole
Then murders, treasons and detested sins,

---

26 rebellion's] Q1–2; rebellious Q3–5, F   29–32] Qq; *not in* F   31 will] Q1–2; would Q3–5   32 succour] *Pope*; succors
Qq   35 power] Qq; friends F   38 and] *Hanmer*; that Qq, F   40 boldly] *Hudson*; bouldy Q1; bloudy Q2–5, F
41 this] Q1, F; his Q2–5   43 light] Qq; Lightning F

21 **double** forked.
21 **mortal** killing.
23 **senseless conjuration** appeal to the unfeeling earth.
24–5 **these stones...soldiers** A paraphrase of
Luke 3.8 and 19.40.
25 **native** home born. Richard was known as
Richard of Bordeaux because he was born there. See
5.6.33.
27–32 For an examination of Carlisle's Biblical
role in this scene see Roy Battenhouse, 'Tudor
doctrine and the tragedy of *Richard II*', *Rice
University Studies* 60 (1974), 31–53, esp. pp. 40–3.
29–32 F's omission of Carlisle's compact theo-
logising diminishes the mildly comic point of
Aumerle's translation.
30 **Else** Otherwise.
31 **we will not** we deny the will of heaven.
33 **we...remiss** Aumerle's point has been

variously put in subsequent centuries as 'Praise the
Lord and keep your powder dry', or 'Praise the
Lord and pass the ammunition.'
34 **security** overconfidence. See 1.3.97 and
2.1.266 n., and *Mac.* 3.5.32–3: 'security...mortals'
chiefest enemy'.
36 **Discomfortable** Bringing discomfort. See
13 n. and 75 n.
37 **the searching...heaven** A phrase used by
Gaunt of Bullingbrook's exile at 1.3.274–5. See for
Richard's emblem of the clouded sun 2.4.21, and for
a Biblical precedent Job 29.13–17.
38 **and** Hanmer's emendation makes good sense
of what was probably a memorial slip by Q1's
Compositor A from the syntax of the previous line.
40 **boldly** Hudson's conjectural emendation of
Q1 fits the context more closely than Q2's 'bloudy'.
41 **this...ball** i.e. the globe of 38.

The cloak of night being plucked from off their backs,   45
Stand bare and naked, trembling at themselves?
So when this thief, this traitor, Bullingbrook,
Who all this while hath revelled in the night
Whilst we were wandering with the antipodes
Shall see us rising in our throne the east   50
His treasons will sit blushing in his face,
Not able to endure the sight of day,
But self-affrighted tremble at his sin.
Not all the water in the rough rude sea
Can wash the balm off from an anointed king.   55
The breath of worldly men cannot depose
The deputy elected by the Lord.
For every man that Bullingbrook hath pressed
To lift shrewd steel against our golden crown
God for His Richard hath in heavenly pay   60
A glorious angel. Then if angels fight
Weak men must fall, for heaven still guards the right.

Enter SALISBURY.

Welcome, my lord. How far off lies your power?
SALISBURY Nor near nor farther off, my gracious lord,
Than this weak arm. Discomfort guides my tongue   65
And bids me speak of nothing but despair.

49] Qq; *not in* F   53 tremble] Q1, F; trembled Q2–5   55 off] Qq; *not in* F   60 God] Qq; Heauen F   63 Welcome]
F; *King* Welcome Qq

47 thief Bullingbrook's conduct is more like a traitor than a thief except as the usurper of Richard's sun image and Richard's suspicion that it is the crown which is to be stolen.

49 While the sun was on the other side of the globe. F's omission of this line may be through accident or possibly incomprehension as a result of Q's slip in printing 'that' at 38.

50 east Richard has sailed in from the west.

51 blushing For shame, and reflecting the angry red of the morning sun.

54–5 water...king Besides the association of Bullingbrook with water, there are Biblical echoes from 1 Sam. 24.6, and 26.9, and Rom. 12.4.

55 balm consecrating oil. With medicinal connotation.

56 breath...men Compare Bullingbrook on the breath of kings, 1.3.214.

57 deputy See 1.2.38.

58 pressed impressed, conscripted.

59 shrewd injurious.

59 golden crown The contrast of steel with gold leads Richard on to gold as money, in 'pay' and 'angel', a gold coin of which there were two to a pound sterling. It replaced the 'noble' which Richard puns on at 5.5.67.

61 a glorious angel Richard is invoking Matt. 26.53. In 52 Jesus says that they who take the sword shall perish with the sword. Richard's contrast between Bullingbrook's conscripts and God's paid angels has a touch of materialism which serves to intensify its impracticality.

62 Weak men The stress is on 'men'.

62 SD Salisbury is not named in Holinshed as the bearer of this news, but 2.4 makes him the obvious character.

63 How far off Richard comes straight to the point – ironically, in the wake of his claim to have angelic support.

64 Nor near No nearer.

One day too late, I fear me, noble lord,
Hath clouded all thy happy days on earth.
Oh call back yesterday, bid time return
And thou shalt have twelve thousand fighting men.   70
Today, today, unhappy day too late
O'erthrows thy joys, friends, fortune and thy state,
For all the Welshmen, hearing thou wert dead,
Are gone to Bullingbrook, dispersed and fled.
AUMERLE Comfort, my liege. Why looks your grace so pale?   75
RICHARD But now the blood of twenty thousand men
Did triumph in my face, and they are fled,
And till so much blood thither come again
Have I not reason to look pale and dead?
All souls that will be safe fly from my side,   80
For time hath set a blot upon my pride.
AUMERLE Comfort, my liege. Remember who you are.
RICHARD I had forgot myself. Am I not king?
Awake, thou coward! Majesty, thou sleepest.
Is not the king's name twenty thousand names?   85
Arm, arm, my name! A puny subject strikes
At thy great glory. Look not to the ground.
Ye favourites of a king, are we not high?
High be our thoughts. I know my uncle York
Hath power enough to serve our turn. But who comes
here?   90

Enter SCROOPE.

SCROOPE More health and happiness betide my liege
Than can my care-tuned tongue deliver him.
RICHARD My ear is open and my heart prepared.
The worst is worldly loss thou canst unfold.

---

67 me] Q1–2; my Q3–5, F   84 coward! Majesty] *This edn*; coward Maiesty Q1; coward, Maiesty Q2–5; sluggard
Maiestie F   85 twenty] Qq; fortie F   90] Qq; Hath...turne. / But...here? F

67 **One...late** Arriving one day too late.
75 **Comfort** Aumerle is responding directly to
Richard's 'Discomfortable cousin' at 36. See 204–8.
76 **twenty thousand** See 1.3.159 n.
76–81 A cross-rhymed quatrain and a couplet, as
at 2.1.9–14.
79 **pale and dead** A doublet: deathly pale.
81 **blot** stain, slur. See 4.1.236.
84 **coward! Majesty** Some punctuation needs

to be supplied to pick up the implication of majesty
as a thing separate from the king's body, as
Northumberland sees it at 2.1.295.
90 SD **SCROOPE** The brother of the Earl of
Wiltshire. See 122 below.
92 **care-tuned** (1) tuned by sorrow, (2) tuned to
the note of sorrow.
92 **deliver** (1) bring, (2) tell.

Say, is my kingdom lost? Why, 'twas my care   95
And what loss is it to be rid of care?
Strives Bullingbrook to be as great as we,
Greater he shall not be. If he serve God
We'll serve Him too, and be his fellow so.
Revolt our subjects? That we cannot mend.   100
They break their faith to God as well as us.
Cry woe, destruction, ruin and decay.
The worst is death, and death will have his day.

SCROOPE   Glad am I that your highness is so armed
To bear the tidings of calamity.   105
Like an unseasonable stormy day
Which makes the silver rivers drown their shores
As if the world were all dissolved to tears,
So high above his limits swells the rage
Of Bullingbrook, covering your fearful land   110
With hard bright steel and hearts harder than steel.
Whitebeards have armed their thin and hairless scalps
Against thy majesty, boys with women's voices
Strive to speak big, and clap their female joints
In stiff unwieldy arms against thy crown.   115
Thy very beadsmen learn to bend their bows
Of double-fatal yew against thy state.
Yea, distaff women manage rusty bills
Against thy seat. Both young and old rebel
And all goes worse than I have power to tell.   120

---

102 and] Qq; Losse F   107 makes] Q1–2; make Q3–5, F   110 covering] Qq, F *(corr.)*; coueting F *(uncorr.)*
112 Whitebeards] Qq; White Beares F   113 boys] Q1; and boies Q2–5, F   117 yew] *Hanmer*; ewe Q1–2; wo Q3–5;
Eugh F

95 care trouble, responsibility. Richard picks up Scroope's 'care' from 92, and plays on it. He repeats the word-play to Bullingbrook at 4.1.194–8.

99 his Bullingbrook's.

100 Revolt our subjects? Do our subjects revolt?

104 armed prepared. With a possible sarcasm about military preparedness.

106–11 The simile brings together the storms (2.1.264), clouds (2.4.21–2), and the elemental imagery of Bullingbrook as water.

109 his Both 'his' (Bullingbrook's) and 'its' (rage).

109 rage (1) flood, (2) anger.

110 Bullingbrook This is the only explicit use

in the play of Daniel's punning use of 'brook' (*Civil Wars*, II, 8).

111 steel A reminder of the contrast with gold 'angels'.

112 Whitebeards See Textual Analysis, p. 190 below.

116 beadsmen Pensioners paid to say prayers.

117 double-fatal Yew is a poison as well as the wood used for longbows.

118 distaff A stick used in spinning wool.

118 rusty Because of the native peace. See 2.3.80.

118 bills Old-fashioned bladed longsticks used by the parish guard.

119 seat (1) position, (2) throne.

RICHARD Too well, too well thou tell'st a tale so ill.
　　　　　Where is the Earl of Wiltshire, where is Bagot,
　　　　　What is become of Bushy, where is Green,
　　　　　That they have let the dangerous enemy
　　　　　Measure our confines with such peaceful steps?　　　125
　　　　　If we prevail their heads shall pay for it.
　　　　　I warrant they have made peace with Bullingbrook.
SCROOPE Peace have they made with him indeed, my lord.
RICHARD Oh villains, vipers, damned without redemption!
　　　　　Dogs, easily won to fawn on any man!　　　　　　130
　　　　　Snakes in my heart blood warmed, that sting my heart!
　　　　　Three Judases, each one thrice worse than Judas!
　　　　　Would they make peace? Terrible hell
　　　　　Make war upon their spotted souls for this!
SCROOPE Sweet love I see, changing his property,　　　　　135
　　　　　Turns to the sourest and most deadly hate.
　　　　　Again uncurse their souls. Their peace is made
　　　　　With heads and not with hands. Those whom you curse
　　　　　Have felt the worst of death's destroying wound
　　　　　And lie full low, graved in the hollow ground.　　　140
AUMERLE Is Bushy, Green, and the Earl of Wiltshire dead?
SCROOPE Ay, all of them at Bristow lost their heads.
AUMERLE Where is the duke my father with his power?

133–4] Qq; Would...make warre / Vpon...this Offence. F　　135 love] Q1–2, F; loue's Q3–4; Ioue's Q5　　138 heads]
Q1, F; head Q2–5　　139 wound] Qq; hand F　　142 Ay] Q1 (I); Ye Q2; Yea Q3–5, F

122–3 The four leading flatterers were on the
Council of Regency under York while Richard was
in Ireland. Richard's naming of Bagot here confirms
that he is not at Bristol as Bullingbrook conjectured
(2.3.164). His travels are obscure until he appears
a prisoner in 4.1. From 141 Aumerle knows that
Bagot was not at Bristol with the others. Richard
seems to know the same, judging by his reference
to only three Judases at 132. An explanation of
Bagot's separate fate is needed between 122 and 132,
and its absence may reflect some incomplete
adjustments to the movements of the minor figures
evident in 2.2.

125 Measure our confines Travel over (with a
hint of possessive measuring) the limits of our
territories.

131 The allusion is to the story of a farmer who
warmed a frozen snake back to life by putting it
under his shirt, and was stung.

132 Three See 122–3 n.

132 Judases Both here and at 4.1.170 it is
possible to overstate the implication that Richard is
comparing himself to Christ by calling his betrayers
Judases. It was a familiar term of abuse in such
circumstances.

133 Would they Did they wish to.

134 spotted (1) sinful (as in 'blot' at 81), and
(2) like the skin of snakes.

135 his property its essence, essential feature.
With a possible play on possessiveness.

138 hands Hands were used in swearing oaths
of loyalty, and in war. See 3.3.36.

139 wound F's 'hand' is most likely a compositor's memory of 'hands' in the previous line. It loses
the rhyme with the homophonic 'ground'.

140 graved (1) in a grave, (2) engraved (like a
memorial).

140 hollow ground The first reference to the
earth as hollow. At 153 it is also barren.

RICHARD No matter where. Of comfort no man speak.
    Let's talk of graves, of worms and epitaphs,   145
    Make dust our paper and with rainy eyes
    Write sorrow on the bosom of the earth.
    Let's choose executors and talk of wills.
    And yet not so, for what can we bequeath
    Save our deposèd bodies to the ground?   150
    Our lands, our lives and all are Bullingbrook's,
    And nothing can we call our own but death,
    And that small model of the barren earth
    Which serves as paste and cover to our bones.
    For God's sake let us sit upon the ground   155
    And tell sad stories of the death of kings,
    How some have been deposed, some slain in war,
    Some haunted by the ghosts they have deposed,
    Some poisoned by their wives, some sleeping killed,
    All murdered. For within the hollow crown   160
    That rounds the mortal temples of a king
    Keeps Death his court, and there the antic sits
    Scoffing his state and grinning at his pomp,
    Allowing him a breath, a little scene
    To monarchise, be feared and kill with looks,   165
    Infusing him with self and vain conceit
    As if this flesh which walls about our life
    Were brass impregnable, and humoured thus

---

155 God's] Qq; Heauens F

146 **rainy eyes** Richard's tears mark a further step in his transition from sun to water. The image suggests tears writing in dry earth.

148–50 See p. 24 above.

153 **model** Used in different senses in the play, at 1.2.28, 3.4.42 and 5.1.11. All four uses share the idea of the model as a microcosm or miniature of what it represents. Here its principal meaning is of a portion, the outline of the body in the grave covering.

154 **paste and cover** a pastry covering, a piecrust. The earth covering a grave (a 'model') was sometimes compared to a piecrust.

155 **the ground** The location for graves, worms and epitaphs (145). In the whole play, apart from Gaunt in his sick chair, the king is the only person to sit. Richard has been seated on the throne in 1.1 and 1.3. Bullingbrook takes his seat after 4.1. Here Richard evidently does sit down, judging from Carlisle's reproof at 178, thus giving up his 'state'. It is doubtful if the courtiers sit with him, since they

maintain the respectful posture of staying hat in hand (171). Richard is the only one to despair, and his sitting while the others remain standing affirms his isolation and his responsibility for his fall.

156 **sad** solemn, serious, as at funerals.

158 **deposed** deprived of life.

160 **hollow** Richard's adjective links the crown with the earth (see 140).

162 **antic** (1) clown, (2) gargoyle.

163 **Scoffing** Ridiculing.

163 **state** (1) regal status, (2) throne (in the 'court' of 162).

164 **scene** picture. With a hint of acting, also implied in the 'antic' clown.

165 **monarchise** act the monarch.

166 **self...conceit** self-made and vain concept of himself.

167–8 **flesh...brass** See Job 6.12: 'Is my flesh of brasse?'

168 **humoured thus** thus wilfully inclined. The subject of the sentence is still death.

Comes at the last and with a little pin
Bores through his castle wall and farewell king!   170
Cover your heads, and mock not flesh and blood
With solemn reverence. Throw away respect,
Tradition, form and ceremonious duty,
For you have but mistook me all this while.
I live with bread like you, feel want,   175
Taste grief, need friends. Subjected thus,
How can you say to me I am a king?

CARLISLE My lord, wise men ne'er sit and wail their woes,
But presently prevent the ways to wail.
To fear the foe, since fear oppresseth strength,   180
Gives, in your weakness, strength unto your foe,
And so your follies fight against your self.
Fear and be slain. No worse can come to fight,
And fight and die is death destroying death
Where fearing dying pays death servile breath.   185

AUMERLE My father hath a power. Enquire of him
And learn to make a body of a limb.

RICHARD Thou chid'st me well. Proud Bullingbrook, I come
To change blows with thee for our day of doom.
This ague fit of fear is overblown,   190
An easy task it is to win our own.
Say, Scroope, where lies our uncle with his power?
Speak sweetly, man, although thy looks be sour.

SCROOPE Men judge by the complexion of the sky
The state and inclination of the day;   195
So may you by my dull and heavy eye.

---

170 through] Q2–5, F; thorough Q1   170 wall] Q1; walls Q2–5, F   178 sit...woes] Qq; waile their present woes F
182] Qq; *not in* F

170 **farewell king** Some editors suggest Richard takes off his crown here. Such a gesture would add to the point he next makes about his courtiers continuing to stand bareheaded.

172 **solemn reverence** gesture of holy respect. See 2.1.123. Doffing the hat was customary in the king's presence and at funerals.

175–6 **bread...grief** See Isa. 30.20.

176 **Subjected** (1) Afflicted, (2) made a subject.

178 **sit** See 155 n.

179 **prevent** anticipate, avoid by anticipating.

182 An accidental omission in F. Carlisle seems particularly prone to such accidents. See 29–32.

183 **No...fight** If you fight, you cannot suffer worse than being slain.

184 **destroying** (1) defying, (2) living in honourable memory. See *JC* 2.2.32–3.

185 **Where** Whereas.

185 **pays...breath** becomes a subject to death.

186 **power** army. In Holinshed he has, but not in 2.2.

189 **change** exchange.

192 **uncle** York is Richard's only surviving uncle after Gaunt's death.

194–7 The cross-rhyme concludes a run of five couplets, to close off Richard's brief surge of hope.

My tongue hath but a heavier tale to say.
I play the torturer by small and small
To lengthen out the worst that must be spoken.
Your uncle York is joined with Bullingbrook   200
And all your northern castles yielded up,
And all your southern gentlemen in arms
Upon his party.
RICHARD   Thou hast said enough.
[*To Aumerle*] Beshrew thee, cousin, which didst lead me
    forth
Of that sweet way I was in to despair.   205
What say you now? What comfort have we now?
By heaven I'll hate him everlastingly
That bids me be of comfort any more.
Go to Flint Castle, there I'll pine away.
A king, woe's slave, shall kingly woe obey.   210
That power I have, discharge, and let them go
To ear the land that hath some hope to grow,
For I have none. Let no man speak again
To alter this, for counsel is but vain.
AUMERLE My liege, one word.
RICHARD   He does me double wrong   215
That wounds me with the flatteries of his tongue.
Discharge my followers, let them hence away
From Richard's night to Bullingbrook's fair day.

                                        Exeunt

203 party] Qq; Faction F   204 SD] *Theobald; not in* Qq, F   211 them] Qq; 'em F   218 SD] F; *not in* Qq

198 torturer...small The rack was an instrument of torture which gradually stretched its victim. The slower the stretching, the greater the pain.

203 party F's 'faction' is a more explicit term for political division. Bushy uses 'faction' of the rebels at 2.2.57, and the F editor may have registered an actor's change. 'Party' is used in a slightly different sense at 3.3.115.

205 Of From.

206 comfort Compare Aumerle at 36, 75, 82. The word picks up 'sweet' from the previous line. See 13 n.

209 Flint Castle The next scene, 3.3, is commonly known as the Flint Castle scene. Holinshed has Conway in his text and Flint in the margin (II, 499). In Holinshed, Northumberland persuades Richard to move from Conway to Flint promising him safe conduct, and then ambushes him on the way when he is unguarded. Flint is near Chester at the northern extremity of Wales.

212 ear plough and sow.

215 double In the wounding and the lies of flattery.

218 Richard gives the sun image up to Bullingbrook.

3.3 *Enter with drum and colours* BULLINGBROOK, YORK, NORTHUM-
BERLAND, *Attendants.*

BULLINGBROOK So that by this intelligence we learn
       The Welshmen are dispersed, and Salisbury
       Is gone to meet the king, who lately landed
       With some few private friends upon this coast.
NORTHUMBERLAND The news is very fair and good, my lord.   5
       Richard not far from hence hath hid his head.
YORK It would beseem the Lord Northumberland
       To say King Richard. Alack the heavy day
       When such a sacred king should hide his head.
NORTHUMBERLAND Your grace ˙mistakes. Only to be brief   10
       Left I his title out.
YORK   The time hath been,
       Would you have been so brief with him he would
       Have been so brief with you to shorten you,
       For taking so the head, your whole head's length.
BULLINGBROOK Mistake not, uncle, further than you should.   15
YORK Take not, good cousin, further than you should,
       Lest you mistake. The heavens are o'er our heads.
BULLINGBROOK I know it, uncle, and oppose not myself
       Against their will. But who comes here?

Enter PERCY.

       Welcome, Harry. What, will not this castle yield?   20

Act 3, Scene 3   0 SD] F; *Enter Bull. Yorke, North.* QQ   11–13] F; *Yorke The . . . with him,* / *He would . . . shorten
you,* QQ   13 *with you*] F; *not in* QQ   17 *o'er*] F; *ouer* QQ   17 *our heads*] Q1–2; *your heads* Q3–5; *your head* F
19 *will*] Q1–3, F; *willes* Q4–5

Act 3, Scene 3

  3.3 Shakespeare compresses Holinshed's account
of the manoeuvres between Conway and Flint. In
the process he eliminates Northumberland's dupli-
city in using force against Richard. This simplifies
Richard's fall by putting the whole onus on his
despair, and emphasises Bullingbrook's military
power (and his popularity) in comparison with
Richard.

  1 intelligence military information. He enters
in mid speech, possibly with a paper (the
'intelligence') in his hand.

  2 The . . . dispersed See 2.4 and 3.1.43 n.

  4 private friends Percy brings their names at
27–9.

  6 hid his head Like the sunset, but also
contemptuously, as York's rebuke underlines.

  12–13 with him . . . with you The F addition
corrects the metre. This seems one of the instances
where F corrected by consulting an authoritative
text.

  13 to as to.

  14 taking . . . head (1) speaking so to the head of
state, (2) taking the head alone instead of the whole
subject, (3) being headstrong.

  15 Mistake not (1) do not take it amiss, (2) do
not misunderstand.

  17 mistake. Most editors read 17 as a
continuous sentence, but thus minimise the
word-play on 'take' and 'mis-take' which runs
through 14–17 and ends in York's assertion of
divine justice waiting to punish the thief.

  20 What A confidently casual enquiry.

  20 this castle Flint. See 3.2.209 n.

PERCY The castle royally is manned, my lord,
      Against thy entrance.
BULLINGBROOK Royally? Why, it contains no king.
PERCY Yes, my good lord.
      It doth contain a king. King Richard lies   25
      Within the limits of yon lime and stone,
      And with him are the Lord Aumerle, Lord Salisbury,
      Sir Stephen Scroope, besides a clergyman
      Of holy reverence; who, I cannot learn.
NORTHUMBERLAND Oh, belike it is the Bishop of Carlisle.   30
BULLINGBROOK Noble lord,
      Go to the rude ribs of that ancient castle.
      Through brazen trumpet send the breath of parle
      Into his ruined ears, and thus deliver:
      Henry Bullingbrook   35
      On both his knees doth kiss King Richard's hand
      And sends allegiance and true faith of heart
      To his most royal person; hither come
      Even at his feet to lay my arms and power,
      Provided that my banishment repealed   40
      And lands restored again be freely granted.
      If not I'll use the advantage of my power
      And lay the summer's dust with showers of blood
      Rained from the wounds of slaughtered Englishmen,
      The which how far off from the mind of Bullingbrook   45
      It is such crimson tempest should bedrench
      The fresh green lap of fair King Richard's land

---

21 royally is] Q1, F; is royally Q2–5   23] *Hudson;* Royally, why it contains no King. Qq; Royally? Why, it containes no King? F   26 yon] Qq; yond F   27 are] Q1; *not in* Q2–5, F   31 lord] F; Lords Qq   33 parle] F; parlee Qq   35–8] *Malone;* H. Bull. on both...hand, / And sends...heart / To his...come Qq; *Henry Bullingbrooke,* vpon... kisse / King...allegeance / And...his Royall...come F

23 Bullingbrook's surprise is a consequence of Shakespeare eliminating the Conway and Flint incident, which in Holinshed brings Richard to Flint as Northumberland's prisoner.

25 King Richard An ironic title in view of the exchange between Percy's father and York at 6–8.

32 rude ribs The imaginary building at which Percy gestures in 26 is personified with ribs (enclosing the heart) and ruined ears, a visual image for the castellations of its towers. The ears are 'tottered' (tattered) at 52.

33 parle truce. See 1.1.192.

35 Either a short line or an extra-metrical phrase. The importance of names, from Bullingbrook's

claim to return as Lancaster (2.3.113) to York's insistence on 'King' Richard, warrants the emphasising pause which the short line gives the bald name.

39 my The change to the first person underlines what Bullingbrook has and his opposite has not.

40 my...repealed the repeal of my sentence of banishment. From this point it is Richard who moves into banishment and nameless exile.

41 lands...again the restoration of my lands.

43 summer's The month was August. See 3.2.146.

47 lap The front of a skirt or body, with a Biblical connotation of fertile land.

My stooping duty tenderly shall show.
Go, signify as much while here we march
Upon the grassy carpet of this plain.   50
Let's march without the noise of threatening drum,
That from this castle's tottered battlements
Our fair appointments may be well perused.
Methinks King Richard and myself should meet
With no less terror than the elements   55
Of fire and water when their thundering shock
At meeting tears the cloudy cheeks of heaven.
Be he the fire, I'll be the yielding water.
The rage be his, whilst on the earth I rain
My waters; on the earth and not on him.   60
March on, and mark King Richard how he looks.

Parle without, and answer within. Then a flourish. Enter on the walls
RICHARD, CARLISLE, AUMERLE, SCROOPE, SALISBURY.

See, see, King Richard doth himself appear
As doth the blushing discontented sun
From out the fiery portal of the east
When he perceives the envious clouds are bent   65
To dim his glory and to stain the track
Of his bright passage to the occident.

---

56 shock] Q1; smoke Q2–5, F   59 whilst] Qq; while F   59 rain] F (raine); raigne Qq   60 waters; on] *Rowe²*; water's on Qq, F   61 SD] F; *The trumpets sound, Richard appeareth on the walls.* Qq   62 See] F; *Bull* See Qq   66 track] Qq; tract F

48 **tenderly** lovingly, respectfully.
52 **tottered** ruined. See 32 n.
53 **fair appointments** handsome military showing.
54–60 Bullingbrook repeats Richard's image of the exchange of positions in the elemental imagery of storm. See p. 25 above.
55 **With** Causing.
56 **thundering shock** Thunder was thought to come from the clash between the elements of fire (lightning) and water (rain). 'Shock' was the term for the impact of warhorses against each other. See 1.3.136 n.
57 **cloudy cheeks** Possibly a visual image for the cherubs depicted at the corners of maps to denote the winds.
58 **yielding water** Fire was the dominant, upward-tending element. 'As weak as water' is a proverbial phrase used in Ezek. 7.17.
59 **rage** See 3.2.109.

59 **rain** Also 'reign', though Ure and other editors will not admit this as a pun here.
61 SD.1 *Parle* A trumpet call.
61 SD.1 **on the walls** Presumably Richard and his followers appear on the balcony or 'tarras' (terrace) above the stage entry-doors in the tiring-house front. Scenes were rarely written for more than two or three actors to appear '*above*' on the balcony. It is visually significant, of course, in giving Richard a height from which he descends in the course of the scene to the 'base court' of the stage platform.
62–7 See *Sonnets* 33 and 34. A red sunrise might aptly be taken as a sign of anger since it commonly precedes a storm. See also illustration 5, p. 26 above.
65 **envious** hostile (to its glory).
66 **stain** See 3.1.14, 3.2.81, and *Sonnets* 33.14: 'Suns of the world may stain, when heaven's sun staineth.'

YORK Yet looks he like a king. Behold, his eye,
　　　　As bright as is the eagle's, lightens forth
　　　　Controlling majesty. Alack, alack for woe　　　　　　70
　　　　That any harm should stain so fair a show.
RICHARD [*To Northumberland*]
　　　　We are amazed, and thus long have we stood
　　　　To watch the fearful bending of thy knee
　　　　Because we thought ourself thy lawful king.
　　　　And if we be, how dare thy joints forget　　　　　　75
　　　　To pay their awful duty to our presence?
　　　　If we be not, show us the hand of God
　　　　That hath dismissed us from our stewardship,
　　　　For well we know no hand of blood and bone
　　　　Can gripe the sacred handle of our sceptre,　　　　　80
　　　　Unless he do profane, steal or usurp.
　　　　And though you think that all as you have done
　　　　Have torn their souls by turning them from us
　　　　And we are barren and bereft of friends
　　　　Yet know: my master, God omnipotent,　　　　　　85
　　　　Is mustering in his clouds on our behalf
　　　　Armies of pestilence, and they shall strike
　　　　Your children yet unborn and unbegot
　　　　That lift your vassal hands against my head
　　　　And threat the glory of my precious crown.　　　　　90
　　　　Tell Bullingbrook, for yon methinks he stands,
　　　　That every stride he makes upon my land
　　　　Is dangerous treason. He is come to ope
　　　　The purple testament of bleeding war,

72 SD] *Rowe ; not in* Qq, F　　91 yon] Qq ; yond F　　91 stands] Qq ; is F　　93 ope] F ; open Qq

68 **Yet** Still, nonetheless.
69–70 **lightens...majesty** sends forth as lightning the majesty which controls the earth. Jove's
instruments of divine justice were bolts of lightning.
　71 **stain** York alters Bullingbrook's term (66).
　72 **amazed** bemused, puzzled.
　73 **watch** wait for.
　73 **fearful** full of fear.
　73 **thy knee** In Holinshed all the rebel lords
knelt to Richard.
　76 **awful** (1) respectful, (2) full of awe.
　76 **our presence** See 1.1.15 n.
　77 **hand** sign and signature.
　80 **gripe** grasp.
　81 **profane** commit sacrilege.
　83 **torn** lacerated.

83 **turning** Similar in spelling and meaning to
'torn', with the added implication of treachery as
in 'turncoat'.
　84 **And** And that.
　87 **Armies of pestilence** A phrase from 2 Kings
19.35, caught up again at 5.3.3.
　87 **strike** afflict, as with plague.
　89 **vassal...head** See 3.2.138 n. Richard is also
using the familiar body politic metaphor of the
body's hands rebelling against the head. See 1 Cor.
1.96–7.
　91 **yon** yonder.
　92 **stride** See 2.3.89, 3.2.17 and 125.
　94 **purple** crimson.
　94 **testament** will or bequest. See p. 28 above.

But ere the crown he looks for live in peace   95
Ten thousand bloody crowns of mothers' sons
Shall ill become the flower of England's face,
Change the complexion of her maid-pale peace
To scarlet indignation and bedew
Her pastor's grass with faithful English blood.   100
NORTHUMBERLAND The King of Heaven forbid our lord the king
Should so with civil and uncivil arms
Be rushed upon! Thy thrice noble cousin,
Harry Bullingbrook, doth humbly kiss thy hand
And by the honourable tomb he swears,   105
That stands upon your royal grandsire's bones,
And by the royalties of both your bloods,
Currents that spring from one most gracious head,
And by the buried hand of warlike Gaunt,
And by the worth and honour of himself,   110
Comprising all that may be sworn or said,
His coming hither hath no further scope
Than for his lineal royalties, and to beg
Enfranchisement immediate on his knees,
Which on thy royal party granted once   115
His glittering arms he will commend to rust,
His barbèd steeds to stables and his heart
To faithful service of your majesty.
This swears he as he is a prince and just,

---

100 pastor's] Qq, F; pasture's *Capell*   119 a prince and just] *conj. Sisson;* princesse iust Q1–2; a Prince iust Q3–5; a
Prince, is iust F

96 **bloody crowns** bleeding heads.

100 **pastor's** priest's (implying pastoral care as
for sheep at grass). See 'stewardship' (78). Some
editors depersonalise to 'pasture's'.

101–14 Northumberland's declaration broadly
follows Holinshed, II, 498. Compare *1H4*
1.3.145–86.

102 **civil and uncivil** ungentle in civil war: a
compressed oxymoron.

103 **thrice noble** Possibly triple because from
Edward III, Gaunt, and from his own right. At
2.2.24 the trebling of the adjective seems to be a
stock intensifier. Perhaps here there is a hint of a
threat in its use for someone less than a king.

105–6 The tomb of Edward III is in Westminster
Abbey.

107 **royalties** royal status, regality.

113 **lineal royalties** See 1.1.58, 2.1.190 and
2.3.119. 'Lineal' might imply not only inheritance

through Gaunt but from Richard, a hint not in
Bullingbrook's instructions to Northumberland at
35–48.

113–14 A paraphrase of Holinshed, II, 501,
where they are spoken by Bullingbrook himself.
Other demands which Northumberland made
according to Holinshed, such as a trial for the
flatterers and for the murderers of Gloucester, both
of which Bullingbrook is shown to pursue in the
play, are omitted here.

114 **Enfranchisement** Restoration of legitimate
authority.

115 **party** part, side of the agreement. See
3.2.203 n.

117 **barbèd** armed with a barb on its head.

119 **a prince...just** C. J. Sisson's conjecture
(*New Readings in Shakespeare*, 2 vols., 1956, II, 24)
makes better sense of Q1's mistake than either Q3
or F. See 2.1.18 n.

And as I am a gentleman I credit him.   120
RICHARD Northumberland, say thus the king returns:
    His noble cousin is right welcome hither,
    And all the number of his fair demands
    Shall be accomplished without contradiction.
    With all the gracious utterance thou hast   125
    Speak to his gentle hearing kind commends.
    [*To Aumerle*] We do debase ourselves, cousin, do we not,
    To look so poorly and to speak so fair?
    Shall we call back Northumberland and send
    Defiance to the traitor and so die?   130
AUMERLE No, good my lord. Let's fight with gentle words,
    Till time lend friends, and friends their helpful swords.
RICHARD Oh God, oh God, that e'er this tongue of mine
    That laid the sentence of dread banishment
    On yon proud man should take it off again   135
    With words of sooth! Oh that I were as great
    As is my grief, or lesser than my name,
    Or that I could forget what I have been,
    Or not remember what I must be now!
    Swell'st thou, proud heart? I'll give thee scope to beat,   140
    Since foes have scope to beat both thee and me.
AUMERLE Northumberland comes back from Bullingbrook.
RICHARD What must the king do now? Must he submit?
    The king shall do it. Must he be deposed?
    The king shall be contented. Must he lose   145
    The name of king? A God's name let it go.

---

127 SD] *Rowe; not in* Qq, F   127 We] Q4–5, F; *King* We Q1–3   127 ourselves] Qq; *our selfe* F   135 yon] Qq; *yond* F   146 of king? A] Q1; *of a King?* Q2–5; *of King? o'* F

121 **returns** gives in answer. Richard has asserted the rights of kingship at 79–100, which Northumberland has countered with the rights of the subject (105–18), while affirming Bullingbrook's royal blood and implying his claim by inheritance (113 n.). Richard now steps back from the confrontation of king's and subject's rights.

126 Northumberland leaves Richard silently, without the ceremony which accompanied his arrival, though with an economy which matches his failure to kneel to Richard at 71.

131 **gentle** (1) soft, (2) noble (the antonym to 'poor' at 128).

136 **words of sooth** (1) truth, (2) appeasing terms.

137 **my name** This is the first instance of Richard thinking of the name and not the reality of the king.

140 **Swell'st thou** (1) Do you beat faster, (2) do you swell with pride.

141 **scope** aim, purpose. With an echo of Northumberland at 112.

141 **beat** (1) punish, (2) defeat, (3) shame by whipping.

143 **What...now?** Once the name is separated from the thing, it can be used, as here, with a two-edged sarcasm, wounding both the enemies who take it lightly and the owner of the name through its lightness. Richard supplies his own answers to the questions throughout this speech of renunciation, confirming the fall begun at 40.

145 **contented** willing, happy to agree.

I'll give my jewels for a set of beads,
My gorgeous palace for a hermitage,
My gay apparel for an almsman's gown,
My figured goblets for a dish of wood,   150
My sceptre for a palmer's walking staff,
My subjects for a pair of carvèd saints,
And my large kingdom for a little grave,
A little, little grave, an obscure grave.
Or I'll be buried in the king's highway,   155
Some way of common trade, where subjects' feet
May hourly trample on their sovereign's head;
For on my heart they tread now whilst I live,
And buried once, why not upon my head?
Aumerle, thou weep'st, my tender-hearted cousin.   160
We'll make foul weather with despisèd tears:
Our sighs and they shall lodge the summer corn
And make a dearth in this revolting land.
Or shall we play the wantons with our woes
And make some pretty match with shedding tears,   165
As thus to drop them still upon one place
Till they have fretted us a pair of graves
Within the earth, and therein laid? There lies
Two kinsmen digged their graves with weeping eyes.
Would not this ill do well? Well, well, I see   170
I talk but idly and you laugh at me.
Most mighty prince, my Lord Northumberland,

166 As] Q1, F; And Q2–5   171 laugh] Qq; mock F

147 **set of beads** a rosary, the equipment of a beadsman and a pilgrim. The alternatives in 147–53 are matched visually, and make the play's most specific allusion to Richard's lavish expenditure. Holinshed takes particular note of his expensive clothing.

149 **almsman** Recipient of charity.

150 **figured** embossed, ornamented.

151 **palmer** Pilgrim who has visited Jerusalem. See p. 4 above.

155 **highway** Another sarcasm. See 1.4.4 where Aumerle plays on 'high' in 'highway'.

156 **trade** (1) commerce, (2) tread.

158 **tread** Homonymic with 'trade'. See Cercignani, p. 78. This instance is a more likely homonym than the dubious rhyme of 'face' with 'peace' dismissed by Cercignani, p. 158.

159 **buried once** once I am buried.

161 **despisèd tears** (1) the tears of those who are despised, (2) tears which are seen as unimportant. Richard now accepts the imagery of water for himself.

162 **they** the tears (rain accompanying the wind of sighs).

162 **lodge** flatten. See *Mac.* 4.1.55: 'Though bladed corn be lodged', and compare 5.1.14.

164 **wantons** flirts.

165 **make** compose.

165 **match** game.

168–9 **There...eyes** The epitaph on the two graves.

170 **ill** (1) evil deed, (2) unhappiness.

What says King Bullingbrook? Will his majesty
Give Richard leave to live till Richard die?
You make a leg and Bullingbrook says ay.   175

NORTHUMBERLAND My lord, in the base court he doth attend
To speak with you. May it please you to come down?

RICHARD Down, down I come, like glistering Phaëton,
Wanting the manage of unruly jades.
In the base court? Base court where kings grow base   180
To come at traitors' calls and do them grace!
In the base court come down. Down court, down king,
For night owls shriek where mounting larks should sing.

                        [*Richard descends*]

BULLINGBROOK What says his majesty?

NORTHUMBERLAND   Sorrow and grief of heart
Makes him speak fondly like a frantic man.   185

       [*Enter Richard below.*]

Yet he is come.

BULLINGBROOK   Stand all apart
And show fair duty to his majesty.
               He kneels down.
My gracious lord.

RICHARD Fair cousin, you debase your princely knee

---

180 court?] F; court, Qq   183 SD] *This edn; not in* Qq, F   185 SD] *Johnson Var.; not in* Qq, F   187 SD] Qq; *not in*
F   189] Qq; Fair Cousin, / You...Knee, F

173 **King Bullingbrook** Granting the title, however sarcastically, is an implicit admission of the separability of name and person. The sarcasm is extended in the trick question of 174, but when Richard supplies the answer himself as he does at 175 he begins the process of filling Bullingbrook's silences with the words which Bullingbrook wants.

175 **make a leg** bow.

176 **the base court** the servants' court. In Holinshed's account of the arrest of Gloucester the term appears several times. Froissart uses it in his account of the Flint Castle episode, and Shakespeare's exploitation of it here may indicate a debt to Froissart as well as Holinshed.

178 **Phaëton** The upstart who could not control the horses of the sun and so burned the earth till Jove struck him with lightning. In Greek the word means 'shining' or 'glittering'.

179 **manage** control (of horses).

179 **jades** vicious horses.

181 **do them grace** (1) be graceful to them, (2) make them good, (3) bow to them.

183 It is nightfall when it should be daybreak, because Richard's sun is setting. Owls were traditionally associated with the devil, and thought to presage death. See *Mac.* 2.2.3.

183 SD The two lines 184–5 allow Richard time to climb down the stairs inside the tiring-house between the balcony and stage level. See 61 SD n. There were no external stairs between the balcony and the stage, so Richard would be invisible while he descended, until he emerged from the stage doors.

185 **fondly** foolishly.

185 **frantic** temporarily out of his mind. See *LLL* 5.1.26.

186 **Yet...come** As elsewhere in Q1 the appropriate stage direction is left to be deduced from the dialogue.

187 **fair duty** (1) honourable respect, (2) ceremonial kneeling.

189 **debase** An extension of the word-play on 'base court' (180).

To make the base earth proud with kissing it.   190
Me rather had my heart might feel your love
Than my unpleased eye see your courtesy.
Up, cousin, up. Your heart is up, I know,
Thus high at least, although your knee be low.

BULLINGBROOK My gracious lord, I come but for mine own.   195
RICHARD Your own is yours and I am yours and all.
BULLINGBROOK So far be mine, my most redoubted lord,
    As my true service shall deserve your love.
RICHARD Well you deserve. They well deserve to have
    That know the strong'st and surest way to get.   200
    Uncle, give me your hands. Nay, dry your eyes.
    Tears show their love but want their remedies.
    Cousin, I am too young to be your father,
    Though you are old enough to be my heir.
    What you will have I'll give, and willing too,   205
    For do we must what force will have us do.
    Set on towards London, cousin, is it so?
BULLINGBROOK Yea, my good lord.
RICHARD   Then I must not say no.

Flourish. Exeunt

199] Qq; *Rich.* Well you deseru'd: / They...have, F   201 hands] Qq; Hand F   204 my] Q1, F; *not in* Q2–5
207] Qq; Set...London: / Cousin...so? F   208 SD] F; *not in* Q1–3; *Exeunt.* Q4–5

191 **Me rather had** I would prefer.
192 **courtesy** Homonymic with 'curtsy', kneeling.
194 **Thus high** Up to Richard's head, and the crown on it.
195 **for mine own** Bullingbrook's seemingly modest claim is as ambiguous as Northumberland's 'lineal royalties' (113), though it does repeat Northumberland's assertion to York at 2.3.147–8.
197 **redoubted** dreaded.
198 **service** (1) duty, (2) loyal service.
202 **their love** the love of those who shed them. York is the only character outside the king's own party to weep for his fall.

203 **too young** Historically both Richard and Bullingbrook were 33.
204 **my heir** Richard enlarges on what both Northumberland at 113 and Bullingbrook at 195 have hinted at.
207 **London** For a coronation, and possibly for the legal sanction of Parliament. In *3H6* much is made of Parliament's role in confirming claims over the succession. See 2.1.172–6: 'He swore consent to your succession, / His oath enrolled in the parliament. / And now to London all the crew are gone / To frustrate both his oath and what beside / May make against the house of Lancaster.'

3.4 *Enter the* QUEEN *with her attendants.*

QUEEN What sport shall we devise here in this garden
    To drive away the heavy thought of care?
LADY Madam, we'll play at bowls.
QUEEN 'Twill make me think the world is full of rubs
    And that my fortune runs against the bias.   5
LADY Madam, we'll dance.
QUEEN My legs can keep no measure in delight
    When my poor heart no measure keeps in grief.
    Therefore no dancing, girl. Some other sport.
LADY Madam, we'll tell tales.   10
QUEEN Of sorrow or of joy?
LADY   Of either, madam.
QUEEN Of neither, girl.
    For if of joy, being altogether wanting
    It doth remember me the more of sorrow,
    Or if of grief, being altogether had   15
    It adds more sorrow to my want of joy.
    For what I have I need not to repeat
    And what I want it boots not to complain.
LADY Madam, I'll sing.
QUEEN   'Tis well that thou hast cause,
    But thou shouldst please me better wouldst thou weep.   20
LADY I could weep, Madam, would it do you good.
QUEEN And I could sing would weeping do me good,
    And never borrow any tear of thee.

Enter a GARDENER *and two* SERVANTS.

    But stay, here come the gardeners.

Act 3, Scene 4   o SD] Qq; *Enter the Queene, and two Ladies.* F   11 joy] *Rowe*; griefe Qq, F   23 SD] F; *Enter Gardeners*
Qq   24 come] Q1; commeth Q2–5; comes F

Act 3, Scene 4

o SD *attendants* F's '*two ladies*' indicates what the playhouse supplied for this scene. The ladies make four offers, but Shakespeare probably did not expect four different ladies to make them.

1 **this garden** The queen's verbal designation for the scene makes it possible that it was staged without other signs of the locality, though see 25 n.

3 **bowls** Bowling alleys were a common feature of Elizabethan gardens.

4 **rubs** A term from bowls, meaning 'hindrances to the run of the bowl'.

5 **against the bias** counter to the weighting of the bowl. Proverbial (Tilley B339).

7 **measure** (1) musical time, (2) a slow dance step.

8 **measure** limit.

18 **boots not** is pointless.

18 **complain** lament.

23 SD F is more specific than Q1. The gardeners have sometimes been played as rustic clowns. See A. C. Sprague, *Shakespeare's Histories*, pp. 40–1.

Let's step into the shadow of these trees.   25
My wretchedness unto a row of pins
They'll talk of state, for everyone doth so
Against a change. Woe is forerun with woe.

GARDENER Go bind thou up young dangling apricocks,
    Which like unruly children make their sire   30
    Stoop with oppression of their prodigal weight.
    Give some supportance to the bending twigs.
    Go thou, and like an executioner
    Cut off the heads of too-fast-growing sprays
    That look too lofty in our commonwealth.   35
    All must be even in our government.
    You thus employed, I will go root away
    The noisome weeds which without profit suck
    The soil's fertility from wholesome flowers.

SERVANT Why should we, in the compass of a pale,   40
    Keep law and form and due proportion,
    Showing as in a model our firm estate,
    When our sea-wallèd garden, the whole land,
    Is full of weeds, her fairest flowers choked up,
    Her fruit trees all unpruned, her hedges ruined,   45
    Her knots disordered and her wholesome herbs
    Swarming with caterpillars?

GARDENER   Hold thy peace.

---

26 pins] F (Pinnes); pines Qq   27 They'll] F; They will Qq   28 change.] F; change Qq   29 young] Q1 (yong); yon Q2–5; yond F   34 too] F; two Qq   38 which] Q1; that Q2–5, F   42 as] Q1, F; *not in* Q2–5

25 **these trees** The naming of the trees makes it easy to use the stage posts for the purpose. See p. 35 above.

26 **My...unto** I will bet my wretchedness against.

26 **a row of pins** Proverbial for insignificance. See *Ham.* 1.4.65.

27 **state** affairs of state.

28 **Against** In anticipation of.

28 **forerun with** heralded by.

29 **young** Q2's 'yon' is probably a misprint for Q1 'yong'. There is no precise indication of the season for this scene. Historically it was summer (September in Holinshed), which would be the right time for 'young' apricots, and would come between the disordered spring and the fall of leaf (48–9). The pruning of which the Gardener speaks at 34 and 57–8 belongs to spring, and Richard's 'fall' (49, 76) to the autumn.

29 **dangling** Grown as standards, apricots would hang on their branches while still small.

31 **prodigal** immense, extravagant. The parable of the prodigal son was extremely popular in the sixteenth century. The word 'prodigal' here develops the idea implicit in 'young' (29).

33 **like an executioner** The comparison of a garden to a kingdom, implicit in Gaunt's 'other Eden, demi-paradise' (2.1.42), has many classical precedents. It develops Bullingbrook's use of a commonplace to describe the flatterers as caterpillars (2.3.165). For the classical precedents see Ure, pp. li–lvii.

40 **pale** fenced enclosure.

42 **in a model** in miniature. See 3.2.153 n.

43–7 The Servant echoes both Gaunt (2.1.42–63) and Bullingbrook (2.3.165).

46 **knots** patterned flowerbeds.

He that hath suffered this disordered spring
Hath now himself met with the fall of leaf.
The weeds which his broad spreading leaves did shelter,   50
That seemed in eating him to hold him up,
Are plucked up root and all by Bullingbrook.
I mean the Earl of Wiltshire, Bushy, Green.

SERVANT What, are they dead?

GARDENER   They are, and Bullingbrook
Hath seized the wasteful king. Oh what pity is it   55
That he had not so trimmed and dressed his land
As we this garden! We at time of year
Do wound the bark, the skin of our fruit trees,
Lest being overproud in sap and blood
With too much riches it confound itself.   60
Had he done so to great and growing men
They might have lived to bear and he to taste
Their fruits of duty. Superfluous branches
We lop away, that bearing boughs may live.
Had he done so, himself had borne the crown   65
Which waste of idle hours hath quite thrown down.

SERVANT What, think you then the king shall be deposed?

GARDENER Depressed he is already, and deposed
'Tis doubt he will be. Letters came last night
To a dear friend of the good Duke of York's   70
That tell black tidings.

QUEEN Oh, I am pressed to death through want of speaking!
Thou, old Adam's likeness set to dress this garden,

---

50 which] Q1; that Q2–5, F   52 plucked] Q1–2; puld Q3–5, F   54–7] *Capell;* They are. / And...king, / Oh...
trimde, / And drest...yeare Qq, F   55 is it] Q1, F; it is Q2–5   57 garden! We] *Capell;* garden, Qq, F   58 Do] Qq;
And F   59 in] Q1; with Q2–5, F   66 of] Qq; and F   67 then] *Pope; not in* Qq, F   69 doubt] Qq; doubted F
70 good] Q1–2; *not in* Q3–5, F

---

48 **suffered** (1) allowed to happen, (2) undergone.

51 As parasites, like ivy.

57–8 **garden!...Do** F's emendation of 'Do' to 'And' looks like an attempt to make sense of Q. Capell's strengthening of the punctuation and his relineation make rather better sense and better metre.

57 **at time of year** in season.

59 **overproud** (1) too fertile, (2) too rich in blood.

60 Without pruning it will put all its growth into wood, not fruit.

65 **crown** Of the tree and of the king.

67 **then** Pope's emendation restores the metre. Ure suggests that the Q1 compositor (A) might have read the abbreviation 'thē' as an accidental repetition.

68 **Depressed** Humbled, lowered in fortune.

69 **'Tis doubt** It is feared. See 'redoubted', 3.3.197.

72 **pressed to death** The medieval punishment for defendants who refused to speak was pressing to death. Also 'oppressed to the point of death'.

73 **old Adam's likeness** Adam was sometimes characterised as the first gardener, as in the adage, 'When Adam delved and Eve span, / Who was then the gentleman?'

How dares thy harsh rude tongue sound this unpleasing news?
What Eve, what serpent hath suggested thee   75
To make a second fall of cursèd man?
Why dost thou say King Richard is deposed?
Darest thou, thou little better thing than earth,
Divine his downfall? Say where, when and how
Camest thou by this ill tidings? Speak, thou wretch!   80
GARDENER Pardon me, madam. Little joy have I
To breathe this news, yet what I say is true.
King Richard he is in the mighty hold
Of Bullingbrook. Their fortunes both are weighed.
In your lord's scale is nothing but himself   85
And some few vanities that make him light,
But in the balance of great Bullingbrook
Besides himself are all the English peers,
And with that odds he weighs King Richard down.
Post you to London and you'll find it so.   90
I speak no more than everyone doth know.
QUEEN Nimble mischance, that art so light of foot,
Doth not thy embassage belong to me,
And am I last that knows it? Oh, thou thinkest
To serve me last that I may longest keep   95
Thy sorrow in my breast. Come ladies, go
To meet at London London's king in woe.
What, was I born to this, that my sad look
Should grace the triumph of great Bullingbrook?
Gardener, for telling me these news of woe   100
Pray God the plants thou graft'st may never grow.
               Exit [*with attendants*]
GARDENER Poor queen, so that thy state might be no worse

---

80 Camest] Q2–5, F; Canst Q1   82 this] Q1; these Q2–5, F   90 you'll] F; you will QQ   100 these] QQ; this F
101 Pray God] QQ; I would F

75 **suggested** tempted.
76 **a second fall** The queen represents Richard as Adam expelled from Eden, not as Christ. See 3.2.132, 4.1.238.
79 **Divine** Prophesy.
83 **hold** grip, wrestling hold.
84–9 Scales are normally associated with justice rather than fortune. The passage, especially 86, has echoes of Ps. 62.9: 'As for the children of men, they are but vain: the children of men are deceitful upon

the weights, they are altogether lighter than vanity itself.'
93 **belong** to relate to.
95 **serve** (1) be servant to (as at dinner), (2) deliver a (legal) document to.
96–101 The queen begins to rhyme as she regains her temper and control.
99 **grace the triumph** adorn the triumphal procession. See *Ant.* 5.2.208–21.
102 **so that** if.

I would my skill were subject to thy curse.
Here did she fall a tear. Here in this place
I'll set a bank of rue, sour herb of grace.   105
Rue even for ruth here shortly shall be seen
In the remembrance of a weeping queen.

Exeunt

4.1 *Enter as to the Parliament* BULLINGBROOK, AUMERLE, NORTHUM-
BERLAND, PERCY, FITZWATER, SURREY, *the Bishop of* CARLISLE, *the*
Abbot of WESTMINSTER, HERALD, *Officers, and* BAGOT.

BULLINGBROOK Call forth Bagot.
    Now, Bagot, freely speak thy mind
    What thou dost know of noble Gloucester's death,
    Who wrought it with the king, and who performed
    The bloody office of his timeless end.   5
BAGOT Then set before my face the Lord Aumerle.
BULLINGBROOK Cousin, stand forth, and look upon that man.
BAGOT My Lord Aumerle, I know your daring tongue
    Scorns to unsay what once it hath delivered.
    In that dead time when Gloucester's death was plotted   10

---

104 fall] Q1; drop Q2–5, F   107 the] Q1, F; *not in* Q2–5   107 SD] Qq; *Exit.* F   Act 4, Scene 1   0 SD] F; *Enter*
Bullingbrooke with the Lords to parliament. Qq   1 Bagot.] F; Bagot. *Enter Bagot.* Qq   9 once it hath] Qq; it hath once F

---

104 fall drop. Q2–5 and F normalise.
105 sour...grace See *Ham.* 4.5.180–2:
'rue...we may call it herb of grace a' Sundays'.
Noting it as sour fits more closely with the imagery
of sweet and sour than with its traditional
associations.
106 Rue Repentance.
106 for ruth out of pity, sorrow.

Act 4, Scene 1
4.1 The basic details of this scene are from
Holinshed, though it crowds seven different events
(II, 501–13) into a single episode. The main events
in Holinshed are (1) Richard signing a form of
abdication; (2) Bullingbrook accepting the throne;
(3) Bagot accusing Aumerle; (4) Fitzwater accusing
Aumerle; (5) Carlisle protesting; (6) Mowbray's
release from exile by Bullingbrook; (7) the
Westminster conspiracy.

0 SD Q1's version is less orderly than F. Both
however emphasise the processional entry to a
meeting of Parliament, the judicial function of

which would require the royal regalia to be carried
at the head of the procession, before the new judge
Bullingbrook. It would also require the presence of
the throne, since Parliament was formally *rex in*
parliamento, the king, lords and commons together.
Since it is a scene exactly balancing 1.1, where the
king hears the charges and countercharges about
Gloucester's death, Bullingbrook should appropria-
tely occupy the throne here as Richard did in 1.1.
On the evidence of 113, however, he must stand
uncomfortably in front of the empty seat while
acting as judge.
    2 freely speak Bullingbrook exactly echoes
Richard at 1.1.17.
    4 wrought...king persuaded the king to agree
to it.
    5 office duty, function.
    5 timeless (1) untimely, (2) enduring in
memory.
    9 unsay deny. See p. 17 above.
    10 dead time (1) fatal time, (2) secret occasion.
See *Ham.* 1.1.65.

I heard you say 'Is not my arm of length,
That reacheth from the restful English court
As far as Calais, to mine uncle's head?'
Amongst much other talk that very time
I heard you say that you had rather refuse   15
The offer of an hundred thousand crowns
Than Bullingbrook's return to England,
Adding withal how blessed this land would be
In this your cousin's death.

AUMERLE   Princes and noble lords,
What answer shall I make to this base man?   20
Shall I so much dishonour my fair stars
On equal terms to give him chastisement?
Either I must, or have mine honour soiled
With the attainder of his slanderous lips.
There is my gage, the manual seal of death   25
That marks thee out for hell. I say thou liest,
And will maintain what thou hast said is false
In thy heart blood, though being all too base
To stain the temper of my knightly sword.

BULLINGBROOK Bagot, forbear. Thou shalt not take it up.   30
AUMERLE Excepting one, I would he were the best
In all this presence that hath moved me so.
FITZWATER If that thy valour stand on sympathy,
There is my gage, Aumerle, in gage to thine.

13 mine] Qq; my F   17–19] Capell; Then Bullingbrookes...withall, / How...death Qq, F   22 him] Q3–5, F; them Q1; my Q2   26 I say] Q1; not in Q2–5, F   33 sympathy] Qq; sympathize F

11–13 Traditionally it was the king's arm which was long enough to carry the sword of justice throughout the land. It was a Greek proverb recorded in Herodotus. Shakespeare probably knew it from Ovid, *Epist.* XVII.166: 'An nescis longas regibus esse manus?' (Do you not know that kings have long hands?). The allusion covertly reasserts the charge made in 1.2 that Richard was guilty of Gloucester's murder.

12 **restful** unmoving.

14 **that very time** Historically Gloucester was dead eleven years before Bullingbrook was banished. Bagot is either wrong or embroidering a doubtful truth with a recognisable lie.

16 **an...crowns** Holinshed (II, 512) more baldly quotes £20,000. Shakespeare's total is £25,000, there being four crowns to a pound sterling. See 3.2.59–61.

17–20 Q1 mislines through need to compress the text in sig. G4ᵛ.

18 **withal** besides.

21 **my fair stars** (1) my good destiny, (2) my good birth.

22 **On equal terms** Aumerle is Bagot's superior in social rank, so would degrade himself by fighting with him.

24 **attainder** dishonourable accusation. See *LLL* 1.1.157.

25 **manual seal** (1) gauntlet, (2) legal affirmation by signature or handshake. See 1.1.69 n.

31 **Excepting one** i.e. except for Bullingbrook.

31 **the best** highest in rank. Aumerle implies that Bullingbrook may be highest-ranked, but he will not call him king.

33 **stand on sympathy** can only confront equals.

34 **in gage** engaged.

By that fair sun which shows me where thou standest   35
I heard thee say, and vauntingly thou spak'st it,
That thou wert cause of noble Gloucester's death.
If thou deniest it twenty times, thou liest,
And I will turn thy falsehood to thy heart
Where it was forgèd, with my rapier's point.   40

AUMERLE Thou dar'st not, coward, live to see that day.
FITZWATER Now by my soul I would it were this hour.
AUMERLE Fitzwater, thou art damned to hell for this.
PERCY Aumerle, thou liest. His honour is as true
In this appeal as thou art all unjust,   45
And that thou art so, there I throw my gage,
To prove it on thee to the extremest point
Of mortal breathing. Seize it if thou darest.

AUMERLE And if I do not may my hands rot off
And never brandish more revengeful steel   50
Over the glittering helmet of my foe!

ANOTHER LORD I task the earth to the like, forsworn Aumerle,
And spur thee on with full as many lies
As may be hollowed in thy treacherous ear
From sun to sun. There is my honour's pawn.   55
Engage it to the trial if thou darest.

AUMERLE Who sets me else? By heaven, I'll throw at all!
I have a thousand spirits in one breast
To answer twenty thousand such as you.

SURREY My Lord Fitzwater, I do remember well   60
The very time Aumerle and you did talk.

---

35 which] Q1; that Q2–5, F   41 to see that] Q1; I to see the Q2–5; to see the F   43 Fitzwater] F; Fitzwaters Qq
52–9] Qq; *not in* F   52 task] Q1; take Q2–5   54 As] *Capell*; As it Qq   55 sun to sun] *Capell*; sinne to sinne Qq
60–2] Qq; My…*Fitz-water*: / I do…time / *Aumerle*…talke. / *Fitz.* My Lord, / 'Tis very…then, F

---

35 that fair sun Bullingbrook. They all show an uneasy consciousness of Bullingbrook's ambiguous 'presence' before the throne. See also 31 and 55.

36 vauntingly boastfully.

39 turn…to reverse…into.

40 rapier's The slimmer sword, with its point more important than its blade, became popular in the 1590s and largely replaced the 'fox' or broadsword.

52–9 The omission by F of the anonymous lord with his fourth gage saves one minor speaking part, and slightly reduces the risk frequent on the modern stage that the rain of gages becomes comic.

52 task burden; i.e. throws down another gage.

53 lies accusations of lying.

54 hollowed shouted.

55 sun to sun sunrise to sunset. The formal time limits for a duel. Q1's misprint derives from a minim error in reading the manuscript.

55 honour's pawn See 1.1.74.

57 sets puts up a stake in challenge. Aumerle implies that duelling is a matter of gambling rather than justice.

57 throw a dice.

59 twenty thousand See 1.3.159 n.

60–5 The F text has to stretch this passage over 10 lines in d1^v in order to fill the cast-off space. The compositor invents 'My lord' at 62. See illustration 15, p. 191 below.

FITZWATER 'Tis very true, you were in presence then
    And you can witness with me this is true.
SURREY As false, by heaven, as heaven itself is true.
FITZWATER Surrey, thou liest.
SURREY   Dishonourable boy,   65
    That lie shall lie so heavy on my sword
    That it shall render vengeance and revenge
    Till thou the lie-giver and that lie do lie
    In earth as quiet as thy father's skull.
    In proof whereof there is my honour's pawn.   70
    Engage it to the trial if thou darest.
FITZWATER How fondly dost thou spur a forward horse!
    If I dare eat or drink or breathe or live
    I dare meet Surrey in a wilderness
    And spit upon him whilst I say he lies   75
    And lies and lies. There is my bond of faith
    To tie thee to my strong correction.
    As I intend to thrive in this new world
    Aumerle is guilty of my true appeal.
    Besides, I heard the banished Norfolk say   80
    That thou, Aumerle, didst send two of thy men
    To execute the noble duke at Calais.
AUMERLE Some honest Christian trust me with a gage.
    That Norfolk lies, here do I throw down this,
    If he may be repealed to try his honour.   85
BULLINGBROOK These differences shall all rest under gage
    Till Norfolk be repealed. Repealed he shall be
    And, though mine enemy, restored again

64] Qq ; *Surrey*: As. . .heauen, / As Heauen. . .true. F   65–6] F ; *one line* Qq   70 my] Q1 ; mine Q2–3, F   76 my] Q3–5,
F ; *not in* Q1 ; the Q2   82 at] Q1, F ; of Q2–5

---

62 in presence present.

65 boy A contemptuous term here.

67 vengeance and revenge A tautology rather than a doublet, meant as an intensifier.

72 fondly foolishly.

72 forward eager. Proverbial (Tilley H638).

74 a wilderness See 1.1.64–6.

76 my Q3 offers a more likely conjecture than Q2 to fill Q1's omission. H. F. Brooks (in Ure) conjectures 'this' on the grounds that Fitzwater has already thrown down one gage and could be stressing the fact that 'this' is his second. But the main stress is on 'bond. . .tie'.

76 bond of faith the bond of my faith which binds. The fact that Fitzwater can throw down a second gage indicates that Shakespeare was thinking of gloves or gauntlets rather than the hoods which Holinshed says were used. But see 83 n.

78 this new world i.e. the world which Bullingbrook now rules.

83 This is Aumerle's second, and the seventh gage in all. Some editors assume that Aumerle has already thrown his second glove down at 57, but that is not a specific challenge. Holinshed says Aumerle borrowed a bystander's hood, a detail Shakespeare evidently thought worth retaining.

85 repealed called back from exile.

85 try (1) test, (2) submit to trial.

86 rest under gage (1) wait to be resolved by the duelling trials, (2) remain engaged.

To all his lands and signories. When he's returned,
Against Aumerle we will enforce his trial.   90
CARLISLE That honourable day shall ne'er be seen.
Many a time hath banished Norfolk fought
For Jesu Christ in glorious Christian field,
Streaming the ensign of the Christian cross
Against black pagans, Turks and Saracens,   95
And, toiled with works of war, retired himself
To Italy, and there at Venice gave
His body to that pleasant country's earth
And his pure soul unto his captain, Christ,
Under whose colours he had fought so long.   100
BULLINGBROOK Why, bishop, is Norfolk dead?
CARLISLE As surely as I live, my lord.
BULLINGBROOK Sweet peace conduct his sweet soul to the bosom
Of good old Abraham. Lords appellants,
Your differences shall all rest under gage   105
Till we assign you to your days of trial.

Enter YORK.

YORK Great Duke of Lancaster, I come to thee
From plume-plucked Richard, who with willing soul
Adopts thee heir, and his high sceptre yields
To the possession of thy royal hand.   110
Ascend his throne, descending now from him,
And long live Henry, of that name the fourth!

---

89 he's] F; he is Qq   91 ne'er] F; neuer Qq   98 that] Q1, F; a Q2–5   102 surely] Q1; sure Q2–5, F   103–4] Qq;
...Soule / To...*Abraham.* / Lords...gage, F   109 thee] Q2–5, F; the Q1   112 Henry...fourth] F; Henry, fourth of
that name Qq

---

89 signories See 3.1.22 n.
92–100 Shakespeare makes the exiled Mowbray
a crusader. Holinshed only says he died in Venice.
Stow says his death happened when he was
returning from Jerusalem, but does not indicate
whether the visit was as a crusader or a pilgrim. See
5.6.49 n. and p. 5 above.
94 Streaming Flying in the wind.
96 toiled with exhausted by.
103–4 Sweet...Abraham See Luke 16.22:
'And it came to passe that the begger [Lazarus]
dyed, and was caried by the Angels into Abrahams
bosome.'
104 Lords appellants See 1.1.4 'appeal'.
106 we The royal pronoun. E. W. Talbert, *The
Problem of Order*, p. 179, takes this as a mark of
Bullingbrook's hypocrisy.
108 plume-plucked stripped of his splendour.

Holinshed notes the costly extravagance of Richard's
wardrobe. 'Plume' probably alludes to Aesop's
fable of the crow dressed in stolen feathers and
shamed when the other birds stripped him of them.
See Dent P441.1.
109 heir See 1.4.35, 36 n. and p. 28 above.
Technically York's statement indicates that Richard
has abdicated, and is not therefore being deposed.
Carlisle's protest which follows is an argument that
Richard cannot abdicate.
112 of...fourth F's reading is stately, emphatic
and metrically correct. On balance, the likelihood
that F made a positive correction either on the
independent authority of the manuscript copy used
to correct Q3, or from a change introduced in the
playhouse, weighs more heavily than Q1 in view of
Compositor A's tendency to scramble phrases in his
memory.

BULLINGBROOK In God's name I'll ascend the regal throne.
CARLISLE Marry, God forbid!

    Worst in this royal presence may I speak,   115
    Yet best beseeming me to speak the truth.
    Would God that any in this noble presence
    Were enough noble to be upright judge
    Of noble Richard. Then true noblesse would
    Learn him forbearance from so foul a wrong.   120
    What subject can give sentence on his king,
    And who sits here that is not Richard's subject?
    Thieves are not judged but they are by to hear
    Although apparent guilt be seen in them,
    And shall the figure of God's majesty,   125
    His captain, steward, deputy, elect,
    Anointed, crownèd, planted many years,
    Be judged by subject and inferior breath
    And he himself not present? Oh, forfend it, God,
    That in a Christian climate souls refined   130
    Should show so heinous, black, obscene a deed!
    I speak to subjects and a subject speaks,
    Stirred up by God thus boldly for his king.
    My lord of Herford here, whom you call king,
    Is a foul traitor to proud Herford's king,   135
    And if you crown him let me prophesy:

---

114 Marry] F3; Mary Qq, F   114 God] Qq; Heauen F   115 may I] Q1, F; I may Q2–5   117 that] Q1, F; *not in* Q2–5
119 noblesse] Q1; nobleness Q2–5, F   122 sits] Q1, Q5, F; sits not Q2–4   126 deputy, elect] Qq; Deputie elect F
129 forfend] Qq; forbid F   133 God] Qq; Heauen F

---

115 Worst Most unfit. Because he is a priest among nobles. Carlisle also remembers Aumerle's 'best' at 31.

115 this royal presence With this sarcasm, Carlisle brings to the surface the uneasiness of the nobles at Bullingbrook's position by the throne. He offers the correct form, 'this noble presence', at 117.

117–49 Carlisle's speech against the abdication of Richard is set in the form of a *sermo humilis*, a classical oration in the Christian lowly style appropriate to a protest against high presumption. After the *exordium* (115–16), he gives a *narratio* (117–22), *explicatio* (123–9), *partitio* (129–31), *amplificatio* (132–5), *refutatio* (136–44), and the *peroratio* (145–9). See John Baxter, *Shakespeare's Poetic Styles*, pp. 184–7.

119 noblesse nobility, of soul as well as rank.

121–9 In Holinshed (II, 512) Carlisle's protest is made after the abdication and is directed specifically against the proposal to bring Richard to trial for the actions confessed in the article of abdication. See 223–7 below. In context here, Carlisle's objection to the notion of judging Richard implies that he has been deposed as an attempted act of justice.

124 apparent evident, clear-cut.

125 figure image.

126 deputy, elect F's reading as one phrase – deputy elect – ignores the sequence from elected to anointed, crowned and planted. Holinshed makes no reference to divine right at all.

128 subject...breath See 1.3.214.

129 forfend (1) forbid, (2) prevent.

134 My...Herford The minimal title Bullingbrook could claim, the name under which he was exiled.

136 let me prophesy Carlisle's warnings are those of the 'Homily Against Disobedience and

The blood of English shall manure the ground
And future ages groan for this foul act.
Peace shall go sleep with Turks and infidels,
And in this seat of peace tumultuous wars   140
Shall kin with kin and kind with kind confound.
Disorder, horror, fear and mutiny
Shall here inhabit, and this land be called
The field of Golgotha and dead men's skulls.
Oh, if you raise this house against this house   145
It will the woefullest division prove
That ever fell upon this cursèd earth.
Prevent it, resist it, let it not be so,
Lest child, child's children, cry against you woe.

NORTHUMBERLAND Well have you argued, sir, and for your pains   150
Of capital treason we arrest you here.
My Lord of Westminster, be it your charge
To keep him safely till his day of trial.
May it please you, lords, to grant the commons' suit?

BULLINGBROOK Fetch hither Richard, that in common view   155
He may surrender. So we shall proceed
Without suspicion.

YORK   I will be his conduct.   *Exit*

138 this] Q1; his Q2–5, F   145 raise] Qq; rear F   145 against this] Q1–2, F; against his Q3–5   148 let] Q1; and let
Q2–5, F   154–317] Q4–5, F; *not in* Q1–3   154 commons'] F (Commons); common Q4–5   155 BULLINGBROOK. Fetch]
F; Fetch Q4–5   156–7] F; *one line* Q4–5   157 SD] F; *not in* Q4–5

Wilful Rebellion' (see Appendix 3, p. 225 below).
For the theological weaknesses of the 1571 Homily
see Roy Battenhouse, 'Tudor doctrine and the
tragedy of *Richard II*', pp. 33–7.
    137 manure The same verb appears in a similar
context in *Caesar's Revenge* 150–1. Other similarities
of phrase at 1.1.109 and 196 and 2.2.142 make it just
possible that Shakespeare knew this academic play,
which was performed by students at Oxford in the
early 1590s.
    141 confound bring to destruction. Allegations
that fathers kill sons and sons their fathers in civil
war were commonplace. See *3H6* 2.5.55–122.
    144 field battlefield, and possibly pasture.
    144 Golgotha Calvary, the hill of execution
outside Jerusalem known as the 'place of skulls'.
See John 19.17, Mark 15.22.
    145 raise call to rebel.
    145 this house…house See Mark 3.25: 'If a
house be divided against itself…' The overt
reference is to the Parliament house (see *3H6*
1.1.71), but there is also a hint of the Houses of York

and Lancaster which fought in the *H6* plays. If it
is a reference to the alternative heir Edmund
Mortimer (see *1H4* 1.3.155–7), it is deeply
submerged. In a production in Oregon in 1980
Carlisle gestured first at the assembled Parliament
and then at heaven, giving point to his invocation
of the divinity of kingship.
    152 Westminster The sources put Carlisle into
the care of the Abbot of St Albans, but in view of
Carlisle's subsequent share in the Westminster
conspiracy the change is an obvious economy.
    154–317 Q1–3 lack these 163 lines, the so-called
'deposition scene'.
    154 the commons' suit A request to publish
the terms of Richard's abdication. Bullingbrook
responds to the request by summoning Richard to
appear. See 271 below. His second sentence (156–7)
in his currently economical style of speaking
acknowledges Carlisle's plea that Richard should
not be judged in his absence (125–9).
    156 surrender give up the crown, abdicate.

BULLINGBROOK Lords, you that here are under our arrest,
　　　　Procure your sureties for your days of answer.
　　　　Little are we beholding to your love   160
　　　　And little looked for at your helping hands.

Enter RICHARD *and York.*

RICHARD Alack, why am I sent for to a king
　　　　Before I have shook off the regal thoughts
　　　　Wherewith I reigned? I hardly yet have learned
　　　　To insinuate, flatter, bow and bend my knee.   165
　　　　Give sorrow leave awhile to tutor me
　　　　To this submission. Yet I well remember
　　　　The favours of these men. Were they not mine?
　　　　Did they not sometime cry 'All hail' to me?
　　　　So Judas did to Christ, but he in twelve   170
　　　　Found truth in all but one, I in twelve thousand none.
　　　　God save the king! Will no man say Amen?
　　　　Am I both priest and clerk? Well then, Amen.
　　　　God save the king, although I be not he,
　　　　And yet Amen if heaven do think him me.   175
　　　　To do what service am I sent for hither?
YORK To do that office of thine own good will
　　　　Which tirèd majesty did make thee offer,
　　　　The resignation of thy state and crown
　　　　To Henry Bullingbrook.   180

158 here are] F; are heere, are Q4–5 161 looked] F; looke Q4–5 161 SD] F; *Enter king Richard.* Q4–5 165 knee]
F; limbes Q4–5 166–70] F; Give...submission: / Yet...men, / Were...hayle / To...twelue, Q4–5 169 sometime]
F; sometimes Q4–5 180 Henry] F; Harry Q4–5

160 **beholding** indebted.
161 SD From here on F stops using *King* for
Richard in speech headings and stage directions.
162 **to a king** Richard announces himself as
having already abdicated. According to
E. W. Talbert, *The Problem of Order*, p. 185, the
assumptions in 162–7 are Lancastrian (pro Bullingbrook), in 167–76 Yorkist (pro Richard), in 177–80
Lancastrian, in 181–91 Yorkist, and in 190–221
Lancastrian, after which Northumberland's intervention turns the focus away from the constitutional
aspects of the deposition.
165 **insinuate** slide forward.
168 **favours** (1) faces, (2) political colours. See
5.3.18.
169 In Matt. and Mark Judas says 'Hail
Master'. In the York and Chester Mysteries Judas
greets Christ in the words Richard uses.

171 **twelve thousand** See 3.2.70, 76.
173 **both...clerk** The clerk said 'amen' to the
priest's prayers. Richard is conducting a decorona-
tion ceremony and acting as his own authority
without a representative of the Church. The phrase
is proverbial (Dent P587.1).
176 **service** (1) homage as a servant, (2) church
service.
177 **office** church ceremony or function.
178 **tirèd** One of several words implying the
clothing (attire) of royalty. See 108, 202, 249.
179 **resignation** The technical act of abdication
in Holinshed is Richard's signing the document
renouncing his title and releasing his subjects from
their oaths of service to him. Here it has a more
visual point as the handing-over of the crown and
withdrawal from the 'state' or throne.

RICHARD Give me the crown. Here, cousin, seize the crown,
　　　　On this side my hand and on that side thine.
　　　　Now is this golden crown like a deep well
　　　　That owes two buckets, filling one another,
　　　　The emptier ever dancing in the air,　　　　　　　　185
　　　　The other down, unseen and full of water.
　　　　That bucket, down and full of tears, am I,
　　　　Drinking my griefs whilst you mount up on high.
BULLINGBROOK I thought you had been willing to resign.
RICHARD My crown I am, but still my griefs are mine.　　190
　　　　You may my glories and my state depose,
　　　　But not my griefs. Still am I king of those.
BULLINGBROOK Part of your cares you give me with your crown.
RICHARD Your cares set up do not pluck my cares down.
　　　　My care is loss of care, by old care done.　　　　195
　　　　Your care is gain of care, by new care won.
　　　　The cares I give I have, though given away.
　　　　They 'tend the crown, yet still with me they stay.
BULLINGBROOK Are you contented to resign the crown?
RICHARD Aye – no. No – aye, for I must nothing be,　　200
　　　　Therefore no 'no', for I resign to thee.
　　　　Now, mark me how I will undo myself.
　　　　I give this heavy weight from off my head
　　　　And this unwieldy sceptre from my hand,

181] F; Sease the Crowne. Q4–5　　182] *Johnson*; Heere Cousin, on this side my Hand, on that side thine. F; Heere
Coosin, on this side my hand, and on that side yours: Q4–5　　188 griefs] F; griefe Q4–5　　200 Aye – no. No – aye,]
This edn; I, no; no, I: F; I, no no I; Q4–5　　201 no 'no'] *Theobald*; no, no, F; no no, Q4–5

181 **Give me the crown** The royal regalia,
brought in with the procession '*as to the
parliament*', has on this evidence not yet been taken
up by Bullingbrook.
　181 **Here...crown** F's repetition of 'Heere
Cousin' may have been either an editorial or
compositorial confusion. It created an extra-metrical
foot in 182 which F tried to remedy by deleting the
'and', an attempt more characteristic of the F editor
than of its compositors. It is possible that there was
some elaboration in the playhouse to clarify a
difficult piece of staging, and that the F text reflects
the change.
　181 **seize the crown** In Holinshed Richard put
his ring on Bullingbrook's hand. Daniel (*Civil Wars*,
II, 119) says ''Tis said with his owne hands he gave
the crowne / To *Lancaster*...' and begged to be
allowed to live as a private man.

183–8 H. R. Patch, *The Goddess Fortuna in
Medieval Literature*, records this simile as a stock
image of fortune (pp. 53–4).
　184 **owes** possesses.
　184 **filling one another** The raising of the full
bucket lowers the other to be filled in its turn.
　194–8 Richard puns on care as (1) obligation, (2)
grief, (3) worry.
　198 **'tend** attend. Behind the word-play is the
proverbial 'crowns have cares' (Tilley c863).
　200 **Aye...aye** No written form can encompass
the nuances of the spoken form of this sentence,
though the Elizabethan habit of writing 'I' for both
'I' and 'aye' does better than the modernised form.
See Mahood, p. 87, and *Rom.* 3.2.45–50.
　202 **undo** (1) destroy, (2) undress.
　203–14 The phrases here are closely based on the
Act of Abdication.

The pride of kingly sway from out my heart.   205
With mine own tears I wash away my balm;
With mine own hands I give away my crown;
With mine own tongue deny my sacred state;
With mine own breath release all duteous oaths.
All pomp and majesty I do forswear;   210
My manors, rents, revenues I forgo;
My acts, decrees, and statutes I deny.
God pardon all oaths that are broke to me;
God keep all vows unbroke are made to thee.
Make me that nothing have with nothing grieved,   215
And thou with all pleased that hast all achieved.
Long mayst thou live in Richard's seat to sit,
And soon lie Richard in an earthy pit.
God save King Henry, unkinged Richard says,
And send him many years of sunshine days.   220
What more remains?

NORTHUMBERLAND   No more, but that you read
These accusations and these grievous crimes
Committed by your person and your followers
Against the state and profit of this land,
That by confessing them the souls of men   225
May deem that you are worthily deposed.

RICHARD Must I do so? And must I ravel out
My weaved-up follies? Gentle Northumberland,
If thy offences were upon record
Would it not shame thee, in so fair a troop,   230
To read a lecture of them? If thou wouldst,
There shouldst thou find one heinous Article
Containing the deposing of a king
And cracking the strong warrant of an oath,

---

209 duteous oaths] F; duties rites Q4–5   211 manors] F; Manners Q4; Mannors Q5   214 are made] F; that sweare
Q4–5   218 earthy] Q4, F; earthly Q5   219 Henry] F; *Harry* Q4–5   220 sunshine] Q4, F; Sun-shines Q5   228 follies]
F; Folly Q4–5

206 **balm** anointing oil. See 3.2.54–5.
209 **duteous oaths** Compare 'duty' at 3.3.48
and elsewhere.
221–6 Holinshed gives the articles in full (II,
502). Northumberland's demand that Richard read
them in Parliament is Shakespeare's invention. It
renews Northumberland's role as Bullingbrook's
strong man.
227 **ravel out** unravel, unweave.

228 **Gentle** (1) Noble, (2) soft-mannered.
231 **read a lecture** recite the list.
232 **heinous Article** Holinshed writes (II, 502)
of '33 solemn articles, heinous to the eares of all
men', and 'these articles, and other heinous and
detestable accusations'.
234 **an oath** Northumberland's oath of allegiance. See 2.2.112, and compare 213–14.

Marked with a blot, damned in the book of heaven.   235
Nay, all of you that stand and look upon me
Whilst that my wretchedness doth bait my self,
Though some of you with Pilate wash your hands,
Showing an outward pity, yet you Pilates
Have here delivered me to my sour cross   240
And water cannot wash away your sin.

NORTHUMBERLAND My lord, dispatch. Read o'er these Articles.

RICHARD Mine eyes are full of tears; I cannot see.
And yet salt water blinds them not so much
But they can see a sort of traitors here.   245
Nay, if I turn mine eyes upon my self
I find myself a traitor with the rest,
For I have given here my soul's consent
T'undeck the pompous body of a king,
Made glory base, a sovereignty a slave,   250
Proud majesty a subject, state a peasant.

NORTHUMBERLAND My lord –

RICHARD No lord of thine, thou haught insulting man,
Nor no man's lord. I have no name, no title,
No, not that name was given me at the font,   255
But 'tis usurped. Alack the heavy day
That I have worn so many winters out
And know not now what name to call myself.
Oh that I were a mockery king of snow
Standing before the sun of Bullingbrook,   260
To melt myself away in water drops.
Good king, great king, and yet not greatly good,
And if my word be sterling yet in England
Let it command a mirror hither straight

---

236 all of] F; of Q4–5   236 upon me] F; vpon Q4–5   249 T'undeck] F; To vndecke Q4–5   250 a sovereignty] F;
and Soueraigntie Q4–5   254 Nor] Q4–5; No, nor F   263 word] F; name Q4–5

238–9 Matt. 27.24. The reference to Pilate is
consistent with the references to Judases at 3.2.132
and 170 in this scene. In the second 'Pilates'
Richard may be punning on 'pilots', guiding
merchandise by water to its destination. Holinshed
puns against the Archbishop of Canterbury as
'prelate' and 'Pilate' (II, 501).

240 delivered The verb used in the Gospels.

245 sort gang, group. Always used contemptuously in Shakespeare.

249 pompous ceremonially dressed.

250 a sovereignty a slave Richard echoes
Gaunt's charge at 2.1.114.

253 haught arrogant, haughty.

256 usurped taken away illegally. Richard is
now attacking the wrongdoing of the deposers.
Some editors have conjectured that this specific
complaint about Richard's name is an allusion to the
Lancastrian claim that he was a bastard child.

263 And if An intensive form ('And' is 'an', the
old form of 'if').

263 sterling of current value.

That it may show me what a face I have   265
Since it is bankrupt of his majesty.

BULLINGBROOK Go some of you, and fetch a looking glass.

                                  [*Exit an attendant*]

NORTHUMBERLAND Read o'er this paper while the glass doth come.

RICHARD Fiend, thou torments me ere I come to hell.

BULLINGBROOK Urge it no more, my Lord Northumberland.   270

NORTHUMBERLAND The commons will not then be satisfied.

RICHARD They shall be satisfied. I'll read enough
When I do see the very book indeed
Where all my sins are writ, and that's my self.

                   Enter one with a glass.

Give me that glass and therein will I read.   275
No deeper wrinkles yet? Hath sorrow struck
So many blows upon this face of mine
And made no deeper wounds? Oh flattering glass,
Like to my followers in prosperity
Thou dost beguile me. Was this face the face   280
That every day under his household roof
Did keep ten thousand men? Was this the face
That like the sun did make beholders wink?
Is this the face which faced so many follies,
That was at last outfaced by Bullingbrook?   285
A brittle glory shineth in this face.
As brittle as the glory is the face,

                  [*Smashes the glass.*]

For there it is, cracked in an hundred shivers.

---

267 SD] *Capell; not in* Qq, F   274 SD] F; *not in* Q4–5   275–85] F; Guie me the Glasse: no deeper...yet? / Hath... this / Face...woundes? / Oh...prosperitie! / Was this the face that...his / Househould...men? / Was...face that faast...follies, / And was...Bullingbrooke? Q4–5   287 SD] *Theobald (Dashes the glass against the ground); not in* Qq, F   288 an] F; a Q4–5

266 his its.

271 commons See 154 n.

273–4 the very...writ See Ps. 139.15: 'in thy booke were al my members written'.

275 For the iconography of mirrors and the self see Ure, 'The looking glass of *Richard II*', *PQ* 34 (1955), 219–24, and Janette Dillon, *Shakespeare and the Solitary Man*, ch. 5. The flattering glass (278) was proverbial (Dent G132.1).

279 followers in prosperity fairweather friends.

282 ten thousand See Holinshed, II, 508.

282 Was...face Both Richard here and Faustus on Helen of Troy have behind them Isa. 14.16: 'Is this the man that brought all lands in fear, and made the kingdoms afraid?'

283 wink shut their eyes.

284 faced put a new face on (as in a cloth facing).

288 shivers fragments.

Mark, silent king, the moral of this sport,
How soon my sorrow hath destroyed my face.   290
BULLINGBROOK The shadow of your sorrow hath destroyed
    The shadow of your face.
RICHARD   Say that again.
    The shadow of my sorrow. Ha, let's see.
    'Tis very true, my grief lies all within
    And these external manners of laments   295
    Are merely shadows to the unseen grief
    That swells with silence in the tortured soul.
    There lies the substance; and I thank thee, king,
    For thy great bounty, that not only givest
    Me cause to wail but teachest me the way   300
    How to lament the cause. I'll beg one boon
    And then be gone and trouble you no more.
    Shall I obtain it?
BULLINGBROOK   Name it, fair cousin.
RICHARD Fair cousin? I am greater than a king,
    For when I was a king my flatterers   305
    Were then but subjects. Being now a subject
    I have a king here to my flatterer.
    Being so great I have no need to beg.
BULLINGBROOK Yet ask.
RICHARD And shall I have?   310
BULLINGBROOK You shall.
RICHARD Then give me leave to go.
BULLINGBROOK Whither?
RICHARD Whither you will, so I were from your sights.
BULLINGBROOK Go some of you, convey him to the Tower.   315
RICHARD Oh good – 'convey'. Conveyers are you all
    That rise thus nimbly by a true king's fall.

292–300] F; Say...sorrow; / Ha...griefe / Lies...manners / Of...vnseene, / Griefe...soule: / And I...King that
not onely giuest / Me...way Q4–5   295 manners] Q4–5; manner F   303 Shall...it?] F; *not in* Q4–5   304 cousin?]
F; Coose, why? Q4–5   305–8] F; For...subiects, / Being...heere / To...beg. Q4–5   310 have?] F; haue it? Q4–5
312 Then] F; Why then Q4–5   316 good –] F (good:); good Q4–5

289 **silent king** Richard emphasises Bullingbrook's increasing taciturnity and his own contrasting command of the stage with words instead of real
power.
    291 **shadow...sorrow** (1) darkness, (2) image,
(3) reflection not the reality.
    297 **swells** An image of pregnancy, as in the
queen's conceit at 2.2.10–66. Her play on 'shadow'
is also related to Richard's.

298 **There** In the soul.
    307 **to** (1) as, (2) be.
    315–16 Richard develops the principal sense of
'convey' as 'to escort' with its two other meanings,
'to transfer the title to property', and 'to steal'. See
Edward II 1.1.200–1.
    317 **nimbly** 'Nimble fingers' was a metonymy
for a thief.

BULLINGBROOK On Wednesday next we solemnly set down
   Our coronation. Lords, prepare yourselves.

        Exeunt [Bullingbrook, Richard, Lords and guards,
        all except] Westminster, Carlisle and Aumerle

WESTMINSTER A woeful pageant have we here beheld.   320
CARLISLE The woe's to come. The children yet unborn
   Shall feel this day as sharp to them as thorn.
AUMERLE You holy clergymen, is there no plot
   To rid the realm of this pernicious blot?
WESTMINSTER My lord,   325
   Before I freely speak my mind herein
   You shall not only take the sacrament
   To bury mine intents but also to effect
   Whatever I shall happen to devise.
   I see your brows are full of discontent,   330
   Your hearts of sorrow and your eyes of tears.
   Come home with me to supper. I will lay
   A plot shall show us all a merry day.

                                  Exeunt

5.1 *Enter the* QUEEN *with her attendants.*

QUEEN This way the king will come. This is the way
   To Julius Caesar's ill-erected tower,
   To whose flint bosom my condemnèd lord

318–19] Q4–5, F; *Bull.* Let it be so, and loe on wednesday next, / We solemnly proclaime our Coronation, / Lords be ready all. Q1–3   319 SD] Qq; *Exeunt.* F   321 woe's] Qq; woes F   325–6 My lord, / Before] *Cam.*; My Lo. before Q1–2 *(one line)*; Before Q3–5, F   331 hearts] Q1; heart Q2–5, F   332–3] *Pope;* ...Ile lay a plot, / Shall... Qq, F Act 5, Scene 1   0 SD] Qq; *Enter Queene, and Ladies* F

318–19 At this point Q1–3 compensate for the cancellation of the deposition scene. The substitution has been variously regarded as clumsy or adroit, though most editors note that the Abbot of Westminster's reference to a pageant is pointless without the deposition scene.

318 **set down** appoint as the time for.

320 **pageant** (1) ceremonial, (2) play-acting.

324 **blot** i.e. the shameful deed of deposition, rather than its perpetrators.

327 **take the sacrament** Holinshed (II, 514) says 'they sware on the holie evangelists'. Daniel says 'The Sacrament the pledge of faith they made.'

332–3 Pope's emendation restores a rhyming couplet to conclude the scene.

333 **plot** plan, design.

Act 5, Scene 1

5.1 In Daniel, but in no other versions, Richard and the queen meet in a London street. Shakespeare's dialogue has verbal resemblances to Daniel's 33 stanzas (*Civil Wars*, II, 66–98). The latter part of the scene, from Northumberland's entry on, is entirely Shakespeare's, apart from the transfer to Pomfret.

2 **Julius...tower** According to Stow (1598) this was the 'common opinion' about the origin of the Tower of London.

2 **ill-erected** built with bad intention and bad effect.

Is doomed a prisoner by proud Bullingbrook.
Here let us rest, if this rebellious earth   5
Have any resting for her true king's queen.

Enter RICHARD *and guard.*

But soft, but see, or rather do not see
My fair rose wither. Yet look up, behold,
That you in pity may dissolve to dew
And wash him fresh again with true love tears.   10
Ah thou, the model where old Troy did stand,
Thou map of honour, thou King Richard's tomb,
And not King Richard! Thou most beauteous inn,
Why should hard-favoured grief be lodged in thee
When triumph is become an alehouse guest?   15
RICHARD Join not with grief, fair woman, do not so,
To make my end too sudden. Learn, good soul,
To think our former state a happy dream,
From which awaked, the truth of what we are
Shows us but this. I am sworn brother, sweet,   20
To grim Necessity, and he and I
Will keep a league till death. Hie thee to France
And cloister thee in some religious house.
Our holy lives must win a new world's crown
Which our profane hours here have thrown down.   25
QUEEN What, is my Richard both in shape and mind

6 SD] F; *Enter Ric.* QQ   25 thrown] QQ; stricken F

8 **My fair rose** We last saw the queen in the
garden scene, 3.4. Hotspur in *1H4* 1.3.175 calls
Richard 'that sweet lovely rose'. The rose among
flowers was regarded as equivalent to the lion among
beasts. See 1.1.174. The water (dew) of grief
belongs more with roses than with lions, though in
29–31 the queen urges Richard to be a lion.

11 **model** groundplan, in little. The meaning is
not the same as in 1.2.28, though the sense of a
miniature representation is there.

11 **old Troy** London was known in popular
mythology as Troynovant – New Troy – from its
alleged foundation by the Trojan Brutus, great-
grandson of Aeneas, founder of Rome according to
Virgil.

12 **map** picture.

13 **inn** temporary lodging.

14 **hard-favoured** harsh-faced.

14 **lodged** The queen has called grief a guest at
2.2.7. The verb is also used of corn blown flat by
a storm.

15 **triumph** See 3.4.99.

15 **alehouse** The cheapest kind of inn.

20 **sworn brother** A member of a brotherhood
(chivalric or monastic).

22 **keep a league** maintain an alliance.

22 **Hie thee** Take yourself.

23 **cloister thee…house** withdraw from a
political to a religious life. Richard considers this
alternative for himself at 3.2.99 and 3.3.147–53. It
parallels the alternatives of pilgrimage or crusade.
See p. 5 above.

24 **new world's crown** In heaven.

25 **thrown** A disyllable, as in F's 'stricken'.

Transformed and weakenèd? Hath Bullingbrook
Deposed thine intellect? Hath he been in thy heart?
The lion dying thrusteth forth his paw
And wounds the earth if nothing else with rage   30
To be o'erpowered, and wilt thou, pupil-like,
Take the correction mildly, kiss the rod,
And fawn on rage with base humility,
Which art a lion and the king of beasts?

RICHARD A king of beasts indeed. If aught but beasts   35
I had been still a happy king of men.
Good sometime queen, prepare thee hence for France.
Think I am dead, and that even here thou takest
As from my deathbed thy last living leave.
In winter's tedious nights sit by the fire   40
With good old folks, and let them tell thee tales
Of woeful ages long ago betid,
And ere thou bid good night, to 'quite their griefs
Tell thou the lamentable tale of me
And send the hearers weeping to their beds.   45
For why! the senseless brands will sympathise
The heavy accent of thy moving tongue,
And in compassion weep the fire out,
And some will mourn in ashes, some coal black,
For the deposing of a rightful king.   50

Enter NORTHUMBERLAND.

NORTHUMBERLAND My lord, the mind of Bullingbrook is changed.

32 the correction] Q1 ; thy correction Q2–5, F   32 correction mildly,] F ; correction, mildly Qq   34 the] Q1 ; a Q2–5,
F   37 sometime] Q3–5, F ; sometimes Q1–2   39 thy] Q1 ; my Q2–5, F   41 thee] Q2–5, F ; the Q1   42 betid] Q1 ; betide
Q2–5, F   43 griefs] Q1 ; griefe Q2–5, F   44 tale] Qq ; fall F   46 sympathise] Q1, F ; simpathie Q2–5

27 Capell conjectures that an adjective may be
omitted before 'Bullingbrook', damaging the
metre. But 'weakenèd' as a trisyllable gives a
perfectly regular rhythm.
29–30 See *Edward II* 5.1.11–15, and 1.1.174 n.
above.
32 correction...kiss Q1 and F differ in punctuation, Q fitting the adverb to 'kiss' and F to
'take'. Ure cites Tyndale (1528) with a precedent
for F's version, though that may signify no more
than the possibility that F is normalising.
32 kiss the rod Proverbial for submissiveness
(Tilley R156).
33–4 The queen demands human anger, not
divine patience of the kind York speaks of at 5.2.33.

Compare the Duchess of Gloucester to Gaunt at
1.2.33–4.
42 betid Q1's spelling is 'betidde'. A rare past
tense, meaning 'happened'.
43 'quite requite, balance.
44 tale Q1's word fits the context well, and is not
a compositor's recollection of 41, since A took over
from S at 43. F's word is a normalisation.
46 brands firewood.
46 sympathise share the feelings of.
47 moving exciting sympathy.
49 some i.e. some brands.
51 Bullingbrook Northumberland still does not
use a respectful title.

You must to Pomfret, not unto the Tower.
And, madam, there is order ta'en for you.
With all swift speed you must away to France.
RICHARD Northumberland, thou ladder wherewithal   55
The mounting Bullingbrook ascends my throne,
The time shall not be many hours of age
More than it is ere foul sin gathering head
Shall break into corruption. Thou shalt think
Though he divide the realm and give thee half   60
It is too little, helping him to all.
He shall think that thou which knowest the way
To plant unrightful kings wilt know again,
Being ne'er so little urged, another way
To pluck him headlong from the usurpèd throne.   65
The love of wicked men converts to fear,
That fear to hate, and hate turns one or both
To worthy danger and deservèd death.
NORTHUMBERLAND My guilt be on my head, and there an end.
Take leave and part, for you must part forthwith.   70
RICHARD Doubly divorced! Bad men, you violate
A twofold marriage twixt my crown and me
And then betwixt me and my married wife.
Let me unkiss the oath twixt thee and me –
And yet not so, for with a kiss 'twas made.   75
Part us, Northumberland: I towards the north
Where shivering cold and sickness pines the clime,
My wife to France, from whence set forth in pomp
She came adornèd hither like sweet May,
Sent back like Hollowmas or short'st of day.   80

66 men] Qq; friends F   72 twixt] Q1, F; betwixt Q2–5   74 twixt] Q1, F; betwixt Q2–5   78 wife] Qq; Queene F

52 **Pomfret** Pontefract Castle. See Holinshed, II, 507.·

53 **there...ta'en** arrangements have been made.

54 **France** Richard's second queen was French. She was returned to her family.

55–9 In *2H4* 3.1.67–79 Bullingbrook quotes these lines as an accurate prophecy. His counsellor Warwick says they were merely 'a perfect guess'.

55 **ladder** See Daniel, *The Civil Wars*, I, 74, and *JC* 2.2.22. Ladders were commonly associated with ambition.

58 **foul...head** The metaphor is of a plague of boils, such as God imposed on the Egyptians and on Job.

60 **Though he** Even though he should.

61 **helping him** since you helped him.

63 **plant** The submerged metaphor is of the Plantagenet line and the Tree of Jesse. See 1.2.13 n. and *3H6* 1.1.48.

67 **one or both** i.e. of the wicked men.

68 **worthy** justifiable.

74 **unkiss the oath** release from the oath (of marriage) by kissing.

77 **pines the clime** afflicts the climate.

80 **Hollowmas** All Hallows (All Saints), 1 November. Occurring six months after May Day, its antithesis, it counted as the start of winter.

QUEEN And must we be divided? Must we part?

RICHARD Ay, hand from hand, my love, and heart from heart.

QUEEN Banish us both, and send the king with me.

NORTHUMBERLAND That were some love, but little policy.

QUEEN Then whither he goes thither let me go.   85

RICHARD So two together weeping make one woe.

      Weep thou for me in France, I for thee here;

      Better far off than, near, be ne'er the near.

      Go, count thy way with sighs, I mine with groans.

QUEEN So longest way shall have the longest moans.   90

RICHARD Twice for one step I'll groan, the way being short,

      And piece the way out with a heavy heart.

      Come, come, in wooing sorrow let's be brief

      Since, wedding it, there is such length in grief.

      One kiss shall stop our mouths, and dumbly part.   95

      Thus give I mine, and thus take I thy heart.

QUEEN Give me mine own again. 'Twere no good part

      To take on me to keep and kill thy heart.

      So, now I have mine own again be gone,

      That I may strive to kill it with a groan.   100

RICHARD We make woe wanton with this fond delay.

      Once more adieu, the rest let sorrow say.

                        Exeunt

5.2 *Enter Duke of* YORK *and the* DUCHESS.

DUCHESS My lord, you told me you would tell the rest,

      When weeping made you break the story off,

---

84 SH NORTHUMBERLAND] F; *King* Qq   87 Weep thou] Q1, F; *Weepe* Q2–5   95 dumbly] Q1, F; *doubly* Q2–5   Act 5, Scene 2   0 SD] Qq; *Enter Yorke, and his Duchesse.* F   2 off] F; *of* Q1; *not in* Q2–5

84 SH NORTHUMBERLAND Many editors adopt the Q1 ascription of the line to Richard, since it continues the stichomythic exchange between husband and wife. But the reference to 'little policy' (unsound politics) is more like Northumberland than Richard, and the queen's next line is certainly addressed to Northumberland.

86–9 Stanley Wells, 'The lamentable tale of *Richard II*', *S.St.* 17 (1982), 1–23, points out that this exchange brings together all the terms of grief in the play, except for 'lament'. The 'lamentable tale' (44) has an edge of blame which makes it less apt here.

88 ne'er the near not together. A proverbial phrase (Dent N135.2). The last word is strictly a comparative ('nearer'). See Wells, *Modernising Shakespeare's Spelling*, p. 26.

92 piece…out lengthen the journey.

95 and dumbly part and then let us part in silence.

101 wanton reckless, unrestrained.

102 Once more adieu Presumably with a third kiss.

Act 5, Scene 2

5.2 The account of Bullingbrook's 'triumph' in entering London, which Charles Kean and his nineteenth-century successors made a stage spectacle, is close to Daniel, *The Civil Wars*, II, 66–70.

Of our two cousins coming into London.

YORK Where did I leave?

DUCHESS   At that sad stop, my lord,
Where rude misgoverned hands from windows' tops   5
Threw dust and rubbish on King Richard's head.

YORK Then, as I said, the duke, great Bullingbrook,
Mounted upon a hot and fiery steed
Which his aspiring rider seemed to know,
With slow but stately pace kept on his course,   10
Whilst all tongues cried 'God save thee, Bullingbrook!'
You would have thought the very windows spake,
So many greedy looks of young and old
Through casements darted their desiring eyes
Upon his visage, and that all the walls   15
With painted imagery had said at once
'Jesu preserve thee! Welcome, Bullingbrook!'
Whilst he from one side to the other turning,
Bare headed, lower than his proud steed's neck,
Bespake them thus: 'I thank you, countrymen',   20
And thus still doing, thus he passed along.

DUCHESS Alack, poor Richard. Where rode he the whilst?

YORK As in a theatre the eyes of men
After a well-graced actor leaves the stage
Are idly bent on him that enters next,   25
Thinking his prattle to be tedious,
Even so or with much more contempt men's eyes
Did scowl on Richard. No man cried 'God save him',
No joyful tongue gave him his welcome home,

---

11 Whilst] Q1; While Q2–5, F   11 thee] F; the Qq   17 thee] F; the Qq   18 from] F; from the Qq   22 Alack] Qq; Alas F   22 rode] Q1; rides Q2–5, F   28 Richard] F; gentle Richard Qq

---

3 cousins nephews.

4 leave stop, leave off.

5 windows' tops high or top windows. Casements (14) do not have 'tops'.

6 King Richard's The duchess keeps the old title, as she does for her son at 41–3.

7 Bullingbrook The entry to London preceded the coronation.

8 a hot…steed See 5.5.77 n.

9 Which…know Which seemed to know who its aspiring rider was.

16 painted imagery Like a tapestry or row of statues recessed in a wall.

18 from one F's emendation improves Q1's

metre, which probably resulted from Q1 Compositor A trying to hold the whole line in his memory while he set it, and so balancing 'the one side' with 'the other'.

20 Bespake Addressed.

23–30 In Holinshed (II, 501) the citizens' attitude to Richard is represented as much more actively hostile. The 'actor' simile, often invoked to augment the idea of Richard as an actor of his kingly role rather than as true king, in fact applies more directly to Bullingbrook.

28 Richard Q1's adjective makes the line an alexandrine. Q1 Compositor A could have taken it from 31.

But dust was thrown upon his sacred head,   30
Which with such gentle sorrow he shook off,
His face still combating with tears and smiles,
The badges of his grief and patience,
That had not God for some strong purpose steeled
The hearts of men they must perforce have melted   35
And barbarism itself have pitied him.
But heaven hath a hand in these events,
To whose high will we bound our calm contents.
To Bullingbrook are we sworn subjects now,
Whose state and honour I for aye allow.   40

Enter AUMERLE.

DUCHESS Here comes my son Aumerle.
YORK   Aumerle that was,
But that is lost for being Richard's friend,
And, madam, you must call him Rutland now.
I am in Parliament pledge for his truth
And lasting fealty to the new-made king.   45
DUCHESS Welcome, my son. Who are the violets now
That strew the green lap of the new-come spring?
AUMERLE Madam, I know not, nor I greatly care not.
God knows I had as lief be none as one.
YORK Well, bear you well in this new spring of time   50
Lest you be cropped before you come to prime.

40 SD] F; *not in* Q1–3; *after* 41 Q4–5

---

33 **badges** Insignia of a noble or 'gentle' (31) man.

37–8 York falls into rhyme when moralising Richard's 'patience' (33) as good Christian policy.

38 **bound** limit, restrict. Cognate with 'band' and 'bond'.

41–116 The gist of the Aumerle plot and its discovery is in Holinshed, II, 515. For its function in Act 5 see Sheldon P. Zitner, 'Aumerle's conspiracy', *SEL* 14 (1974), 239–57. Its burlesque presentation of the question of loyalty and its comic relief before the conclusion suggest that its frequent elimination from productions is a mistake.

41 **my** Alan E. Craven ('Simmes' Compositor A and five Shakespeare quartos', *SB* 26 (1973), 37–60, p. 58) conjectures that Q1 Compositor A normalised 'our' into 'my', possibly influenced by 46. But 'my' is perfectly correct.

43 **you...now** Holinshed (II, 513) notes that after the abdication the Dukes of Aumerle, Surrey and Exeter lost their dukedoms, which Richard had given them. This is the only acknowledgement in the play of the consequences of the Parliament-scene quarrels.

44 **truth** troth, loyalty.

45 **new-made** York, besides keeping Bullingbrook's name, insists that he has been 'made' a king, and has not attained the crown by birth or succession.

46–7 An allusion to new flatterers, and also to the 'sun' of Bullingbrook making a new spring.

50 **bear you well** bear yourself honourably.

51 **cropped** cut, reaped. With a hint of the garden imagery about pruning too-fast-growing sprays (3.4.34).

What news from Oxford? Do these jousts and triumphs hold?

AUMERLE For aught I know, my lord, they do.

YORK You will be there, I know.

AUMERLE If God prevent it not I purpose so.   55

YORK What seal is that that hangs without thy bosom?

    Yea, lookst thou pale? Let me see the writing.

AUMERLE My lord, 'tis nothing.

YORK   No matter then who see it.

    I will be satisfied. Let me see the writing.

AUMERLE I do beseech your grace to pardon me.   60

    It is a matter of small consequence,

    Which for some reasons I would not have seen.

YORK Which for some reasons, sir, I mean to see.

    I fear, I fear –

DUCHESS   What should you fear?

    'Tis nothing but some band that he is entered into   65

    For gay apparel 'gainst the triumph day.

YORK Bound to himself? What doth he with a bond

    That he is bound to? Wife, thou art a fool.

    Boy, let me see the writing.

AUMERLE I do beseech you pardon me. I may not show it.   70

YORK I will be satisfied. Let me see it, I say.

    He plucks it out of his bosom and reads it.

YORK Treason, foul treason! Villain! Traitor! Slave!

DUCHESS What's the matter, my lord?

YORK Ho, who's within there? Saddle my horse!

    God for His mercy, what treachery is here!   75

---

52 Do...hold?] Qq; Hold those Iusts & Triumphs? F   55 it] *Capell;* not in Qq, F   58 see] Qq; sees F   65 band] Qq; bond F   66 'gainst] Q1; against Q2–5, F   66 day] Q1; not in Q2–5, F   71 SD] Qq; *Snatches it* F   73 What's] F; What is Qq   74 who's] F; who is Qq   75 God] Qq; Heauen F

52 **Oxford** The Abbot of Westminster's con-spiracy was to kill Bullingbrook during the tourna-ment at Oxford (Holinshed, II, 514).

52 **Do...hold?** Q1's line has twelve syllables, and F has evidently adjusted to correct the metre. But the result is clumsy.

55 **it** Capell's insertion restores the metre to a line with a fairly obvious Q1 omission not restored by F.

56 The rolled paper was inside Aumerle's shirt but the attached seal hung outside. It is described thus in Holinshed, II, 515.

60 **pardon me** allow me the discourtesy of not showing it.

65 **band** See 1.1.2. York plays on the word at 67 with 'Bound' and 'bond', sufficiently to warrant F modernising the spelling here. But 1.1.2 suggests that 'band' was the authorial spelling.

66 **'gainst** (1) until, (2) in readiness for.

67–8 **What...bound to?** A bond acknowledg-ing Aumerle's debts would be in the hands of his creditor.

69 **Boy** An angry monosyllable but also a reminder of the obligation of filial obedience.

75 **God...mercy** See 2.2.98.

DUCHESS Why, what is't, my lord?

YORK Give me my boots, I say! Saddle my horse!
　　　Now by mine honour, by my life, my troth,
　　　I will appeach the villain.

DUCHESS　　　　　　　　　　　What is the matter?

YORK Peace, foolish woman!   80

DUCHESS I will not peace. What is the matter, Aumerle?

AUMERLE Good mother, be content. It is no more
　　　Than my poor life must answer.

DUCHESS　　　　　　　　　　　Thy life answer?

YORK Bring me my boots! I will unto the king.

His man enters with his boots.

DUCHESS Strike him, Aumerle! Poor boy, thou art amazed.   85
　　　Hence, villain! Never more come in my sight.

YORK Give me my boots, I say.

DUCHESS　　　　　　　　　Why York, what wilt thou do?
　　　Wilt thou not hide the trespass of thine own?
　　　Have we more sons, or are we like to have?
　　　Is not my teeming date drunk up with time,   90
　　　And wilt thou pluck my fair son from mine age
　　　And rob me of a happy mother's name?
　　　Is he not like thee? Is he not thine own?

YORK Thou fond mad woman,
　　　Wilt thou conceal this dark conspiracy?   95
　　　A dozen of them here have ta'en the sacrament
　　　And interchangeably set down their hands

---

76 is't] F; is it Qq   78 mine] Qq; my F   78 by my life, my troth] *Pope;* by my life, by my troth Q1; my life, my troth Q2–5, F   81 Aumerle] Qq; Sonne F   84 SD] Qq; *Enter Seruant with Boots.* F   88 thou not] Q1, F; not thou Q2–5   93 thee] Q2–5, F; the Q1

---

78 Pope's adjustment smoothes the metre. The Q1 compositor seems to have made this kind of unauthorised repetition also at 18, and at 2.2.88.

79 **appeach** (1) inform against, (2) publicly proclaim.

81 **Aumerle** F's 'sonne' reduces the force of the duchess's sticking to her son's former title in this scene, but changing to 'Rutland' before Bullingbrook in the next (5.3.95).

84 **boots** Long leather riding-boots were the garb of the traveller. Ross and Willoughby on their entry at 2.3.56 would have been booted, as presumably would the more leisurely travellers at the beginning of the scene and in Richard's contingent in 3.2.

85 **him** i.e. the servant.

85 **amazed** stunned, confused.

89 **Have...sons** Historically York had a second son, Richard, who is the traitor Cambridge of *H5* and brother of the Duke of York (Aumerle) who dies at Agincourt.

90 **teeming date** capacity for giving birth.

96 **A dozen** In Holinshed only six signed the bond.

96 **sacrament** See 4.1.327.

97 **interchangeably** So that each signatory had a copy signed by all.

To kill the king at Oxford.
DUCHESS   He shall be none.
We'll keep him here, then what is that to him?
YORK Away, fond woman! Were he twenty times my son   100
I would appeach him.
DUCHESS   Hadst thou groaned for him
As I have done thou wouldst be more pitiful.
But now I know thy mind – thou dost suspect
That I have been disloyal to thy bed
And that he is a bastard, not thy son.   105
Sweet York, sweet husband, be not of that mind.
He is as like thee as a man may be,
Not like to me or any of my kin,
And yet I love him.
YORK   Make way, unruly woman!   *Exit*
DUCHESS After, Aumerle! Mount thee upon his horse,   110
Spur post, and get before him to the king
And beg thy pardon ere he do accuse thee.
I'll not be long behind. Though I be old
I doubt not but to ride as fast as York,
And never will I rise up from the ground   115
Till Bullingbrook have pardoned thee. Away, be gone.
                                                          Exeunt

5.3 *Enter* BULLINGBROOK [*as king*], PERCY *and other lords.*

BULLINGBROOK Can no man tell of my unthrifty son?
'Tis full three months since I did see him last.

98–9] F; *Du. He...heere,* / *Then...him?* Qq   100–1 YORK *Away...appeach him*] Qq; *as prose* F   101–2] *Rowe; Du.*
Hadst...done, / *Thou...pittifull.* Qq, F   107 *as a*] Q1 *(Hunt., Capell, Petworth),* F; *as any* Q1 *(Huth)*   108 *to*] Q1,
F; *not in* Q2–5   108 *or any*] Q1 *(Hunt., Capell, Petworth); or a* Q1 *(Huth); nor any* F   116 SD] *Rowe; Exit* F; *not
in* Qq   Act 5, Scene 3   0 SD] F; *Enter the king with his nobles.* Qq   1 SH BULLINGBROOK] F; *King H.* Qq   1 *tell*]
F; *tell me* Qq

98 none not one of them.
101 groaned In the act of giving birth.
108 The historical duchess was Aumerle's
stepmother.
110 After Go after him. Exclamations are
compressed throughout this exchange.

Act 5, Scene 3
1 SH BULLINGBROOK The authorial Q
copy changes the new king's name here, the first

time we could expect to see him wearing the crown.
The F playhouse copy retains the regular speech
heading.
1 tell F's omission improves the metre. Q1's
Compositor A has normalised his reading of the line.
1 my unthrifty son The estrangement between
Bullingbrook and his son is reported by Holinshed,
Halle, Fabyan and Stow. Historically the prince was
only twelve in 1399.

If any plague hang over us 'tis he.
I would to God, my lords, he might be found.
Enquire at London 'mongst the taverns there,   5
For there they say he daily doth frequent
With unrestrainèd loose companions,
Even such, they say, as stand in narrow lanes
And beat our watch and rob our passengers,
Whilst he, young, wanton and effeminate boy,   10
Takes on the point of honour to support
So dissolute a crew.
PERCY My lord, some two days since I saw the prince
    And told him of those triumphs held at Oxford.
BULLINGBROOK And what said the gallant?   15
PERCY His answer was he would unto the stews
    And from the commonest creature pluck a glove
    And wear it as a favour, and with that
    He would unhorse the lustiest challenger.
BULLINGBROOK As dissolute as desperate! Yet through both   20
    I see some sparks of better hope in him
    Which elder years may happily bring forth.
    But who comes here?

Enter AUMERLE *amazed.*

AUMERLE   Where is the king?
BULLINGBROOK   What means
    Our cousin, that he stares and looks so wildly?
AUMERLE God save your grace. I do beseech your majesty   25

---

4 God] Qq; heauen F   9 beat...rob] Qq; rob...beat F   10 Whilst] *Capell;* Which Qq, F   11–12] F; *one line* Qq
14 those] Qq; these F   16 unto] Q1, F; to Q2–5   20–2] *Capell; King H.* As...both, / I see...hope, which...
yeares, / May...heere? Qq, F   21 sparks] Q1, F; sparkles Q2–5   21 in him] *This edn; not in* Qq, F   22 years] Qq;
dayes F   23 SD amazed] Qq; *not in* F   23–4 What...wildly?] *Capell; one line* Qq; What...stares / And...wildely?
F

---

3 **plague** An allusion to Richard's prophecy at
3.3.86–7.
3 **hang over** threaten. Plagues were sent from
heaven, and so fell downwards on the people.
9 **watch** night guard.
9 **passengers** travellers.
10 **Whilst** Capell's emendation makes sense of
a manuscript misreading shared by Q and F.
10 **young...boy** Daniel, *The Civil Wars*, I, 70,
calls Richard 'this wanton young effeminate'. The
prince is compared with Richard in *1H4* 3.2.60–85
and 93–4 by his father.
11 **Takes...honour** Makes it a test of his kind
of honour.

14 **held** to be held.
15 **gallant** man of fashion, man about town.
Sarcastic.
16 **stews** brothel quarter.
18 **favour** token of allegiance. If the 'gages' of
1.1 and 4.1 were gauntlets, the point the prince
makes would be even sharper.
21 **in him** The defective metre suggests that
something has been omitted in this line. Most
editors reline 20–2.
22 **happily** by chance, by good fortune.
23 SD **amazed** The Q copy uses the adjective
from 5.2.85.

To have some conference with your grace alone.
BULLINGBROOK Withdraw yourselves, and leave us here alone.
                              [*Exeunt Percy and lords*]
        What is the matter with our cousin now?
AUMERLE For ever may my knees grow to the earth, [*Kneels.*]
        My tongue cleave to the roof within my mouth,   30
        Unless a pardon ere I rise or speak.
BULLINGBROOK Intended or committed was this fault?
        If on the first, how heinous e'er it be
        To win thy after love I pardon thee.
AUMERLE Then give me leave that I may turn the key   35
        That no man enter till my tale be done.
BULLINGBROOK Have thy desire.
        The Duke of YORK *knocks at the door and crieth.*
YORK [*Within*] My liege, beware, look to thyself.
        Thou hast a traitor in thy presence there.
BULLINGBROOK Villain, I'll make thee safe.   40
                              [*Draws his sword.*]
AUMERLE Stay thy revengeful hand. Thou hast no cause to fear.
YORK [*Within*] Open the door, secure foolhardy king.
        Shall I for love speak treason to thy face?
        Open the door or I will break it open!

                         Enter YORK.

BULLINGBROOK What is the matter, uncle? Speak.   45
        Recover breath. Tell us how near is danger,
        That we may arm us to encounter it.
YORK Peruse this writing here and thou shalt know
        The treason that my haste forbids me show.
AUMERLE Remember, as thou read'st, thy promise past.   50
        I do repent me. Read not my name there.

---

27 SD] *Capell; not in* Qq, F   29 SD] *Rowe; not in* Qq, F   30 the] *Dyce;* my Qq, F   35 I may] Q2–5, F; May Q1
37 SD] Qq; *Yorke within.* F   40 SD] *Johnson; not in* Qq, F   42 SD] *Capell; not in* Qq, F   44 SD] F; *not in* Qq
45–6] *Johnson Var.; King.* What...breath, / Tell...daunger, Qq, F   49 treason] Qq; reason F

29 SD Compare York at 2.3.155–6.
30 See Ps. 137.6: 'If I doe not remember thee,
let my tongue cleave to the roof of my mouth.'
30 the roof Another Q1 compositorial slip (by
A), by infection from the 'my' later in the line.
31 Unless a pardon Aumerle is using the
compressed speech of the end of the previous scene.
It fits his breathlessness.

40 safe harmless; i.e. make him so by killing
him.
42 secure overconfident.
43 for...treason out of my love for you call you
a fool.
49 my haste the lack of breath that results from
my haste.

My heart is not confederate with my hand.
YORK It was, villain, ere thy hand did set it down.
　　　I tore it from the traitor's bosom, king.
　　　Fear and not love begets his penitence.   55
　　　Forget to pity him, lest thy pity prove
　　　A serpent that will sting thee to the heart.
BULLINGBROOK Oh heinous, strong and bold conspiracy!
　　　Oh loyal father of a treacherous son!
　　　Thou sheer, immaculate and silver fountain,   60
　　　From whence this stream through muddy passages
　　　Hath held his current and defiled himself,
　　　Thy overflow of good converts to bad,
　　　And thy abundant goodness shall excuse
　　　This deadly blot in thy digressing son.   65
YORK So shall my virtue be his vice's bawd
　　　And he shall spend mine honour with his shame,
　　　As thriftless sons their scraping fathers' gold.
　　　Mine honour lives when his dishonour dies,
　　　Or my shamed life in his dishonour lies.   70
　　　Thou kill'st me in his life. Giving him breath
　　　The traitor lives, the true man's put to death.
DUCHESS *(Within)* What ho, my liege! For God's sake let me in!
BULLINGBROOK What shrill-voiced suppliant makes this eager cry?
DUCHESS [*Within*] A woman and thy aunt, great king. 'Tis I.   75
　　　Speak with me, pity me, open the door!

62 held] Q1–2; hald Q3–5; had F　73 SD] F; *not in* Qq　73 God's] Qq; heauens F　74 voiced] Q3–5, F; voice Q1–2
75 SD] Capell; *not in* Qq, F　75 thy] Qq; thine F

52 **hand** signature. Aumerle extends the images
of heart and tongue, and heart and hand, of
1.3.253–6, 2.3.50 and elsewhere.
53 **it** i.e. his signature.
56 **Forget to pity** Forget your promises to
forgive.
56 **thy** Alan E. Craven conjectures a compositorial addition ('Simmes' Compositor A and five
Shakespeare quartos', *SB* 26 (1973), 37–60, p. 58).
It certainly intrudes on the metre.
57 See 3.2.131. York echoes Richard's image
about traitors, giving point to the Aumerle plot as
a parody of the question of loyalty.
60 **sheer** pure.
62 **held** F alters a slip introduced in Q3 but
without reference to any authoritative source copy.
65 **This deadly blot** (1) this sin, (2) this
signature on paper.

65 **digressing** (1) divergent (of a stream), (2)
transgressing (of sin).
66 **bawd** procurer, pander.
67 **spend** (1) expend (semen), (2) spend
(money).
71 **in his life** By granting him pardon and
allowing him to live. York repeats himself twice over
in 70–2.
74–5 The rhymes which begin here run for the
whole of the duchess's intrusion, for 32 couplets.
The rhymes, together with the stage actions of
hammering at the door and kneeling, are charac-
teristics which bring the scene very close to the few
surviving examples of the jig or knockabout act
which commonly followed the performance of a
public-theatre play on the Elizabethan stage. The
comic burlesque manner of the scene is unavoidable
in performance.

A beggar begs that never begged before.

BULLINGBROOK Our scene is altered from a serious thing,
    And now changed to 'The Beggar and the King'.
    My dangerous cousin, let your mother in.   80
    I know she's come to pray for your foul sin.

YORK If thou do pardon whosoever pray,
    More sins for this forgiveness prosper may.
    This festered joint cut off, the rest rest sound.
    This let alone will all the rest confound.   85

                Enter DUCHESS.

DUCHESS Oh king, believe not this hard-hearted man.
    Love loving not itself none other can.

YORK Thou frantic woman, what dost thou make here?
    Shall thy old dugs once more a traitor rear?

DUCHESS Sweet York, be patient. Hear me, gentle liege. [*Kneels.*]   90

BULLINGBROOK Rise up, good aunt.

DUCHESS   Not yet, I thee beseech.
    For ever will I walk upon my knees
    And never see day that the happy sees
    Till thou give joy, until thou bid me joy
    By pardoning Rutland, my transgressing boy.   95

AUMERLE Unto my mother's prayers I bend my knee. [*Kneels.*]

YORK Against them both my true joints bended be. [*Kneels.*]
    Ill mayst thou thrive if thou grant any grace.

DUCHESS Pleads he in earnest? Look upon his face.
    His eyes do drop no tears, his prayers are in jest,   100
    His words come from his mouth, ours from our breast.
    He prays but faintly, and would be denied.

---

81 she's] F; she is Qq   84 rest rest] Qq; rest rests F   85 SD] F; *not in* Qq   90 SD] *Rowe; not in* Qq, F   92 walk]
Qq; kneele F   96 SD] *Rowe; not in* Qq, F   97 SD] *Rowe; not in* Qq, F   98] Qq; *not in* F   101 words] Q1, F; words
do Q2–5

---

79 'The…King' The title might refer either to
a ballad of the kind published in broadsheet form
or to a jig. Presumably Bullingbrook is thinking of
some version of the story of King Cophetua and the
Beggar Maid. See *LLL* 4.1.65–80, and the link with
Richard at 5.5.32–4.

84 festered…off Amputation to heal the body
politic.

85 let alone left untreated.

85 confound (1) infect, (2) destroy.

87 Love…itself York is incapable of loving
anyone because of his own self-hatred.

89 once…rear give life a second time.

92 walk F's reading may be a compositor's
association with 'knees'.

94 joy be joyful.

95 Rutland The duchess is not completely
'frantic'. See 5.2.81 n.

98 The omission of this line in F must be
accidental, since it shares a rhyme.

100 in jest See 1.3.95.

We pray with heart and soul and all beside.
His weary joints would gladly rise, I know.
Our knees still kneel till to the ground they grow.   105
His prayers are full of false hypocrisy,
Ours of true zeal and deep integrity.
Our prayers do outpray his – then let them have
That mercy which true prayer ought to have.
BULLINGBROOK Good aunt, stand up.
DUCHESS   Nay, do not say 'stand up',   110
Say 'pardon' first, and afterwards 'stand up'.
And if I were thy nurse thy tongue to teach
'Pardon' should be the first word of thy speech.
I never longed to hear a word till now.
Say 'pardon', king. Let pity teach thee how.   115
The word is short, but not so short as sweet.
No word like 'pardon' for kings' mouths so meet.
YORK Speak it in French, king. Say 'pardonne moy'.
DUCHESS Dost thou teach pardon pardon to destroy?
Ah, my sour husband, my hard-hearted lord,   120
That sets the word itself against the word,
Speak 'pardon' as 'tis current in our land.
The chopping French we do not understand.
Thine eye begins to speak – set thy tongue there,
Or in thy piteous heart plant thou thine ear   125
That, hearing how our plaints and prayers do pierce,
Pity may move thee 'pardon' to rehearse.
BULLINGBROOK Good aunt, stand up.
DUCHESS   I do not sue to stand.
Pardon is all the suit I have in hand.
BULLINGBROOK I pardon him, as God shall pardon me.   130
DUCHESS Oh happy vantage of a kneeling knee!
Yet am I sick for fear. Speak it again.

---

105 still] Qq; shall F   109 prayer] Qq; prayers F   110 SH BULLINGBROOK] Q2–5, F; *yorke* Q1   111 Say] Qq; But
F   125 thy] Q1 *(Hunt., Capell, Petworth)*, F; this Q1 *(Huth)*   130 God] Qq; heauen F

---

112 **And if** See 4.1.263 n.
118 **'pardonne moy'** A transliteration of the
French pronunciation. Its meaning in French,
'excuse me', is the opposite of the duchess's
meaning.
119 **teach…destroy** By using the word against
the word (see 5.5.13–14).
123 **chopping** logic-chopping, shifting mean-

ings. The home of Ramist rhetoric, which could
be parodied as chop-logic, was in Paris.
127 **rehearse** recite, repeat by rote learning.
The duchess is extending the nurse image of 112–13.
129 **all…hand** (1) plea I am making, (2) my
hand of cards.
131 **happy vantage** fortunate perspective.

Twice saying 'pardon' doth not pardon twain,
But makes one pardon strong.
BULLINGBROOK   With all my heart
I pardon him.
DUCHESS   A god on earth thou art.   135
BULLINGBROOK But for our trusty brother-in-law and the abbot,
With all the rest of that consorted crew,
Destruction straight shall dog them at the heels.
Good uncle, help to order several powers
To Oxford or where'er these traitors are.   140
They shall not live within this world, I swear,
But I will have them if I once know where.
Uncle, farewell, and cousin too adieu.
Your mother well hath prayed, and prove you true.
DUCHESS Come, my old son. I pray God make thee new.   145

                                        Exeunt

5.4 *Enter* EXTON *and* SERVANTS.

EXTON Didst thou not mark the king, what words he spake?
'Have I no friend will rid me of this living fear?'
Was it not so?
SERVANT   These were his very words.
EXTON 'Have I no friend?' quoth he. He spake it twice,

134–5 With...heart / I...him] *Pope*; I pardon him with all my hart Qq, F   136 and] Qq; *not in* F   143 too] Q6;
not in Qq, F   145 God] Qq; heauen F   **Act 5, Scene 4**   0 SD] F; *Manet sir Pierce Exton, & c.* Qq   3 These] Qq;
Those F

133 **twain** double, divide. An echo of her own
two uses at 119.
134–5 Pope's emendation restores the couplet
rhyme lost by Q's mislineation.
135 **A...earth** The conclusion of the farcical
scene and its rhymes is ironical in view of the terms
of 'sacred' kingship invoked by Carlisle at 4.1.125–8.
The phrase was a cliché implying mercy (Dent
G275.1, Tilley M898).
136 **trusty** trustworthy. The sarcasm brings the
action back to political realities with some force.
136 **brother...abbot** The Duke of Exeter and
the Abbot of Westminster. See 2.1.281 and
4.1.332–3.
137 **consorted crew** A contemptuous term,
linking the 'sort' of traitors at 4.1.245 with the
'crew' at 12 in this scene.
139 **several** separate.
143 **too** Q6 adds a word conjecturally in order to

regularise the metre. In a rhyming passage this
seems more than usually desirable, although in this
instance an unusual triple rhyme is established.
144 **prove** (1) may you prove, (2) you must
prove.
145 **my old son** my unreformed son. The
duchess is echoing the rite of baptism.

Act 5, Scene 4
5.4 The stage direction in Q1 suggests that a
scene or exchange at the end of 5.3 has been deleted,
since Exton and others have no opportunity in the
present text of 5.3 to enter after the stage is cleared
at 27. F's stage direction makes it a new scene, but
F fails to note it as one otherwise, marking 5.5 which
follows as 5.4. The evidence of F's incomplete
adjustment strengthens the assumption that Q1
shows a deletion incompletely recorded. The
material for this brief scene is in Holinshed, II, 517.

And urged it twice together, did he not?   5
SERVANT He did.
EXTON And speaking it, he wishtly looked on me
    As who should say 'I would thou wert the man
    That would divorce this terror from my heart',
    Meaning the king at Pomfret. Come, let's go.   10
    I am the king's friend, and will rid his foe.

                               Exeunt

5.5 *Enter* RICHARD *alone.*

RICHARD I have been studying how I may compare
    This prison where I live unto the world,
    And for because the world is populous
    And here is not a creature but myself
    I cannot do it. Yet I'll hammer't out.   5
    My brain I'll prove the female to my soul,
    My soul the father, and these two beget
    A generation of still breeding thoughts,
    And these same thoughts people this little world
    In humours like the people of this world,   10
    For no thought is contented. The better sort,
    As thoughts of things divine, are intermixed
    With scruples, and do set the word itself
    Against the word –
    As thus: 'Come, little ones', and then again   15

---

7 wishtly] Q1–2; wistly Q3–5, F   11 SD] Q4–5; *not in* Q1–3; *Exit.* F   **Act 5, Scene 5**   5.5] *Scoena Quarta.* F
0 SD *alone*] QQ; *not in* F   1 I may] Q1; to Q2–5, F   5 hammer't] F; hammer it QQ   13 word] QQ; Faith F
14 the] Q1, F; thy Q2–5   14 word] QQ; Faith F   14–15] Capell; *one line* QQ, F

---

7 Bullingbrook looks directly at Exton in Daniel's account, not in Holinshed.

7 wishtly longingly. The Q1 spelling is acceptable, although the F version had a wider provenance.

Act 5, Scene 5

5.5 The details of the murder are in Holinshed, II, 517. The soliloquy, the music and the groom with his story of roan Barbary are in no source.

8 generation family, offspring.

8 still breeding always producing offspring. It has been suggested that the construction makes it an antonym of 'stillborn'.

9 this little world i.e. the prison, a microcosm of the great world.

10 In humours In a variety of (unbalanced) temperaments.

11 no...contented Thought, being man's capacity for God-like and therefore moral reasoning, was inherently melancholic. See 2.2.31.

13 scruples small doubts.

13–14 do set...the word See 5.3.121. F's alterations seem either designed to intensify the point or to avoid an echo of the previous use of the phrase. The half-line may indicate an imperfectly recorded emendation in the Q copy, or possibly a compositor's adjustment to fill out a short page (ending at 18, sig. 13ᵛ).

15–17 The nature of the contradictory thoughts in the Bible indicates that the essential question is entering heaven.

15 'Come, little ones' Matt. 19.14, Luke 18.16.

'It is as hard to come as for a camel
To thread the postern of a small needle's eye.'
Thoughts tending to ambition, they do plot
Unlikely wonders: how these vain weak nails
May tear a passage through the flinty ribs   20
Of this hard world my ragged prison walls,
And, for they cannot, die in their own pride.
Thoughts tending to content flatter themselves
That they are not the first of Fortune's slaves,
Nor shall not be the last, like silly beggars   25
Who, sitting in the stocks, refuge their shame
That many have and others must set there,
And in this thought they find a kind of ease,
Bearing their own misfortunes on the back
Of such as have before endured the like.   30
Thus play I in one person many people,
And none contented. Sometimes am I king,
Then treasons make me wish myself a beggar,
And so I am. Then crushing penury
Persuades me I was better when a king,   35
Then am I kinged again, and by and by
Think that I am unkinged by Bullingbrook,
And straight am nothing. But whate'er I be
Nor I nor any man that but man is
With nothing shall be pleased till he be eased   40
With being nothing.
                    The music plays.
                  Music do I hear?

17 postern] Q1–2, F; small postern Q3–5   17 small needle's] Qq; Needles F   27 set] Q1–2; sit Q3–5, F
29 misfortunes] Qq; misfortune F   31 person] Q1; prison Q2–5, F   32 I] Q1, F; I a Q2–5   33 treasons make] Qq;
Treason makes F   38 be] Qq; am F   41 SD] Qq; *Musick* F *(after 38)*

16–17 Matt. 19.24, Mark 10.25, Luke 18.25. All give slightly varying forms of this statement.

17 Q3 inserts a second 'small' before 'postern', with a standard slip of compositorial memory. F eliminates both, possibly as an over-correction, but possibly to get rid of the apparent metrical awkwardness which arises if 'needle' is read as a disyllable. It was generally pronounced as a monosyllable, 'neele'. See Cercignani, p. 317.

18 ambition earthly (as distinct from heavenly) progress.

21 ragged jagged, rugged.

22 their own pride of thwarted ambition.

23 Thoughts...content Compare 11. The allusion is to acceptance and Christian patience.

26 refuge find refuge for.

27 set sit, be set. Here as at 1.2.47 Q1 reads 'set' while F normalises to 'sit'. The two words were commonly confused.

39–41 An ornate way of making the proverbial point that there is no peace for mankind on earth.

41 SD In the 1590s when *R2* was first staged, the public playhouses appear not to have used a 'music room' on the balcony above the stage but to have played behind the hangings in the tiring-house at stage level. The most likely kind of music would be wind (recorders) and strings.

Ha, ha, keep time! How sour sweet music is
When time is broke and no proportion kept.
So is it in the music of men's lives.
And here have I the daintiness of ear   45
To check time broke in a disordered string,
But for the concord of my state and time
Had not an ear to hear my true time broke.
I wasted time and now doth time waste me,
For now hath time made me his numbering clock.   50
My thoughts are minutes, and with sighs they jar
Their watches on unto mine eyes, the outward watch,
Whereto my finger like a dial's point
Is pointing still, in cleansing them from tears.
Now sir, the sound that tells what hour it is   55
Are clamorous groans that strike upon my heart,
Which is the bell. So sighs and tears and groans
Show minutes, times and hours. But my time
Runs posting on in Bullingbrook's proud joy
While I stand fooling here, his Jack of the clock.   60
This music mads me. Let it sound no more,
For though it have holp madmen to their wits
In me it seems it will make wise men mad.
Yet blessing on his heart that gives it me,
For 'tis a sign of love, and love to Richard   65
Is a strange brooch in this all-hating world.

46 check] Qq; heare F   46 a] Q1, F; *not in* Q2–5   50 me] Q1, F; *not in* Q2–5   56 that] F; which Qq   58 times and hours] Qq; Houres, and Times F   60 of the] Qq; o' th' F

42 **Ha, ha** An exclamation, not laughter.
43 **proportion** The metronomic beat of polyphonic music.
46 **check** reprove.
46 **time broke** a false or out-of-place note. See E. W. Naylor, *Shakespeare and Music*, p. 32.
46 **string** stringed musical instrument.
47 **the concord...time** See p. 34 n. 6 above. This passage about time focuses the large number of references to time and the seasons in the play.
49 **waste** decay. See 2.2.3 n.
50 **numbering clock** A clock telling the hours and minutes, as distinct from a sundial or hourglass.
51 **jar** knock themselves onwards.
52 **watches** waking periods.
52 **outward watch** (1) viewer, (2) sentry, (3) watching clockface.
53 **dial's point** hand on the clockface.
54 **still** (1) continually, (2) motionless.

55 **Now sir** Richard is numbering the details of his concept to his imaginary listener.
58 **times** marks on the dial.
58 **times and hours** F tidies up the sequence wrongly.
58 **my time** Richard's life on earth, as distinct from himself as the clock.
60 **Jack...clock** Figure which strikes the bell to sound the hours.
61 **mads** maddens.
62 **holp** helped.
62 **madmen...wits** Music was used to heal mad Lear by Cordelia in *Lear* 4.7.24. See also *Per.* 3.2.91 and *Temp.* 1.2.392–4.
63 **wise men** i.e. such as Richard, producer of the wisdom displayed in the clock conceit.
65 **to** for. Ironic in view of what is to follow.
66 **brooch** jewel. Usually worn in the hat.

Enter a GROOM *of the stable.*

GROOM Hail, royal prince!
RICHARD   Thanks, noble peer.
        The cheapest of us is ten groats too dear.
        What art thou? And how comest thou hither
        Where no man never comes but that sad dog   70
        That brings me food to make misfortune live?
GROOM I was a poor groom of thy stable, king,
        When thou wert king, who, travelling towards York,
        With much ado at length have gotten leave
        To look upon my sometime royal master's face.   75
        Oh, how it erned my heart when I beheld
        In London streets that coronation day
        When Bullingbrook rode on roan Barbary,
        That horse that thou so often hast bestrid,
        That horse that I so carefully have dressed.   80
RICHARD Rode he on Barbary? Tell me, gentle friend,
        How went he under him?
GROOM So proudly as if he disdained the ground.
RICHARD So proud that Bullingbrook was on his back.
        That jade hath ate bread from my royal hand,   85
        This hand hath made him proud with clapping him.
        Would he not stumble, would he not fall down,
        Since pride must have a fall, and break the neck
        Of that proud man that did usurp his back?
        Forgiveness! Horse, why do I rail on thee,   90
        Since thou, created to be awed by man,
        Wast born to bear? I was not made a horse

66 SD] Qq; *Enter Groome.* F   70 never] Q1–4; euer Q5, F   76 erned] Qq; yern'd F   79 bestrid] F; bestride Qq
83 he] Qq; he had F

67–8 royal…noble…groats Richard puns on
the names of three coins. Two royals were
equivalent to a pound sterling; so were three nobles.
Ten groats was the difference between them.
Richard is now noble, not royal. This word-play on
coins was attributed to Queen Elizabeth in the
eighteenth century.
68 cheapest i.e. the cheaper of the two, Richard
himself.
75 sometime royal formerly royal. A comment
on Richard's word-play on coins at 67–8.
76 erned made ache.

77 that…day Historically 13 October 1399.
This is not the same journey as the one described
by York at 5.2.7–10 when Bullingbrook was
mounted on 'a hot and fiery steed'. Neither
reference to the horse is in any of the sources.
78 Barbary A proper name, derived from a
breed of Arab horses.
81 gentle Richard claims that his visitor is
noble, not a groom.
85 jade vicious horse. See 3.3.179.
86 clapping patting.
88 pride…fall Prov. 16.18.

And yet I bear a burthen like an ass,
Spurred, galled and tired by jauncing Bullingbrook.

Enter KEEPER *to Richard with meat.*

KEEPER Fellow, give place. Here is no longer stay.　　　　95
RICHARD If thou love me 'tis time thou wert away.
GROOM What my tongue dares not, that my heart shall say.　　*Exit*
KEEPER My lord, wilt please you to fall to?
RICHARD Taste of it first as thou art wont to do.
KEEPER My lord, I dare not. Sir Pierce of Exton,　　　　100
　　Who lately came from the king, commands the contrary.
RICHARD The devil take Henry of Lancaster, and thee!
　　Patience is stale, and I am weary of it!
　　　　　　　[Beats the Keeper.]
KEEPER Help, help, help!

*The murderers [*EXTON *and Servants] rush in.*

RICHARD How now! What means death in this rude assault?　　105
　　Villain, thy own hand yields thy death's instrument.
　　Go thou and fill another room in hell.
　　　　　Here Exton strikes him down.

94 Spurred, galled] Qq; Spur-gall'd F　　94 SD] *This edn; Enter one to Richard with meate.* Qq; *Enter Keeper with a Dish*
F　　99 art] Q1–4; wert Q5, F　　103 SD] Rowe; *not in* Qq, F　　104 SD] Qq; *Enter Exton and Seruants* F　　106 thy own]
Q1–4; thine owne Q5, F　　107 SD *Here*] Qq; *not in* F

93 **burthen** An alternative spelling of 'burden'.
94 **Spurred, galled** F's 'spur-galled' is a
normalisation. It was used by Nashe, *Pierce
Penilesse* (1592), Francis Quarles, *Hieroglyphikes*
(1638), and other writers.
94 **tired** wearied (not 'dressed').
94 **jauncing** prancing, bouncing, hard-riding.
The Nurse in *Rom.* 2.5.52 uses 'jaunsing'.
94 SD **meat** food.
95 **Fellow** The keeper addresses the groom
according to his status, unlike Richard.
95–7 A triple rhyme.
99 **Taste...first** A formality at the royal table.
Flattery was commonly described as a poisoned cup.
101 **lately** Pope emends to 'late' in order to
improve the metre. The speech may have been
designed as prose, though if so it would be the only
prose in the play, and a sharp contrast to the
preceding rhymes.
103 The culmination of the theme of Richard's
patience (see 5.1.33–4 n. and 5.2.33 and 37–8 n.)
brings its emphatic rejection. 'Stale' was used

particularly of drink, as in Hamlet's 'weary, stale,
flat and unprofitable' (*Ham.* 1.2.133), possibly by
association with the 'stale' or urine of horses and
cattle. It had more force than its present meaning.
See *OED* sv *a* 2a, b.
103 SD Rowe's stage direction is conveniently
uncommitted. According to Holinshed, Richard
struck the keeper on the head with the carving
knife.
105 **Death** A personification.
105 **this rude assault** Richard perhaps implies
that poison would have been more gentle.
106–7 According to Holinshed, Richard seized a
pike from one of the eight murderers, and killed four
of them before Exton, standing on Richard's chair,
struck him down from behind. The words suggest
that Shakespeare halved the number of Richard's
victims, and probably expected the number of
murderers to be halved too. This memorable scuffle
is the only fight in the play, for all the confrontations
of Acts 1, 3 and 4.
107 **room** empty space.

That hand shall burn in never-quenching fire
That staggers thus my person. Exton, thy fierce hand
Hath with the king's blood stained the king's own land.   110
Mount, mount my soul. Thy seat is up on high
Whilst my gross flesh sinks downward, here to die. [*Dies.*]
EXTON As full of valour as of royal blood.
Both have I spilled. Oh, would the deed were good,
For now the devil that told me I did well   115
Says that this deed is chronicled in hell.
This dead king to the living king I'll bear.
Take hence the rest and give them burial here.

Exeunt

5.6 *Flourish. Enter* BULLINGBROOK, YORK, *with other Lords and attendants.*

BULLINGBROOK Kind uncle York, the latest news we hear
Is that the rebels have consumed with fire
Our town of Ciceter in Gloucestershire,
But whether they be ta'en or slain we hear not.

Enter NORTHUMBERLAND.

Welcome, my lord. What is the news?   5
NORTHUMBERLAND First, to thy sacred state wish I all happiness.
The next news is I have to London sent

112 SD] *Rowe; not in* Qq; F   118 SD] *Rowe; Exit.* F; *not in* Qq   Act 5, Scene 6   5.6] *Scæna Quinta.* F   0 SD] F;
Enter Bullingbrooke with the duke of Yorke. Qq

109 **staggers** makes stagger.
109 **my person** Implies 'my royal person'.
110 **the king's blood** Compare 68 where he
ironically denies his 'royal' value.
111 **seat** (1) royal throne, (2) place in heaven.
112 **sinks downward** The idea that the soul,
like air or fire, rises while the body (earth) falls is
related to the elemental imagery, the concept of the
king's two bodies and the implication of Christian
martyrdom. See p. 24 above and 1.1.37–8.
115–16 Holinshed, II, 517, mentions Exton's
feelings of guilt.
118 **the rest** See 106–7 n. At least two bodies
besides Richard's had to be removed.

Act 5, Scene 6
5.6 The material is compressed from Holinshed,
II, 515–17.

0 SD *Flourish* F's marking of this entry to be
heralded by a fanfare of trumpets is not matched at
5.3, which also shows 'King' Bullingbrook after his
coronation. It is doubtful if F was making a point
about Bullingbrook not being king until after
Richard's death, and there may therefore have been
a flourish at 5.3.0 which F does not record.
1 SH BULLINGBROOK *King* in Q1.
3 **Ciceter** Cirencester. Holinshed spells it
Cicester or Circiter.
6 **thy sacred state** Northumberland is more
reverent to Bullingbrook's face than behind his back
in 5.1. It is the symbolic chair of state, the throne,
which he actually salutes. He would probably
accompany such a salute by kneeling, in contrast to
his behaviour to Richard at 3.3.72.
7 **next** (1) nearest, (2) most pressing.

The heads of Salisbury, Spencer, Blunt and Kent.
The manner of their taking may appear
At large discoursèd in this paper here.   10
BULLINGBROOK We thank thee, gentle Percy, for thy pains,
And to thy worth will add right worthy gains.

Enter Lord FITZWATER.

FITZWATER My lord, I have from Oxford sent to London
The heads of Broccas and Sir Bennet Seely,
Two of the dangerous consorted traitors   15
That sought at Oxford thy dire overthrow.
BULLINGBROOK Thy pains, Fitzwater, shall not be forgot.
Right noble is thy merit, well I wot.

Enter PERCY *and* CARLISLE.

PERCY The grand conspirator, Abbot of Westminster,
With clog of conscience and sour melancholy   20
Hath yielded up his body to the grave.
But here is Carlisle living, to abide
Thy kingly doom and sentence of his pride.
BULLINGBROOK Carlisle, this is your doom:
Choose out some secret place, some reverend room,   25
More than thou hast, and with it joy thy life.
So, as thou livest in peace die free from strife.
For though mine enemy thou hast ever been
High sparks of honour in thee have I seen.

Enter EXTON *with a coffin.*

EXTON Great king, within this coffin I present   30

8 Salisbury, Spencer, Blunt] F; Oxford, Salisbury, Blunt Q1; Oxford, Salisbury Q2–5   11–12] Qq, F *(corr.)*; not in
F *(uncorr.)*   12 SD FITZWATER] Q6; *Fitzwaters* Qq, F   17 Fitzwater] Q6; *Fitz.* Qq; *Fitzwaters* F   18 SD] F; *Enter
H. Percie.* Qq   29 SD a] F; *the* Qq

8 **Salisbury...Kent** The names are from
Holinshed, II, 515. Q1's list is clearly wrong. Either
the author misremembered Holinshed, or the Q1
compositor (A) took up the intrusive 'Oxford' from
13 below. Q2 adjusted by omission, and F corrected
by reference either directly to Holinshed or, if Q1's
error came from the compositor, to its authoritative
manuscript.

10 **At...discoursèd** Described in full.

12 **worthy** (1) well-deserved, (2) substantial.

14 The names are from Holinshed, II, 515. The
attribution of the various tasks to Northumberland,
Fitzwater and Percy is Shakespeare's.

15 **consorted** See 5.3.137. Fitzwater almost
echoes the description Richard levelled at him
amongst others at 4.1.245.

16 **dire** dangerous.

20 **clog** burden.

22 **abide** await.

23 **doom** (1) punishment, (2) fate.

25 **reverend room** hermit's cell or monastery.
The alternative form 'reverent' (Q1–3) means
respectful, while 'reverend' (Q4–5) means worthy of
reverence.

26 **More** i.e. more worthy of reverence.

26 **joy** enjoy.

Thy buried fear. Herein all breathless lies
The mightiest of thy greatest enemies,
Richard of Bordeaux, by me hither brought.
BULLINGBROOK Exton, I thank thee not, for thou hast wrought
A deed of slander with thy fatal hand   35
Upon my head and all this famous land.
EXTON From your own mouth, my lord, did I this deed.
BULLINGBROOK They love not poison that do poison need.
Nor do I thee. Though I did wish him dead,
I hate the murderer, love him murderèd.   40
The guilt of conscience take thou for thy labour,
But neither my good word nor princely favour.
With Cain go wander through shades of night
And never show thy head by day nor light.
Lords, I protest my soul is full of woe   45
That blood should sprinkle me to make me grow.
Come mourn with me for what I do lament,
And put on sullen black incontinent.
I'll make a voyage to the Holy Land
To wash this blood off from my guilty hand.   50
March sadly after. Grace my mournings here
In weeping after this untimely bier.

Exeunt

35 slander] Q1; slaughter Q2–5, F   43 through shades] Q1; through the shade Q2–5, F   47 what] Qq; that F
51 mournings] Qq; mourning F   52 SD] F; *not in* Qq

31 **buried fear** Compare 'living fear', 5.4.2.
31 **breathless** See 1.3.214.
33 **Richard of Bordeaux** See 3.2.25 n. Exton
will not admit the name of king.
34 **I...not** Holinshed does not mention Bullingbrook's repudiation of Exton.
35 **A...slander** A deed of murder which will
slander the new king's name.
37–40 The precedents for this kind of disavowal
go back to Henry II over the murder of Thomas a
Becket, and to Elizabeth herself, who disowned
Secretary Davison's order to execute Mary Queen
of Scots. E. Daunce, *A Briefe Discourse* (1590), cites
examples including David, Canute and Cesare
Borgia.
41 **guilt** (1) a guilty conscience, (2) payment
(gilt) for the deed.
43 **Cain** See 1.1.104, and Gen. 4.12, 14.
43 **through** A disyllable. Q2 adjusts for the
metre, unnecessarily.
46 **sprinkle** As water on a plant – or on a child
in the baptismal rite.

48 **incontinent** immediately.
49 Bullingbrook's vow is introduced here by
Shakespeare. In Daniel it is not mentioned until the
king is on his deathbed. The terms in which it is
announced indicate that he is thinking of a
pilgrimage of expiation. By the beginning of *1H4*
(1.1.19–27) it has turned into a crusade. See p. 5
above.
50 **wash...off** See 4.1.238.
52 **this untimely bier** Holinshed (II, 517)
records the respect paid to Richard's coffin. After
the body had lain in state for three days 'There was
a solemne obsequie doone for him, both at Paules,
and after at Westminster, at which time, both at
dirige overnight, and in the morning at the masse
of *Requiem*, the king and the citizens of London were
present.' Funeral processions following a coffin
were the standard conclusion to a tragedy, as here.
The finale nicely balances the sense of an ending in
the fall of princes with the visual evidence of a guilty
king and the object of his guilt which makes the
launching point for the next play in the sequence.

TEXTUAL ANALYSIS

The first publication of *King Richard II* was a quarto which appeared in 1597 from the press of Valentine Simmes for the bookseller Andrew Wise. The Stationers' Register contains an authorisation dated 29 August 1597, and the publication would have followed quickly after. The title page of this first quarto (Q1) reads

THE / Tragedie of King Ri- / chard the se- / cond. / *As it hath beene publikely acted* / *by the* *right Honourable the* / *Lorde Chamberlaine his Ser-* / *uants.* / [Simmes's device] / LONDON / Printed by Valentine Simmes for Androw Wise, and / are to be sold at his shop in Paules church yard at / the signe of the Angel. / 1597.

The copy for this first edition seems to have been authoritative, and it may be that popular demand led the acting company which owned the play, Shakespeare's company, to release it to the press. Its popularity is indicated by the two further printings which Wise undertook in the following year. Wise probably had a steady and legitimate arrangement with Shakespeare's company for printing popular plays. He also produced an edition of *Richard III* in 1597 sometime after the *Richard II*, in 1598 he published *1 Henry IV*, and in 1600 *Much Ado about Nothing* and *2 Henry IV*.

Richard II Q2 (1598) and Q3 (1598) are both reprints of Q1 by the same printer. Q2 was the first of Shakespeare's plays to appear with his name on the title page. All three early quartos issued by Wise omit the central section of 4.1, lines 154–317, the so-called 'deposition scene' in which Richard appears and hands over his crown to Bullingbrook. The omission is roughly cobbled over in the quartos, which possibly contain the version approved by the stage censor, the Master of the Revels. It seems likely that some authority censored the deposition scene from the published text, but there is no evidence to indicate what was done on stage.

The deposition scene first appeared in 1608 in the fourth quarto (Q4), which was issued by Matthew Law, who had acquired the rights to the play from Wise on 21 June 1603. The new quarto, printed by William White, had two versions of its title page. One of them, which only survives in a single copy (the Malone copy in the Bodleian Library; see illustration 2, p. 8 above), advertised its new contents:

THE / Tragedy of King / Richard the Second: / With new additions of the Parlia- / ment Scene, and the deposing / of King Richard, / As it hath been lately acted by the Kinges / Maiesties seruantes, at the Globe. / By *William Shake-speare.* / [White's device] / AT LON-DON, / Printed by W.W. for *Matthew Law*, and are to be / sold at his shop in Paules Churchyard, / at the signe of the Foxe. / 1608.

The other version copies the earlier quartos, even continuing to call the actors 'the Lord Chamberlaine his seruantes', the name they gave up in 1603 when they became the King's Men. This title page was cancelled, and replaced by the version advertising the deposition, in the course of printing. Three surviving copies of Q4 lack any title page, which suggests that they originally had the cancel leaf with the deposition scene advertised. Apart from the deposition scene, Q4's text was taken from Q3, and was not so scrupulous a reprint as the earlier quartos. Law issued a fifth quarto (Q5) in 1615, printing from a copy of Q4.[1]

The editors who prepared the printer's copy for the First Folio (F) in 1623 supplied their printer with copy from the quartos, but with a good deal of emendation. Their basic text was a copy of Q3; however, another text with some authority – evidently one that had been used in the playhouse – was collated with the printed quarto. The nature of the text collated with Q3 is difficult to ascertain. It may have been a manuscript, possibly even the promptbook, or it may have been a printed text emended by reference to the promptbook. Certainly the Folio text which resulted from the collation shows playhouse influences. It omits some passages (1.3.129–33, 238–41, 267–92; 3.2.29–32; and 4.1.52–9) which look like acting cuts, together with some isolated lines (2.2.77, 3.2.49 and 182, and 5.3.98), and regularises many of the stage directions and speech headings to make it a more manageable acting text. As the clearest evidence of playhouse influence, F consistently replaces references to 'God' with 'heaven'. The 1606 'Acte...to Restraine Abuses of Players' which ordered the actors to avoid profanity applied only to performance, not to printed texts, and Q4 (1608) and Q5 (1615) alter none of the profanities in the earlier quartos. The F text, on the other hand, does so throughout except for a section (1.3.11–25) corresponding to about a page of the quarto text. F therefore most likely reflects playhouse practices from the period 1606–22.

The major difference of F from Q1 is of course its restoration of the deposition scene. F's version of 4.1.154–317 is certainly the best text of the passage to have survived. The version which first appeared in Q4 and was reprinted in Q5 is clearly inferior, and has instances of mislineation and mishearing which suggest it is a hasty transcript probably made from dictation. The Folio text restores the metre and corrects at least 23 verbal errors. The evidence seems to indicate that for at least this section of the text the editor who prepared the copy for the Folio printer had a manuscript sufficiently clean and superior to the quarto version to persuade him to dispense with the quarto altogether for that part of the text. The independent authority of the Folio here, together with the coherence it gains from its links with the playhouse, makes it an invaluable check on the occasional stumblings which happened when the manuscript which formed the copy for Q1 was being put into print. The difficulty is in ascertaining when the Folio version has the authority of the author behind it and when it has only the plausibility of an actor's, the book-keeper's or the Folio editor's guesswork.

The feature of F which most clearly differentiates it from Q1 is its stage directions. In general Q1's stage directions are authorial where F's are theatrical. The F directions

---

[1] The printing of the quartos has been minutely studied by A. W. Pollard, who first identified Q3 as a separate edition from Q2 in his facsimile edition of Q3, *A New Shakespeare Quarto. The Tragedy of King Richard II. Printed for the third time by Valentine Simmes in 1598*, 1918. Detailed information about the printing of the successive quartos is in Black, pp. 355–77.

tend to be more systematic than the quarto, and more elaborate when they specify details of staging such as trumpet calls. The Q directions are the more elaborate or descriptive in the scene entries of 1.2, 1.3, 1.4, 2.1, 2.4 and 5.5. They are also more descriptive at 1.3.6 and 25, 4.1.319, 5.2.71, 5.3.23 and 37, and throughout 5.5 (Richard's death scene) at 41, 66, 94, 97, 104 and 107. F has more elaborate scene entries for 2.3, 3.2, 3.3, 4.1, 5.3 and 5.6, all involving massed entries, but otherwise expands Q only at 3.3.61 and 5.3.73. It adds trumpets to Q's directions at 1.3.117 (where the text calls for them), 122 and 247, 2.1.223, 3.3.208 and 5.6.0, adds trumpets together with military drums at 3.2.0, and drums at 3.3.0.

As we should expect from a text based on playhouse copy, the Folio stage directions also tidy up the quarto's inconsistencies. In five places (1.3.6, 2.1.68, 3.1.0, 5.1.6 and 5.6.18) F augments Q's list of the characters entering, and in a dozen other instances it supplies entry directions which in Q are evident only from the dialogue, at 2.1.146, 2.2.40, 72 and 85, 2.3.56, 67 and 80, 5.2.40 and 5.3.44 and 85. F also supplies exits at 2.2.147, 2.4.17 and 24, 3.2.218, 3.3.208, 5.2.116, 5.4.11, 5.5.118 and 5.6.52. On the other hand, in four of these instances – 2.2.147, 5.2.116, 5.4.11 and 5.5.118 – F supplies a singular *Exit* where plural *Exeunt* is required. F's systematising of the Q directions is some way from being perfect. It also omits an *Exeunt* which is in Q at 1.3.308, and shares with Q the omission of necessary entry or exit directions at 2.2.107, 3.1.35, 4.1.267 and 287, and 5.3.27. Both F and Q provide singular exits at 3.4.101 and 107 where plural *Exeunt* is needed.

F makes a few other attempts to tidy up the Q staging. At the end of 1.1 it sends Gaunt out before Richard's final speech, so that he does not have to exit and immediately re-enter for the next scene with the Duchess of Gloucester. In 1.4.23 it makes an attempt to tidy up some confusion about the characters on stage caused by Bushy's entrance at 52, and it supplies walk-on characters such as 'attendants' and the queen's ladies. Q, especially in 2.2 and 2.3, tends to omit stage directions for entries which are signalled in the dialogue, and has only two explanatory directions, *he kneeles downe* for Bullingbrook at 3.3.187 (which F omits), and *the musike plaies* at 5.5.41. Where the dialogue indicates a gesture, such as the casting down of the gages at 1.1.69 and 146, and in 4.1, and Richard throwing down his warder at 1.3.117, neither Q nor F provides any directions, though F supplies a *within* at 5.3.73.

In general for this edition the more elaborate stage direction, whether from Q or F, is given in the text, though where the variations are unimportant Q has been preferred. A few explanatory directions have been added where the dialogue does not make them obvious. F's *Exit Gaunt* at 1.1.195 has been retained, and the Aumerle *Exit* at 1.3.249 supplied, since they reflect the system of continuous staging which minimised scene breaks. Similarly, where F names walk-on characters not given in Q, the extra names are included. At 5.4.0, where the Q direction indicates either an omission or a change of mind in the course of composition, F's regularised entry has been used.

Speech headings for the most part follow the pattern of the stage directions. F is largely consistent while Q makes an effort to accommodate the change in the name of king from Richard to Bullingbrook. Q's opening entry names *King Richard*, and follows it with the speech heading *King*. He is uniformly *King* until the entry at 3.3, where he is called *Richard*, although the speech headings remain *King*. On his next appearance in Q1 (which omits his entry for the deposition scene), at 5.1, he enters as *Ric.* and is *Rich.* in the first speech heading, but then reverts to *King*. In 5.5 he enters as *Richard* and is *Rich.* in the speech headings throughout the scene. The Folio text begins 1.1. like Q with an entry as *King Richard*, and the speech heading *King*. In 1.3, 1.4 and 2.1, he enters as *King* but is given the speech heading *Rich.* or *Ric.* throughout, and thereafter he invariably enters as *Richard* and speaks as *Rich.* The Folio uses his identifying name for its speech headings consistently after the opening scene.

Bullingbrook is also given his identifying name, as *Bul.* or *Bull.* throughout the Folio text, although in the first two acts the quarto's more variable pattern seems to have influenced the Folio. At his entry in 1.3 he is called *Hereford*, and at 2.3 *the Duke of Hereford*, where in Q he is *Duke of Hereford* in 1.3 and *Hereford* in 2.3. Q calls him *Duke of Hereford* in the entry direction in 3.1, but reverts to the original *Bullingbrooke* in 3.2 and 4.1. In Act 5, unlike F the quarto texts acknowledge his new title with the direction in 5.3.0 *Enter the King*, and the speech headings *King H.* or *King*. In 5.6 he enters as *Bullingbrooke* but is given the speech heading *King*. Presumably the Q headings reflect the author's sense of the changes produced by the events of the play while F's consistency reflects the needs of the playhouse. All the other speech headings, even that for Aumerle once he has been demoted to Rutland, are consistent in both Q and F.

In the quarto texts after Q1 and in F some small verbal changes most likely reflect the early editor's or compositor's preferences. Q2, for instance, four times changes Q1's 'which' into 'that' (2.3.14, 3.4.38 and 50, and 4.1.35). In the Folio, one 'that' becomes 'which' (1.3.306) and one 'which' is altered into 'that'. F consistently makes Q 'yon' into 'yond' (2.3.53, 3.3.26, 91, 135, and 3.4.29) and prefers 'mine' or 'thine' before a vowel to the quarto 'my' or 'thy' (1.1.191, 1.3.14, 3.1.24, 4.1.70, 5.2.78, 5.3.75 and 5.5.106), though it once puts 'my' for the quarto 'mine' (4.1.13). Sometimes F puts 'ye' for 'you'. Q1's 'whilst' was altered to 'while' twice in Q2 (3.1.22 and 5.2.11), and once in F (3.3.59).

F's major change from the quarto versions, apart from the stage directions and the substantive emendations, is the introduction of elisions to help the metre. The clearest instances are at 1.3.39, 2.2.25 and 127, 3.3.17 and 93, 3.4.27 and 90, 5.2.73, 74 and 76, and 5.3.81. Occasionally, too, F attempts to adjust quarto mislineation.

There is evidence for F's text having been edited by a mind concerned to make sense of the difficulties and ready to emend in order to make the text more easily comprehensible, particularly in Acts 1, 3 and 5. Some attention was evidently paid to metre, and some to verbal confusions, where F finds a way through the muddles of the quarto texts, while in some places F merely normalises the quarto's words. At 1.3.82 Q 'adverse' changes to F 'amaz'd', possibly by infection from the next line. At 140 'pain of life', a phrase repeated thirteen lines below, where F makes no change, is normalised into 'pain of death'. At 226 'sullen' becomes 'sudden'. At 2.3.124 Q's 'cousin' becomes in F 'Kinsman'. At 3.2.43 'light' becomes 'Lightning', possibly by a dim memory from 1.3.79. At 85 'twentie' becomes 'fortie'. At 139 'wound' becomes 'hand'. At 203 'party' becomes 'Faction'. At 3.3.91 'stands' becomes 'is', and at 171 Q 'laugh' becomes 'mock'. At 4.1.145 Q 'raise' becomes F 'rear'. At 5.1.25 Q 'thrown' (probably disyllabic) becomes F 'stricken', a definite disyllable. More routinely, at 66 'men' becomes 'friends'. At 5.3.22 'yeares' becomes 'dayes'. At 92 the painful 'walke' on knees becomes 'kneele'. At 105 'still' becomes 'shall', and at 5.5.46 'check' becomes 'heare'. These alterations may have been changes introduced by the players and recorded in the promptbook, or perhaps wilful adjustments made by a literary-minded editor of the copy prepared for the Folio printers. More positive examples of F editing include the change of Q's 'Woodstock' at the beginning of 1.2 into the more recognisable 'Glouster' which is the form of all the subsequent references in Q as well as F. The consistent censoring which turned Q 'God' into F 'heaven' may also be evident in the two instances where Q 'word' at 5.5.13 and 14 is altered by F into 'Faith', and in political rather than religious terms with Q's 'power' at 3.2.35, which F makes into 'friends', and Q's 'coward' of Richard at 3.2.84 which F softens to 'sluggard'.

Richard E. Hasker's analysis of the printing of F led him to the view first proposed by Fredson Bowers that the source used by the F printer was a copy of Q3 supplemented near the end by a few leaves from a copy of Q5.[1] This made-up copy, he considered, had been serving in the playhouse for some years as the promptbook before it was given to the printer. Service in the playhouse would explain the alteration of oaths and stage directions, and the normalisation of words and metre. Players' alterations would presumably have been registered in the prompt copy. There is substantial evidence to support this theory. Certainly F does adopt a sufficient proportion of the errors introduced by Q3 to make its debt to Q3 likely. While restoring 120 or so of Q1's readings it incorporates over 100 Q3 errors. The availability of a specially adapted playhouse copy of Q3 would also help to explain why, faced with the defective nature of the copy's last pages, the printers did not use a complete copy of Q5 for the whole play, but instead used it just to supplement their version of Q3. The difficulty of this theory is that it calls either for an outstandingly careful book-keeper in the playhouse, who corrected the 120 Q3 errors recorded correctly in F, or for a Folio editor who had access to some manuscript source which supplied him with the necessary corrections.

The question of who edited the copy which the F printer used is complicated by the deposition scene, for which F had a text distinctly superior to Q4 and Q5. This led Ure to conclude[2] that a manuscript promptbook was collated with Q3 to make the copy for F, since the manuscript of the deposition scene was evidently available, and therefore the whole text would most likely have been on hand, Ure also reckoned that Hasker's theory – that a copy of Q3 was prepared as a printed promptbook – is unnecessarily complex and does not account for the survival of uncorrected Q3 errors in F. Recent evidence about the thoroughness of the editing done in the process of

---

[1] Richard E. Hasker, 'The copy for the First Folio *Richard II*', *SB* 5 (1952), 53–72. J. K. Walton, *The Quarto Copy for the First Folio of Shakespeare*, 1971, pp. 116–17, rejects the case for any use of Q5.

[2] Ure, pp. xxv–xxvii.

preparing copy for the Folio[1] supports Ure's view. I would add a few instances where F has altered the Q3 reading apparently by reference to a manuscript, since F reproduces misreadings characteristic of manuscript texts. The gratuitous change in F at 3.2.112 of Q's 'White beards' to 'White Beares' looks like the d/e misreading common with the reversed e of the Elizabethan Secretary hand. Similar preferences for a misread manuscript over the printed text (understandable in a collating editor making the quantity of alterations he incorporated in the F copy) might include 1.3.71 vigour/rigor, 226 sullen/sudden, 1.4.28 smiles/soules, 2.1.118 chasing/chafing, 283 Ramston/Rainston, 2.2.124 unpossible/impossible, 3.3.66 tracke/tract and 4.1.33 sympathy/sympathize. None of these is readily explicable as anything other than a manuscript misreading, except perhaps for 2.1.283, where Q's 'Ramston', the name which appears in Holinshed, might have been infected for the F compositor by the 'Rainold' of line 279, four lines before. In one instance, 2.1.102, F's 'incaged' corrects a Q manuscript misreading 'inraged'.

If the made-up copy of Q3 used as the basis for F's copy was the playhouse promptbook itself, as Hasker claims, it would give the Folio text a substantial degree of authority, as a reflection of the settled playhouse version of the play – the performing text, as distinct from the author's draft which lies behind Q1. But it seems more likely that F is the result of a collation between a raw copy of Q3 and a playhouse manuscript. Only the existence of an incompletely corrected copy of Q3 would adequately explain such features of F as the incompletely altered stage directions (a promptbook would need better stage directions than F supplies), the insertion of a superior version of the deposition scene, the failure to correct over a hundred Q3 errors and the indications that the F copy-editor relied on a manuscript source to make at least some gratuitous corrections to Q3. The indifferent variants and the adjustments of metre as well as the stage directions suggest that the copy which the F editor collated with Q3 was a manuscript promptbook.

There is one awkwardness in this theory. If the F editor had access to a manuscript with authority close to that of the Q1 copy, it is strange that he allowed so many of Q3's errors to pass into the Folio text. Equally, we might reasonably expect to find superior readings in F whenever the quarto printers manifestly misread their copy. In fact F corrects Q1 authoritatively only in about half of the more than 200 places where Q3 is evidently in error, and a proportion of these corrections could have been merely commonsensical. In several places the F editor can be seen making his own conjectural emendations of his defective Q3 copy without reference to anything like Q1 (see Commentary on 1.1.77, 1.3.265, 2.1.18, 2.2.3, 2.3.77, 3.3.119, 3.4.29 and 5.5.17). Presumably the F editor had a degree of confidence in his own abilities sufficient to allow him more freedom in his conflation of printed text and manuscript than would please seekers after the authentic Shakespeare.

Two considerations offer guidelines for the correction of the Q1 and F texts. The first is our knowledge of the compositors, their practices in setting each text and their known types of error. The second is the regularity of the play's metre. Neither offers really secure guidance.

---

[1] See for instance Eleanor Prosser, *Shakespeare's Anonymous Editors*, 1981, esp. p. 162.

Some careful work has been done in recent years identifying the stints of the compositors in Simmes's and the Folio printing-houses. For both the Q and F printings, the problems of spacing consequent on miscalculation of cast-off copy and the standard rates of error for both teams of compositors are reasonably well established. In Q1 the first eight pages, up to 1.1.204, were set sequentially, and subsequent formes set by casting-off, with the outer pages of each forme set first. A standard page had 37 lines, but on eight of the 73 pages the compositor had to squeeze in an extra line. In forme D, the uncorrected state of the text (the Petworth copy) has 37 lines at D1^v and D3^v where the corrected version supplies a thirty-eighth (2.1.186 and 2.2.33). Despite the extra lines in the corrected state, the effects of the compositor compressing his copy appear in mislineations and the omission of some entry and exit stage directions – for instance, Green's entry on D3^v at 2.2.40. Half-lines tend to be tacked on to the line preceding, as at 2.2.60–1. The Folio text was similarly set by cast-off copy, and the effects of this method are visible at 4.1.60–5, for instance, where six type-lines of Q3 are stretched over ten lines of D1^v in F, which also invents a superfluous 'My Lord' at 62 to fill an extra line. Q1's compression of copy and F's stretching seem to have met at 2.1.186–8, on a page where Q1 (D1^v) had to squeeze in an extra line, and F (c3^r) had to spread Richard's half-line over two lines.

The compositor's adjustments made to fit the available space are fairly easily

Sur. My lord Fitzwater, I do remember well
The very time (Aumerle) and you did talke.
Fitz. Tis very true you were in presence then.
                                  And

King Richard the second.

And you can witnes with me this is true.
Sur. As false,by heauen, as heauen it selfe is true.
Fitz. Surrie thou liest.   (sword,
Sur. Dishonorable boy, that lie shall lie so heauie onmy

Surrey. My Lord *Fitz. water* :
I do remember well, the very time
Aumerle, and you did talke.
    Fitz. My Lord,
'Tis very true : You were in presence then,
And you can witnesse with me, this is true.
    Surrey. As false, by heauen,
As Heauen it selfe is true.
    Fitz. Surrey, thou Lyest.
    Surrey. D shonourable Boy ;
That Lye, shall lie so heauy on my Sword,

F (sig. d1^v)

15 4.1.60–6: the quarto text is compressed into six lines, while the Folio text, at the end of the page, is expanded to fill eleven.

identified. It has also proved possible by comparing texts printed from other printed texts to identify the average rates of error in setting by the compositors of both Q1 and F.[1] Unlike casting-off problems, though, the identification of specific errors is not greatly helped by such knowledge. Two compositors set Q1. One of them, Compositor S, with an average error-rate in setting from printed copy of one mistake in 48 lines, set 15½ pages, while the other, Compositor A, with an above-average rate for Elizabethan compositors of one mistake in 17 lines, set 53½ pages.[2] The Folio text was largely set by two compositors, one of whom had a minimal error-rate, chiefly of small literals, and set 2.3.7 to 3.4.53 and 4.1.72 to 5.2.6. The other man, the much-abused Compositor B who set half the entire Folio, had a highish error-rate and was notable for taking liberties with his copy, as he evidently did at 4.1.60–5 when in trouble over casting-off.[3]

Unfortunately, knowing the error-rate of each compositor, and even knowing that one of the Q1 pair was three times more likely to introduce an error than the other, does not do much except increase our uneasiness over the reliability of the text as we have it in the quarto. There are some passages in Compositor A's stints of Q1 where he seems to have botched his copy in the fashion recognisable in his stints with other quartos, notably 1.3.136, 2.1.254, 2.2.88, 5.3.1 and 5.5.17. Knowledge of his habits of misremembering helps to give a shape to conjectural emendations. But they are still only conjectures.

Richard II is almost alone amongst Shakespeare's plays in being entirely in verse. It has more rhymes, more declamation and more formally structured speeches such as oaths, curses, lamentations and proclamations than any of the tragedies. Besides the couplet rhymes ending scenes or major speeches, there are runs of as many as 21 successive couplets and even cross-rhymes. The main variations from the decasyllabic line are occasional half-lines and extra-metrical exclamations. Half-lines are a classic editorial dilemma, since they interfere with the regularity of the metre and therefore invite the suspicion that the text must be corrupt. And yet the poets certainly used half-lines either to introduce or end speeches, sometimes linked to the half-line of another speech (as in *Richard II* 1.1.162 and 173, where the half-lines rhyme) and sometimes not. To a large extent it is a chicken-and-egg problem, resting on the *a priori* assumption that half-lines were a frequent feature of versification and can therefore be accommodated in modernised editions. The difficulty is knowing how frequent they were. *A priori* adoption of them by previous generations of editors only confuses the evidence.[4]

---

[1] For the compositors of Q1, see Alan E. Craven, 'Simmes Compositor A and five Shakespeare quartos', *SB* 26 (1973), 37–60, esp. p. 49, and 'Two Valentine Simmes compositors', *PBSA* 67 (1974), 161–71. For the Folio compositors see Charlton Hinman, *The Printing and Proofreading of the First Folio of Shakespeare*, 2 vols., 1963, esp. I, 10–11, and II, 513, and Paul Werstine's analysis of Compositor B in Gary Taylor and Michael Warren (eds.), *The Division of the Kingdoms*, 1983, pp. 248–72.

[2] Q1 Compositor S, probably the senior man, set sig. A *seriatim* (up to 1.1.204), and subsequently 1.3.175–2.1.125, 3.3.169–203, 5.1.5–42, 5.2.83–113, 5.3.34–69, 5.5.56–90 and 5.6.35–end. Compositor A set the rest.

[3] Hinman regards the stint 3.4.54–4.1.71 as possibly taken by Compositor C instead of B.

[4] For a general survey of this question see Fredson Bowers, 'Establishing Shakespeare's text: notes on short lines and the problem of verse division', *SB* 33 (1980), 74–130. For a look at some non-Shakespearean evidence, see Andrew Gurr (ed.), *Philaster*, 1969, pp. xxxi–lxxxii, and Appendix B.

For this edition, where Q1 and F differ or where there is other evidence of metrical irregularity, rather more freedom has been taken in adjusting Q's or F's metre than is nowadays usual. In eight cases (2.2.93–5, 3.2.90 and 133–4, 3.3.189 and 199, 4.1.60–2 and 103–4, and 5.2.100–1) the Q1 lineation has been adopted. In five cases (2.2.50–1, 2.3.28–9, 3.3.11–13, 5.2.98–9 and 5.3.11–12) the F lineation has been preferred. In eighteen other instances the text has been emended, often on the precedent of Pope or Capell, the eighteenth-century editors who most readily assumed that defective metre signalled a misrepresentation of the original. That is not a principle which should necessarily be adopted too widely. In *Richard II*, however, with its emphatic use of verse and the frequency of its rhymes, it seems consistent with the nature of the play's language.

APPENDIX 1
SHAKESPEARE'S USE OF HOLINSHED

Ideally this appendix should reprint the 28 double-column pages of Holinshed's *Chronicles...of England, Scotlande, and Irelande* which was Shakespeare's basic source for *Richard II*. Only by scrutinising the choices Shakespeare made, both of what to include and what to omit, and seeing where he felt it necessary to supplement Holinshed from *Woodstock* or *The Civil Wars*, can we appreciate the artistic and political considerations which went into the making of *Richard II*. Holinshed was a formidably scrupulous and thorough historian, but his presentation of Richard was clearly not to the taste either of Shakespeare's dramatic art or of his politics. It is illuminating to see what happened to the contents of those 28 pages as Shakespeare consulted the alternative authorities – he looked at more for this play than any other – and put together his personal view of the reign.

Bullough's *Narrative and Dramatic Sources* and Ure's edition of the play reprint only those parts of Holinshed where Shakespeare's debt is evident. Reasonably comprehensive and accurate reprints are available in book form, however,[1] and since it might seem to burke editorial responsibility merely to reprint the basic material for a comparison of Holinshed's Richard with Shakespeare's, this appendix attempts to detail what was included in the play from the primary source, and what omitted. There is a risk that my interpretation of reasons for the inclusions and omissions may be too subjective and reflect preconceptions open to challenge. The careful reader will also refer to Holinshed's full original text.

Rafael Holinshed's formidable *Chronicles* made extensive and well-acknowledged use of previous histories, not least the much more tendentious Edmund Halle, whose account of the dynastic wars which preceded the Tudor line began with the combat between Bullingbrook and Mowbray, where Shakespeare's account starts. Holinshed was more objective than Halle in one sense. He sought to chronicle facts rather than to shape his material with the openly providential gloss of Halle's account. Halle's work was entitled *The Union of the Two Noble and Illustre Famelies of Lancaster and Yorke*, and made orderly patterns in its account by representing the sequence of events from Richard's fall to Henry VII's accession as a divinely ordained alternation between harmony and chaos, periods of peace followed by periods of war. Holinshed's chronicle grew out of a different principle. His work began as a grandiose project for a compendium of the history and geography of the world. Commercial restraints narrowed it to a history and geography of Britain, and its first edition in 1577 contained Holinshed's histories of England and Scotland, plus a geographical 'Description' of

---

[1] *Holinshed's Chronicle as used in Shakespeare's Plays*, ed. Allardyce and Josephine Nicoll, 1927, 1955; *Holinshed's Chronicles: Richard II, 1398–1400, Henry IV and Henry V*, ed. R. S. Wallace and Alma Hansen, 1917, 1923.

England, Wales and Scotland by William Harrison, and Richard Stanyhurst's 'Description' and history of Ireland. In a compendium there was no call for the political tendentiousness of Halle, though Holinshed's account of the period of English history covered by Halle does lean heavily on the earlier work.

The 1587 edition of Holinshed, which Shakespeare read, was an even looser compendium than the first. It appeared after Holinshed's death and its compiler threw in a fairly random array of historical pieces to augment the original. In outward appearance it offers itself as an even less systematic collection than the first edition, and it says something for Shakespeare's interest in reading between the lines that he accorded the work so much respect. By doing so, in the one section on the dynastic wars of York and Lancaster, he took Holinshed at his best. As a devoted antiquarian and sharp-nosed investigator of sources, Holinshed made his account of the years from 1398 to 1485 into a monument for its own time. In dealing with some periods, he could be faulted for an uncritical acceptance of myth-making and hearsay with the result that his narrative lost coherence. But his chronicle of what to him was recent English history is firm, clear and judicious. Shakespeare was equally judicious in relying on it.

The 28 pages of Holinshed which cover the ground of Shakespeare's play are crammed with detail which is only occasionally laced with comment and authorial judgement. Holinshed left out nothing, and generally allowed the facts to speak for themselves. Bullingbrook's acquisition of the crown from Richard and the attempt to make Richard condemn his own misdeeds he regarded as 'heinous', and said so. But on the whole he provided the best possible quarry for a literary form which records what men do, and not what they ought to do.

The complete account of Richard's reign occupies 95 pages (II, 415–509), or approximately 140,000 words. Shakespeare uses directly only the last 17 pages of this account and the first 9 of the following account of 'Henrie the Fourth, cousine germane to Richard the second, latelie deprived'. Shakespeare begins with p.493, where Holinshed described 'K. Richard his evill government', as the marginal gloss puts it. Nobles and commons alike 'began to feare' for their estates and their lives. The nobles appealed to the flatterers, 'by whose naughtie counsell they understood the king to be misled', in the hope that they might change their counsel or that Richard, 'having knowledge what evill report went of him, might mend his manners misliked of his nobles'. But the quarrel between Bullingbrook and Mowbray intervened and made all this 'in vaine'.

Holinshed said that the initial accusation and counter-accusation were read out to the king, who asked each duke to comment and then ordered a formal hearing to be held six weeks later at Windsor. Shakespeare's opening presents this formal repetition of the complaints each duke made against the other. It thus becomes a ceremonial occasion. Shakespeare resisted, here and elsewhere, the easy temptation to make Holinshed's reported confrontation into a spontaneous and exclamatory exchange. He follows Holinshed in presenting a formal scene, with the appellants appearing before Richard 'sitting there in his seat of justice' as Holinshed put it. His only substantial changes are the introduction of Gaunt and the mood of the king.

In Holinshed, when Richard heard the knight who spoke for Bullingbrook offer to test the truth of his charge 'within lists' against Mowbray, the king 'waxed angrie' and asked Bullingbrook to confirm his spokesman's statement. In Shakespeare Richard is controlled and seeks to soothe the anger of both contestants. The play also ignores Holinshed's report that once the gages were thrown down Richard 'swore by saint John Baptist, that he would never seeke to make peace betwixt them againe'. Shakespeare's Richard is less peremptory, more controlled and calculating.[1]

Holinshed then moved straight on to describe the ceremonies of the combat day. Shakespeare inserts 1.2, the dialogue between Gaunt and the widowed Duchess of Gloucester. This scene serves several artistic and political functions. It augments the role of Gaunt, whom Holinshed only mentioned at his death, and it clarifies the importance of Gloucester's murder as the underlying argument in the quarrel between Bullingbrook and Mowbray. By so doing it hints at Richard's private feelings as Bullingbrook's implicit target and the special link with Mowbray as his agent in the murder. It sets out Gaunt's choice of patient Christian pilgrimage against his son's active revenge or crusading. It also introduces the first of the three female characters, a grieving duchess who anticipates the grieving queen of the middle scenes in the play and balances the other emotional duchess of the last scenes.

Holinshed described the ceremonial where Aumerle acted as Constable and Surrey as Marshal. He described the costumes and colours of each combatant, his horse and his 'chaire' or pavilion. The appellant, 'the duke of Hereford', came first and formally answered the Constable and Marshal's challenge. Richard came next 'into the field with great triumph', a French earl in his company to witness the combat. Mowbray, 'the duke of Norfolke', followed. Shakespeare's version tidies up the ceremonial, introducing Richard first in the seat of justice, and allowing Richard control of the ceremony. He instructs the Marshal and he directs the sequence of events up to the point where, exactly as in Holinshed, he stops the combat by throwing his warder down. Shakespeare then telescopes events, reducing the two hours of debate in Council before judgement is given to a few moments, and making Richard rebate four of Bullingbrook's years of exile as soon as Mowbray has departed. He does not alter the sequence of events, though again Gaunt's contribution is all Shakespeare. Holinshed's account of Mowbray effectively ended here, with an account of his wanderings in Germany and death in Venice, and a note that he died 'melancholie', having hoped for better support from the king in the dispute with Bullingbrook. Holinshed made no mention of Jerusalem in connection with Mowbray's exile and death.

The historian's account of Bullingbrook's exile included the story of Richard stopping his marriage to the French king's cousin. Shakespeare omits any reference to the period of exile, concentrating instead on Richard's abuse of Bullingbrook's property rights at home. Before Holinshed came to that, however, he gave a striking

---

[1] Holinshed also reports disagreement amongst his sources over the date appointed for the combat at Coventry, between a Monday in August or St Lambert's day, 17 September, or 11 September. Shakespeare chose the alternative which could be most concisely named and had some appropriate connotations.

half-column to Richard's misrule. Applying his favourite pejorative, 'heinous', to Richard's intervention over Bullingbrook's marriage, which Shakespeare refers to only in passing at 2.1.167–8, he went on to comment 'And how are the malicious tormented with egernes of revenge against them whome they maligne, wringing themselves in the meane time with inward pangs gnawing them at the hart?' A note followed about a three-mile stretch of river disappearing from its channel on New Year's Day of that year which was taken to signify subjects revolting from their natural prince. The next paragraph described the business of blank charters. Out of these hints Shakespeare made 1.4, with its jealous king describing Bullingbrook's departure from England, and his announcement of the blank charters. The end of the scene prepares for the extended treatment in 2.1 of Holinshed's next paragraph, about the death of Gaunt and Richard's seizure of his property.

Holinshed's next two paragraphs need to be quoted in full. They give the bones – Gaunt's death, Richard's seizure and York's protest – out of which Shakespeare made the first great dramatic confrontation in the play.

In this meane time, the duke of Lancaster departed out of this life at the bishop of Elies palace in Holborne, and lieth buried in the cathedrall church of saint Paule in London, on the northside of the high altar, by the ladie Blanch his first wife. The death of this duke gave occasion of increasing more hatred in the people of this realme toward the king, for he seized into his hands all the goods that belonged to him, and also received all the rents and revenues of his lands which ought to have descended unto the duke of Hereford by lawfull inheritance, in revoking his letters patents, which he had granted to him before, by vertue whereof he might make his attorneis generall to sue liverie for him, of any maner inheritances or possessions that might from thenceefoorth fall unto him, and that his homage might be respited, with making reasonable fine: whereby it was evident, that the king meant his utter undooing.

This hard dealing was much misliked of all the nobilitie, and cried out against of the meaner sort: but namelie the duke of Yorke was therewith sore mooved, who before this time, had borne things with so patient a mind as he could, though the same touched him verie neere, as the death of his brother the duke of Glocester, the banishment of his nephue the said duke of Hereford, and other mo injuries in great number, which for the slipperie youth of the king, he passed over for the time, and did forget aswell as he might. But now perceiving that neither law, justice nor equitie could take place, where the kings wilfull will was bent upon any wrongfull purpose, he considered that the glorie of the publike wealth of his countrie must needs decaie, by reason of the king his lacke of wit, and want of such as would (without flatterie) admonish him of his dutie; and therefore he thought it the part of a wise man to get him in time to a resting place and to leave the following of such an unadvised capteine, as with a leden sword would cut his owne throat.

By linking his account of the seizure with Richard's malice against Bullingbrook, Holinshed left little room for question about a motive for the seizure. Shakespeare's creation of Gaunt on his deathbed turns his Richard into a poseur whose boast to his flatterers about financing the Irish wars from Gaunt's coffers is inflated beyond all bounds by his hysterical fury at Gaunt's reproofs. York's withdrawal thus changes into a protest against the crucial political mistake which Richard's emotional state drove him to unawares.

Holinshed's next few paragraphs detailed Richard's misrule, how he 'set to farme the realme of England, unto sir William Scroope earle of Wiltshire, and then treasurer of England, to sir John Bushie, sir John Bagot, and sir Henrie Greene knights'. The details are all of financial exactions, except for a curious point about legal irregularities and trial by combat:

manie of the kings liege people were through spite, envie, and malice, accused, apprehended, and put in prison, and after brought before the constable and marshall of England, in the court of chivalrie, and might not otherwise be delivered, except they could justifie themselves by combat and fighting in lists against their accusers hand to hand; although the accusers for the most part were lustie, yoong and valiant, where the parties accused were perchance old, impotent, maimed and sicklie. Whereupon not onelie the great destruction of the realme in generall, but also of everie singular person in particular, was to be feared and looked for.

Shakespeare makes no use of this charge, vivid though it was. On the other hand one wonders about the next paragraph. It was Holinshed's only reference to the crusades and has nothing directly to do with Richard or the troubles of his reign. It simply stated that at this time the Bishop of Chalcedon came to England asking for contributions to help the Emperor of Constantinople against the Turks. In the context of Richard's personal extravagance and his exactions the implication about Richard's misuse of his wealth is clear, though Holinshed did not add any comment. Shakespeare's motif of crusades and pilgrimages might have begun there.

The Irish campaign next took more than a page of Holinshed's account, none of which Shakespeare uses. The change from reportage to dialogue makes him leap not only past Ireland but past the appeal made to Bullingbrook to return while Richard was still in Ireland. Holinshed says this appeal by nobility and prelates was 'devised with great deliberation and considerable avise'. Shakespeare gives us only the news that Bullingbrook has landed with a strong body of supporters. From Holinshed's note about the dispute in his source authorities over how much support Bullingbrook landed with, Shakespeare takes the highest figure. This detail, together with the reception of the news by Northumberland and the other northern lords, shows how popular Bullingbrook's action is. Shakespeare's changes, however, give the initiative for his return wholly to Bullingbrook himself.

The gist of the return is similar in chronicle and play, including the flight of the flatterers, Bullingbrook's declaration that he came back only for his inheritance and to remove the flatterers from the king, their execution, and York's ineffective manoeuvres. Shakespeare emphasises the comic *senex* characterisation of York by depriving him of the 'puissant power' he commanded according to Holinshed, who maintained that York's passivity resulted from his knowledge that his troops were unreliable and 'there was not a man that willinglie would thrust out one arrow against the duke of Lancaster'. Shakespeare also picks out Holinshed's own parenthesis over Bullingbrook's name, 'the duke of Hereford or Lancaster, whether ye list to call him', and gives it to Berkeley.[1] Choosing this when he passes over so many other vivid details gives us some confirmation for seeing a thematic emphasis on names.

Through the first two acts Shakespeare constructs an alternation of major public scene and small private grouping, with two of each in each act. The third act changes the pattern as it builds to the two climaxes, at Flint and in Parliament. Shakespeare

[1] 2.3.76.

in 2.1–3 follows Holinshed fairly closely, fleshing out the details of localities and names, and compressing rather than eliminating the main features of the historical account. Worcester's dispersal of the royal Household, which comes after Richard's return from Ireland in Holinshed, Shakespeare puts into the list of troubles in 2.2. Holinshed's account of 'K. Richard in utter despaire', as the marginal gloss describes him, included the point that when he told his soldiers to disperse they begged him to stand firm, with the result that he stole away from them at night to Flint Castle. Shakespeare compresses the subsequent comings and goings, which lasted several weeks, but his only radical change is to free Richard to make his own doom. The key incident in Holinshed, where Northumberland tricked Richard into venturing out of Conway Castle and then ambushed him, so putting him totally into Bullingbrook's power, vanishes. In the play, Richard stands on Flint walls with enough power to choose military confrontation if he has the nerve.

Holinshed's description of the meeting between Richard and Bullingbrook at Flint occupied most of p. 501. Shakespeare's version in 3.3 holds close to the history, keeping Northumberland's function as intermediary and the descent to what Holinshed called the 'utter ward' and Shakespeare, probably after Froissart, the 'base court'. Holinshed's version of the meeting was succinct:

Forthwith as the duke got sight of the king, he shewed a reverend dutie as became him, in bowing his knee, and comming forward, did so likewise the second and third time, till the king tooke him by the hand, and lift him up, saieng; 'Deere cousine, ye are welcome.' The duke humblie thanking him said; 'My sovereigne lord and king, the cause of my comming at this present, is (your honor saved) to have againe restitution of my person, my lands and heritage, through your favourable licence.' The king hereunto answered; 'Deere cousine, I am readie to accomplish your will, so that you may injoy all that is yours, without exception.'

The play keeps faith with the chronicle's bald account, while enhancing its implications.

Holinshed followed this with the journey to London and the great welcome given to the duke. The only reference to Richard contrasts the one suit he wore all through the journey with the sumptuous clothing he usually decked himself in. Shakespeare invents for York in 5.2 the citizens' abuse of Richard on the entry to London, just as he takes from Daniel the queen's reception of him in 5.1. From 3.4 onwards Shakespeare deploys Holinshed more radically, adjusting the sequence of events, adding a scene with the queen and inventing detail not in Holinshed. By far the greatest invention is the structure of 4.1 and its climax – the deposition.

4.1 compresses several events from Holinshed. Seven pages (502–8) were devoted largely to transcripts of the five principal documents, the articles of objection, the instrument of the Parliamentary commissioners for Richard's deposition, Richard's instrument of resignation, the published announcement of the deposition and the Archbishop of Canterbury's oration. From these Shakespeare uses only the name of the articles which Northumberland urges Richard to read, and the gist of Richard's instrument of resignation, incorporated in his speech (4.1.202–14) of renunciation. He invents Richard's arrival in Parliament to depose himself in person, and thus translates what was done in private on to the public stage.

The Parliament scene (4.1) as a whole puts together five separate events from Holinshed. Out of the early events in the account of Henry IV's reign, Shakespeare takes Bagot's testimony in Parliament together with a subsequent hearing in which Aumerle defended himself against the charge that he was implicated in Gloucester's murder and the subsequent rain of counter-charges and gages (p. 512). From p. 514 he took the Westminster plot which closes the Parliament scene. Into the largely invented fourth event, Richard's abdication, he inserts a fifth, Carlisle's protest, which Holinshed reported as made in Parliament after Richard's resignation had led the House of Commons to demand that a judgement should be passed on him and that 'the causes of his deposing might be published through the realme for satisfieng of the people'. By inserting Carlisle's speech, Shakespeare adds the claim to Richard's divine right which Holinshed never made. Shakespeare gives to Northumberland the voice of the demand on behalf of the Commons, and makes him the antagonist to Carlisle's protest.

What Shakespeare omits from the chain of events is noteworthy here. Even though the dynastic problem (created by Bullingbrook's accession to the throne ahead of the more direct heirs to Richard) is central to the later plays in the *Henry IV* sequence, Bullingbrook's attempt to claim a right by succession disappears, together with any mention of the Yorkist line surviving in the Mortimer family, both of which were detailed by Holinshed (p. 511). More intriguingly, Bagot's direct implication of Richard in Gloucester's murder vanishes, as does his accusation against Mowbray. Instead Aumerle becomes Bagot's chief target. In Holinshed Aumerle's principal involvement was not only being overheard to wish Bullingbrook dead but being preferred by Richard over Bullingbrook as his heir. Shakespeare also changes Mowbray's role. In Holinshed's report of the exchanges in Parliament Mowbray became potentially a key witness, and was summoned to return home. His death was only mentioned in the summary of the year's crop of deaths, along with the Duchess of Gloucester. Mowbray's noble death as a crusader is all Shakespeare.

The final four pages of Holinshed's account, up to Richard's death, gave Shakespeare the bones of Act 5. Richard's removal from the Tower to Pomfret Castle, the Westminster plot and the tourney at Oxford where Bullingbrook was to be assassinated, York's discovery of Aumerle's share in the plot, the plot's overthrow, the Exton story of Richard's murder and the penitent funeral for Richard are all in Holinshed. Shakespeare adds the queen and the Duchess of York, the Groom who visits Richard at Pomfret, the story of roan Barbary, and Bullingbrook's concern for his roistering heir, together with Harry Percy's youth counterbalancing Prince Harry. Some details about the Oxford plotters disappear, as of course do the alternative versions of Richard's death. Holinshed's only mention of Richard's queen in all these 28 pages occurred here, when the Oxford conspirators went to where she was staying near Reading and told her that Richard had escaped and was backed by 100,000 soldiers at Pomfret. She proved more gullible than the townsfolk at whom the rumour was directed, and who were not to be moved to rebellion.

Holinshed offered two alternative versions of Richard's death besides the Exton story. One claimed that Richard was starved to death, the other that he starved himself. These versions, said Holinshed, were 'the common fame', but the truth was that immediately after the Westminster plot was crushed 'king Henrie, to rid himselfe of anie such like danger to be attempted against him thereafter, caused king Richard to die of a violent death, that no man should afterward faine himselfe to represent his person, though some have said, he was not privie to that wicked offense'. The Exton story in Shakespeare of course leaves the verdict as open as Holinshed left it. The final paragraph in Holinshed detailed the elaborate funeral arrangements, including the display of his coffin in all the towns between Pomfret and London: 'his face discovered, was shewed to all that coveted to behold it'.

APPENDIX 2: From
THE FIRST FOWRE BOOKES OF THE CIVILE
WARS BETWEEN THE TWO HOUSES OF
LANCASTER AND *YORKE,* by Samuel Daniel (1595)

The text of the first edition of Daniel's epic poem, the 1595 version, has never been reprinted. Bullough, *Narrative and Dramatic Sources,* III, gives substantial excerpts and a summary of the omitted sections. This text corrects some minor errors in Bullough and adds a number of stanzas which Bullough omits. The copy-text is British Library c.117.bb/3.

The argument of the first booke

> *What times forgoe* Richard *the seconds raigne;*
> *The fatall causes of this civile warre*
> *His Unckles pride, his greedie Minions gaine,*
> Glosters *revolt, & death delivered are:*
> Herford *accusd, exild, calld backe againe,*
> *Pretends i'amend what others Rule did marre.*
> *The King from* Ireland, *hastes but did no good,*
> *Whilst strange prodigious signes fortoken bloud.*

1

I sing the civil warrs, tumultuous broyles,
And bloudy factions of a mighty land:
Whose people hauty, proud with forain spoyles
Upon themselves, turn back their conquering hand:
Whilst Kin their Kin, brother the brother foyles,
Like Ensignes all against like Ensignes band:
Bowes against bowes, the Crowne against the crowne,
Whil'st all pretending right, all right throwen downe.

2

What furie, ô what madness held you so
Deare people to too prodigall of bloud?
To wast so much and warre without a foe,
Whilst *France* to see your spoyles, at pleasure stood;
How much might you have purchased with lesse wo?
T'have done you honour & your Nephews good,
Yours might have beene what ever lies betweene
The *Perenei* and *Alps, Aquitayne, & Rheine...*

30

Of these *John* Duke of *Lancaster* was one,
(Too great a subject growne, for such a state
The title of a king & what h'had done
In great exploits his mind did elevate
Above proportion kingdoms stand upon,
Which made him push at what his issue gate)
The other *Edmund Langley*, whose milde sprite
Affected quiet and a safe delight.

31

With these did interpose his proud unrest
Thomas of woodstocke, one most violent,
Impatient of command, of peace, of rest,
Whose brow would shew, that which his hart had ment:
His open malice and repugnant brest
Procur'd much mischiefe by his discontent:
And these had all the charge of king and state,
Till by himselfe he might it ordinate...

55

And long it was not ere he apprehendes
The Duke, who close to *Calice* was convei'd,
And th'Earles of *Arundell* and *Warwike* sendes,
Both in close prisons strongly to be laid;
And soone the Duke his life unquiet endes,
Strangled in secret ere it was bewraide;
And *Arundell* was put to publike death,
But *Warwike* by great meanes he banisheth...

58

For like a Lion that escapes his bounds
Having bin long restraind his use to straie,
Raunges the restles woods, staies on no ground,
Riottes with bloudshed, wantons on his praie:
Seekes not for need but in his pride to wound,
Glorying to see his strength and what he may;
So this unbridled king freed of his feares
In libertie himself thus wildly beares.

59

For standing on himselfe he sees his might
Out of the compasse of respective awe,
And now beginnes to violate all right,
While no restraining feare at hand he saw:
Now he exactes of all, wasts in delight,
Riots in pleasure, and neglects the law;
He thinkes his crowne is licensd to do ill
That lesse should list, that may do what it will.

60

Thus b'ing transported in this sensuall course
No frend to warne, no counsell to withstand,
He still proceedeth on from bad to worse,
Sooth'd in all actions that he tooke in hand
By such as all impiety did nurse,
Commending ever what he did commaund:
Unhappy kings that never may be taught
To know themselves or to discerne their fault.

61

And whilst all sylent grieve at what is donne,
The Duke of Herford then of courage bold
And worthily great John of *Gaunts* first sonne
Utters the passion which he could not hold,
In sad discourse upon this course begun,
Which he to *Mowbray* Duke of Norfolke told,
To th'end he being great about the king
Might doe some good by better counselling.

62

The faithles Duke that presentlie takes hold
Of such advantage to insinuate
Hastes to the king, perverting what was told,
And what came of good minde he makes it hate:
The king that might not now be so controld
Or censur'd in his course, much frets thereat;
Sendes for the Duke, who doth such wordes deny
And craves the combate of his enemy.

63

Which straight was granted, and the daie assign'd
When both in order of the field appeare
To right each other as th'event should find,
And now both even at point of combate were
When lo the king changd sodenly his mind,
Casts downe his warder and so staies them there,
As better now advisd what waie to take
Which might for his assured safety make.

64

For now considering (as it likely might)
The victorie should hap on *Herfords* side,
A man most valiant and of noble sprite,
Belov'd of all, and ever worthy tride:
How much he might be grac'd in publique sight
By such an act as might advance his pride,
And so become more popular by this,
Which he feares, too much he already is.

65

And therefore he resolves to banish both,
Though th'one in chiefest favour with him stood,
A man he dearly lov'd and might be loth
To leave him that had done him so much good:
Yet having cause to do as now he doth
To mitigate the envie of his bloud,
Though best to loose a friend, to rid a foe,
And such a one as now he doubted so.

66

And therefore to perpetuall exile hee
Mowbray condemnes; *Herford* but for ten years:
Thinking (for what the wrong of this decree
Compard with greater rigour lesse appeares)
It might of all the better liked be:
But yet such murmuring of the fact he heares,
That he is faine foure of the ten forgive,
And judg'd him sixe yeares in exile to live.

67

At whose departure hence out of the land,
O how the open multitude reveale
The wondrous love they bare him underhand,
Which now in this hote passion of their zeale
They plainely shewde that all might understand
How deare he was unto the common weale:
They feard not to exclaime against the king
As one that sought all good mens ruining...

[The multitude lamented Bullingbrook's departure:]

70

Ah must we leave him here; that here were fit
We should retaine the pillar of our state;
Whose vertues well deserve to governe it,
And not this wanton young effeminate?
Why should not he in regall honour sit,
That best knowes how a realme to ordinate?
Yet one daie ô we hope thou shalt bring backe
Dear *Bullingbrooke* the justice that we lacke.

71

Thus muttred lo the malecontented sort
That love kings best before they have them still,
And never can the present state comport,
But would as oft change as they change their will:
For this good Duke had wonne them in this sort
By suckring them and pittying of their ill,
That they supposed straight it was one thing,
To be both a good man, and a good king...

[Gaunt died and the king seized his possessions. Richard sailed to Ireland; Bullingbrook landed.]

88

And com'd to quiet shore but not to rest,
The first night of his joyfull landing here
A fearfull vision doth his thoughts molest,
Seeming to see in wofull forme appeare
A naked goodly woman all distrest,
Which with ful-weeping eies and rent-white haire,
Wringing her hands as one that grievd and praid,
With sighes commixt, with words it seem'd shee said.

89

O whither dost thou tend my unkind sonne?
What mischiefe dost thou go about to bring
To her whose *Genius* thou here lookst upon,
Thy mother countrey whence thy selfe didst spring?
O whither dost thou in ambition run,
To change due course by foule disordering?
What bloudshed, ô what broyles dost thou commence
To last for many wofull ages hence?

90

Stay here thy foote, thy yet unguilty foote,
That canst not stay when thou art farther in,
Retire thee yet unstaind whilst it doth boote,
The end is spoile of what thou dost begin:
Injustice never yet tooke lasting roote,
Nor held that long impiety did win:
The babes unborne, shall ô be borne to bleed
In this thy quarrell if thou doe proceede

91

This said she ceast, when he in troubled thought
Griev'd at this tale and sigh'd, and this replies:
Deare Country ô I have not hither brought
These Armes to spoile but for thy liberties:
Tho sinne be on their head that this have wrought
Who wrongd me first, and thee doe tyrannise;
I am thy Champion and I seeke my right,
Provokt I am to this by others spight.

92

This this pretence saith shee, th'ambitious finde
To smooth injustice, and to flatter wrong:
Thou dost not know what then will be thy mind
When thou shalt see thy selfe advanc'd and strong.
When thou hast shak'd off that which others binde
Thou soone forgettest what thou learnedst long:
Men doe not know what then themselves will be
When as more then themselves, themselves they see.

93

And herewithall turning about he wakes,
Lab'ring in sprite, troubled with this strange sight:
And musd a while, waking advisement takes
Of what had past in sleepe and silent night.
Yet hereof no important reck'ning makes
But as a dreame that vanisht with the light:
The day designes, and what he had in hand
Left it to his diverted thoughts unskand.

94

Doubtfull at first, he warie doth proceed
Seemes not t'affect, that which he did effect,
Or els perhaps seemes as he ment indeed,
Sought but his owne, and did not more expect:
Then fortune thou art guilty of his deed,
That didst his state above his hopes erect,
And thou must beare some blame of his great sin
That left'st him worse then when he did begin.

95

Thou didst conspire with pride, and with the time
To make so easie an assent to wrong
That he that had no thought so hie to clime,
(With favoring comfort still allur'd along)
Was with occasion thrust into the crime,
Seeing others weakenes and his part so strong:
And ô in such a case who is it will
Do good, and feare that may live free with ill...

115

Red fiery dragons in the aire doe flie,
And burning Meteors, poynted-streaming lights,
Bright starres in midst of day appeare in skie,
Prodigious monsters, gastly fearefull sights:
Straunge Ghosts, and apparitions terrifie,
The woefull mother her owne birth affrights,
Seeing a wrong deformed infant borne
Grieves in her paines, deceiv'd in shame doth morn.

116

The Earth as if afeard of bloud and woundes
Trembles in terror of these falling bloes:
The hollow concaves give out groning sounds
And sighing murmurs to lament our woes:
The Ocean all at discord with his boundes,
Reiterates his strange untimely floes:
Nature all out of course to checke our course,
Neglects her worke to worke in us remorse...

The second booke

8

So flocke the mightie with their following traine
Unto the all-receiving *Bullingbrooke*,
Who wonders at himselfe how he should gaine
So manie hearts as now his partie tooke,
And with what ease and with how slender paine,
His fortune gives him more then he could looke,
What he imagind never could be wrought
Is powrd upon him, farre beyond his thought.

9

So often things which seeme at first in shew,
Without the compasse of accomplishment,
Once ventred on to that successe do growe,
That even the Authors do admire th'event:
So manie meanes which they did never knowe
Do second their designes, and doe present
Straunge unexpected helpes, and chiefly then
When th'Actors are reputed worthy men...

[Richard muses to himself:]

17

O if my youth hath offred up to lust
Licentious fruits of indiscreet desires
When idle heate of vainer yeares did thrust
That fury on: yet now when it retires
To calmer state: ô why should you distrust
To reape that good whereto mine age aspires?
The youth of Princes have no bounds for sinne
Unlesse themselves do make them bounds within.

18

Who sees not that sees ought (wo worth the while)
The easie way that greatnesse hath to fall
Environd with deceit, hem'd in with guile,
Sooth'd up in flattery, fawned on of all;
Within his owne living, as in exile,
Heares but with others eares or not at all:
Even made a pray onely unto a few,
Who locke up grace that would to others shew.

19

And who as let in lease doe farme the crowne,
And joy the use of *Majestie* and might,
Whilst we hold but the shadow of our owne,
Pleasd but with shewes, and dalied with delight:
They as huge unproportion'd mountaines growne
Betweene our land and us, shadowing our light,
Bereave the rest of joy and us of love,
And keepe downe all to keepe themselves above...

22

Thus he complaind, when lo from *Lancaster*
(The new intituled *Duke*) with order sent
Ariv'd *Northumberland*, as to conferre
And make relation of the *Dukes* intent:
And offred there, if that he would referre
The controversie unto *Parlament*,
And punish those that had abusd the State,
As causers of this universall hate,

23

And also see that justice might be had
On those the Duke of *Glosters* death procur'd,
And such removd from councell as were bad,
His cosin Henrie would, he there assur'd,
On humble knees before his grace be glad
To aske him pardon to be well secur'd,
And have his right and grace resto'rd againe,
The which was all he laboured t'obtaine.

24

And therefore he a Parley doth exhort,
Perswades him leave that unbeseeming place
And with a Princely hardines resort
Unto his people, that attend his grace:
They ment the publique good and not his hurt,
And would most joifull be to see his face:
He layes his soule to pledge, and takes his oth
The ost of Christ an ostage for his troth...

[Richard considers the request:]

38

Thus he: when that good Bishop thus replies
Out of a mind that quiet did affect,
My Lord, I must confesse as your case lies,
You have great cause your subjects to suspect
And counterplot against their subtelties,
You all good care and honestie neglect
And feare the worst what insolence maie doe,
Or armed fury maie incense them to.

39

But yet my Lord, feare maie as well transport
Your care beyond the truth of what is ment,
As otherwise neglect maie fall too short
In not examining of their intent:
But let us weigh the thing which they exhort,
Tis Peace, submission, and a parlament,
Which, how expedient tis for either part
Twere good we judgd with an unpartiall hart.

40

And first for you my Lord, in griefe we see
The miserable case wherein you stand
Void here of succour, helpe or majestie,
On this poore promontory of your land,
And where how long a time your grace may be,
Expecting what may fall into your hand
We know not: since th'event of things do lie
Clos'd up in darknes far from mortall eie.

41

And how unfit it were you should protract
Long time in this so dangerous disgrace,
As though that you good spirit and courage lackt
To issue out of this opprobrious place:
When even the face of kings do oft exact
Feare and remorse in faulty subjects base,
And longer stay a great presumption drawes
That you were guilty or did doubt your cause.

42

What subjects ever so inragd would dare
To violate a Prince, t'offend the bloud
Of that renowmed race, by which they are
Exalted to the glorie of this good?
What if some things by chaunce misguided were,
Which they have now rebelliously withstood?
They never will proceed with that despight
To wracke the state, and to confound the right.

43

Nor doe I thinke that *Bullingbrooke* can be
So blind ambitious to affect the crowne,
Having himselfe no title, and doth see
Others, if you should faile, must keepe him downe:
Besides the Realme, though mad, will never gree
To have a right succession overthrowne,
To raise confusion upon them and theirs
By prejudicing true and lawfull heires.

44

And now it may be fearing the successe
Of his attempts, or with remorse of mind,
Or else distrusting secret practises,
He would be glad his quarrell were resignd;
So that there were some orderly redresse
In those disorders which the Realme did find:
And this I thinke he now sees were his best
Since farther actions farther but unrest.

45

And for th'impossibility of peace
And reconcilement which my Lords objects;
I thinke when doying injurie shall cease
(The cause pretended) then surcease th'effects:
Time and some other Actions may increase
As may divert the thought of these respects;
Others law of forgetting injuries
Maie serve our turne in like calamities.

46

And for his oath my Lord I thinke in conscience,
True honour would not so be found untrue,
Not spot his bloud with such a fowle offence
Against his soule, against his God and you:
Our Lord forbid that ever with th'expence
Of heaven and heavenly joies that shall insue,
Mortality should buy this little breath
T'indure the horror of eternal death.

47

And therefore as I thinke you safely maie
Accept this proffer, that determine shall
All doubtfull courses by a quiet waie;
Needfull for you, fit for them, good for all:
And here my sov'raigne to make longer stay
T'attend for what you are unsure will fall,
May slippe th'occasion and incense their will,
For feare that's wiser then the truth doth ill.

48

Thus he perswades even of a zealous mind,
Supposing men had spoken as they ment,
And unto this the king likewise inclinde
As wholy unto peace and quiet bent,
And yeelds himselfe to th'earle, goes, leaves behind
Safety, Scepter, honor, government:
For gone, all's gone, he is no more his owne;
And they rid quite of feare, he of the crowne...

53

To *Flint* from thence unto a restles bed
That miserable night he comes convayd,
Poorely provided, poorely followed,
Uncourted, unrespected, unobayd:
Where if uncertaine sleepe but hoovered
Over the drooping cares that heavy weigh'd,
Millions of figures fantasie presents
Unto that sorrow, wakened griefe augments...

55

The morning light presents unto his view
Walking upon a turret of the place,
The truth of what he sees is prov'd too true;
A hundred thousand men before his face
Came marching on the shore which thither drew:
And more to aggravate his fowle disgrace,
Those he had wrongd or done to them despight
As if they him obrayd, came first in sight.

56

There might he see that false forsworne vile crue,
Those shameles agents of unlawfull lust,
His *Pandars, Parasites*, people untrue
To God and man, unworthy any trust:
Pressing unto that fortune that was nue
And with unblushing faces formost thrust
As those that live in sun-shine of delights,
And flie the winter when affliction lights.

57

There he beheld how humbly diligent
New adulation was to be at hand,
How ready *Falshood* stept, how nimbly went
Base-pickthanke *Flattery* and prevents command:
He saw the great obay, the grave consent,
And all with this new-raisd *Aspirer* stand,
Which when he saw and in his sorrow waid
Thus out of griefe unto himselfe he said.

58

O faithlesse *Cosen*, here behold I stand
Spectator of that act my selfe have plaid,
That act of rule which now upon thy hand
This wavering mutability hath laid:
But *Cosen*, know the faith of this false land
Stands sworne to me, that faith they have betraid
Is mine, tis mine the rule, thou dost me wrong
T'usurpe the government I held so long.

59

And when thou hast but tride what I have found,
Thou maist repent t'have bought command so deare,
When thou shalt find on what unquiet ground
Greatnes doth stand, that stands so high in feare:
Where infinite occasions do confound
The peace of minde, the goode thou look'st for here:
Of fatall is th'ascent unto a crowne!
From whence men come not downe, but must fall downe.

60

O you that cherish fat iniquity,
Inriching sinne, with store, and vice with gaine
By my disgrace, see what you get thereby
To raise the bad, to make the good complaine:
These vipers spoile the womb wherein they lie,
And have but impudence a grace to gaine,
But bodies and bold browes no mindes within
But minde of ill, that knowes but how to sin.

61

And for the good which now do take thy part
Thou maiste rejoyce, for th'others I am glad
To thinke they may in time likewise subvart
The expectation which of thee men had:
When thou shalt find how difficult an art
It is to rule and please the good and bad:
And feele the grievance of this fatall sort,
Which still are borne for court are made in court.

62

More griefe had said: when lo the Duke he saw
Entring the *Castle* come to parle there,
Which makes him presently from thence withdraw
Into a fitter place some other where:
His fortune now inforst an yeelding awe
To meete him, who before in humble feare
Would have been glad t'have staid, and to prepare
The grace of audience, with attendant care.

63

The *Duke* when come in presence of his king,
Whether the sight of majestie did breed
Remorse of wrong which reverence did bring;
Or whether but to formalize his deed,
He kneeles him downe even at his entering,
Rose, kneeles againe (for craft will still exceed)
When as the king approcht, put off his hood
And welcomd him, though wishd him little good.

64

To whom the *Duke* thus said: my Lord I know
That both unlookt for, and unsent unto
I have presumed to come hither now;
But this your wrong and rigor drave me to,
And being come I purpose now to shew
You better how to rule, and what to doe:
You have had time too much to worke our ill,
But now redresse is planted in our will.

65

As you shal please deare cosin said the king,
You have me in your powre, I am content
And I am pleasd, if my disgrace may bring
Good to my countrey which I ever ment:
But yet God grant your course held in this thing
Cause not succeeding ages to repent.
And so they left: the *Duke* had hast to go,
It was no place to end the matter so...

69

He that in glorie of his fortune sate,
Admiring what he thought could never be,
Did feele his bloud within salute his state,
And lift up his rejoicing soule to see
So manie hands and harts congratulate
Th'advancement of his long'desir'd degree:
When prodigall of thankes in passing by
He resalutes them all with cheerefull eie.

70

Behind him all aloofe came pensive on
The unregarded king, that drooping went
Alone, and but for spight scarce lookt upon,
Judge if he did more envy or lament:
O what a wondrous worke this daie is done,
Which th'image of both fortunes doth present,
In th'one to shew the best of glories face,
In th'other worse then worst of all disgrace.

71

Now *Isabell* the young afflicted Queene,
Whose yeares had never shew'd her but delights,
Nor lovely eies before had ever seene
Other then smiling joies and joyfull sights:
Borne great, matcht great, liv'd great and ever beene
Partaker of the worlds best benefits,
Had plac'd her selfe, hearing her Lord should passe
That way where shee unseene in secret was.

72

Sicke of delay and longing to behold
Her long mist love in fearfull jeoperdies,
To whom although it had in sort beene told
Of their proceeding, and of his surprize,
Yet thinking they would never be so bold
To lead their Lord in any shamefull wise,
But rather would conduct him as their king,
As seeking but the states reordering.

73

And forth shee looks: and notes the formost traine
And grieves to view some there she wisht not there,
Seeing the chiefe not come, staies, lookes againe,
And yet she sees not him that should appeare:
Then backe she stands, and then desires was faine
Againe to looke to see if he were nere,
At length a glittring troupe farre off she spies,
Perceives the thronge and heares the shoots & cries.

74

Lo yonder now at length he comes (saith shee)
Looke my good women where he is in sight:
Do you not see him? yonder that is hee
Mounted on that white courser all in white,
There where the thronging groupes of people bee,
I know him by his seate, he sits s'upright:
Lo now he bows: deare Lord with what sweet grace:
How long have I longd to behold that face?

75

O what delight my hart takes by mine eie?
I doubt me when he comes but something neare
I shall set wide the window: what care I
Who doth see me, so him I may see cleare?
Thus doth false joy delude her wrongfully
Sweete lady in the thing she held so deare;
For nearer come, shee findes shee had mistooke,
And him shee markt was *Henrie Bullingbrooke*.

76

Then *Envie* takes the place in her sweet eies,
Where sorrow had prepard her selfe a seat,
And words of wrath from whence complaints should rise,
Proceed from egar lookes, and browes that threat:
Traytor saith shee: i'st thou that in this wise
To brave thy Lord and king art made so great?
And have mine eies done unto me this wrong
To looke on thee? for this staid I so long?

77

O have they grac'd a perjur'd rebell so?
Well for their error I will weepe them out,
And hate the tongue defilde that praisde my fo,
And loath the minde that gave me not to doubt:
O have I added shame unto my woe?
Ile looke no more; *Ladies* looke you about,
And tell me if my Lord bee in this traine,
Least my betraying eies should erre againe...

83

Thus as shee stoode assur'd and yet in doubt,
Wishing to see, what seene she grievd to see,
Having beliefe, yet faine would be without;
Knowing, yet striving not to know twas he:
Her hart relenting, yet her hart so stout
As would not yeeld to thinke what was, could be:
Till quite condemnd by open proofe of sight
Shee must confesse or else denie the light.

84

For whether love in him did sympathize
Or chance so wrought to manifest her doubt,
Even just before, where she thus secret prize,
He staies and with cleare face lookes all about:
When she: tis ô too true, I know his eies
Alas it is my owne deare Lord, cries out:
And with that crie sinkes downe upon the flore,
Abundant griefe lackt words to utter more.

85

Sorrow keepes full possession in her soule,
Lockes him within, laies up the key of breath,
Raignes all alone a *Lord* without controule
So long till greater horror threatneth:
And even in daunger brought, to loose the whole
H'is forst come forth or else to stay with death,
Opens a sigh and lets in sence againe,
And sence at length gives words leave to complaine:

86

Then like a torrent had beene stopt before,
Teares, sighes, and words, doubled togither flow,
Confusdly striving whether should do more
The true intelligence of griefe to show:
Sighes hindred words, words perisht in their store,
Both intermixt in one together grow:
One would do all, the other more then's part
Being both sent equall agents from the hart.

87

At length when past the first of sorrowes worst,
When calm'd confusion better forme affords
Her hart commands her words should past out first,
And then her sighes should interpoint her words;
The whiles her eies out into teares should burst,
This order with her sorrow she accords,
Which orderles all forme of order brake,
So then began her words and thus she spake.

88

O dost thou thus returne againe to mee?
Are these the triumphs for thy victories?
Is this the glory thou dost bring with thee
From that unhappy Irish enterprise?
O have I made so many vowes to see
Thy safe returne, and see thee in this wise?
Is this the lookt for comfort thou dost bring,
To come a captive that wentst out a king?

89

And yet deare Lord though thy ungratefull land
Hath left thee thus, yet I will take thy part,
I do remaine the same under thy hand,
Thou still dost rule the kingdome of my hart;
If all be lost, that government doth stand
And that shall never from thy rule depart:
And so thou be, I care not how thou be,
Let greatnes goe, so it goe without thee.

90

And welcome come, how so unfortunate,
I will applaud what others do dispise,
I love thee for thy selfe not for thy state,
More then thy selfe is what without thee, lies:
Let that more go, if it be in thy fate,
And having but thy selfe it will suffize:
I married was not to thy crowne but thee,
And thou without a crowne all one to mee.

91

But what doe I heere lurking idlie mone
And waile apart, and in a single part
Make severall griefe which should be both in one,
The touch being equall of each others hart?
Ah no sweete Lord thou must not mone alone,
For without me thou art not all thou art,
Nor my teares without thine are fullie teares,
For thus unjoyn'd, sorrow but halfe appeares.

92

Joine then our plaints & make our griefe ful griefe,
Our state being one, ô lets not part our care,
Sorrow hath only this poore bare reliefe,
To be bemon'd of such as wofull are:
O should I rob thy griefe and be the thiefe
To steale a private part, and severall share,
Defrauding sorrow of her perfect due?
No no my Lord I come to helpe thee rue...

96

Shee that was come with a resolved hart
And with a mouth full stoor'd with words wel chose,
Thinking this comfort will I first impart
Unto my Lord, and thus my speech dispose:
Then thus ile say, thus looke, and with this art
Hide mine owne sorrow to relieve his woes,
When being come all this prov'd nought but winde,
Teares, lookes, and sighes doe only tell her minde.

97

Thus both stood silent and confused so,
Their eies relating how their harts did morne
Both bigge with sorrow, and both great with woe
In labour with what was not to be borne:
This mightie burthen wherewithall they goe
Dies undelivered, perishes unborne;
Sorrow makes silence her best oratore
Where words may make it lesse not shew it more.

98

But he whom longer time had learn'd the art
T'indure affliction as a usuall touch:
Straines forth his wordes, and throwes dismay apart
To raise up her, whose passions now were such
As quite opprest her overchardged hart,
Too small a vessell to containe so much,
And cheeres and mones, and fained hopes doth frame
As if himselfe believ'd, or hop'd the same...

115

Then to the towre (where he remained) went
The *Duke* withall the *Peeres* attended on:
To take his offer with his free consent,
And testifie his resignation:
And thereof to informe the parlament
That all things might more formally be done:
And men might rest more satisfide thereby
As not done of constraint but willingly.

116

And forth h'is brought unto th'accomplishment
Deckt with the crowne in princely robes that day,
Like as the dead in other landes are sent
Unto their graves in all their best array:
And even like good did him this ornament
For what he brought he must not beare away,
But buries there his glory and his name
Intombd for evermore in others blame.

117

And there unto th'assembly of these states
His sorrow for their long indured wrong
Through his abusd authority relates,
Excuses with confessions mixt among:
And glad he saies to finish all debates
He was to leave the rule they sought for long,
Protesting if it might be for their good
He would as gladly sacrifice his bloud.

118

There he his subjects all in generall
Assoyles and quites of oth and fealty,
Renounces interest, title, right and all
That appertaind to kingly dignity;
Subscribes thereto and doth to witnes call
Both heaven and earth, and God and saints on hie,
And all this did he but t'have leave to live
The which was all he crav'd that they would give.

119

Tis said with his owne hands he gave the crowne
To *Lancaster*, and wisht to God he might
Have better joy thereof then he had knowne,
And that his powre might make it his by right:
And furthermore he crav'd of all his owne
But life to live apart a private wight;
The vanity of greatnes he had tride
And how unsurely standes the foote of pride.

120

This brought to passe the lords returne with speed
T'acquaint the Parlament with what is done,
Where they at large publisht the kings owne deed
And manner of his resignation:
When *Canterbury* urgd them to proceed
Forthwith unto a new election,
And *Henry* make his claime both by discent
And resignation to the governement.

121

Who there with full and generall applause
Is straight proclaimd as king and after crownd,
The other cleane rejected by the lawes,
As one the Realme had most unworthy found.
And yet ô *Lancaster* I would thy cause
Had had as lawfull and as sure a ground
As had thy vertues, and thy glorious worth
For *Empire* borne, for *Government* brought forth...

The third booke

20

Yet reverent *Carlile* thou didst there oppose
Thy holy voice to save thy Princes bloud,
And freely check'st this judgement and his foes,
When all were bad, yet thou dar'st to be good:
Be it inrold that time may never lose
The memory how firme thy vertues stood,
When powre, disgrace, nor death could ought divart
Thy glorious tongue, thus to reveale thy hart.

21

Grave, reverent Lords, since that this sacred place
Our *Aventine, Retire*, our holy hill;
This place, soule of our state, the Realmes best grace
Doth priviledge me speake what reason will:
O let me speake my conscience in this case
Least sin of silence shew my hart was ill,
And let these walles witnes if you will not,
I do discharge my soule of this foule blot.

22

Never shall this poore breath of mine consent
That he that two and twenty yeeres hath raignd
As lawfull Lord, and king by just discent,
Should here be judgd unheard, and unaraignd
By subjects two: Judges incompetent
To judge their King unlawfully detaind,
And un-brought forth to plead his guiltles cause,
Barring th'annointed libertie of lawes.

23

Have you not done inough? blush, blush to thinke,
Lay on your harts those hands; those hands too rash,
Know that this staine that's made doth farther sinke
Into your soules then all your blouds can wash,
Leave with the mischiefe done and do not linke
Sin unto sin, for heaven, and earth will dash
This ill accomplisht worke ere it be long,
For weake he builds that fences wrong with wrong.

24

Stop there was his too vehement speech with speed,
And he sent close to warde from where he stood:
His zeale untimely deem'd too much t'exceed
The measure of his wit and did no good:
They resolute for all this doe proceed
Unto that judgement could not be withstood:
The king had all he crav'd or could compell,
And all was done we will not say how well...

55

Kinges (Lordes of times and of occasions)
May take th'advantage when, and how they list,
For now the Realme with these rebellions
Vext, and turmoyld, was thought would not resist
Nor feele the wound, when like confusions
Should by this meanes be stayd, as all men wist,
The cause be'ing once cut off, that did molest
The land should have her peace, and he his rest.

56

He knew this time, and yet he would not seeme
Too quicke to wrath, as if affecting bloud;
But yet complaines so far, that men might deeme
He would twere done, and that he thought it good;
And wisht that some would so his life esteeme
As rid him of these feares wherein he stood: *This Knight*
And therewith eies a knight, that then was by,   *was Sir Pierce*
Who soone could learne his lesson by his eie.   *of Exton*

57

The man he knew was one that willingly
For one good looke would hazard soule and all,
An instrument for any villanie,
That needed no commission more at all:
A great ease to the king that should hereby
Not need in this a course of justice call,
Nor seeme to wil the act, for though what's wrought
Were his own deed, he grieves should so be thought...

63

The morning of that day, which was his last,
After a weary rest rysing to paine
Out at a little grate his eyes he cast
Uppon those bordering hils, and open plaine,
And viewes the towne, and sees how people past,
Where others libertie makes him complaine
The more his owne, and grieves his soule the more
Conferring captive-Crownes with freedome pore.

64

O happie man, saith hee, that lo I see
Grazing his cattel in those pleasant fieldes!
O if he knew his good, how blessed hee
That feeles not what affliction greatnes yeeldes,
Other then what he is he would not bee,
Nor chaung his state with him that Scepters weildes:
O thine is that true life, that is to live,
To rest secure, and not rise up to grieve.

65

Thou sit'st at home safe by thy quiet fire
And hear'st of others harmes, but feelest none;
And there thou telst of kinges and who aspire,
Who fall, who rise, who triumphs, who doe mone:
Perhappes thou talkst of mee, and dost inquire
Of my restraint, why here I live alone,
O know tis others sin not my desart,
And I could wish I were but as thou art.

66

Thrice-happie you that looke as from the shore
And have no venter in the wracke you see,
No sorrow, no occasion to deplore
Other mens travayles while your selves sit free.
How much doth your sweet rest make us the more
To see our misery and what we bee?
O blinded greatnes! thou with thy turmoyle,
Still seeking happie life, mak'st life a toyle.

67

But looke on mee, and note my troubled raigne,
Examine all the course of my vext life;
Compare my little joyes with my long paine,
And note my pleasures rare, my sorrowes rife,
My childhood spent in others pride, and gaine,
My youth in daunger, farther yeares in strife,
My courses crost, my deedes wrest to the worst,
My honour spoild, my life in daunger forst.

68

This is my state, and this is all the good
That wretched I have gotten by a crowne,
This is the life that costes men so much bloud
And more then bloud to make the same their owne,
O had not I then better beene t'have stood
On lower ground, and safely lived unknowne,
And beene a heardsman rather then a king,
Which inexperience thinkes so sweet a thing.

69

O thou great *Monarch*, and more great therefore
For skorning that whereto vaine pride aspires
Reckning thy Gardens in *Illiria* more
Then all the Empire; took'st those sweet retires:
Thou well didst teach, that ô he is not poore
That little hath, but he that much desires;
Finding more true delight in that small ground
Then in possessing all the earth was sound.

*Dioclesian
the Emperor*

70

But what do I repeating others good
To vexe mine owne perplexed soule the more?
Alas how should I now free this poore bloud
And care-worne body from this state restore?
How should I looke for life or lively-hood
Kept here distrest to die, condemnd before,
A sacrifice prepared for his peace
That can but by my death have his release?

71

Are kings that freedom give themselves not free,
As meaner men to take what they maie give?
O are they of so fatall a degree
That they cannot discend from that and live?
Unlesse they still be kings can they not bee,
Nor maie they their autority survive?
Will not my yeelded crowne redeeme my breath?
Still am I fear'd? is there no way but death?

72

Scarce this word death had sorrow uttered,
But in rusht one, and tels him how a knight
Is come from court, his name delivered.
What newes with him said he that traiterous wight?
What more removes? must we be farther lead?
Are we not sent inough yet out of sight?
Or hath this place not strength sufficient
To guard us in? or have they worse intent?...

[The murderers attack Richard, who defends himself 'Lion-like' but is struck down by the 'coward knight'.]

80

Monster of men, ô what hast thou here done
Unto an overpressed innocent,
Lab'ring against so many, he but one,
And one poore soule with care, with sorrow spent?
O could thy eies indure to looke upon
Thy hands disgrace, or didst thou then relent?
But what thou didst I will not here devine
Nor straine my thoughts to enter into thine.

81

But leave thee wretch unto blacke infamie,
To darke eternall horror, and disgrace,
The hatefull skorne to all posterity,
The out-cast of the world, last of thy race,
Of whose curst seed, nature did then deny
To bring forth more her faire workes to deface:
And as asham'd to have produc'd that past
She staies her hand, and makes this worst her last...

85
And thus one king most nere in bloud allide
Is made th'oblation for the others peace:
Now onely one, both name and all beside
Intirely hath, plurality doth cease:
He that remaines, remaines unterrifide
With others right; this day doth all release:
And henceforth he is absolutely king,
No crownes but one, this deed confirmes the thing...

APPENDIX 3: AN HOMILIE AGAINST DISOBEDIENCE AND WILFULL REBELLION

The Homilies were composed to be read in all the churches in the land on every Sunday and holy day. The first book of homilies appeared in 1547, six months after Henry VIII died. Three of its twelve sermons were by Cranmer. Mary replaced this book with thirteen homilies of her own. Under Elizabeth the original twelve were revived and others were subsequently added. A *Second Book* containing another 21 homilies which appeared in 1563 was revised by Elizabeth herself. In 1571 the last and longest of them all, the 'Homily Against Rebellion', joined the *Second Book*, having been issued separately in the previous year. It was designed as a counter to the Papal Bull of 1570, *De Visibili Monarchia*, and rebellions such as the northern risings led by the Earls of Northumberland and Westmorland in 1569. The Pope's edict in 1570 was a major assault on heresy. It excommunicated heretical monarchs and even suggested that Catholic subjects of such monarchs might be justified in assassinating them. The 'Homily Against Rebellion' put the Church of England's and the English government's case against political insurrection, basing it on religious arguments.

The extract which follows is taken from the one-volume folio edition of all the Homilies published with James's authority in 1623, the year of the Shakespeare First Folio. Both folios were carefully and respectfully edited, with in the Homilies scrupulous marginal notes showing the Scriptural authorities used by the authors. These notes are included as footnotes in this text, which is from the beginning of the Homily.

AN HOMILIE AGAINST
disobedience and wilfull
rebellion

The first part.

As GOD the Creatour and Lord of all things appointed his Angels and heavenly creatures in all obedience to serve and to honour his majesty: so was it his will that man, his chiefe creature upon the earth, should live under the obedience of his Creatour and Lord: and for that cause, GOD, assoone as hee had created man, gave unto him a certaine precept and law, which hee (being yet in the state of innocency, and remayning in Paradise) should observe as a pledge and token of his due and bounden obedience, with denunciation of death if hee did transgresse and breake the sayde Law and commandement. And as GOD would have man to be his obedient subject, so did he make all earthly creatures subject unto man, who kept their due obedience unto man, so long as man remayned in his obedience unto GOD: in the which obedience if man had continued still, there had beene no poverty, no diseases, no sickenesse, no death, nor other miseries wherewith mankinde is now infinitely and most miserably afflicted and oppressed. So heere appeareth the originall kingdome of GOD over Angels and man, and universally over all things, and of man over earthly creatures which GOD had made subject unto him, and with all the felicity and blessed state, which Angels, man, and all creatures had remayned in, had they continued in due obedience unto GOD their King. For as long as in this first kingdome the subjects continued in due obedience to GOD their king, so long did GOD embrace all his subjects with his love, favour, and grace, which to enjoy, is perfect felicity, whereby it is evident, that obedience is the principall vertue of all vertues, and indeed the very root of all vertues, and the cause of all felicitie. But as all felicitie and blessednesse should have continued with the continuance of obedience, so with the breach of obedience, and breaking in of rebellion, al vices and miseries did withall breake in, and overwhelme the world.[1] The first authour of which rebellion, the root of all vices, and mother of all mischiefes, was *Lucifer*, first GODS most excellent creature, and most bounden subject, who by rebelling against the Majestie of GOD, of the brightest and most glorious Angel, is become the blackest and most foulest fiend and devill: and from the height of heaven, is fallen into the pit and bottome of hell.[2]

Here you may see the first authour and founder of rebellion, and the reward thereof, here you may see the graund captaine and father of rebels, who perswading the following of his rebellion against GOD their Creatour and Lord, unto our first Parents *Adam* and *Eve*, brought them in high displeasure with GOD, wrought their exile and banishment out of Paradise, a place of all pleasure and goodnesse, into this wretched earth and vale of misery: procured unto them, sorrowes of their mindes, mischiefes, sicknesse, diseases, death of their bodies, and which is farre more horrible then all worldly and bodily mischiefes, he had wrought thereby their eternal and everlasting death and damnation, had not GOD by the obedience of his Sonne Jesus Christ repaired that, which man by disobedience and rebellion had destroyed, and so of his mercy had pardoned and forgiven him: of which all and singular the premisses, the holy Scriptures doe beare record in sundry places.[3]

Thus doe you see, that neither heaven nor paradise could suffer any rebellion in them, neither be places for any rebels to remaine in. Thus became rebellion, as you see, both the first and the greatest, and the very first of all other sinnes, and the first and principall cause, both of all worldly and bodily miseries, sorrowes, diseases, sicknesses, and deathes, and which is infinitely worse then all these, as is said, the very cause of death and damnation eternall also. After this breach of obedience to GOD, and rebellion against his Majestie, all mischiefes and miseries breaking in therewith, and overflowing the world, lest all things should come unto confusion and utter ruine, GOD foorthwith by lawes given unto mankind, repaired againe the rule and order of obedience thus by rebellion overthrowne,[4] and besides the obedience due unto his Majesty, hee not onely ordained that in families and housholds, the wife

---

[1] Matt. 4.9, 25, 41; John 8.44; 2 Pet. 2.4.
[2] Rev. 12.7; Gen. 3.1 ff.; Wisd. of Sol. 2.24; Gen. 3.8, 9 ff., 17 and 23, 24.
[3] Rom. 5.12 ff., and 19 ff.   [4] Gen. 3.17.

should be obedient unto her husband, the children unto their parents, the servants unto their masters:[1] but also, when mankind increased, and spread it selfe more largely over the world, hee by his holy word did constitute and ordaine in Cities and Countreys severall and speciall governours and rulers, unto whom the residue of his people should be obedient.[2]

As in reading of the holy Scriptures, we shall finde in very many and almost infinite places, as well of the olde Testament, as of the new,[3] that Kings and Princes, as well the evill as the good, doe raigne by Gods ordinance, and that subjects are bounden to obey them: that GOD doth give Princes wisedome, great power, and authority: that GOD defendeth them against their enemies, and destroyeth their enemies horribly: that the anger and displeasure of the Prince, is as the roaring of a Lyon, and the very messenger of death: and that the subject that provoketh him to displeasure, sinneth against his own soule: With many other things, concerning both the authority of Princes, and the duetie of subjects. But heere let us rehearse two speciall places out of the new Testament, which may stand in stead of all other. The first out of Saint *Pauls* Epistle to the Romanes and the thirteenth Chapter,[4] where hee writeth thus unto all subjects. Let every soule be subject unto the higher powers, for there is no power but of GOD, and the powers that be, are ordeined of GOD. Whosoever therefore resisteth the power, resisteth the ordinance of GOD, and they that resist, shall receive to themselves damnation. For Princes are not to be feared for good works, but for evill. Wilt thou then be without feare of the power? Doe well, so shalt thou have praise of the same: For he is the minister of GOD for thy wealth: But if thou doe evill, feare: for he beareth not the sword for nought, for he is the minister of GOD to take vengeance upon him that doth evil. Wherefore ye must be subject, not because of wrath onely, but also for conscience sake: for, for this cause ye pay also tribute, for they are GODS ministers, serving for the same purpose. Give to every man therefore his duty: tribute, to whom tribute belongeth: custome, to whom custome is due: feare, to whom feare belongeth: honour, to whom ye owe honour. Thus far are S. *Pauls* words. The second place is in S. *Peters* Epistle, and the second Chapter,[5] whose words are these, Submit your selves unto all maner of ordinances of man for the Lords sake, whether it bee unto the King, as unto the chiefe head, either unto rulers, as unto them that are sent of him for the punishment of evil doers, but for the cherishing of them that doe well. For so is the will of GOD, that with well doing ye may stoppe the mouthes of ignorant & foolish men: as free, and not as having the libertie for a cloake of maliciousnesse, but even as the servants of GOD. Honour all men, love brotherly fellowship, feare GOD, honour the King. Servants, obey your masters with feare, not onely if they be good and courteous, but also though they be froward. Thus farre out of Saint *Peter*.

By these two places of the holy Scriptures, it is most evident that Kings, Queenes, and other Princes (for hee speaketh of authoritie and power, be it in men or women) are ordeined of GOD, are to bee obeyed and honoured of their subjects: that such

---

[1] Gen. 3.16.   [2] Job 34.30 and 36.7.
[3] Eccles. 8.2 and 10.16, 17 and 20; Ps. 18.50 and 20.5 and 21.1; Prov. 8.15.
[4] Rom. 13.   [5] 1 Pet. 2.

subjects, as are disobedient or rebellious against their Princes, disobey GOD, and procure their owne damnation: that the government of Princes is a great blessing of GOD, given for the common wealth, specially of the good and godly: For the comfort and cherishing of whom GOD giveth and setteth by princes: and on the contrary part, to the feare and for the punishment of the evill and wicked. Finally, that if servants ought to obey their masters, not onely being gentle, but such as be froward: as well and much more ought subjects to be obedient, not onely to their good and courteous, but also to their sharpe and rigorous Princes. It commeth therefore neither of chance and fortune (as they terme it) nor of the ambition of mortal men and women climbing up of their owne accord to dominion, that there bee Kings, Queenes, Princes, and other governours over men being their subjects: but all Kings, Queenes, and other governours are specially appoynted by the ordinance of GOD.[1] And as GOD himselfe, being of an infinite Majestie, power, and wisedome, ruleth and governeth all things in heaven and earth, as the universall Monarch and onely King and Emperour over all, as being onely able to take and beare the charge of all: so hath hee constituted, ordeyned, and set earthly Princes over particular Kingdomes and Dominions in earth, both for the avoyding of all confusion, which els would be in the world, if it should be without governors, and for the great quiet and benefite of earthly men their subjects, and also that the Princes themselves, in authoritie, power, wisedome, providence, and righteousness in governement of people and countreys committed to their charge, should resemble his heavenly governance, as the majestie of heavenly things may by the baseness of earthly things bee shadowed and resembled. And for that similitude, which is betweene the heavenly Monarchie, and earthly Kingdomes well governed, our Saviour Christ in sundry parables saith,[2] that the Kingdom of heaven is resembled unto a man, a king: and as the name of the king, is very often attributed and given unto GOD in the holy Scriptures, so doeth GOD himselfe in the same Scriptures sometime vouchsafe to communicate by Name with earthly Princes, terming them gods: doubtlesse for that similitude of governement which they have or should have, not unlike unto GOD their King. Unto the which similitude of heavenly governement, the neerer and neerer that an earthly Prince doth come in his regiment, the greater blessing of GODS mercy is he unto that countrey and people over whom he reigneth: and the further and further that an earthly prince doth swarve from the example of the heavenly government, the greater plague is he of GODS wrath, and punishment by GODS justice, unto that countrey and people, over whom GOD for their sinnes hath placed such a Prince and governour. For it is indeede evident, both by the Scriptures, and dayly by experience, that the maintenance of all vertue and godlinesse, and consequently of the wealth and prosperity of a kingdome and people, doeth stand & rest more in a wise and good Prince on the one part, then in great multitudes of other men being subjects: and on the contrary part, the overthrow of all vertue and godlinesse, and consequently the decay and utter ruine of a Realme and people doth grow and come more by an undiscreete and evill governour, then by many thousands of other men being subjects. Thus say the holy Scriptures,[3] Well

[1] Ps. 10.16 and 45.6 ff., and 47.2; Eccles. 17.
[2] Matt. 18.23 and 22.12; Ps. 10.16 and 45, and 47.2 ff.; Matt. 22.13 and 25.34; Ps. 82.6.
[3] Eccles. 10.16; Prov. 16 and 29; Eccles. 10.

is thee, O thou land (saith the Preacher) whose King is come of Nobles, and whose princes eate in due season, for necessity, and not for lust. Againe, a wise and righteous King maketh his Realme and people wealthy: and a good, mercifull, and gracious Prince, is as a shadow in heate, as a defence in stormes, as deaw, as sweete showres, as fresh water springs in great droughts.

Againe the Scriptures, of undiscreet and evill Princes, speake thus, Woe be to thee (O thou land) whose King is but a child, and whose Princes are early at their bankets. Againe, when the wicked doe raigne, then men goe to ruine. And againe, A foolish Prince destroyeth the people, and a covetous King undoeth his Subjects. Thus speake the Scriptures,[1] thus experience testifieth of good and evill Princes.

What shall Subjects doe then? shall they obey valiant, stout, wise, and good Princes, and contemne, disobey, and rebell against children being their Princes, or against undiscreet and evill governours? God forbid: for first what a perilous thing were it to commit unto the Subjects the judgement which Prince is wise and godly, and his governement good, and which is otherwise: as though the foot must judge of the head: an enterprise very heinous, and must needs breed rebellion. For who else be they that are most inclined to rebellion, but such haughtie spirits? from whom springeth such foule ruine of Realmes? Is not rebellion the greatest of all mischiefes? And who are most ready to the greatest mischiefes, but the worst men? Rebels therefore the worst of all Subjects are most ready to rebellion, as being the worst of all vices, and farthest from the duetie of a good Subject: as on the contrary part the best Subjects are most firme and constant in obedience, as in the speciall and peculiar vertue of good Subjects. What an unworthy matter were it then to make the naughtiest Subjects, and most inclined to rebellion and all evill, judges over their Princes, over their government, and over their counsellers, to determine which of them be good or tolerable, and which be evill, and so intolerable, that they must needs be remooved by rebels, being ever ready as the naughtiest subjects, soonest to rebell against the best Princes, specially if they be yong in age, women in sexe, or gentle and curteous in government, as trusting by their wicked boldnesse, easily to overthrow their weaknesse and gentlenesse, or at the least so to feare the mindes of such Princes, that they may have impunitie of their mischievous doings.

But whereas indeede a rebell is worse then the worst prince, and rebellion worse then the worst governement of the worst prince that hitherto hath beene: both rebels are unmeete ministers, and rebellion an unfit and unwholsome medicine to reforme any small lackes in a prince, or to cure any little griefes in government, such lewd remedies being far worse then any other maladies and disorders that can bee in the body of a common wealth. But whatsoever the prince bee, or his governement, it is evident that for the most part, those princes whome some subjects doe thinke to bee very godly, and under whose governement they rejoyce to live: some other subjects doe take the same to bee evill and ungodly, and doe wish for a change. If therefore all subjects that mislike of their prince, should rebell, no Realme should ever bee without rebellion. It were more meete that rebels should heare the advise of wise men, and give place unto their judgement, and follow the example of obedient subjectes,

---

[1] Eccles. 10.16; Prov. 28 and 29.

as reason is that they whose understanding is blinded with so evill an affection, should give place to them that bee of sound judgement, and that the worst should give place to the better: and so might Realmes continue in long obedience, peace, and quietnesse. But what if the Prince be undiscreete, and evill indeed, and is also evident to all mens eyes, that hee so is? I aske againe, what if it be long of the wickednesse of the Subjects, that the Prince is undiscreete and evill? Shall the Subjects both by their wickednesse provoke GOD for their deserved punishment, to give them an undiscreet or evill Prince, and also rebell against him, and withall against GOD, who for the punishment of their sinnes did give them such a Prince? Will you heare the Scriptures concerning this point? GOD (say the holy Scriptures)[1] maketh a wicked man to raigne for the sinnes of the people. Againe, GOD giveth a Prince in his anger, meaning an evill one, and taketh away a Prince in his displeasure, meaning specially when hee taketh away a good Prince for the sinnes of the people: as in our memorie hee tooke away our good *Josias* king *Edward* in his yong and good yeeres for our wickednesse. And contrarily the Scriptures doe teach,[2] that GOD giveth wisedome unto Princes, and maketh a wise and good King to raigne over that people whom he loveth, and who loveth him. Againe, if the people obey GOD, both they and their king shal prosper and be safe, els both shall perish, saith GOD by the mouth of *Samuel*.

Here you see, that GOD placeth as well evil Princes as good, and for what cause he doth both. If wee therefore will have a good Prince, either to be given us, or to continue: now we have such a one, let us by our obedience to GOD and to our Prince move GOD thereunto. If we will have an evill Prince (when GOD shall send such a one) taken away, and a good in his place, let us take away our wickednesse which provoketh GOD to place such a one over us, and GOD will either displace him, or of an evill Prince make him a good Prince, so that wee first will change our evill into good. For will you heare the Scriptures?[3] The heart of the Prince is in GODS hand, which way soever it shall please him, he turneth it. Thus say the Scriptures. Wherefore let us turne from our sinnes unto the Lord with all our hearts, and he will turne the heart of the Prince, unto our quiet and wealth: Els for Subjects to deserve through their sinnes to have an evill Prince, and then to rebell against him, were double and treble evill, by provoking GOD more to plague them. Nay let us either deserve to have a good Prince, or let us patiently suffer and obey such as wee deserve. And whether the Prince be good or evill, let us according to the counsell of the holy Scriptures, pray for the Prince, for his continuance and increase in goodnesse, if he be good, and for his amendment if he be evill...

[1] Job 34.10.   [2] 2 Pet. 2.9; Prov. 16.   [3] Prov. 21.

APPENDIX 4: *ENGLANDS PARNASSUS*, COMPILED BY ROBERT ALLOTT (1600)

Allott's book supplies 2,439 passages from more than 85 English poets, arranged under 284 headings beginning with *Angels* and ending with *Youth*. The running title is 'The Choysest Flowers of our English Poets'. The name of the poet is given under each flower, not always accurately. There are seven quotations from *Richard II*, four of them ascribed to Shakespeare.

page 3   *Angels*

5   Weake men must fall, for heaven stil gards the right.

                                        W. Shakespeare.   (3.2.62)

page 54   *Death*

311   – The toongs of dying men
        Inforce attention like deep harmony,
        Where words are scarce, they are sildom spent in vaine:
        For they breath truth, that breath their words in paine.
        He that no more must say, is lissened more,
        Then they whom youth & ease have taught to glose:
        More are mens ends markt, then their lives before.
        The setting sunne and musick at the close,
        As the last tast of sweet is sweetest tast,
        Writ in remembrance more, then things long past.

                                        W. Shakespeare.   (2.1.5–14)

page 113   *Good name*

605   The purest treasure mortall times affoord,
        Is spotlesse reputation, that away,
        Men are but guilded trunkes, or painted clay.

                                        W. Shakespeare.   (1.1.177–9)

page 156   *Kings*

862   Not all the water in the rough rude sea
        Can wash the balme from an anoynted King:
        The breath of worldly men cannot depose
        The deputie elected by the Lord.

                                        W. Shakespeare.   (3.2.54–7)

54 *THE CHOYSEST FLOVVERS*

Sad life worſe then glad death, and greater croſſe.
To ſee friends graue, then dead, the graue ſelfe to en-
        Ed. Spencer.   (groſſe.

---- In wretches ſudden death at once
There long-ſome ill is buried with their bones.
        Th. Hudſon. Tranſl.

Death is to him that wretched life doth lead
Both grace and gaine; but he in hell doth lie
That liues a loathed life, and wiſhing cannot die.
        Ed. Spencer.

Death is moſt lonely ſweet and amiable:
But captiu'd life for fouleneſſe admirable.
        I. Marſton.

----- The toongs of dying men
Inforce attention like deep harmony,
Where words are ſcarce, they are ſildom ſpent in vaine:
For they breath truth, that breath their words in paine.
He that no more muſt ſay, is liſſened more,
Then they whom youth & eaſe haue taught to gloſe:
More are mens ends markt, then their liues before.
The ſetting ſunne and muſick at the cloſe,
As the laſt taſt of ſweet is ſweeteſt taſt,
Writ in remembrance more, then things long paſt.
        W. Shakeſpeare.

Delaie.

On the one ſide doubt, on the other ſate Delaie,
Behind the gate, that none her might eſpie:
Whoſe manner was, all paſſengers to ſtaie,
And entertaine with her occaſions ſlie.
Through which, ſome loſt great hope vnheedilie,
Which neuer they recouer might againe: And

16 A page from *England's Parnassus*

And others quite excluded forth did lie,
Long languishing there, in vnpittied paine,
And seeking often entrance afterward in vaine.
Ed. Spencer.

----Daunger growes by lingring till the last,
And phisicke hath no helpe when life is past.
Th. Watson.

----Oft things done, perhaps, do lesse annoy
Then may the doing, handeled with delay.
S. Daniell.

Delaie in close awaite
Caught hold on me, and thought my steps to stay,
Faining stil, many a fond excuse, to prate:
And time, to steale the treasure of mans day,
Whose smallest minute lost, no riches render may.
Ed. Spencer.

----Times delay new hope of helpe still breeds.
Idem.

----Fearfull tormenting
Is leaden seruitor, to dull delay.
W. Shakespeare.

He that will stop the brooke must then begin
When sommers heat hath dried vp the spring:
And when his pittering streames are low and thin,
For let the winter aid vnto them bring,
He growes to be of watry flouds the king:
And though you damme him vp with loftie rankes,
Yet will he quickly oueiflow his bankes.
R. Greene.

Ill newes deferring, is a plague as great as an ill newes.
Ab. Fraunce.

E 4   Delay

page 280 *Of Sorrow*

1557   Fell sorrowes tooth never ranckles more,
        Then when it bites, but launcheth not the sore.

                                    S. Daniell.   (1.3.301–2)

1560   – Snarling sorrow hath lesse powre to bite
        The man that mocks at it, and sets it light.

                                    Ed. Spencer.   (1.3.291–2)

page 348 *Of Albion*

1927   This royall throne of Kings, this sceptred yle,
        This earth of majestie, this seate of Mars,
        This other Eden, this demi-paradise,
        This fortresse built by nature for her selfe,
        Against intestion and the hand of warre,
        This happie breede of man, this little world,
        This precious stone sette in the silver sea,
        Which serves it in the office of a wall,
        Or as a Moate defensive to a house,
        Against the envie of lesse happier lands,
        This nurse, this teeming wombe of royall Kings,
        Fearde by their breede, and famous by their byrth,
        Renowned in their deedes as farre from home,
        For charitie, service, and true chivalrie,
        As is the Sepulchre in stubborne Jewrie.

                                    M[ichael]. Dr[ayton].   (2.1.40–55)

READING LIST

All books mentioned in abbreviated form in the notes to the Introduction and the Commentary are listed here in full. The list includes useful reference works and a selection of books and articles which might be found useful in further studies of the play. It does not include articles which deal with specific details and which are given in full at the appropriate point in a Commentary note.

Albright, Evelyn M. 'Shakespeare's *Richard II* and the Essex conspiracy', *PMLA* 42 (1927), 686–720

Bailey, Richard W. (ed.). *Early Modern English: Additions and Antedatings to the Record of English Vocabulary 1475–1700*, 1978

Baldwin, T. W. *Shakspere's 'Small Latine & Lesse Greeke'*, 2 vols, 1944

Barkan, Leonard, 'The theatrical consistency of *Richard II*', *SQ* 29 (1978), 5–19

Barroll, J. Leeds. 'A new history for Shakespeare and his time', *Shakespeare Quarterly* 39 (1988), 441–64

Baxter, John. *Shakespeare's Poetic Styles*, 1980

Berger, Jr., Harry. '*Richard II* 3.23: an exercise in imaginary audition', *ELH* 55 (1988), 755–96

Bergeron, David M. 'The Hoby letter and *Richard II*: a parable of criticism', *Shakespeare Quarterly* 26 (1975), 477–80

'*Richard II* and carnival politics', *Shakespeare Quarterly* 42 (1991), 33–43

Black, Matthew W., and Metz, G. Harold. *The Life and Death of King Richard II: A Bibliography to supplement the New Variorum Edition of 1955*, 1977 (includes entries up to 1973)

Boris, Edna Zwick. *Shakespeare's English Kings, The People and the Law*, 1978

Brooke, Nicholas (ed.). *Richard II: A Casebook*, 1973

Bullough, Geoffrey (ed.). *Narrative and Dramatic Sources of Shakespeare*, III, 1960 (material on *Richard II* on pp. 353–497)

Calderwood, J. L. *Metadrama in Shakespeare's Henriad: 'Richard II' to 'Henry V'*, 1979

Campbell, Lily B. *Shakespeare's 'Histories': Mirrors of Elizabethan Policy*, 1947 (includes pp. 176–94 the debate about the succession, 1594–1601)

Cercignani, Fausto. *Shakespeare's Works and Elizabethan Pronunciation*, 1981

David, Richard. *Shakespeare in the Theatre*, 1978

Dent, R. W. *Shakespeare's Proverbial Language: An Index*, 1981

Dillon, Janette. *Shakespeare and the Solitary Man*, 1981 (ch. 5 is on *Richard II*)

Dollimore, Jonathan. 'Introduction' to *Political Shakespeare*, ed. Jonathan Dollimore and Alan Sinfield, 1985, p. 88

Dutton, Richard. 'Buggeswords: the case of Sir John Hayward's *Life of Henry IV*', in *Licensing, Censorship and Authorship in Early Modern England*, 2000, pp. 162–91

Edwards, Philip. 'Person and office in Shakespeare's plays', *Proceedings of the British Academy* 56 (1972), 93–109 (Annual Shakespeare Lecture for 1970)

Fleischer, Martha Hester. *The Iconography of the English History Play*, 1974 (includes the state, the garden, trial by combat)

Forker, Charles R. (ed.). *Richard II, 1780–1920*. Shakespeare: The Critical Tradition, 1998. [Forker's edition of *Richard II* for the Arden 3 series appeared in March 2002]

Fussner, F. Smith. *The Historical Revolution: English Historical Writing and Thought 1580–1640*, 1962

Gordon, Donald J. 'Name and fame: Shakespeare's *Coriolanus*', *Papers Mainly Shakespearean*, ed. G. I. Duthie, 1964, pp. 40–57 (on name and identity)

Greenblatt, Stephen, (ed.). *The Power of Forms in the English Renaissance*, 1982.

Hakola, Liisa. *In One Person Many People. The Image of the King in Three RSC Productions of William Shakespeare's 'King Richard II'*, 1988

Hamilton, Donna B. 'The state of law in *Richard II*', *Shakespeare Quarterly* 34 (1983), 5–17

Harris, Kathryn M. 'Sun and water imagery in *Richard II*: its dramatic function', *SQ* 21 (1970), 157–65

Hart, Jonathan. *Theater and World: the Problematics of Shakespeare's History*, 1992

Healy, Margaret. *William Shakespeare: Richard II*, Writers and their Work, 1998

Hinman, Charlton. *The Printing and Proofreading of the First Folio of Shakespeare*, 2 vols, 1963

Hodgdon, Barbara. *The End Crowns All: Closure and Contradiction in Shakespeare's History*, 1991

Humphreys, A. R. 'Shakespeare and the Tudor perception of history', *Stratford Papers on Shakespeare 1964*, ed. B. W. Jackson, 1965, 51–70

Richard II, 1967 (Studies in English Literature series)

Kantorowicz, Ernest H. *The King's Two Bodies: A Study in Medieval Political Theology*, 1957

Kelly, Henry Ansgar. *Divine Providence in the England of Shakespeare's Histories*, 1970

Kernan, Alvin B. '*The Henriad*: Shakespeare's major history plays', *Yale Review* 59 (1969), 3–32 (reprinted in *Modern Shakespearean Criticism*, ed. Alvin B. Kernan, 1970, pp. 245–75)

Kinney, Arthur. 'Essex and Shakespeare vs. Hayward', *Shakespeare Quarterly* 44 (1993), 464–6

Knowles, Ronald. *Shakespeare's Arguments with History*, 2001

McManaway, James G. '*Richard II* at Covent Garden', *SQ* 15 (1964), 161–75

MacKenzie, Clayton G. 'Paradise and paradise lost in *Richard II*', *Shakespeare Quarterly* 37 (1986), 318–39

Maguire, Laurie E. *Shakespearean Suspect Texts: The 'Bad' Quartos and Their Contexts*, 1996

Mahood, M. *Shakespeare's Wordplay*, 1957 (esp. ch. 3)

Merrix, Robert P. 'Shakespeare's Histories and the new bardolators', *SEL* 19 (1979), 179–96

Muir, Kenneth. *The Sources of Shakespeare's Plays*, 1977 (pp. 46–66)

Naylor, E. W. *Shakespeare and Music*, 1931

Norbrook, David. '"A liberal tongue": language and rebellion in *Richard II*', in *Shakespeare's Universe: Renaissance Ideas and Conventions*, ed. John M. Mucciolo, 1996, pp. 37–51

Ornstein, Robert. *A Kingdom for a Stage: The Achievement of Shakespeare's History Plays*, 1972 (esp. ch. 5)

Patch, H. R. *The Goddess Fortuna in Medieval Literature*, 1927

Pater, Walter. 'Shakespeare's English Kings', *Scribner's Magazine*, 5 April 1889, 506–12 (reprinted in *Appreciations*, 1889, pp. 192–212)

Patterson, Annabel. *Reading Holinshed's Chronicles*, 1994

Pierce, Robert B. *Shakespeare's History Plays: The Family and the State*, 1971

Pollard, A. W. *A New Shakespeare Quarto. The Tragedy of King Richard II. Printed for the third time by Valentine Simmes in 1598*, 1918

Prior, Moody E. *The Drama of Power: Studies in Shakespeare's Plays*, 1973

Rabkin, Norman. *Shakespeare and the Common Understanding*, 1967

Rackin, Phyllis. 'The role of the audience in Shakespeare's *Richard II*', *Shakespeare Quarterly* 36 (1985), 262–81

Stages of History: Shakespeare's English Chronicles, 1990

Ribner, Irving. *The English History Play in the Age of Shakespeare*, 1957, rev. edn, 1965 (traces the evolution of the history play, emphasising Shakespeare's innovations)

Riggs, David. *Shakespeare's Heroical Histories: Henry VI and its Literary Tradition*, 1971 (identifies different schools of sixteenth-century historiography, against Tillyard)

Rossiter, A. P. (ed.). *Woodstock: A Moral History*, 1946

Sanders, Wilbur. *The Dramatist and the Received Idea: Studies in the Plays of Marlowe and Shakespeare*, 1968 (esp. ch. 9)

Schoenbaum, S. '*Richard II* and the realities of power', *S.Sur.* 28 (1975), 1–13

Scouten, A. H. *The London Stage 1660–1800, Part 3: 1729–1747*, 1961

Shewring, Margaret. *Richard II: Shakespeare in Performance*, 1996

Sprague, Arthur C. *Shakespeare's Histories: Plays for the Stage*, 1964

Talbert, E. W. *The Problem of Order*, 1962 (includes pp. 146–200, 'Shakespeare's deposition of Richard II')

Tilley, M. P. *A Dictionary of the Proverbs in England in the Sixteenth and Seventeenth Centuries*, 1950

Tillyard, E. M. W. *Shakespeare's History Plays*, 1944

Trousdale, Marion. *Shakespeare and the Rhetoricians*, 1982

Tuck, Anthony. *Richard II and the English Nobility*, 1973

Van Lennep, William. *The London Stage 1660–1800, Part 1: 1660–1700*, 1965

Vickers, Brian (ed.). *Shakespeare: The Critical Heritage I: 1623–1692*, 1974 (reprints the preface and five scenes from Tate's version of *Richard II*)

Wells, Stanley. *Modernising Shakespeare's Spelling*; with Gary Taylor, *Three Studies in the Text of 'Henry V'*, 1979

Yachnin, Paul. 'The powerless theater', *English Literary Renaissance* 21 (1991), 49–74

Yeats, W. B. 'At Stratford-on-Avon', *Essays and Introduction*, 1961, pp. 96–110